A GIRL GREW UP IN RUSSIA

Elisaveta Fen has also written
  Rising Tide
  A Russian Childhood
  A Beginner's Russian Reader
  A Beginner's Russian Conversation
  A Russian Family
  A Russian Family on Holiday

The photograph of the author
was taken when she was $11\frac{1}{2}$ years old

ELISAVETA FEN

A GIRL
GREW UP
IN RUSSIA

READERS UNION

Newton Abbot 1972

First published 1970 by André Deutsch Limited

This edition was produced in 1972 for sale to its members
only by the proprietors, Readers Union Limited, PO Box 6,
Newton Abbot, Devon, TQ12 2DW. Full details of
membership will gladly be sent on request

Reproduced and printed in the UK
for Readers Union by Redwood Press
Limited, Trowbridge & London

Contents

Mine were my faults, and mine be their reward.
My whole life was a contest, since the day
That gave me being, gave me that which marr'd
The gift – a fate, or will, that walk'd astray;
And I at times have found the struggle hard,
And thought of shaking off my bonds of clay;
But now I fain would for a time survive,
If but to see what next can well arrive.

Byron

'Shades of the Prison House'

Preparation should blunt the sharp point of pain, but it can prolong the agony. I was told at least a year ahead that when I reached the age of eleven, I was to become a boarder at the school in the town of M* where my sister had been a boarder, yet throughout that year I continued to hope, quite unreasonably, that somehow I might escape this fate. I asked my mother more than once why I could not be a day pupil and live in a family, like my brother. She told me that she would be less worried about my well-being if I were a boarder, because I would be looked after by people experienced in the job: she mentioned cleanliness, good food and good manners . . . This explanation struck me even then as unsatisfactory, as ignoring my most important needs, and because I was unable to put my thoughts into words, I merely repeated with tears that I would much rather live in a family. The prospect of being taught good manners offended my pride, while the mention of food aroused the fear of being made to eat up all that was put on my plate. But my mother continued to say that she knew of no suitable family with a girl of my own age into whose care she could confidently place me, and that the family with whom my brother was living was not the right one for me.

After repeated discussions of this kind, I began to realize that she could not be swayed by pleading, and to sense the meaning of the inevitable. It was like a dark storm cloud on the horizon, approaching slowly but inexorably. Soon it would envelop and engulf me; I would be lost in it, desolate and utterly alone. The image of the school as a place

I*

of confinement where I would be in the power of complete strangers dominated my thoughts; it superseded the memory of it as an object of curiosity where I had been taken once or twice to visit my sister, and as a place of excitement and triumph when I went there for my entrance examinations. While absorbed in play or reading, I could forget my approaching doom, but suddenly the thought returned with a sickening shock, such as one feels when reminded of the loss of a loved person. It often kept me awake at night after I had gone to bed. Things could never be the same again. The serenity of my last months at home was corroded by these attacks of dreadful anticipation.

When the dreaded day came and — at the end of it — the parting from my mother in the school reception hall, I cried bitterly and made her promise that she would not leave me there for longer than one term. My trust in her, already somewhat shaken, suffered a further blow when I found later that she had never intended to keep that promise. The governess on duty, whose face I could hardly see through my tears, took me to the boarders' study-room, well lit but dreary with its polished brown benches and long black tables at which the boarders did their homework. She showed me my place and the drawer in which I could keep my books, pens and pencils, and I tried to read, but could not concentrate for the hum of voices all around me and the pressure of distress on my throat and eyes.

Desolate as I was, I did not anticipate that my sense of bereavement would turn to despair that night when I found that I could not see the sky from my bed in the school dormitory. At home the windows of my bedroom opened on to an orchard, and the curtains were never drawn. When the lamp was put out, the darkness was not complete: even on the darkest night there were gleams of light in the sky, and now and again a star trembled on the edge of a cloud. I used to lie and gaze at it until my eyes became glued with sleep.

In the school dormitories the lower panes of tall windows were painted over with white paint. My dormitory was on the first floor and faced a building of four storeys across the street. One could probably see the sky if one stood on the window-sill, but that was one of the many things that were forbidden. Besides, white cotton blinds were always pulled half-way down, so that the room could not be overlooked from above, and that made me feel, in some obscure way, as if I had been suddenly cut off from all natural things among which I had lived until then.

On many a night after that first night I lay in bed in that lofty, aseptic room, painted in green and white, with cold, highly polished parquet floor, thinking of the game I used to play at home after dark, throwing a ball up into the sky. I used to play it by myself, yet I did not feel alone because I could hear familiar voices in conversation on the veranda behind me. I flung my ball towards the shimmering stars and, with my head thrown back, followed its ascent up and up into the luminous dusk until it disappeared out of sight at what seemed to be an incredible height, the height I could never reach when throwing it up in daylight. Then, just as incredibly, it descended into my open hands like a gift from heaven, and up it went again and again, until I felt light-headed with delight and ravished, through drinking in all that starlight, so that I staggered and lost my balance and sank down happily on the fine sand of the garden path.

There were five girls beside myself in the small dormitory. Of these one was friendly, one aloof, two hostile and one isolated and inaccessible. This last one, a rebellious little girl called Ania Orlovskaia, provided me with one of those object lessons that become, despite their triviality, real landmarks on one's journey towards the 'wisdom' — if such it is — of later years. But the chain of incidents which led to this was started off, quite innocently, by myself — by my dislike of the yellow, scratchy pea soup.

The two hostile girls were Mílochka and Fatima. Mílochka was a doll-faced child with large, round, blue eyes and a long plait of fair hair; Fatima a dark, swarthy Tartar girl from beyond the Volga who looked mature for her years. The friendly girl was Tania Pánova, and the aloof one, Stassia, a pale slender child with a long Polish surname. She, Fatima and Mílochka were second-year boarders, old stagers compared to myself and the other two who were new to the school. Fatima and Mílochka looked down on Tania and myself, and they positively despised Ania Orlovskaia.

I was told as soon as I arrived that Mílochka was very pretty and that she was the favourite of Fräulein Schmiedel. Fräulein Schmiedel was one of the three governesses who lived at the school and supervised the boarders, the three Parcae who held the threads of our daily lives in their hands, who watched us at our meals and studies and during our leisure, or whatever passed under that name. Each was on duty on one day out of three. Mademoiselle Saburova was elderly, distinguished-looking and remote. Her manner towards us verged on the disdainful. On her days we were obliged to talk French, and if a girl was heard speaking Russian, she was set to learn a column of French vocabulary before going to bed that night. Otherwise Mademoiselle Saburova took very little notice of us, reading a French book at her own little table, while the girls got on with their homework.

Mademoiselle Vinogradova was a slender person with a soft, light voice, much younger than Mademoiselle Saburova. On her duty days we spoke Russian. She treated us as persons rather than as mere pupils in her charge, and spoke to us often with a smile. The study-room had a relaxed atmosphere when she was on duty, and she was the only one of the three to whom I felt I could bring a difficulty and ask a question in connection with my homework.

Fräulein Schmiedel, the third governess, was short and plump and had piggy eyes and red cheeks. Her homely looks were deceptive: she was a small army sergeant in petticoats. The worst thing about her was her voice. While Mademoiselle Saburova drawled, Fräulein Schmiedel barked, and her bark was gruff and loud. It usually made me jump as if I were doing something forbidden, and it took me some time to discover that her bark was worse than her bite and that the older girls were not frightened of her. The rule about speaking German on her duty days was frequently broken, and the study-room was at its noisiest and least tidy. Now and again the Fräulein would flare up in a temper and set half the room memorizing lines of German text — too many for her to check before the pupils' bed-time, and so ineffective as a deterrent.

It was this woman who favoured Mílochka and called her by her Christian name, which is in Russian also a term of endearment, while the rest of us were called by our surnames. The advantages of being Fräulein Schmiedel's favourite were brought sharply into focus, as far as I was concerned, one evening soon after I had become a boarder. The Fräulein was presiding over our supper and she allowed Mílochka to leave her plate of pea soup untouched. I hated pea soup, and Mílochka's success gave me the courage to ask permission to do the same. But Fräulein Schmiedel came down on me like a ton of bricks. Did I have to ape Mílochka? she demanded. Frightened but indignant, I replied that I was not aping anybody: I never liked pea soup and had never been made to eat anything I disliked at home. Fräulein Schmiedel retorted that I had no right at my age to use the word 'never', and that I must have been spoiled at home. 'I promise you that you won't get any spoiling here while I'm on duty,' she added.

I managed to swallow my tears and a few spoonfuls of soup before my plate was mercifully removed by the kind maid Sasha who was serving at table. After that I had to struggle through a large helping of beef rissoles and macaroni. The sweet course of *kissiel* went down more easily, and at last the ordeal of supper was over. We formed into pairs and transferred ourselves into the study-room where we had to do our homework for next morning's lessons. As I was taking out my books, still smarting under Fräulein Schmiedel's reprimand, I heard Mílochka and Fatima tittering together, then Mílochka said loudly: 'Girls, we've got a monkey at our table!'

Tania, Stassia and Ania looked at me. 'Yes, her!' continued Mílochka. 'She apes people. Fräulein Schmiedel said so.'

My reasonable self was telling me to ignore this provocation, but a part of me which felt passionately about 'truth' and 'justice' burst out in protest: 'It isn't true!'

'You don't mean to say that Fräulein Schmiedel isn't speaking the truth?'

That was Fatima, the Tartar girl from over the Volga. She was speaking with a sly smile and narrowed eyes. I felt there was something almost diabolical about Fatima. She was a Muslim – not a Christian. Muslims had tortured Christians; Tartars had invaded and oppressed Russia. Fatima, I was sure, could be as cruel as those Muslims and Tartars of old. She certainly thought up much more wounding things to say than the spiteful but silly Mílochka.

'I'll tell you what – if Rayévskaia is a monkey, then her parents must be apes!'

This gratutious insult made me leap to my feet in an impulse to do something – I knew not what – to the offender. But in doing this, I made the bench scrape the floor and drew Fräulein Schmiedel's attention to our table. She demanded to know what was happening. I was too ashamed to explain: Fatima had dared to insult my parents! She had dared – and I could do nothing to her!

The governess called us up to her table and insisted on an explanation. In the end I managed to tell her that Fatima was saying things about my parents, but I could not bring myself to repeat what she had said. Ania Orlovskaia then blurted out the offending phrase. Fräulein Schmiedel told Fatima that she was very silly, but added that I was silly too, to take notice of such nonsense. Mílochka, who had started it all, escaped reprimand altogether.

As we returned to our table, Fatima muttered that she hated sneaks and tell-tales. She probably meant me, but Ania, who happened to be next to her, flared up and stamped hard on her foot under the table. Fatima yelled, and that started another inquest. The outcome of it all

was that Ania was told to stand by the wall in punishment for hurting
Fatima, and Fatima was given some German lines to learn, for calling
Ania names.

Ania Orlovskaia was a very plain little girl, snub-nosed, freckled,
with wisps of straight ginger hair sticking out from her head in every
direction. She could easily have passed for a sulky, resentful little peasant
boy, and the boarders' uniform, a long-skirted dress and white lawn
cape, looked ridiculous on her. I was not attracted to her, but the
unfairness of the punishment to which she was subjected made my heart
go out to her in sympathy, especially as I felt she was suffering partly on
my account. I writhed inwardly as I imagined myself in her place: I
would have preferred to face the wall rather than the room full of
people, but Ania amused herself by making faces at the girls who
happened to look at her. There was some tittering, then Fatima complained in an aggrieved voice that Orlovskaia was preventing her from
learning her German lines. Ania shouted that Fatima was telling fibs.
Fräulein Schmiedel told Ania to turn her face to the wall; she obeyed
but continued looking round over her shoulder and putting out her
tongue at Fatima, who again complained. In the end Fräulein Schmiedel
barked out an order to one of the older girls to take Orlovskaia to the
dormitory and have her put to bed.

As Ania was led out, resisting and shouting that she did not want to
go to bed, she became for a few moments, despite her freckles and snub
nose, a young heroine in my eyes, then a victim, led to execution. My
imagination balked at the thought of what was going to happen next, for
I did not believe this was the end of the incident. And very soon the
older girl returned to report that Ania refused to go to bed and that she
was hysterical. Fräulein Schmiedel sent a message to the matron, asking
her to give Ania some valerian drops, and soon afterwards sent the whole
of our table to bed half an hour early.

As we approached the small dormitory through the big girls' much
larger one, I could hear Ania's angry wail. She was sitting on her bed,
half undressed, her hair hanging over her eyes, glaring at the two
female figures standing over her. These were the old chambermaid
Dasha and the matron, who was holding a glass half full of brownish
liquid. 'Take it away!' Ania was shouting. 'I won't drink your beastly
drops! Go away, both of you!'

Dasha darted towards us as soon as she saw us come in and shepherded
us into the washing-room.

This Dasha must have been about seventy years old when I first knew her, and she had looked after more than one generation of boarders. A tiny, bent figure with thin silvery hair, half covered with a white headkerchief, she was the only motherly person in the place and more like a family nanny than an ordinary maid. Someone in the administration of the school, perhaps our wise and kindly director, assigned her the task of looking after the younger boarders, maybe so that she could save them from feeling utterly lost in the wilderness of coldly unrelated classrooms, halls and dormitories. She did this by just being herself, a small source of spontaneous feeling whose warmth prevented us from growing emotionally numbed. The very way she talked of nothing in particular in her quiet old voice could soothe a homesick child. On the evening of Ania's outburst, however, even she was less serene than usual. I heard her muttering as she undid my plaits and began to comb my hair.

'Lord help and preserve us! What's come over our Anichka?'

Fatima growled resentfully: 'She's not *ours* . . . She's been here only a week, and I hope they'll expel her!'

'It's a sin to talk like that, dearie,' Dasha reproved her, mildly.

When we returned to the dormitory, Ania was still sitting on her bed, but now the dumpy figure of Fräulein Schmiedel had joined the white-clad matron. I could not hear what the governess was saying to Ania because Ania was crying loudly. She was repeating between sobs: 'I don't want to and I won't!'

I slipped into my bed as quickly as I could, drew the bedclothes up to my chin and lay tense, watching, ready to stop my ears if there were any shouting. Then Fräulein Schmiedel's voice pierced the noise of crying. 'Very well, then, I shall have to report you to the *Nachálnitsa*,' she said and walked, almost ran, out of the room.

Peeping over the edge of my blanket, I saw Dasha stroking Ania's back, whispering to her, obviously doing her best to get her into bed. But Ania was too far gone in her mood of defiance to respond even to Dasha. Instead of doing what she was asked, she had slipped down and was sitting on the floor, her face buried in the bedclothes, crying.

We did not often see the *Nachálnitsa*, the headmistress, except at prayers in the assembly hall. She was not the type of person to inspire fear even in the most timid of girls. Her voice and manner were very gentle and she looked benevolent. She always wore a uniform dress of mid-blue stiff silk with a shawl of black lace over her shoulders and black lace mittens on her hands. A small gold watch was pinned to her corsage and a lorgnette in a gold frame hung from her waist on a black ribbon.

I was told that she had been a 'Smolny pupil'; that is, she had been educated in one of the exclusive boarding schools for girls in St Petersburg. She certainly had the exquisite manners and affectations of that type of school. She always addressed a girl as *dóoshechka* — little soul — and would often pat the young ones on the cheek. When I was old enough to form an opinion of her, I found her as she looked — a sweet-tempered, unassertive, rather sentimental person — yet her voice could be decisive when there was a question about expelling a pupil from the school.

What will she decide about Ania? What will she do? I knew that the others in their beds were, like myself, wondering and waiting for her arrival in a state of barely tolerable suspense.

She came at last, walking faster than usual, with a rustle of her silk skirts, and went straight to Ania, still huddled on the floor by her bed. In the hushed silence of the dormitory we heard her soft, precise voice saying in tones of unusual urgency:

'*Dóoshechka*, you must not sit on the floor — you will catch a chill. Please get up and get into your bed at once.'

Ania's voice, several notes deeper than *Nachálnitsa's* and muffled by the bedclothes, came in reply: 'I don't want to. I want to catch a chill!' '*Dóoshechka*, be reasonable! You must get into bed. I don't think you can be well. I shall have to write to your parents about this!'

Ania emitted a long, loud wail. The headmistress made a sign to Dasha, who was standing by, and now made another attempt to raise Ania on to her bed. This time, inexplicably, Ania allowed herself to be lifted and lay on the bed, face downwards. The headmistress watched Dasha undress her, and as soon as Ania was inside the bedclothes, she turned and walked out, accompanied by Fräulein Schmiedel and the matron.

For the first time since I became a boarder I was diverted from the contemplation of my own misery by thoughts about the predicament of another. My feelings about Ania were confused. I marvelled at her pluck in defying the authority of the adults on whose goodwill she had to depend. Yet I found her so plain and pitiful in her defiance that my admiration for her courage was mingled with revulsion. I could not imagine myself doing the sort of thing Ania seemed to be doing so readily: putting her tongue out at the other girls, saying 'I won't' to *Nachálnitsa*, sitting on the floor when told to go to bed. She behaved like a big baby, really, and if I had been subjected to the same treatment, I would have felt deeply humiliated. But did it mean that she was brave and I — a coward? Why did she not care what anybody thought of her? With these questions in my mind I fell asleep for the first time without the tears of homesickness burning my eyes.

At a quarter past seven the clamour of the morning bell crashed into my dreams, and my first thought on waking was of Ania. Across the room, she seemed to be still fast asleep, the tufts of her ginger hair showing between the pillow and the bedclothes she had drawn over her face. When I returned from the washing-room, she was awake, and the matron was standing over her, thermometer in hand. One of the older girls, detailed to plait my hair, called me at that moment, and then the rush to get dressed in time for prayers, breakfast and the beginning of lessons diverted my thoughts from Ania's predicament until lunch time.

She was not there at lunch and someone whispered that she had been taken to the *lazaryet*, the school sickbay in a separate house, which stood between the main building and the garden. That evening her bed was empty, and a few days later we were told that her mother had come and taken her away.

Was her mother *asked* to take her away? With a triumphant snigger, Fatima hinted as much, but I was fast learning to mistrust Fatima. All the same, what happened to Ania was an object lesson to me. I understood that she had been judged 'unsuitable' as a boarder, and a thought, blinding and alarming like lightning, flashed through the gloom of my depression. Was this a way out for me? But, like lightning, it was gone in a second, leaving me more depressed than ever. I knew that I could not put up that kind of show and go through with it. If Ania was brave, then I was a coward; if she felt no shame, then I had the capacity of feeling ashamed enough for both of us. The school was indeed a prison, but I had to look for another, more dignified way of escape.

Coming to Terms

A naturalist once described a lion cub which tried to push its head through the iron bars of a cage so persistently that its nose bled, yet it went on trying for the rest of the night. A young child under constraint will struggle hard against the much greater strength of an adult. The struggle ends in exhaustion; for a time, the cub or the child gives it up. Then comes the renewal of strength and hope, and the struggle to get free begins anew — until despair sets in.

The letters I wrote to my mother during my first two or three months at the school were just such hopeless rushes at the bars of the cage, desperate calls for rescue. Some of those she kept ended in a threat of suicide: if she did not take me away, I would throw myself out of the window and kill myself.

My imagination pictured her sitting in a circle of light, in a familiar room, reading my letter. I saw the birthmark on her cheek, her lips slightly pursed in concentration, her ash-blonde hair softly shining in the lamplight. The longing that filled my heart was bitter and the tears that sprang to my eyes were tears of outrage as well as of grief. She could not miss me as much as I missed her, otherwise how could she remain unmoved by my pleading? Or did she not believe that I would do what I threatened to do?

Did I myself believe it? As I gazed down into the school yard, its cobbles faintly blue and glistening in the rain, I could almost feel their hard, wet impact on my forehead, could almost see the ground rushing to meet me as I hurled myself out of the window into its terrifying embrace. The window panes at the back of the school were not painted over, but the eye, seeking escape from the confining walls, was not cheered by what it saw outside. A large section of the yard was filled with stacks of birchwood billets, cut and ready for use as fuel in the many class-room stoves. Beyond these was the fence separating the yard from the school garden, a sad garden with unfriendly, unclimbable trees, whose only function seemed to be keeping out the sunlight. On the right, the school extended its pale stuccoed walls with their rows of tall windows. On the left there was a shorter wing containing kitchen and store-rooms; a length of a brick wall with a door, always locked, leading into a side street, and a separate house with the sauna baths on the ground floor and the sickbay on the first. Nowhere was there a look-out on to a wider world, an open space, comforting to the eye. All one could hope to see if one stood watching for half an hour would be one of the maids passing between the kitchen and the sickbay, or the porter Kondratiy carrying a basketful of firewood. With a sinking feeling at the pit of my stomach, I wondered how long I might be lying there, with my head split open in a pool of blood, before anyone discovered that I had done this fascinatingly daring thing — 'committed suicide'. The very words seemed to pierce me with a sensation of triumph and pain.

But a closer look at the school windows should have convinced me that I had better wait until the Christmas holidays for an opportunity of throwing myself under a train. It was autumn, and the heavy casements were firmly shut and bolted; it would have taken me several minutes to unfasten one of them, and I would have been seen, for certain, before I had time to carry out my plan. Besides, each letter I wrote home was like Noah's white dove, which might return with a message of liberation. Then my mother's reply came, and, like my own letters to her, became stained with tears, for each was a confirmation of my growing realization that she did not really intend to rescue me.

She usually gave me the news of the household which she knew would interest me: the news of my favourite horses and my cat, and of the friends who had been enquiring after me or had asked to be remembered. This was, as a rule, followed by the admonition not to fret, to remember that she always prayed for me, and by the reminder that Christmas was not really far away and that Maxim, the coachman, was already looking out for a tall, thick fir tree to cut down at the proper time. The images of loved and familiar things thus evoked made the thought of suicide painfully irrelevant: if I killed myself I could never go home again, never see or do all that her letter promised. Yet I still shed tears over it — to me Christmas still seemed aeons of time away.

The school felt like a prison to me, but our letters were not censored. We sealed and stamped them ourselves and took them down to the entrance hall where they were collected and posted by one of the porters. I should have been outraged if it had been otherwise, for I had been taught to regard reading other people's letters as something shabby, on a par with eavesdropping or peeping through key-holes. I remember feeling ashamed if, by accident, I happened to read a few words on a postcard addressed to someone else. And so I was shattered when one afternoon Fräulein Schmiedel held up a postcard, one of a bunch deposited by the porter Kondratiy on her table for distribution, and called out loudly: 'This is for you, Rayévskaia! Signed "your devoted Edward". You're starting early — receiving letters from young men!'

She had looked at the signature! She may have even read what was on the card!

'He . . . she . . . is really a girl . . . ' I stammered, reeling inwardly under the blow.

'A girl? Why does she call herself "Edward" then?'

'It's . . . it's a game we used to have.'

'What game?'

Did she really expect me to explain? I saw a grin on Fatima's face, and I felt angry with her, with Fräulein Schmiedel for this brutal incursion into the intimacy of my past life, with the writer of the post-card for the embarrassment she was causing me, and with myself — for leaving her my address and for the ungenerous feeling towards her which now possessed me.

'The game was pretending to be characters from books,' I said at last.

'This is illiterate writing. Whoever Edward is, he — or she — cannot spell,' said the governess.

This was the end of the incident as far as she was concerned. But to me it brought a wave of nostalgia for the play companions I had left behind and whom I did not particularly value when I had them.

Until my brother left home to go to school at M* when I was eight and a half, he and his friends had been my constant playmates. There were no girls at hand. After my brother's departure, I was thrown upon my own resources to a very large extent, and I made good use of them: inventing my own games, composing poems and stories, making excursions into the neighbouring fields and meadows. Then a family came to live opposite us in town and I became friendly with the children, two girls and a boy.

One of the girls, whom I liked best of the three, was younger than I, and she accepted my leadership. So did two Jewish girls of poor families, who attached themselves to me during one of my solitary walks and whom I afterwards brought into the house. Hanka, who had signed herself 'your devoted Edward', was one of them. During the summer when we lived on our country estate, two peasant girls from the village, called Mashka and Varka, became my play companions. In all these friendships I was the dominant partner, the giver rather than the recipient of favours, so it was a new experience for me suddenly to become a member of two large groups — the boarders and the day girls — and to be wooed by Margóolina, a little Jewish girl with whom I shared a double desk in my class.

Of the two groups I preferred the day girls who were all friendly, or at least looked so. There were forty of them and it took me some time to sort them out. The four of us, boarders, were distributed over the class-room, conspicuous among the dark brown and black of the day girls' uniforms — brown serge frocks and black alpaca pinafores. We were distinguished from them by our white lawn capes and sleeves, attached by tapes to the short sleeves of our brown dresses, and by the length of our skirts which reached down to the ankles. Another distinguishing feature was our shoes, of soft glossy cloth, with only toes and heels of leather. They made no noise as we walked, and their unsuitability for any rough walking in country or town appeared to symbolize the sheltered condition of our existence in the school.

The school was one of a group run by a special department, known as the Department of the Empress Mary, and the boarders' part, which was not large — about fifty girls in all — was modelled on those more famous boarding schools for girls in the capitals, called the Institutes for the Daughters of Nobility. Foreign languages were an important part of the curriculum, and the appointment of 'dames-de-classe' laid emphasis on the teaching of good manners. A dame-de-classe did not teach anything; she stayed with her class the whole day and right through the years the girls spent at school. Like the boarders' governesses, she watched over our good behaviour, but unlike them, she gave us conduct marks. I soon discovered that to obtain less than full marks, that is, twelve, was almost unheard-of.

Our dame-de-classe was Anna Avdyéevna, a product of one of the Institutes. She was young, perhaps not much older than twenty, and her appointment to our school was, I think, her first. I did not know her age at the time, but even if I knew it, it would not have made any difference to the feelings she inspired in me. To a child an adult is as impressive at eighteen as he is at thirty or even fifty, for he appears as a person of infinitely superior experience and knowledge.

Anna Avdyéevna was such a person to me. She made the decision as to who was to sit beside whom; she appointed monitors and assigned their duties for the week. They wore rosettes of blue ribbon and had to bring out and put away the class register, collect exercise books after a dictation, issue class library books and carry Anna Avdyéevna's messages to other members of the staff.

She herself had a small desk facing the class in one corner of the room, to the side of and a little behind the teacher's dais. From her place she could watch the girls during lessons and control whispered conversations, giggling, passing of notes or prompting. A glance, a frown or a shaking of the head was usually enough, but very occasionally she would act silently and quickly by walking up to the suspected rule-breaker and confiscating whatever should not have been there.

She was a tall, plumpish young woman with dark eyes and hair which she did in a high upward sweep. Her complexion was unhealthily pasty, and her mouth full-lipped and pale. I discovered much later that she was not really intelligent and that she had very definite ideas as to the kind of relationship which should exist between the girls in her class and herself. I was a rather guileless child and quite ready to respond to straightforward, reasonable demands: I wanted to please Anna Avdyéevna and conform to her standards of conduct in class. I could not foresee that her special interest in me was to make me into a rebel.

Stassia, the Polish girl, had to practise the piano for half an hour every night. She usually went to the upstairs hall which was used for gym lessons and for religious services on special occasions when the whole of the school would be present. She said it was 'rather lonely up there', and at once I thought I should like to accompany her, and escape the confinement of the study-room, so wearisome after the freedom I had enjoyed at home. The boarders had no other room where they could play games or read, and when they had finished their homework, they could only stay at their places, reading or sewing, always under the eye of the governess on duty. Even if she seemed absorbed in her book or her piece of embroidery, the knowledge that she could look up and watch you whenever she chose, constrained and created tension.

Mademoiselle Vinogradova was on duty when I plucked up my courage to ask her whether I could keep Stassia company while she practised the piano upstairs. She said, yes, I could go, but we must not chat and waste Stassia's practice time.

Before I came to the school, I persuaded my mother not to have me taught music there — because my sister had told me that the boarders' music teacher was very bad-tempered. I loved music however, and it often moved me to tears. At the age of seven or eight I dreamed of being a musical prodigy, like Mozart or Haydn, whose childhood was described in one of the books I had been reading. Mozart could compose at the age of three — but when I put my fingers on the keys of the piano and waited for inspiration, no melody poured out from under my hands, and, deeply discouraged, I did not try again.

Reading came easily to me, but musical notation bewildered me by its complexity, and I admired Stassia, who could extract from this maze of black dots and circles, with or without tails, the beautiful sounds of Mozart's sonatinas. And after she had played her practice pieces and scales, I would ask her to play 'something longer' and she would treat me to one of 'The Seasons' by Chaikovsky, or to a part of a Beethoven sonata. My favourite piece however, was the transcription of the funeral march from the 'Eroica'.

The large empty hall was lit with a single lamp which shone on the open score and on Stassia's grave, thin, almost transparent face. Her hands looked too small for the sounds she produced and caused to reverberate from the bare walls with a resonance that sent a shudder down my spine. While she played, I walked up and down the hall, from the patch of lamplight into the shadows and back, mourning over the unknown hero who was a part of myself, the music and my emotions carrying me along like a flood. I took my predicament very tragically: my mother had betrayed me; she had handed me over to the gaolers; my life was no longer my own — I might just as well be dead! Before I died, I would leave a letter asking that this march be played at my funeral . . . The abreaction was complete and brought an immediate, though temporary relief.

Stassia showed no surprise at my choosing such tragic music as my favourite listening piece. Compared to myself, she was quite settled at the school but, although we had never talked about it, I knew by her looks that she had passed through the same searing experiences I was going through. Playing what I asked was her act of friendship, and I was aware of that, and grateful without telling her so.

A grown-up, who should have known better, lacked the insight which made Stassia's company such a help to me in my time of need. One evening while Stassia was playing and I sitting beside her, the door at the end of the hall opened before the next girl was due to arrive for her piano practice.

'Look who's come!' whispered Stassia. 'It's Anna Avdyéevna!'

It was indeed our *dame-de-classe*. We were surprised to see her because she had nothing to do with the boarding school and lived in rooms or a flat of her own. She came straight towards us. We stood up and dropped our curtseys.

'Go on with your music,' she said to Stassia. 'I don't want to interrupt you. I've just come to see . . .'

She did not finish her sentence, but looking down at me with a smile, asked: 'Has your sister written you from Petersburg?'

My sister, who entered the Women's University in Petersburg in the same year as I became a boarder, had lavished affection on me and treated me with even greater tenderness than my mother. To be reminded of her so suddenly brought all my dammed-up grief to the surface. My eyes filled with tears and I could not speak. I shook my head. Anna Avdyéevna put an arm round my shoulders and led me away from Stassia, to the far end of the hall.

'Tell me about home,' she murmured.

I was in agony. Tears were streaming down my cheeks and I was making desperate efforts to prevent myself breaking into sobs. I was deeply ashamed of myself for weeping like an infant before this stranger, ready to blame her for thus wringing my heart; and wanting to free myself from this embrace which was not the embrace I longed for.

I told her nothing. In the end she let me go with a sigh.

'When you write to your sister remember me to her,' she said. Her eyes were no longer moist with sympathy and she took her leave by gravely inclining her head, which at once restored the distance between us. We curtseyed again. As the door closed after her, Stassia flopped back on to her stool and gave a huge shrug.

'Whatever did she come up here for?'

'Why was she in the building at all?' I muttered, my tear-stained face half turned away.

'I know why,' said Stassia. 'She came to see her aunt, Mademoiselle Saburova. But why come up here?'

I had no explanation to offer. I had no idea at the time that she had come for *my* sake. I did not know then that my sister, knowing that Anna Avdyéevna was to take charge of my class, had spoken to her about me. I do not know what she had told her: perhaps that I was imaginative and affectionate, and that I was bound to be very homesick. Anxious to make the transition from home to school easier for me, she may have recommended me to Anna Avdyéevna's special care. The consequence of this well-meant démarche proved to be far-reaching, and in subsequent years I had reasons to reproach my sister for having, unwittingly, done me a really bad turn. But more than a year had to pass before I began to realize it.

Homesickness is a kind of bereavement and, like bereavement, it can be cured, it seems, only by the passage of time. As in bereavement there is a painful sense of loss, not only of the familiar presence of persons and things loved, but of a part of oneself.

It was not long before I became aware of a change in myself, of the girl called *Rayévskaia* being different from the girl called *Léda*, of my boarding-school self being quite distinct from the person I had been at home. It was not merely the change in my appearance: the looking-glass reflected a thinner face with fair hair combed back and tightly plaited, instead of in a page-like fringe; nor the long dress which made me feel I dared no longer run or jump. When I saw a long empty corridor stretching before me, I still felt the impulse to race along it, but a glimpse of a mid-blue dress at the other end made me check myself at once, clasp my hands in front of me — as all the boarders were taught to do — and walk demurely, dropping a curtsey as I passed a teacher or a *dame-de-classe*. I was learning reserve and caution and quickly losing my natural spontaneity.

I was also losing some of my self-respect: partly because I despised concealment and pretence, and was ashamed of being afraid, and partly because I could not control my distress and so easily dissolved in tears whenever my family or home were mentioned in my presence.

I doubt that grief is relieved by sharing it — unless it is shared with someone very dear. The knowledge that Tania Pánova, like myself, cried herself to sleep in her bed every night did not make my bereavement any easier to bear: when I saw her looking miserable my own misery was made more intense. Comforting was what we both needed, but we dared not comfort one another, half-ashamed of giving in to grief, half-aware that the quality of comforting we needed could only come from a loved adult, and that a child cannot really console another child in the same predicament.

It is curious how well we kept our distance from one another, protecting our bruised sensitivity from well-meaning but clumsy probes in the way a sore finger or a broken arm is protected by being held out of reach of rough contacts, strenuously avoiding any approaches that could cause pain. And even if we were so inclined, our daily routine provided

very few opportunities for confidences. We were up at a quarter past
seven, in our class-rooms by eight-forty-five, and at our lessons until
half past three, with only half an hour's break for lunch at midday. We
had our main meal at four o'clock, and after that were transferred to the
study-room where we settled down to our homework at once. The
governess on duty checked what we had done by calling us to her table
and making us recite the poem or the list of words in a foreign language,
and if any time were left before bed at nine, we could read, sew or draw,
still in the same room, still under the surveillance of the same person.
We were not supposed to leave the room unless it was to go to the
lavatory, and for that we had to ask permission.

Nor was there much relaxation when eventually we were getting
ready for bed. Dasha combed our hair; twice a week she did this with a
fine comb, to make sure that we had not picked up any of 'those eggs'
from the day pupils. She meant lice, of course; she was convinced that
some of the day girls from less privileged homes had lice in their hair.
'You can see them white specks on their black hair,' she told us. And
she knew by experience that homesick children seem to attract vermin,
which multiply and thrive on their lowered vitality. Now and again
she had the doubtful satisfaction in finding one or two in a girl's hair;
then paraffin oil had to be rubbed into the skin and the head tied up in a
clean kerchief to prevent the oil staining the pillowcase. If the hair was
clean, Dasha would plait it for the night, then kiss the top of the girl's
head and say: 'As pure as gold!' and send her off to bed, feeling warm
inside. Dasha's even-glowing, unselective affection did not enfeeble: it
made me, for one, feel less of a waif than I had felt hitherto.

During that first term, in fact during the whole of that first year at
school, I made no close friends, although I was on friendly terms with
Stassia and Tania and later with an older girl, Yuzia. It seems that self-
pity and a craving for the affection I had left at home allowed no room
for a deeper feeling towards any new person. My class-room neighbour,
Margóolina, made a fuss of me from the first day: she opened my desk
for me, helped me to put my books inside it, sharpened my pencil and
made me a gift of a sheet of glossy coloured paper to put round one of
my books, but all these attentions merely embarrassed me. I needed the
attention and affection of an older, more important person to repair my
damaged self-esteem, to restore my capacity for showing positive feeling.
The person in a position to do this was our *dame-de-classe*.

The desk I shared with Margóolina was in the second row on the left
side of the class-room. Anna Avdyéevna's own table was on the same

side, facing us. I was thus very much in her line of vision, and I soon
noticed that her moist brown eyes, which she often raised from her
piece of embroidery, now and again rested on me with an expression of
great benevolence, and her full, rather colourless lips moved slightly,
sketching a smile when our eyes happened to meet. I did not quite trust
my observation at first: she could be smiling to her thoughts or looking
at someone behind me. Yet, as this went on, my heart, hungry for
affection, began to stir in response. A few weeks passed, and I found
myself, half-consciously, waiting for this exchange of glances and for
her smile, though I still dared not smile back. I was genuinely shocked
when Margóolina, closing her desk with a bang at the end of a day of
lessons, remarked a little provocatively: 'I'll tell you something,
Rayévskaia. You're Anna Avdyéevna's favourite. She's always looking
at you.'

I blushed to the roots of my hair, so flattering and yet alarming was
this piece of information — or accusation — for I knew that 'favourites'
were regarded with envious hostility and suspicion by other girls.
Mílochka was an awful example of their breed.

'Keep quiet!' I turned on Margóolina. 'I'm nobody's favourite!'

'You're mine!' she retorted disarmingly. 'Don't be cross! *You* can't
help it. You've done nothing . . . you haven't been making up to her.
But everyone can see that she likes you best of the class.'

I closed my desk and went in front of her as we trooped out of the
class-room, past Anna Avdyéevna who was standing in the doorway. In
passing her, we all dropped our farewell curtseys, for we were not going
to see her until the following morning. My face was still flushed after my
brief argument with Margóolina, and, as I raised my eyes to our *dame-de-
classe*, hers suddenly turned grave with concern. She made me a sign to
wait.

Hot with embarrassment, I stepped back, trying not to look at
Margóolina as she turned to curtsey on her way out. When the last of
the girls was out of the room, Anna Avdyéevna spoke to me at once in
a voice of an almost velvety softness.

'Rayévskaia, are you all right? Your face is so flushed. Have you a
headache?'

'No, Anna Avdyéevna.'

'Are you sure?' she insisted. 'You look as if you had a temperature.'

I repeated my denial. Then she did something which literally made
my head swim. She placed her hand on my forehead and held it there
for several seconds. No one had done this to me for weeks — weeks that

seemed like an eternity. Her hand was soft and cool, and in its shadow treacherous tears quickly gathered under my eyelids. She took away her hand and I still dared not move, hanging my head, as if guilty of some indefinable transgression.

'No, you haven't a temperature,' she said. 'Still, if by any chance your head begins to ache tonight, I should report at once to the matron. You promise?'

I promised, now longing to escape, both from the hot cloud of emotion which enveloped me, and from the reprimand which I was sure to earn if I were late for the boarders' tea.

Stassia was waiting for me at the top of the stairs.

'It's Fräulein Schmiedel's day,' she told me.

As if I did not know! But I understood what she wanted to say: the Fräulein was bound to come down on me like a ton of bricks, and Stassia stayed behind so that she could share the weight of it with me. It was far, far easier to face a scolding in company with a friend, than to stand before an accusing voice in helpless, humiliating isolation. But as we entered the dining-room, the governess happened to be talking to *her* favourite, Mílochka, and we were able to slip into our seats without her noticing us. In fact, when she turned to speak to me, it was to give me pleasant news.

'Rayévskaia, a parcel for you came this afternoon. You can have it after you've finished tea.'

A parcel from home to a homesick child is not just a collection of dainties, an occasion for gorging and for buying popularity with one's classmates — it is a part of home itself, and to open it brings a lump to the throat and makes one hesitate to break into these carefully packed *krendielkí* and slabs of strawberry cake. My mother's hands had touched them only a day or two ago; they came from a familiar cupboard in a familiar room; they revived memories of happy moments round the tea-table . . . I carried the parcel to the study-room, cradled in my arms like a baby. But here was Fatima, watching me like a lynx, implying by her watchfulness that I would be 'a greedy pig' unless I offered her the first choice of whatever there might be in it. And I was impressionable enough to feel that it would indeed be mean of me not to offer her the choice. Slowly I unpicked the stitches, unwrapped the coarse linen into which the box had been sewn — Aniuta, my former nursemaid, now a maid of my mother's, must have done this careful packing and sewing. Dear, tiresome Aniuta! How annoying she could be at times with her remarks about manners, telling me not to swing my legs because it

meant 'giving a swing to the devil!' I wondered whether she missed me.
I peeped inside the box: yes, it was *krendielkí*, strips of rich, sweet pastry
twisted into a variety of shapes. 'They smell good!' said Fatima's voice
behind me. I closed the lid. 'Don't you want to taste them?' Fatima
asked, suavely.

'Not yet. In the dormitory.'

That evening, half grudgingly, half enjoying it, I offered *krendielkí*
around the small dormitory. That old Dasha accepted one gave me the
most pleasure, while Mílochka's supercilious 'No, thank you,' was both
offensive and satisfying, for I had been expecting it. Was I becoming
worldly wise? Hardly so, as much of what happened later will show.

Red Letter Days

The desk calendar in my father's study at home had a page for every day of the week. Under the boldly printed date and the name of the day, names of men and women appeared in small print, the names of saints and martyrs whose memory was venerated on that day. A child born into a peasant family would be baptized with the name of the saint on whose day he was born, and for the rest of his life that day would be celebrated as his 'name-day'. Educated families did not follow this custom of naming: they chose their children's names freely but they celebrated their name-day all the same.

Some names appeared in the calendar several times in the year: there had been more than one Mary, more than one John among the saints, so the names of Ivan and Maria were the commonest in Russian villages. My name appeared only once, on March 23rd, old style, two days before the Holy Day of Annunciation, when you bought caged birds in the market place and released them, to share with you the joy at the tidings Archangel Gabriel brought to Virgin Mary. Such Holy Days and Sundays were printed on the calendar in red, and there was excitement in coming upon them as you turned the pages, an anticipation of celebrations and rituals connected with them. Less interesting were red-letter days indicating the name-day or birthday of the Tsar, for all that happened on such days was the display of national flags on buildings and my father putting on his parade uniform to attend the service at the cathedral.

At my boarding school, however, such days were observed as a very special kind of holiday, particularly the name-day of our patroness, the Dowager Empress, María Fyódorovna. No lessons were held on that day. In the morning we were issued with a fresh set of fine cambric white cape and sleeves, and a white pinafore fringed with lace. After breakfast we were taken to the upper hall for a religious service. I remember the strong impression it made on me the first time. The hall where Stassia practised her music and where on one day a week we did our gym, was transformed into a chapel, with a praying desk set below the portraits of the Imperial couple. The desk was covered with a cloth of gold brocade and on it lay the book of the Gospels with the ends of bright-coloured ribbons hanging down from between its pages. The boarders led the way, walking demurely in pairs, and ranged themselves facing the praying desk. The staff followed and stood on one side. Then the Headmistress entered in a flurry of silk skirts, accompanied by the Director, both wearing their decorations. We curtseyed deeply to them while they bowed gravely in our direction. Immediately after them *bátiushka*, our school priest, strolled in, a deacon at his elbow. He looked splendid in his blue and silver *risa*, no longer an avuncular figure who smiled at us benevolently, almost indulgently, in the class-room.

The acolyte handed him the censer, and at once he began to swing it and to pray in his deep, rich voice. He prayed that the Lord might grant health and long life to her Imperial Majesty, the Dowager Empress María Fyódorovna, that He guard, preserve and protect her to the end of her days. He offered the same prayers for the Emperor Nikolái, his wife, the Empress Alexandra Fyódorovna, his son, the heir to the throne, the Grand Duke Alexéy, and 'the whole of the Imperial family'. I thought it was most unfair that his daughters were not mentioned by name, though I myself thought the little boy much more attractive than his sisters. The Grand Duchesses, Olga, Tatiana, Maria and Anastasia, with their long straight hair and large hats, did not match my mental picture of a fairy princess; in fact, I thought them rather plain and dowdy.

The '*moliében*', or prayers for health, lasted barely twenty minutes, and we went down to our study-room, to spend the rest of the day — alas! — in boredom, relieved only by a special midday meal with a huge meringue pie for a sweet course and a distribution of chocolates and sweet biscuits at tea time. The Headmistress did this herself, beaming benevolence as she told us: 'From her Imperial Majesty, the Empress Maria Feódorovna!' with such an obvious delight that, in my innocence, I took it that the gifts came to us straight from the palace itself. Mílochka

and Fatima guffawed with derision when, in an unguarded moment, I
voiced this belief.

'You *are* a baby!' said Fatima. 'The Empress only gives money for the
sweets and pastries to the Headmistress: she doesn't *buy* them herself!'

On ordinary Sundays we were taken to a church service at an
orphanage. The orphanage chapel was open to the general public, but
most of them went to the Cathedral, so that we were spared 'the
common crush' . . . and 'the vulgar curiosity' our uniform aroused
among the passers-by. They certainly stared at us as we walked through
the streets in a crocodile, the chief porter, Klementiy, leading the way,
and two governesses, one at the side, the other at the tail of the procession. We walked past the hotel where my mother and I stayed when
she brought me — it seemed so very, very long ago — to visit my sister
at this same boarding school, and again, on the fateful day of my entrance
examinations; past my brother's *Ghymnasia* in the main street . . . And
all the time I was conscious of my captivity, oppressed by the knowledge
that I could not step off this pavement, turn round to look at that
passing cab, stop to gaze at these shop windows without immediately
being told not to, and having to keep in step with the others. As I look
back at it from this distance in time, I believe my sense of desolation
could stand comparison with the dejection of the prisoners in *Fidelio*,
trudging round and round their prison yard.

Nor was the orphanage a place calculated to raise a child's spirits.
Its smaller inmates, all girls, pressed around us as we took off and piled
our bonnets, overcoats and galoshes on to the wooden forms in their
bare dining-hall. I did not fail to notice that their uniforms were a poor
copy of our own: they, too, had white capes and sleeves, but their
frocks were made of coarse grey cotton, not of fine wool like ours.
Conscious of the social chasm which divided us, I saw in their freckled
faces and round eyes the same awareness of 'not belonging' which was
oppressing me, and I was stung with pity for them. Was I more fortunate
than they, who had no parents at all? I knew I was, yet the thought of
their unhappiness merely increased the poignancy of my own.

The chapel into which we were shepherded was bright, almost gay
with the shining gilt of the iconostasis, and warm with the glow of many
burning candles. The orphanage girls filled most of the available space
on the left side, while we took our privileged places on the right, in
front of the rest of the congregation. Opposite us there was a particularly pleasant painting of Jesus: in his sky-blue robes He looked as if He
could not refuse anything you asked Him. If only He could make this

service half an hour shorter, how much better I could pray to Him! But it went on and on, and first my feet, then my back and the whole of my body began to ache. I began to wish that I would faint: perhaps then they would not take me to church next Sunday . . . Myriads of ants started running up my legs. The choir sang 'Lord, have mercy upon us!' for the hundredth time. Our *bátiushka*, who was also the priest and confessor at the orphanage, went in and out of the Royal Gates at least a dozen times. The scent of melting wax and of incense made the air visible above the candle flames: it trembled and flowed upwards in thin wisps.

At last the *bátiushka* came out of the Holy of Holies with a silver cross in his hands. We headed the queue for kissing the cross, and a few minutes later, stretching and yawning out of sight of the governesses, we were back in the orphanage dining-hall, pulling on our galoshes and digging our overcoats out of a pile. The orphanage girls gazed after us wistfully as we trooped out of their door. I wondered if they thought we were lucky to be going out into the streets. If they only knew!

Oh, the boredom of those Sundays at the boarding school! I had never been bored at home, though I might have felt sad at times: there was always so much to see, to do and think about. At school we only had a few games: tiddley-winks, snakes and ladders, a pack of cards — but interest in these did not last for more than a couple of hours. Reading was a way out of boredom, but as far as I remember, even at that age I found a contrast between the world of fantasy and the real world too painful to seek this form of escape as a matter of course. Happy stories did not make me forget my own unhappiness, sad ones intensified my feeling of loss. Of my dormitory companions only Fatima and Tania Pánova stayed at the school on Sundays; the others were taken out by friends or relatives. Fatima was no friend of mine, and Tania was as depressed as myself. Casting around for relief, I wrote my mother, asking if anyone she knew could take me out on Sundays. She thought of Olia Rodiónova, the daughter of my father's former assistant, who was a day girl at the school and lived with her relations. Olia's big cousin was also a pupil at our school, and one Sunday she came to take me to their house.

I had known Olia at home before either of us came to the school, but I found her too timid and slow, and was more friendly with her younger sister. We had hardly spoken to one another in class. She was far from bright, but I felt even her company would be preferable to spending the whole of Sunday in the study-room, not suspecting that any home could be as dreary as Olia's cousin's proved to be.

I went there on several Sundays. Olia had nothing to say. We played cards, tiddley-winks and snakes and ladders. Tea was served on a table covered with cold oilcloth, unappetizing tea with bread cut too thick and jam full of sharp bits of crystallized sugar. The evening came, but for some reason the lighting of the lamp was delayed. We sat at the table waiting for nothing in particular. Across the street an uncurtained window of a house was lit up brightly, and I could see two children, a boy and a girl, leaning over a table, playing some game and laughing. A woman — their mother, no doubt — came in and spoke to them, smiling. She poured something into cups; the children drank. From where I was looking the room seemed extremely cosy and the children so obviously enjoying themselves, that my heart contracted with an envious pain, and I longed to be in their place, not to be myself, to know no more of Olia's cousin, of the boarding school, of the life that was mine and that I found intolerable.

When at last Olia's cousin brought me back to school, I barely found the words to thank her. That Sunday outing had been a torment; I did not want to have another. Wearily, I was looking forward to the hour which at home I used to do my best to postpone — the hour of going to bed. I hurried through the usual preparations, was first in the queue for Dasha to comb my hair. 'Did you enjoy yourself at Rodiónova's cousin's?' Fatima asked me, slyly. I did not reply.

The bed was cold to get into, but, curled into a ball, I soon got warm, and here at last, in a place of my own, between pillow, sheets and blankets, I felt almost secure — secure from intrusion, observation and the demands of all those people around me. The small *lampáda* before the icon of the Virgin in the corner of the room glowed in semi-darkness. It was of red glass, like the one at home, but higher up and further away. My bed stood end to end with Tania's, and for the rest of the night it became my castle, with the enemies, Fatima and Mílochka, kept out, and a friend, Tania Pánova, guarding the entrance. At home I used to like staying awake, weaving fantasies, playing wordless games, but here I wanted to fall asleep as soon as possible. When my eyes closed and sleep descended upon me, my weightless body floated up to the ceiling and through it, into the starlit space, a realm where the familiar and the new became mysteriously interwoven and blended in a fascinating pattern of a dream. And there I stayed, free, until the clanging of the morning bell shattered the intricate pattern and the mystery, and brought me down, back into my bed, the bed I had to leave promptly to begin another day, so much like the one before it and the one that was to follow . . .

My only real red-letter days at school were the days when my uncle Fyodor came to visit me. The first time it happened, half-way through my first term at school, I was bowled over with surprise and excitement, hardly believing, in my slough of despair, that anything so good could happen to me.

I was half-heartedly trying to draw in the study-room one Saturday afternoon when the junior porter, Kondratiy, came in and spoke quietly to the governess in charge. She called me.

'Rayévskaia, your uncle is here to see you. You can go down with Kondratiy.'

I jumped up in a flurry, aware that all the girls at my table were looking at me with interest, and some, no doubt, with envy. I almost forgot to curtsey to the governess and thank her as I left the room, and as I clattered down the iron stairs, I thought with horror that, if I had forgotten, she might have stopped me, in punishment, from seeing my uncle. I ran into the reception hall – and there he was, large, blond and balding, in features so obviously my mother's brother, that I had to laugh through my tears as I hung upon his neck.

We sat in the corner by a window and I opened the box of chocolates he had brought me, excellent chocolates, for Uncle Fyedia did not share the idea some adults have about children not appreciating quality. We played the game of 'guessing the filling': if you guessed it correctly you could have another chocolate straight away. Then I sat on his knee and played with his long moustaches – a game that took me back to my earliest years. I pulled them down, put them up, twisted them into a variety of shapes and giggled at the changed appearance this gave him, while he frowned, squinted or stared to make himself look even more different, which sent me into fits of laughter. I asked him to move his ears, a trick that to my mind verged on the miraculous, and he did it, as he used to do when I was quite small. I pulled out his gold watch from his breast pocket, and he opened the back lid and let me see the tiny cogs and wheels moving at different speeds. But this – disastrously – reminded him of time. He had to go. Already? Seeing my face, he asked: 'Isn't it Sunday tomorrow?'

'Oh, yes!'

'Then I will take you out to lunch and tea . . . We will get your brother to come, too.'

That night I could not go to sleep for a long time with excitement.
Having lunch with Uncle Fyedia meant going to a restaurant, a place
for grown-ups which I found impressively attractive. The chairs were
so large and heavy that the waiter had to move one out for me and push
it under me as I sat down. The spoons, forks and knives were also large
and heavy, but I managed them myself somehow. The table-cloth and
the napkin which stood up, stiff like a soldier, on my plate, were of
shiny whiteness. There were large palms in pots opposite each tall
window, and a pair of especially big ones flanking the door, which was
opened and shut by a porter in a maroon coat with brass buttons. The
people sitting at tables were mostly men in dark suits or uniforms, a
few women, each with a male escort, well-dressed and perfumed, and
no children except myself. One woman smiled at me, and several of the
men exchanged greetings with my uncle.

We had *bouillon* with *pirozkhí*. The *bouillon* was very hot and I burnt
my mouth with the first spoonful, which reduced my enjoyment of
what followed – roast hare with mashed beetroot and cranberry
jelly. I struggled with my knife and fork over a table too high for me.

'Shall I cut it up for you, *báryshnia*?' a respectful voice asked behind
me.

I looked round: it was the kindly waiter who had moved my chair for
me. My first impulse was to say 'no' to this rather humiliating offer, but
my uncle nodded and the waiter, snatching up another knife and fork,
promptly separated the meat from the bone, cut it all up and put the
plate back in front of me with a flourish.

The best part of the meal was of course the sweet course: a large
portion of icecream, mixed with bits of crystallized fruit and topped
with a thick layer of whipped cream. It seemed incredible that Uncle
should choose to eat jam pancakes instead, as if one could not have jam
pancakes any time at home! But he said icecream made him feel too
cold inside.

After lunch Uncle and I went to his hotel where he read through some
papers while I stood by the window looking out into the street. No
white paint on these panes! And the street was busy with a lot of things
to watch. Cabs passed, quiet on their rubber tyres, the horses' hoofs
clop-clopping on the cobbles – a sound I loved to hear. These people
in cabs, people walking along the pavements, their faces seen dimly in
the gathering dusk, who were they? . . . Where were they going? . . .
I wished I could follow them, peep inside their houses as they opened
their doors, see their children, ask them their names. There was a

toy-shop on the opposite side of the road with dolls, and carts, and drums in the window. There was also a pastrycook's with a display of tempting cakes and boxes of sweets. People were buying them — for whom? The bell above the door tinkled as they went in and out. All this life going on, and I just watching — but presently I, too, shall be in the street, still a free child, walking with Uncle to a café where we will meet my brother for tea.

My brother Vladímir, or Vova as we called him, was older than I by four years. His visits to my school were a trial to both of us. I do not know whether he came because my mother had asked him to, or because he really wanted to see me, but the balance of my feelings at that time was so precarious that merely seeing him made me cry. Self-conscious and inexpert in the art of consolation, he could think of nothing to say except: 'Don't cry!' and there we stood, facing each other between the window and the grand piano, in the only corner of that vast impersonal room where one could have some illusion of privacy. When in the end I managed to control my tears, we still found nothing to say to one another, our lives away from home being so different as to defy all attempts at communication. The visit was supposed to last no more than half an hour, and as soon as the hands of the clock above the door moved to three, my brother picked up his cap and gave me a wet kiss on the cheek, unhappily, yet obviously relieved to get away. I cried again, to see this living link with home slipping away from me. 'It's not so very long till Christmas,' he managed to say once, and I was grateful to him for that.

How different the mood when Uncle and I met him outside the café! We saw him pacing up and down, a tall, thin boy with flaxen hair, delicate complexion and lean, almost sunken cheeks. He raised his peaked cap to my uncle, smiling self-consciously; then they embraced and I received a peck on my cheek.

'Well now, Vladímir!' said my uncle. 'You look ready for a meal. Come inside, quickly.'

The café was Zavádsky's, the best in M*, as I soon learned from my schoolmates. My uncle ordered cups of chocolate, *pirozkhí* fried in deep fat, pastries and finally icecream. My brother ate a prodigious meal, leaving me way behind in the race. My uncle sipped a cup of black coffee. How could he drink something so bitter with such evident pleasure?

'How's your Latin, Vladímir?' he asked my brother.

Why did boys have to learn Latin, as well as French and German, and girls only French and German?

'It's my best subject . . . five plus . . . ' my brother muttered, his mouth full.

Why did boys have 'five' as the highest mark at their schools and the girls 'twelve'.

I was thinking while they talked. The sky outside grew dark and the street lights came on.

'Well, children, it's time to say good-bye for the present.'

We came out. My uncle hailed a cab.

'I'm taking your sister back to her golden cage,' he told my brother. 'Can I give you a lift?'

'No, thank you, Uncle. I'm going in the opposite direction. I'll walk.'

We exchanged a feeble kiss and I climbed into the cab, my uncle helping me. As it jerked forward and my head lolled against the padded back, I watched my brother's slender grey-coated shape stride away into the greyness of the autumn evening, my heart aching with pity for him, for myself, and for the passing of this rare, red-letter day. A memory floated up: my parents in the drawing-room of our house at B*, looking through the window at my brother, still in his short-trousered suit, walking along the street. 'There he goes, nodding as usual,' said my father and they both laughed affectionately at his peculiar, head-nodding gait. A sharp pang of jealousy shot through me at the sudden awareness of how much they loved him. Now he walked holding himself very straight, and there was only me to watch him, and only uncle to watch me disappear a few minutes later behind the heavy double doors of the school.

Because my brother used to tease and sometimes bully me, I came to think of him as an antagonist rather than as a friend, despite the fact that he had been my constant play companion before he left home to go to school. My sister, eight years older than I, was affectionate and maternal towards both of us, but she treated me with a special tenderness. She liked giving me pet names, sometimes taking them from a book, sometimes inventing them. The latest of these was *króshka*, a Russian word for 'mite' or 'crumb', and it was as 'my darling *króshka*' that she addressed me in her letters. The year I went to boarding school she was admitted as a student to *Bestoózhevskiye Koorsy*, the Women's University in Petersburg, and it was from there that she wrote me, doing her best to amuse and comfort me. Professor Viengérov, who lectured to them on Pushkin, had a long white beard and was tiny, like the *Chernomór* who stole Ludmila from Russlan on their wedding night. The French lecturer,

Monsieur Laronde, was almost round in shape and looked and talked like a purring cat. But he was a treacherous cat and could snarl and scratch, especially at dark-haired girls. He was said to give passes only to blondes. 'So, dear *kroshka*, you would be all right with him . . . '

She wrote of the short days and long nights of Petersburg, of noiseless streets paved with wooden blocks, of the wonderful theatres, of the curly white chrysanthemums standing on her desk which Goga had brought her . . . Did I remember Goga? She mentioned that she had posted a parcel of nice things for me to eat, which she bought at the Yelisyéev's, a splendid shop in the Nevsky Prospect, and she ended by reminding me that Christmas was approaching fast and begging me not to be sad. She 'embraced and kissed me many times'.

I could almost feel her soft cheek against mine as I read these words, and of course I cried a little over her letter, but for a while it took my thoughts away from home, as I imagined her walking along the Nevsky, all bright lights and lacquered horse-carriages with coachmen in livery. I thought of Goga, her schoolboy friend, who had failed his finals at the *Ghymnasia* and had to enter a military school in Petersburg. He gave her white chrysanthemums, rare and expensive flowers . . . was he in love with her and she with him? But this was only a fleeting thought, a faint prick of curiosity: love between grown-ups was still a closed book to me which I was not ready to open. My thoughts turned to the parcel which I knew would arrive in a day or two.

A parcel from Petersburg! No other girl in my dormitory could boast of a prospect like this! My sister knew what would please me: she sent me a box of *pastilá* — little bars of fruit-flavoured marshmallow — a box of *marmaládd*, another kind of fruit sweets of delectably natural flavour, and a box of *tianoóchki*, a kind of soft, creamy fudge, every bar of which could be pulled out to twice its length without breaking it. My delight in the pretty pictures on the boxes, of children playing with young foals or lambs in flowered meadows, was almost as great as in the sweets themselves.

I wrote the same evening to thank her and tell her of my continuing misery. But was it in fact as acute as it had been six weeks or even a month ago? Time was doing its reviving and deadening work. My pain had become deadened, a mere dull ache in the background of my mind; my interest in people and things was reviving. Class work helped me to recover my sense of reality, and the praise of the teachers was gradually restoring my damaged self-esteem. I liked my lessons. Russian language became, perhaps inevitably, my favourite subject.

The teaching methods in my school — as in most Russian schools of the day — were of a formal kind; a more or less identical pattern was repeated day after day. At the start of a lesson the teacher explained the contents of the next one and set us our homework. Then she called our names from the register, and the pupil she called had to give an account of what she had prepared of the contents of the previous lesson. She had to hold forth until she had nothing more to say. The plight of one who had not done her homework can easily be imagined: she might find herself standing completely silent in front of the waiting teacher, surrounded by the half-sympathetic, half-derisive audience of her classmates. The teacher gave marks for every 'call out' and entered them in the register against the pupil's name. In the course of a lesson there was time only for a few interrogations of this sort, and a fair proportion of pupils, especially those whom the teacher knew to be able and conscientious, might be 'called out' no more than three or four times in the whole term. All the pupils, however, had to take dictation and write compositions in class and at home, and no one could count on escaping the teacher's attention indefinitely. Some teachers had the reputation of catching pupils out by 'calling' them on two consecutive occasions. The French teacher, Vera Petrovna, dry-voiced, precise, with an unhealthy yellowish complexion, was reputed to be capable of such treacherous behaviour. Not so Maria Ivánovna, our teacher of Russian, a somewhat untidy, plumpish woman, who walked with a waddle and had loose strands of hair hanging about her face. I was drawn towards her from the start.

The first composition she set us during my first term was on the usual school theme of the summer holidays. As the previous summer had been my last summer of freedom, I wrote with abandon about St John's night in the country, when peasant youths and girls jump over bonfires holding hands, to see whom they would marry, and girls alone float wreaths of wild flowers with lighted candles on them down the woodland stream, to see who would die that year and who would prosper. I wrote about myself, describing how I went into a dark wood, half-believing that I would find the blue flower of the fern which blooms only on the Eve of St John's, and makes the ground transparent, showing you where the buried treasure lies.

When Maria Ivánovna brought back the corrected essays, I saw that mine was on the top of the pile, and my heart leapt with premonition. Could it be the best of the lot? Surely, it could not be the worst! My mother had thought a great deal of my poems and fairy-tales and proudly showed them to her friends and acquaintances . . .

Maria Ivánovna read it aloud to the whole class from beginning to end, stressing the passages she thought were particularly well-written and taking an obvious pleasure in doing so. I did not know where to look or what to do with my face, imagining that everyone had guessed whose composition it was and was watching me to see how I would behave. I wondered if I looked stupidly pleased, and felt now hot, now cold all over, with a prickly sensation spreading from my head to the whole of my body. Most of all I wondered whether Anna Avdyéevna was looking at me and what she was thinking about my composition, but I dared not glance in her direction. Why was the emotion that possessed me so like shame? When my mother used to read my stories to her friends I listened through a chink in the door to their laughter and comment. I remember one of them saying: 'Could she have copied all this from some book or other?' and I ran off, weeping with helpless anger, humiliation and disgust. From that moment I saw that person as my enemy. What I wrote was so much a part of myself that I took the slightest criticism as an attack on my integrity. Praise, on the other hand, gave me a feeling of wonderful elation.

'It's the best composition by an eleven-year-old that I've read for years,' said Maria Ivánovna. 'In fact, it's quite outstanding – command of language, imagination, feeling for nature, it has it all . . . '

I hardly heard what she said afterwards about other essays, waiting tensely for the moment when my own would be returned to me. My heart was thumping when I opened my book and saw the marks – twelve plus – and the word 'excellent' in red ink under the last line of my sprawling writing. Margóolina was peeping at it over my shoulder.

'Ooh!' she whispered. 'You're going to be her favourite!'

She had said exactly the same thing about Anna Avdyéevna. I threw a quick glance in her direction. Her chin tucked into her high collar, she was looking straight at me and smiling her most seductive smile. I felt myself blushing violently and promptly looked away.

When the break came, my classmates crowded round me, to see what marks I had been given for my essay. The little crowd parted when Anna Avdyéevna came up, too.

'Can I borrow your composition, Rayévskaia? I should like to read it myself.'

She read it during the next lesson instead of doing her embroidery, and I watched her surreptitiously, instead of attending to the lesson. Her lips were creased slightly as if she could not make up her mind whether to smile or not, and when now and again she glanced up at me,

her eyes seemed to be swimming in oil. Did she really like my composition or was she merely amused? The torments of hope and doubt I
went through during that half-hour were a true foretaste of the joys and
pains of authorship, more intense perhaps than anything I have felt since.
It seemed wrong to write about myself; it was embarrassing and frightening to reveal myself to all and sundry, yet I could not help writing
about what I thought and felt . . .

I need not have tormented myself. Anna Avdyéevna liked my composition. She asked me if I had written stories. Yes, I had. My sister had
told her, she said, that I wrote poems as well. I admitted I had. Could
she see them? I told her that I had left them at home.

'Haven't you written any since you came to the boarding school?'
I shook my head. She was silent for a moment.

'I see,' she said. 'You're missing the fields and woods you like so
much. Well, they'll still be there when you go home. You'll recover
your inspiration. You have talent. You have so much in front of you.'

Again I stayed awake longer than usual that evening. The words of
my Russian teacher and of Anna Avdyéevna went on echoing in my
mind. 'The best composition I've read for years.' 'You have talent. You
have so much in front of you' — So much . . . of what? Was I right then,
when I thought of myself as a poet? My mother and sister said I was —
but then, they were very fond of me. My father, on the other hand, had
said: 'Everyone writes poetry when they're young', while my brother
teased me by getting hold of my poems and reciting them with mock
solemnity. But now these grown-up women, who had no reason to
flatter me, were saying . . . It must be true! I could become like Pushkin,
like Lermontov — poet and writer in one. Different though, because I
was a girl . . . the first great woman writer and poet in Russia! The
first . . . shall I become famous? Shall I recite my poems in a great hall
from a dais garlanded with flowers? Will the people in the audience
present me with bouquets? Will they all applaud and call out my name?
This — if it happened — was worth living for . . .

And — to forestall the future — some of it did happen. I did recite my
poems from a dais in a great hall — in Petrograd, at the age of seventeen.
Anna Ahmatova was one of the participants in that 'Evening of Women
Poets' arranged by a professor at the Women's University, who had
married a cousin of mine. And the audience applauded me more than
they applauded Ahmatova — probably because I was so young. And one
man presented me with a bouquet of flowers. But the time was February
1917, a few days before the revolution. The audience was mostly

women; there were many empty seats in the hall; and the youth who gave me flowers was my ill-fated admirer from childhood days, Shoora Martýnov, who was so plain and eccentric that his attentions only embarrassed me. Such are the dreams that 'come true' . . .

Christmas at Home

I awoke one morning, surprised at the brightness of the room, and noticed that the cornices of the house opposite were white with snow. By lunch-time it melted, leaving everything darker than before. It was the first December snow — December, the month of Christmas! I shall go home for the whole three weeks . . . and after that — perhaps — my mother would let me be a day pupil!

At home I had been vividly aware of the change of seasons: the first snow, the first rooks, the first snowdrops . . . Leaves whirling down from trees in the autumn — I watched them dance in the air. Birds, gathering on roofs and telegraph wires—I stopped to listen to their excited twittering before they set off for warmer skies. Streams swelling with rain, snow melting, may-bugs buzzing in the branches of birch trees, dragonflies over the water, the red moon rising from lilac bushes, sunsets and summer lightning — all the wealth of nature was mine. Now, spending so much time indoors, I hardly knew what was happening outside.

On one dreary evening, after I had drawn a house and a boat, and was looking at them with disgust, wondering why I could not draw them better, I noticed Stassia threading tiny imitation pearls and sewing them on to a piece of red velvet. I asked her what she was making.

'A present for my mother,' she replied.

'You give presents to your mother?'

This surprised me. In my family we never gave presents to our elders. It seemed so obvious that we could not because all the money we ever had was our parents' money. The privilege of making presents was entirely theirs.

'I give Christmas presents to all members of my family,' said Stassia with a touch of pride in her voice.

'But *what* do you give them? What is this you're making?'

'This will be – when I've finished it – a tiny velvet mule, to hang up on the wall by the bed. My mother will keep her watch in it during the night.'

I could picture to myself my mother's pleasure on receiving something made by myself, but . . .

'Do you give a present to your father as well?' I asked, my imagination boggling at the thought.

'Yes, I've told you – to everybody – my brothers and sisters, too.'

'*What* – do you give your father?'

Stassia shrugged her shoulders.

'Oh! . . . anything. He's not particular. Last Christmas I gave him a blotting pad. I cut triangles out of a piece of blue leather and stuck them on the corners of a piece of thick cardboard, then I put a sheet of yellow blotting paper over it. It looked quite nice.'

'And he uses it?'

'Of course.'

This was something which took me quite a time to digest. The distance which my father's reserved and taciturn personality had estab lished between us from my earliest days made such intimacy appear to me impossible. My father accepting a present from me! He, who, as I knew, regarded celebration of name-days, birthdays and giving of presents as so much silly nonsense . . . And anyway, what could I give him? Unless of course I made him a blotter, as Stassia did for her father . . .

Curious how this seed took root in my mind, germinated and finally grew into a determination to give Christmas presents to every member of my family – including my father! Now I was not quite so eager that the weeks separating me from Christmas would flash by: I wanted, I needed, time to prepare my gifts.

Stassia became my inspiration and adviser, while Zoya Dmítrevna, the sewing mistress, acted as a sympathetic provider of practical help.

This was comforting, for she was something of an anomaly in the highly conventional setting of our school: this slender, dark-haired woman, whose way of moving and wearing her clothes was more that of an opera singer than of a teacher of little girls. She was temperamental, unpredictable, liable to flare up if she felt a girl behaved as if her subject had no importance. But when I told her I wanted to make something for my sister and mother, she became quite enthusiastic. She cut out a comb case which she thought would do nicely for my sister and an oval mat which she was sure my mother 'would adore' to use on her dressing table. Then she designed simple cross-stitch patterns for me to embroider on these things during her sewing lessons. But what about the men of the family? I did not want to ape Stassia by making a blotter for my father, but I was very tempted to imitate her by making a mule to serve as a case for his watch. Such a present seemed fantastically unsuitable, but the idea fascinated me. I consulted Stassia. She did not seem at all surprised. Yes, of course she would help me to make it. She cut the mule out of cardboard, and I covered it with a piece of red velvet and stitched the decorations of pearl beads over it. There still remained a present for my brother. What could I make for him? A blotter? . . .

'Must you *make* a present for him? Why not buy him something from a shop?' suggested Stassia.

But how could I get him something from a shop? When we were taken for a walk through the town, we could not stop and look at shop windows, and in any case I had no money to buy anything. Fortunately, my uncle Fyodor came to see me a few weeks before the Christmas holidays, and when we were out together, I saw a pretty paperweight in a stationer's window, a statuette of a chestnut horse rearing, with mane and tail flying out as if in the wind. I fell in love with it; my uncle bought it for me — and then I remembered how my brother's technical drawings got blown all over the room when the window was open . . .

It was a difficult decision, for I hated parting with the little horse, but I consoled myself with the thought that I would still see it, rearing up on his desk. Thus the problem of my brother's present was solved — at some cost to myself. Perhaps the sacrifice we least like to make does the most good to our character . . .

On the evening of December 17th old Dasha collected the clothes we took off before going to bed, made us identify our own in the special wardrobe where they were kept, then laid them beside our beds. On the morning of the eighteenth, having dressed, we could hardly refrain from eyeing one another, surprised at finding how different we all looked out of uniform. I stared at my own legs, unfamiliar in their black stockings, after having been concealed for months under the long school dress. I felt tense, restless, waiting for my mother to come for me some time before lunch. She was arriving by train from B* — but there had been a heavy fall of snow in the night, and Fatima was holding forth, telling us how last Christmas holidays trains had been delayed for hours by a snow storm. Tania's mother was coming all the way from the country by horse sleigh, and by twelve o'clock Tania was in tears, convinced that she would not arrive until the next day, or even the day after. Tania's distress made me feel alarmed and tearful, too.

Then, as the strain of waiting was growing almost unbearable, one of the senior girls put her head through the door and called us. Behind her stood Kondratiy, the junior porter, ready to take our cases down.

In our rush downstairs we nearly forgot to report our departure to the governess on duty, and when she told us we were expected back on January 8th, we just gasped out our thanks and raced on — to meet that eternity of bliss — three weeks at home!

In the reception hall two women were sitting on chairs with their backs to the light, but though my mother was wearing unfamiliar winter clothes and I could not see her face, I knew at once which of the two she was and I ran straight up to her, forgetting to say good-bye to Tania, not even turning my head to see what *her* mother was like. Nor was she less oblivious of me than I of her. I am sure her face, like mine, was buried in her mother's bosom, tears streaming from her eyes. When I could see through my tears, I looked up at my mother's face and laughed — because she was wearing a short, wide-meshed veil, and the brown birthmark above one of her eyebrows fitted neatly into one of the meshes. Her green-grey eyes were fixed on me with an expression of anxious scrutiny. How very much the same she seemed! How strange that she was here, looking so much the same!

'Are you quite well?' she asked. 'You look pale. Have you had a bad cold or something?'

She had brought my own overcoat with my ermine bonnet and muff. I pressed them against my cheek before putting them on: they could have been friendly little animals with their soft white fur and tiny black tails.

'This coat is almost too short for you,' said my mother. 'I only hope that your new party frock will fit.'

I was having a new party frock! 'What colour, Mamma?'

'White, on a blue silk sheath . . . You wanted a blue one this time, didn't you?'

I knew my mother preferred pink for me, but my sister thought pink rather vulgar, so I felt divided.

'Yes, I had a pink one last year,' I said.

A two-horse sleigh was waiting outside. We picked my brother up at his lodgings on the way to the station. He, too, was ready, waiting, in his uniform overcoat, light grey with shiny buttons, and a *bashlýk* loose over his back. My mother could not prevail on him to put it over his ears.

We had lunch at the station restaurant before boarding the train. My brother wolfed his food while I toyed with mine, and my mother sighed as she watched us both and commented on my brother's looking pale and thin.

In the train my brother entertained her with stories of the jokes his schoolmates played on the German teacher, while I sat on the little table by the window watching the countryside. It was deep in snow and looked deserted except for the occasional heavy flight of a crow disturbed by the approaching train. Here and there the whiteness was broken by a group of trees, or a sudden view of brown log houses, always some distance from the railway. The air was still and the trees stood motionless, the tangle of their branches transparent against the pale sky tinged with green; the distant huts looked like mushrooms springing up from a field silvery with dew. When the train entered a forest of firs and pines, the movement of air it produced dislodged layers of snow from the broad, sloping branches. The snow slid off and fell silently, breaking into lumps some of which rolled down the slope towards the train and became snowballs before stopping at the bottom. I peered into the shadowy tunnels and caverns under the trees: there the snow was speckled and strewn with fallen pine and fir needles. In some places I noticed a string of small shallow footprints, and I thought with delight of the wild animal — a fox or a hare — which must have passed there.

Suddenly I began to recognize familiar landmarks:a windmill, its sails motionless against the darkening sky, a clump of ash trees, a stretch of wattle fencing, then a few lights . . .

'Is this B*, Mamma? Is it?'

'Yes, of course it's B*,' said my brother, a seasoned traveller between school and home.

'Next stop B*! Next stop!' called out a passing conductor.

My mother hurriedly looked round for small objects that might be left on the seats. My brother put on his peaked cap, adjusted it. 'Mamma, look! Is it straight?'

Yes, it was B*. The dear little station, a yellow and white house with tall, low-set windows, clumps of lime trees at each end, paraffin lamps in glass lanterns on wide-spaced lamp posts . . . The platform was powdered with freshly fallen snow.

'Vova, go and call the porter. Hurry!'

But my brother did not know how to hurry, and before he reached the end of the corridor, two or three porters had already erupted into it and were shouting their way along it. Our friend, Number One, was in the lead. He touched his cap to us, grinned, and in a few seconds had all our luggage in his hands, under his arms and hanging over his shoulder on a strap.

'Your coachman's here, *bárynia*,' he told my mother.

Maxim! He was standing by the greys' heads, wearing his blue padded coat, a fur cap and huge mitts. The greys were covered with blue nets, to prevent the snow thrown up by their hooves flying into our faces. He took off his cap when we appeared and, giving the greys an order which they appeared to understand, hurriedly came to hold back the bearskin cover of the seat.

'Wish you good health — *zdráveia zheláiu, bárynia, báryshnia, paních*!' (This curious mixture of Russian and Polish address was always used by servants in Bielorussia.) He answered my joyous greeting by the familiar military phrase — *zdráveia zheláiu* — and as he fastened the cover round us, I could see by the glint in his eye and the expression on his face that he was pleased to see me almost as much as I was to see him

The sky had turned violet, and the whiteness around us was tinged with lilac as we drove home. A silent voice inside me was singing in tune with the gentle music of the harness bells. Some of the houses we passed had their lights already on with their shutters still open, and I caught glimpses of Christmas trees and of tinsel decorations on the walls. We drove through the centre of the town; familiar shops flashed by; suddenly the great mass of the Catholic church loomed up above me. Beyond the railings of the church enclosure with its great birch trees I could see the front of our house, the porch, the row of windows, unlit, but dimly shining with the light of a lamp burning in one of the farther rooms. Maroossia, my sister, would be sitting in the *zala*, reading, or playing the piano. She used to dance the waltz round the *zala* with me in her arms when I was small . . . My heart now danced with the thought of embracing her.

My father, too, would be at home . . . At the thought of him my heart stopped dancing: it seemed to sway back and forth, as if poised precariously on its toes.

The front door was unlocked as usual. We went straight in. I ran through the empty, half-lit drawing-room, calling out: 'Maroossia, where are you?' We collided in the doorway of the *zala*. Her cheeks were warm and soft. She laughed but her eyes were moist as I hung on her neck.

'*Króshka*! I knew it was you when I heard the sleigh bells!'

The firm masculine steps approaching made me release her. My father came out of his study just as my mother and brother entered the room in my wake. He embraced my mother, asked whether she was tired after her journey, then turned to my brother and kissed him on the cheek with some remark which I failed to hear clearly. As he bent over me, I saw the glow of pleasure in his face, but somehow knew that I was not the cause of it. His moustache touched my cheek while my lips made the sound of a kiss, partly in the air. The flutter in my breast gave way to a faint, hollow ache.

The fir tree standing in the corner of the *zala* was a spectacle to raise my spirits again. It was beautifully thick and had a long straight spar at the top, adorned by a star which touched the ceiling. Boxes of decorations were standing, ready to be used, at the foot of the tree.

I was eager to start decorating it at once. My mother, however, thought it was not the thing to do after a tiring journey, and my protests that I was not in the least tired were ignored. My mother said she would much rather I tried on my new party frock — in case it needed alterations. There was to be a children's Christmas party at the Club, held every year, and almost certainly invitations to several private houses.

Aniuta, as brisk and sharp-eyed as ever, helped me with it, and tied the blue silk sash behind my back.

'It suits *báryshnia* ever so!' she remarked to my mother.

She called me *báryshnia*! The days were over when, as my nursemaid, she presumed to teach me manners by making use of some of her peasant lore. 'Don't scatter bread about, Lédochka,' she used to say. 'It's God's gift. It's a sin to leave it lying on the floor and have it trod on.' Or: 'Don't swing your legs like that! When you do this you're giving the devil a swing and he's glad!'

I came out into the drawing-room where my mother and sister were sitting. To my relief, the males of the family were not there.

'Walk to the end of the room. Now turn,' said my mother. 'Turn round slowly. Is it even all round?' she asked my sister.

I lingered in front of a tall mirror scrutinizing my appearance. The dress was very pretty, and I liked the blue sash, but wondered whether it would look even nicer if the bow were tied where I could see it — at the side. Little Lord Fauntleroy, whose story I had recently read and much enjoyed, wore his sash tied at the side. But my mother said only boys did that . . . How I wished I could have curly hair like him! Mine was so straight and fine that it blew out in all directions forming a kind of halo around my head.

My brother came into the room and seeing me in my party dress before a looking-glass, said: 'Hm, hm!' with a scoffing intonation. My sister at once drew him away and made him practise reversing waltz steps with her. I followed them into the *zala* where the floor was bare and polished, and the air fragrant with the scent of the fir tree. Maroossia sang a waltz tune while my brother wheeled her round and round, looking terribly solemn. I waltzed on my own, keeping out of their way. My mother came out of the drawing-room and watched us for a few minutes. She told my brother to keep his shoulders back a little more, then reminded us that it was getting late and the supper was on the table in the dining-room.

I had hardly had time to look at my own room since I entered the house, and now, about to go to bed, I stood gazing around me, comparing what I remembered with what I saw. The room looked very much as I had left it, only more tidy. All the familiar things were in their places: a low toy cupboard in the far corner – as a small child I used to be frightened of something vague and creepy which might emerge from it in semi-darkness . . . A picture of a dark-haired girl in oriental clothes carrying a pitcher – I had asked for a doll like her once, when I was ill in bed, and cried secretly and bitterly when they gave me the usual, inane-looking, blue-eyed and flaxen-haired thing. The ruby-red *lampáda* in the corner which made the silver casement over the image of the Virgin shine in the dark . . . My bed with my own quilt of wild silk in a blue and gold pattern, made in Samarkand . . . My bed where I had dreamed so many dreams, some full of excitement and delight, some terrifying . . . As I got inside it, I whispered my name – all the caressing variations on it my mother and sister were in the habit of using: Léda, Lédochka, Ledóosha, Ledóonia – as if to make sure that it was she who was I, and not that person whom at school they called 'Rayévskaia'. I was conscious of a different self who was looking at my room with the eyes almost of a stranger, standing outside, hoping to be admitted.

What were going to be my dreams tonight? I no longer had the dreams of ghosts which only a year or so ago made me dread going to sleep. I still had, however, recurrent dreams from which I awoke with a thumping heart. That first night of coming home from school I dropped off to sleep feeling the motion of the train, seeing the great fir trees, heavy with snow, and the white carpet underneath them, marked with the footprints of small animals, glide past me.

My dream began most pleasantly with a ride on horseback. The horse was my father's Sultan on whose back I had sat only once – in the stable

yard with Maxim holding the bridle. Now Sultan was prancing, obedient
to my hand, along a snowy forest track. I knew that forest track, for I
had walked and ridden along it in my former dreams, and I fully
expected, as we turned the curve of the path, to see a white-columned
house at the end of it, rather like our own house in the country, only
grander and mysterious. We turned the curve — and there it was, and
I knew I had to enter it.

Sultan stopped in front of the porch. I jumped off with fantastic ease
and tip-toed up the wide steps, my heart half-stopping with curiosity
and fear. The double door opened silently at a gentle push. The large
hall was empty with three doors in it, all firmly closed. I tip-toed across
it and opened the door in front of me. It led into a long room where all
the furniture was covered with dust sheets, and as I was gazing around it,
twilight came on. There had been no life, no sound until then — when I
heard the front door open and footsteps approaching across the hall.
Knowing that I must escape before I was seen, I raced towards the door
at the opposite end, fumbled with the handle, struggled with its weight,
and slipped through only just in time . . . But the pursuer had heard
me and was running now . . . Another room, another door . . . a
succession of rooms and doors, each more difficult to open, heavier than
the one before . . . My heart was in my mouth, the pursuer close on my
heels . . . And then the last, small, shabby-looking door through which
I crashed just as the pursuer's hand was touching my shoulder! . . .
The frosty night air blew into my face, the snow squeaked under my
feet, there were stars above the tops of the great fir trees . . . It was all
over, the strange attraction of the empty house, the pursuit and the
terror. The light was coming back . . . I was waking up. Where was I?

I opened my eyes. The window panes were white, and my heart sank.
These school dormitory windows — white, like the eyes of blind beggars
I had seen in the streets . . . But no! the whiteness was the sparkling,
fluffy whiteness of hoar frost, not of white paint. I was in my own room,
after all! Outside my windows was our orchard, lovely and immaculate
after a fresh fall of snow. I could run out into it without asking anyone's
permission, and wade through the snow up to my knees, and make a
snowman, and stand under a young cherry tree and shake it, so that it
shed its garment of hoar frost over me like a shower of silver spangles.
I was *free* again!

The pleasure of these first few days at home was marred for me by a
worrying thought: how would my presents be received by my family,

especially by my father and brother? I meant this presentation to be a secret until the last moment, but it weighed so much on my mind that I had to tell my sister about it. I also told her that I just could not face handing them out myself — I could not face what might be an amused or a reluctant acceptance. I feared humiliation more than anything else.

My sister was, as always, comforting and reassuring. She talked it over with my mother, and they decided the best thing would be to put the presents on the breakfast table on Christmas morning, each with a slip of paper saying to whom and from whom, and leave everyone to pick up his own.

But before Christmas morning there was Christmas Eve and the late evening church service. I had often seen my mother and sister go to church on ordinary Saturday evenings: my mother said she enjoyed choir singing at Evensong better than at a Sunday morning service. My sister used to fast for a week before Christmas and Easter. My mother did not approve of fasting for young people who were still growing. Nor did she take me to church except occasionally or on great Holy Days: standing on one's feet through a long service, as everyone had to, she regarded as too tiring for any child.

How right she was! A mere half-hour's standing made me fidgety; and the ordinary service, conducted in Old Slavonic, with many repetitions of the same phrases, intoned in the same manner, bored me; for the meaning of what was happening remained unintelligible and was not explained to me until much later in my life. My mother, by not taking me with her, was also, no doubt, protecting herself from embarrassment, for on one occasion at least she had to stop me from tracing with my finger the outline of a cross embroidered on the priest's garment.

The Great Holy Days were, however, different: the service had a solemn splendour and the events it commemorated were familiar — they stirred imagination. On that first Christmas home from school, having tasted the real unhappiness and pain of separation, I was eager for the kind of experience which, I had been told, gave one strength and comfort, and I was full of reverent curiosity about religion and the church. I begged my mother to take me to the late Christmas Eve service which she and my sister were going to attend, and after some persuasion she agreed to do so.

The story of the Infant Jesus born in Bethlehem is a marvellous one to tell a child. I particularly liked being told about the star which appeared to the shepherds guarding their flocks in the desert. I was transported to that wild, distant place under the infinite starlight, and I watched with them, awed and amazed, the great new star rising above the horizon, and saw and heard the angel telling them to go to Bethlehem and worship the newborn Child. With them I trudged along stony paths, following the star, until it stopped above the stable in which the Child lay.

Christmas Eve! The day charged with expectancy above all days. Anticipation of what was going to take place in church was blended with the excitement of preparations for the supper that was to follow – the sacred blended with the profane. I had to make sure that they had not forgotten to put hay under the tablecloth on the dining-room table before they set it for supper. My mother had said more than once that this custom, probably pagan in origin but later linked up with the Birth in the manger, was tiresome and she wished to abandon it. Glasses would not stand upright on the uneven surface and liquids were spilt over the cloth. But to me Christmas Eve would not be real unless this custom were followed, so I went to investigate. I found the dining-room fragrant with the scent of hay, and Aniuta sweeping some stray blades of dry grass from under the table. The scent immediately conjured up the picture of summer meadows and myself riding through them on horseback – an image that made me happy.

Aniuta told me that my sister was already dressing for church and asked: would I like her to help me on with my gaiters? On the way to my room I met our cook, Galaktyón, and could not refrain from asking him whether he had remembered to make the *kootiyá* for supper.

'But of course, *báryshnia*!' he replied. 'How can we do without the *kootiyá* on Christmas Eve? I've made one that size!' And he showed with his hands the size of a small haystack. Unlike most cooks, Galaktyón was inexhaustibly cheerful; he was my second favourite among the servants after the coachman, Maxim.

Maxim drove us to church in a large, two-horse sleigh. The service had already begun when we came in, but this mattered little because there was always plenty of coming and going in the early part of the service. Here and there people were praying singly, on their knees before their chosen icon, crossing themselves and touching the floor with their foreheads. Others were bringing their small candles to the huge candlesticks that stood in front of the iconostasis. They lighted them from the already burning candles, stuck them into empty sockets, crossed themselves, went up to the icon and kissed it, then crossed themselves again and withdrew.

No one had told me in so many words, but I knew that the candle was their present to the Saint or to Jesus Himself, a request not to be forgotten, or to be good to the person for whose health or well-being they had been praying. And I knew that it was the same to Jesus whether the candle was a beautiful one in pale wax with a thread of gold in it which cost fifty kopecks, or a two-kopeck one in dark yellow wax, so thin that it went crooked in the hand of the old woman in a black shawl even before she had had time to light it.

'Would you like to put up a candle?' my sister whispered into my ear.

'Oh, yes!' I was eager but also apprehensive that I might do something wrong, in full view of all the people now assembled in the body of the church. I crossed the few feet of the floor separating me from the nearest big candlestick blazing with light and heat, and as I stood before it, I realized that not a single socket among its many was free. I did not know what to do, and my embarrassment grew when I noticed that my candle, though moderately thick, was becoming soft and bending in the hot grip of my hand.

My sister came to my help. I saw her hand stretching over my shoulder, removing one of the guttering stumps and uncovering a little pool of hot wax at the bottom of the socket. Now I did not need to heat the end of my candle — I could just put it straight in. My sister blew out the burning stump, then just as confidently took out another, making room for her own candle. She straightened out several crooked ones, crossed herself and signed me to come back with her.

From my place beside my mother I watched my candle burning before the great bejewelled image of the Virgin. What did I put it up *for*? Was it to ask that I need not go back to the boarding school?

The knowledge that I had to go back after the holidays was like a thorn buried deeply in my flesh, unheeded most of the time, then suddenly making itself felt as a jab of blunt pain. I turned to look at my mother, wondering if I could still sway her to grant me my wish, but her praying face looked remote and unaware of the pleading in my eyes. I glanced at my sister; she, too, was praying, but responded with a rapid look out of the corner of her lustrous brown eye. How sweet she looked in her little fur cap with her tipped-up nose, her faintly outlined eyebrows and the delicate colour in her cheeks! A strong wave of tenderness for her welled up in me . . . I decided to pray for her — her happiness, her success in passing the examinations at the *Koorsy* and obtaining the highest credits . . .

But hard as I tried, I found it impossible to concentrate on prayer for

more than a few minutes. The church was now packed with people and
ablaze with many candles. The choir was singing louder and more
joyously. It was glorifying the birth of Jesus and his Mother, the Virgin
Mary. A rapt observer, I watched the comings and goings of the priests
who swung their censers at the icons, then at the congregation, and
intoned their prayers, while the choir sang their responses. Their
fervour went on increasing until in an explosion of sound came the
familiar words: 'Glory to God in Heaven, peace on this earth and goodwill among men!'

Goodwill! . . . Goodwill? Never to dislike anybody? Never to feel
angry? To love one's enemies? To love Fatima, Mílochka, Fräulein
Schmiedel? . . . For a moment even that seemed possible. For a moment
I felt as if I were floating on a flood of warmth and light. My head swam.
I must have swayed on my feet because my sister glanced at me with
alarm and put out her hand towards me.

But it passed away — the ecstasy and the dizziness. The service continued, but I was now conscious of my aching legs and back, and I saw
with relief the Royal Gates flung open and Father Ioann come out with
a silver cross in his hands. Father Ioann, small, slender, with streaks of
yellow in his white beard, looked quite impressive in his blue and silver
vestments, and different from the *bátiushka* who came to our house to
play cards with my father, and at whose house we visited. Now he was
looking at us without a sign of recognition, but one of his acolytes
motioned us to come forward to kiss the cross, and protected us with
his broad back and strong arms against accidental jostling.

Maxim was waiting outside with the sleigh, and as we drove back, I
stared at the star-filled sky above us.

'Which is the star of Bethlehem?' I asked. And as no reply came for
a few moments, I pointed at one, low above the horizon, which was
burning with a quivering blue light. 'Is that the one?'

'I think that is Venus, *króshka*.' My sister was letting me down gently.
'The star of Bethlehem appeared only to the shepherds . . . nearly two
thousand years ago . . . '

When we got home the supper was set out on the table, a lenten
meal, abundant and varied but without meat, milk, eggs or butter.
There was the inevitable salt herring, neatly cut into portions and
trimmed with rings of raw onion; a salad of potatoes, beetroot and
cucumber preserved in brine; fish fried in oil; sardines; fritters with
prunes, and, of course, the central and most important dish of all — the
kootyiá. This was boiled rice piled up in the shape of a conical mound,

to be eaten last with a honey sauce. No one could tell me what *kootyiá*
really meant, but it was a traditional dish for the Christmas Eve
supper, and no Christmas would have been right without it.

While we were still at supper, the front door bell rang, and Aniuta,
who had run to open it, came back with a look of half-apology and
half-excitement, announcing the star-bearers.

I jumped up from my seat. My father glanced at me, and I sat down
again.

'Shall we have them in?' my mother asked, addressing all of us.

My father said nothing. My brother shrugged. I nodded emphatically.

'We can't just turn them away from the door, can we?' said my
sister.

'Oh, well, let them in then,' my mother told Aniuta.

All of us got up from the table except my father who never showed
any interest in things of that sort. As we reached the drawing-room, the
star-bearers entered the hall through the front door, bringing with them
a strong scent of frost and snow. Seven or eight young boys in thick
padded coats and felt boots were led by one with a large cardboard star
fixed to a short pole. The centre of the star was a colour print representing the adoration of the Magi. It was transparent and glowing with
the light of a candle placed behind it. Each arm of the star was of a
different colour, also semi-transparent and illuminated from the back.
The effect of the whole was magical, as far as I was concerned.

There was a moment of silence as the boys grouped themselves in a
tight bunch and stood staring at us. Then all at once they burst into song.

'Christ is being born, glory to God! Christ is coming down from
Heaven! Rejoice! Christ has come down to our earth, rise in joy! Sing
the glory of God, let the whole of the earth sing, let all men sing with
joy, sing the glory of God!'

Their voices were raw and husky with the cold, their hair hung
shaggily from under their caps; as they sang, they turned away to mop
their noses with their coat sleeves. And yet the glow of the star,
reflected back on their faces, imparted to them an innocence almost of
angels. I could hardly recognize them as the same boys whom I had seen
about the streets in the summer, clambering over fences, chasing stray
cats with stones and shouting swear words at one another. Surely, goodwill was going to prevail this Christmas! Surely they deserved to be given
at least twenty kopecks for their singing and the labour they had put
into the making of this splendid star.

I did not in fact see what my mother put into the cap the smallest of the boys held out after they had finished singing; the leader was too much on his dignity to betray his pleasure or disappointment. On a sign from him the boys broke into song again, a song of thanks and good wishes to the giver and her family. Then one of them blew out the candle behind the star, and as the light and colour vanished from it, I felt suddenly let down, shocked by the ease with which magic could be destroyed. As the boys trooped out into the frosty night, one of them carrying over his shoulder the uncouth object on a pole, an assemblage of triangles of coloured paper crudely glued together, I wished he had not blown out that candle, but walked with it right through the town, singing, holding it aloft . . .

My mother called me back to the supper table, and as I passed the door of the *zala*, my spirits rose again at the sight of the *yolka* in its freshly decorated splendour with many candles all ready to be lit.

'Let us light it tonight!' I begged as if my life depended on it.

My mother thought it was too late for that, but my sister and even my brother supported me, and in the end she consented. All the candles on the tree were connected by an inflammable thread which had to be lit at one end to carry the flame from one wick to another. I claimed the privilege of putting a match to the first candle. A small blue flame ran along the thread and each small candle sprang into life the moment it reached the wick, until the whole of the tree was lit up and held us all standing around in admiration.

Then my mother called out in alarm: there was a smell of burning resin – a loose end of the thread trailed and smouldered, setting light to a branch . . . My sister hastened to blow it out.

'These inflammable threads are dangerous. We mustn't use them again,' said my mother.

Through the open door of the *zala* I could see my father in the drawing-room, with his back to us in a rocking chair, smoking a cigarette.

'Papa cannot see the *yolka*,' I said quietly.

'He's not interested,' said Maroossia.

My mother called him by his Christian name. It was strange to hear him called thus as if he were a boy.

'Vitya, come and look at the *yolka*. It's alight.'

Unhurriedly, he responded to her call, came and stood in the doorway for a few moments. I turned to see whether he looked pleased: I must have wished, without knowing it, that he should share the feeling the lighted Christmas tree aroused in me – a magical feeling – of wonder, delight and awe, a special Christmas feeling. But his face gave no indication that he felt anything of that sort: he was simply doing what my mother had asked him to do. A minute or so passed without anyone speaking, then he turned and went back to his chair. My mother followed him.

'It's well past your bedtime, *króshka*,' said my sister.

We blew out the candles, I with regret, my brother with an obvious enjoyment. Like the star of the carol singers the tree suddenly looked stripped of its glory, and a sadness descended on me. Bright beginnings and sad endings — did everything happen that way? Things and feelings changed towards the end. Was the *end* itself a sad thing, or was it the *change*?

As I tossed about in my bed half an hour later, I found myself searching for rhymes in a poem which I was trying to compose — comparing joy with a flame, a flame that flares up, wavers, and is all the time threatened with extinction.

Two Parties and a Memory

Why was Christmas morning always so quiet? You awoke and lay with your eyes open, wondering what the time could be. There was not a sound to be heard in the whole house, not a sign of movement indoors or out of doors. The bedroom windows were bright — not with sunshine but with the brightness of snow outside. As you lay there, looking at the cornice of snow overhanging the eaves, a large, dark-coloured bird fluttered across the window and dusted it with snow . . .

On that first Christmas morning home from school I woke up with a slight shock of alarm. Was it late? Were they all up already? Would I have time to put my presents on the breakfast table before anybody came to the dining-room? But the house was absolutely still, just as it had been on all Christmas mornings I could remember. I got out of bed, extracted my small parcels from the chest of drawers where they had been concealed under some linen, and crept out of my room across the day nursery to the dining-room, where I put my parcels beside each person's plate already set for breakfast. Then I returned to my room to look for my own Christmas presents.

Russian children were not brought up on stories of Father Christmas, not even of Saint Nicholas like Dutch and German children. The old *D'ed Moróz* of the fairytales was not a specially Christmas figure. We knew that whatever we received came from our parents and there was no mystery about it. Nor was there the custom of adults exchanging presents at Christmas or of children giving presents to their parents. So my decision to imitate Stassia (who was Polish and a Catholic) was quite a new departure and I felt very nervous about it.

My presents were on a chair beside my bed. It was a measure of my concern for the fate of my own gifts that I had not looked at them before. They were a splendidly bound book from my mother (Bibliotèque Bleu-et-Argent, a story in French by Madame de Ségur), and a box of chocolates from Yelisyéev's of Petersburg, as well as a picture, from my sister. The picture was of an extremely pretty dark-haired boy in a red velvet suit sitting on a rock. I guessed at once that it must be a portrait of Lord Byron as a child: my sister had spoken of Byron to me — she had been attending a course of lectures on him — and I knew she admired him very much. He was soon also to become one of my heroes. There were no presents from the males of my family. This was not unexpected, but I felt a faint twinge of triumph, imagining their surprise when they received one from *me*!

I dressed without waiting for Aniuta to call me and was in the dining-room before anybody else. Aniuta brought in the samovar. She had seen the parcels on the table and was curious about them.

'Whatever are these?' she asked me. 'And you up so early, lovey! Did you bring them from school with you?'

'It's a surprise,' I put her off impatiently.

Then my mother and sister came in. I kissed them, thanking them for my presents. They unwrapped their parcels and were lavish in praise for my painstaking embroidery. But the critical moment came when my father took his seat at the head of the table. I doubt that he would have noticed the small packet near his plate if my mother had not drawn his attention to it.

'Look, Vitya, what Leda made for me,' she said, showing him my handiwork. 'She embroidered it very nicely, I think.'

My father looked. 'What is it for?' he asked.

'A dressing-table mat. And look: there's something she made for you as well.'

As he looked uncomprehending, she picked up the parcel by his plate, unwrapped it and displayed the miniature velvet mule embroidered with imitation pearls.

My father gazed at it, obviously puzzled.

'What is it for?' he asked again.

My mother explained. The expression on my father's face changed slowly to something which looked like embarrassment.

'Made it herself? . . . ' he repeated my mother's words. 'Yes . . . I see . . . it's quite well made . . . '

Flushed to the roots of my hair, I felt tremendously relieved. He had not asked: 'But what use is it to me?' I did not expect him to smile or even look at me. He put it beside his plate. Perhaps he would even use it for his watch when he went to bed . . .

Meanwhile my brother had unwrapped his present and was weighing it up on the palm of his hand.

'A nice lump of metal! A weighty present from my young sister!' he clowned. 'I'm not accustomed to being so favoured. Thanks all the same. I promise not to throw it at you when you annoy me . . . '

'More likely that she'll be tempted to throw it at you,' my sister joked.

The ordeal was over. Now only the pleasant things lay ahead, and the first on the list was the Club Christmas party on Boxing Day, which in Russia we called simply the Second Day of Christmas.

My hair was put in curlers the night before, and as I had not had my hair curled ever before, I awaited the results with some anxiety. I was hoping for heavy clusters of curls such as I had seen in the pictures of Greek gods, and when the curlers were taken out I was shocked to see my hair spreading around my face like a cloud of pollen. My sister, murmuring that it was too fine for curlers, gathered it away from my forehead and tied the flying strands on the top of my head with a bow of blue ribbon. I studied myself closely in a full-length mirror, wishing I could have a different face, a really pretty one, perhaps a little more like Mílochka's.

My brother came in. He was wearing his 'parade' school uniform, a long dark-blue tunic with white metal buttons. He commented mockingly on my vanity, but as soon as I withdrew from the looking-glass, he went up to it and turned about, studying his own reflection. 'I must see if this tunic really fits . . . ' he muttered.

My sister, in a white tulle dress with long sleeves and a high collar, joined us, and again they practised waltz steps while I watched. I loved the waltz — but I liked dancing it with a grown-up partner who could carry me along. My brother looked awkward . . . boys had no ear for rhythm . . . I hoped M. Rodiónov, my father's assistant who had taught me all the dances before I went to boarding school, would ask me to waltz with him.

The windows of the club house were glowing brightly through the trees as our sleigh stopped before the porch. My father was not with us: he would be arriving later, when the children's party was over, and the grown-ups would gather in the other rooms to play cards or snooker.

In the vestibule, two men in white gloves were helping people to take off their wraps, heavy overcoats and galoshes. As we emerged from them, my mother looked us over and told my sister to powder her nose. It looked rather red and my sister was obviously embarrassed by it. My brother passed a comb through his perfectly smooth blond hair. The sounds of shuffling feet and of a polka being played came from the adjoining room. We entered, I walking ahead of my mother, my brother and sister following.

The children, with their hands linked to form a ring, were walking round the Christmas tree. Monsieur Rodiónov was in charge: four of his own children were among them. On seeing us, he came up to greet my mother, and after kissing her hand, he kissed mine as well . . . I flushed with the unexpectedness of this gesture, and as he led me towards the ring, wondered why he had done that. Was it because I was at the boarding school? . . . or because he liked the way I looked? . . . or . . . But before I could solve this puzzle he inserted me into the ring between two grinning boys in my brother's school uniform and urged us all to go faster, faster round the tree.

The two boys were undoubtedly brothers, both wearing tightly belted black tunics with white metal buttons, both showing slightly rabbity teeth. Their faces were vaguely familiar. Where had I seen them before? Slowly, a memory emerged. Surely it must have been in Father Ioann's orchard above the frog pond, on a hot June Sunday morning? These boys — much younger then — in sailor suits, with their nurse-maid . . . I must have come there with my mother, perhaps after church, and while she was talking to our hosts indoors, I strolled out into the orchard and saw a strawberry. A single ripe strawberry, glowing red among the green of the leaves . . .

The boys with their nurse were walking in front of me. I waited for them to turn the corner at the end of the path, and when they disappeared behind the lilac bushes, I walked back, drawn by that strawberry as by a magnet. Dare I? It would be stealing . . . Nela, Father Ioann's daughter, who prided herself on her gardening, would notice at once . . . Suddenly the temptation was too strong for me. I crouched, plucked the strawberry and put it in my mouth. It was only half-ripe, green on the underside, and its sour taste pricked my tongue. I rose to my feet with a thumping heart, turned to go . . . How did that wretched nursemaid manage to come back so quietly? She was standing on the path a few feet away staring at me. She rolled her head from side to side in a gesture of disapproval.

All my blood seemed to rush to my head. Humiliated, ashamed, I did not know whether to go forward or retreat. Some power — I expect a kind of pride — made me go forward. The girl did not wait for me, she went ahead and I followed. In a summer house, perched on a steep bank above the frog pond, her two charges were sitting, chattering, swinging their legs. I sat down on a separate bench. The nursemaid ignored me. She was holding an unripe apple in her hand which she offered first to one of the boys, then to the other. They did not want it. Then suddenly she tossed it into my lap. It was a gesture of scorn, and I knew it, and it stung me to the quick. She wanted to show me that because I stole the strawberry, she expected me to covet the apple as well.

I did not touch it, I let it roll off my lap on to the ground. No one picked it up. The nursemaid said something to the boys and they all laughed. I slid off my seat and walked away, trying not to run.

How long ago was all that? The memory had haunted me for years — or was it months? When it was still fresh, I wondered every time I met Father Ioann or one of his family whether they knew about the strawberry and what they thought of me. Will they forever think of me as a contemptible little thief? Had Nela told my mother? What if my father got to know of it? How ashamed they would be of having me as their daughter! I really felt contemptible and deeply upset at having 'ruined my reputation' with Father Ioann and his family. Then the memory faded . . . And now I was not even sure that these boys were the same boys. If they were, would they recognize me? They showed no sign of it: they clutched my hands, one on each side, and we all wheeled round the *yolka*, now left, now right, under Monsieur Rodiónov's expert direction. On a sign from him the polka tune changed into a march, then into a gallop, and stopped with a flourish. It was the end of the *horovód*.

The ring broke up and we all returned to our mothers, who were watching us from a row of chairs set against the walls. But my mother hardly had time to mop my forehead with her handkerchief and to smooth back my hair when the band struck the tune of a *vienghérka*, and I saw one of my partners in the ring coming towards me with his toothy smile. He bowed clicking his heels, and murmured the accepted formula of invitation: 'May I ask you? . . . '

I had so hoped that Monsieur Rodiónov would ask me: with him I could be sure of dancing well. With this unknown partner not much bigger than myself how could I be certain of not making a mess of it? But I had to accept him because it had been impressed on me that you should not offend anyone by a refusal unless you were very tired or unwell. So with some misgivings I took his proffered arm and we joined some young couples already doing their steps on the floor.

My partner knew the steps but he did not have a good ear for rhythm, so that his hopping and heel-clicking failed to synchronize with my steps or with the beat which accompanied them. I felt acutely embarrassed and avoided looking at him or around me.

When he took me back to my mother after the end of the dance, I sat uneasily on the edge of my chair, trying to catch Monsieur Rodiónov's eye. He had danced the *vienghérka* with his daughter Olia, the slow one, perhaps because no one else had asked her . . . I wished the next dance to be a waltz, but not unless he asked me to dance it with him.

The band struck up a waltz, 'On the Hills of Manchuria' – but it was my partner of the *vienghérka* whom I saw picking his way across the room in my direction. I looked the other way, desperately hoping, almost praying: 'God, please make him ask someone else.'

A voice said: 'May I ask you? . . . '

I tried not to hear and continued looking the other way. My mother touched my shoulder.

'Leda, someone's asking you to dance . . . '

The boy standing before me was not the one I had expected to see. He was much older though not much taller, more thick-set, with an egg-shaped, closely cropped head and small, deep-set eyes. The other boy, whom he had beaten by a fraction of a second, had not had time to change direction and was standing a step or two behind, looking very self-conscious.

The bigger boy bowed and murmured his name: 'Martýnov'.

'Go on,' said my mother. I went with a sinking heart.

The steps my partner did were surely those of the polka, not of the waltz! He leaped about like a grasshopper, completely out of time with the music, clearly unconscious of his incompetence. Desperately I did my best to swing in rhythm with the music – he jerked me out of it by his wild hops. I tried to get free of him – he clutched me harder still. I was scarlet with shame – what an exhibition we made of ourselves! 'I'm feeling faint . . . ' I pleaded, remembering that this was a permitted way of escaping from an impossible partner – but he did not hear me. Finally, beside myself with frustration, I wrenched myself from his grasp and ran across the floor to my mother, leaving him gaping in the middle of the room.

'What is the matter?' asked my mother.

'He can't dance the waltz . . . he can't dance at all . . . ' I gasped.

'You shouldn't have left him like that all the same,' said my mother. 'Should she, Monsieur Rodiónov?'

'Would you like a turn with me, Lédochka?' asked a welcome voice.

My rescuer and my mentor! He knew how well I could dance because he had taught me. From the depths of dejection I was all at once raised to the heights of bliss.

My toes hardly touching the floor, my body completely at one with the rhythm of movement, I saw the room full of whirling couples, the lights and the Christmas tree as a world out of this world. I was ravished and only wished it could go on for ever. 'Please, God, let it go on . . . please don't let the band stop!'

'Are you dizzy?' Monsieur Rodiónov asked as I clung to his arm while he led me to a chair beside my mother's.

'No, not at all, not in the least,' I assured him. I wanted my mother to talk to him and keep him until the next dance began: I dreaded the Martýnov boy coming and asking me to dance again. But perhaps he would not dare after that waltz . . .

He did dare. As soon as the band started playing a *chardash*, he came up and stood before me, looking not in the least embarrassed, his piggy eyes fixed on me with a curious intensity.

'May I have this dance?'

I took my courage in both hands, blushed violently and blurted out: 'I can't . . . I'm not feeling very well . . . '

He blushed, too, because, I thought, he saw that I was lying, bowed and shuffled off. I felt sorry about hurting him, but I noticed – and disliked – the way he walked with his knees half-bent and his long arms swinging by his sides. He joined a small thin woman who was sitting on the other side of the room, and a few moments later I saw them dancing together. She was teaching him the *chardash*, and he was floundering hopelessly, just as he had done when dancing with me. How wrong, I thought, to ask people to dance with him before he had learned the steps.

The threat of his invitation hung over me for the rest of the evening. There was a respite during the interval when Christmas presents were raffled and a young man with a blue rosette in his lapel went around announcing that a beautiful talking doll had to be won. I coveted that doll, but I drew a ticket which provided me with a pencil case no more attractive than the one I already had. The doll was won by a boy who immediately passed it on to his delighted sister. I wondered what 'luck' really meant and whether there was anything special about people who won the best things in lotteries. I have never been one of them, and my conviction that 'luck' never favoured me grew from the seed sown at that Christmas party many years ago.

The party ended with the distribution of 'little bags' made of bright coloured satin and containing sweets, nuts and an orange. All the time I was aware — or imagined — that the boy Martýnov was watching me from afar, and when the time for our departure was signalled by the band playing a cheerful march, I saw him making his way towards us against the stream of people drifting towards the exit. He was pulling his mother along with him, and she followed, smiling, one arm through the sleeve of her overcoat and a frilly woollen hat slipping sideways off her head. I tugged at my mother's arm, wanting her to leave before they had time to reach us, but she shook her head.

'Don't be impatient. It's best to wait until there's more room in the vestibule.'

The boy Martýnov and his mother were now within speaking distance from us. He pulled her forward and she spoke to my mother, a little breathlessly.

'May I introduce myself? Martýnova, Evdokíya Petróvna . . . This is my son, Shoora. He wants me to tell you that he is having a little Christmas party on the twenty-seventh, and we would be delighted if your son and daughters would care to come.'

Madame Martýnova and my mother shook hands. The invitation was accepted.

'Do you know this Shoora Martýnov?' my mother asked my brother on the way home. 'Is he older than you or younger? It's hard to tell.'

'He's older by a class. He's supposed to be rather clever, but some people say that he's mad.'

'What do you mean? Mad?'

'Well, it's his manner, I suppose. The way he talks and gesticulates when he's excited. Anyway, that's what I've heard others say.'

'Mad or not, he certainly was determined to dance with our Leda,' said my mother.

'I don't envy her,' my brother said.

It was with a mixture of curiosity and reluctance that I saw the date of the Martýnov party arrive. My brother, who was to accompany me, disliked the prospect and showed his annoyance by referring to Shoora as my 'simian admirer'. Deep down I was flattered by the evidence of Shoora's admiration, but at the same time distressed by his ugliness and his inability to dance. I would not be able to refuse him at his own party — and the foretaste of this ordeal made me shrivel up inside.

Anticipation or foresight, habit or inborn trait, whatever you call this propensity, it can be a blessing, but more often is a kind of curse. How often have I forestalled harrowing experiences in imagination only to discover that what really happened was much less trying and dramatic. And how rarely have people and places I have pictured to myself before I saw them come up to my expectations. Often they have proved to be so different that their effect was to put right out the bright burning flame of anticipation. It took me half my life to train myself not to anticipate too eagerly, too vividly and with too much haste.

The Martýnov party proved to be much less of a trial and more of a bore than I had expected. Theirs was a rather dreary drawing-room with a thin, almost bedraggled Christmas tree, and with Madame Martýnova acting as the music-maker, mistress of ceremonies and head-waitress, all in one. There were about half-a-dozen other children, all younger than myself and very much younger than their host, who took little notice of them and showered all his attentions on me.

To my great relief there was no proper dancing because none of the other guests could dance. We played games: musical chairs, blind man's buff, 'the damaged telephone' and such like. Madame Martýnova thumped away at the piano and urged her young visitors to enjoy themselves. They were not very responsive. My brother, silent and conspicuously bored, cast an occasional glance at the plates of sandwiches and pastries displayed on the sideboard but not yet offered for consumption. Shoora, beaming with satisfaction, always managed to throw himself on to a chair next to me in the game of musical chairs; to sit beside me and whisper into my ear when playing at 'damaged telephone'. It was always his hands that tied a handkerchief over my eyes when I had to be the 'blind man', and he succeeded in getting himself caught by me every time I groped around the room.

He protested loudly when at ten o'clock their maid reported that our sleigh had come for us. My brother had made sure that Maxim would fetch us not later than the proverbial 'children's hour'. But Madame Martýnova would not let us leave before she had rapped out a farewell march on her long-suffering piano. And we all had to take away the 'little bags' with nuts and an orange which she had prepared for us. I was made very self-conscious by being presented, in addition to the bag, with a small fretwork box lined with red satin, a gift which the other guests eyed with curiosity but without enthusiasm.

'Shóorochka made it himself,' Madame Martýnova said proudly. 'It was to be presented to the queen of the party, so Lédochka receives it tonight!'

I curtseyed and thanked the hostess; I could not bring myself to thank Shoora, who was fixing me with his bright, piggy eyes. He rushed to help me with my overcoat in the lobby; he knelt on the floor to put on my snow boots for me. He was eager to serve — but his parting remark was quite unanswerable and made me hot with embarrassment.

'It's been a good party, hasn't it?' he said.

'What an ass!' my brother growled as he drew his chin inside his fur collar and leaned back in the jerkily moving sleigh. 'He's supposed to be clever but he says such asinine things. Fancy praising his own party! He's got to boast about something every time.'

I did not reply. I knew he had been bored at the party and was blaming me for it, and I felt vaguely guilty about it all. But what could I do? I had not wanted Shoora Martýnov to become my 'admirer'. Nor did I want this fretwork box which I was holding inside my muff. What use could I make of it? I had no jewellery, no rings or bracelets, and I hated the small ruby earrings my mother liked me to wear. Could I put them inside the box and forget them? But my mother would not allow that.

I listened to the soothing, delicate jingling of the harness bells and pondered. Mother and son had been so proud of giving me the little box because 'he made it himself'. She called me 'the queen of the evening'. Why? I felt an inner movement of revulsion and withdrawal from this unasked-for and unwelcome obligation – the obligation to accept an unwanted gift and to be grateful for it.

To be a Girl

That first Christmas from school stands out in memory as a kind of watershed, a dividing line between true childhood and the beginnings of adolescence. The things that happened during that holiday, the succession of parties, the keenness of my partners on dancing with me, Shoora Martýnov's conspicuous devotion, his mother's flattery in calling me 'the queen of the party', all this made me aware of my femininity, of the pleasures, as well as the snags, of being liked by the opposite sex. I had had fleeting experience of power over others before: in play with my girl companions in town or country, I usually led and they followed. But now for the first time I realized that I could have power not because I produced good ideas for play or for adventure, but because I was a girl — and of this I felt half-proud and half-ashamed.

Inevitably, I threw glances at myself whenever I passed a mirror. No, decidedly, I did not look like a queen, nor even a princess — not as I pictured them in my imagination. They would not have such straight hair, such a large mouth. Nor did I want to queen it over people like Shoora Martýnov — so unattractive to look at, so unenviable a subject! Over whom, then? A photograph I saw in an illustrated magazine gave me an idea. It represented the Tsar's family on a visit to the Kremlin. In some sort of procession the four daughters of the Tsar followed their parents on foot, but the heir to the throne, the Grand Duke Alexéy, was carried by his personal servant, the sailor Doroshénko. That strong, big man was obviously devoted to him: he would do anything the boy wanted. To command anyone like that would indeed be a pleasure . . .

But who could it be? And then I thought of Ivan, our new manservant.

Ivan had been engaged since I went to boarding school. He was a ginger-headed fellow of about twenty-five, with a freckled face and a pleasant tenor voice, and he was being 'broken into service' by Piotr, my father's valet. Piotr himself used the expression 'breaking in', as if Ivan were a wild horse. I heard him remark that Ivan came to our house 'straight from the plough'. As I found out later, this was not really true, for Ivan had done his spell as a conscript in the Army and had some of his country uncouthness rubbed off him. True to his army training, he stood to attention when he saw my mother or father approach, and he replied to orders or questions with military phrases, such as: '*Tóchno tak*' ('Exactly so') instead of 'Yes', '*Nikak nyet*' ('In no way so') instead of 'No', and '*Sloóshayus*' ('I obey') instead of 'I will'. In other ways he remained unsophisticated and spontaneous, and his behaviour on occasions gave rise to some rather endearing anecdotes.

My mother told us how once he stood stock still and silent after she had asked him to go and buy two pounds of 'cooking' butter.

'What are you waiting for, Ivan?' she asked.

'Wh-what butter did you say, *bárynia*?' he stammered. He had never heard the phrase used to distinguish the butter for cooking from 'cream' butter, served at table.

My brother had another story. Piotr had told him that Ivan was a fair shot and knew a place not far out of town where a hare or two could be found. My brother was in bed when Ivan brought in a pair of shoes he had just polished, and they entered into a conversation about shooting. 'Ivan got so excited about it that he came closer and closer to me,' my brother said, 'and suddenly he plonked himself down on my bed, just missing my feet, and went on talking. Just then Piotr looked in. You should have seen his face! His jaw fell, he started winking and jerking his head at Ivan to get him on his feet. But Ivan was not looking his way at all. He jumped up pretty fast, though, when Piotr hissed at him.'

Despite these stories, my own experience of Ivan's naïveté took me by surprise. I was having a late breakfast alone one morning and he served me with a boiled egg. I broke the shell: the white looked a little discoloured, and I turned to Ivan for advice.

'Look, Ivan, I wonder if it's quite fresh?'

He took it from me, put it to his lips, sipped a little, then, handing it back to me, said calmly: 'It's all right, *báryshnia*.'

I was taken aback for a moment, then picked up my spoon and ate the egg in silence, wondering whether I should say anything about it to anybody. I was getting fond of Ivan and had never really liked Piotr.

That Christmas time Ivan was sent to fetch me from one of the parties at a house so near ours that it was not worth the trouble of harnessing a horse to a sleigh. It was a night of full moon, with the moonlight so strong that everything around sparkled as if sacks of diamonds had been shaken out over the snow, and looking up, one saw white clouds and blue-black sky. The road, polished by the runners of many sleighs, was shiny and slippery. The splendour of this scene following upon the excitement of the party made me feel as if I could fly. But in reality, my feet were slithering, and the shawl my mother had sent with Ivan to be put over my head and shoulders against the night frost, was making me clumsy and constricted. Suddenly the wish to test my power over Ivan, the longing to be carried like the heir to the throne came over me. I stopped, clutching at his sleeve.

'Ivan, I'm tired. Will you carry me?'

He looked a little surprised, then grinned and without a word picked me up and carried me. His boots made a squeaky noise on the snow; now and again he slipped or stumbled, but quickly regained his balance. Then we both laughed, and I pointed out to him his shortened shadow with my head sticking above his shoulder, following us along the bright road. What a strange feeling it was! He was stronger than me, yet I could command him. He was taller than I, but as he held me up, I could almost look down on him. I was in his power, and he – in mine. Exhilarated, I was yet aware of the effort it cost him, and I felt remorse – then alarm. What if my father came to know of this?

The street had been empty until that moment when I heard the snow squeak under another pair of feet and saw a human shape appear in the distance.

'Ivan, please put me down,' I said quickly.

'Why, *báryshnia*? I can carry you right up to the house and up the steps of the porch.'

'No, please, I'd rather walk now.'

He complied, blew out his breath and laughed.

'You're not all that heavy, *báryshnia*,' he said.

I thought that the man who passed us gave us a curious look, and I wondered whether he had seen. He might be thinking: 'Fancy a big girl like that being carried! What's the matter with her?'

The house was only a few yards away now, and I hung on to Ivan's arm as we took a run and tried to slide along the polished surface of the road.

Laughing, we raced up the steps of the porch, Ivan helping me to keep a step ahead of him. We pushed open the first of the double front doors, then, suddenly, Ivan pulled himself up, took off his cap and stepped back with the words: 'I wish you good night, *báryshnia*!' He remembered what Piotr called 'the due respect', and did not come into the house with me wearing his sheepskin coat and boots, but went back to the gates of the courtyard and across it to the servants' quarters where he slept.

Aniuta helped me off with my clothes.

'You're perspiring a lot,' she remarked, wonderingly. 'Have you been running or something?'

'It's that shawl,' I retorted, half-truthfully.

I wondered if Ivan, in his simplicity of soul, might not tell Piotr about having carried me, and whether the story would reach my father's hearing. So next day I watched Piotr's impassive face for signs of disapproval, but discovered none: Ivan must have thought that carrying me home from a party was a task too ordinary to be mentioned to anyone. Dear, sensible Ivan!

Time stood still during the first few days of the holiday, then it rushed madly towards the end. It was a most painful wrench to leave home again, but this time I was facing it with my teeth clenched rather than with tears of despair. I cried, of course, when I said good-bye to my mother and sister, but a kernel of hardness began to form deep inside me, a fruit of the discovery that my mother had not taken my unhappiness as much to heart as I imagined and hoped she would. She did not promise that next term would be my last at the boarding school; she merely reminded me that the Shrovetide holiday – *Máslennitsa* – was less than six weeks away. Her image in my mind, all kindness, protection and refuge from every danger or threat, which had been a part of my childhood world, was slowly changing. My heart was hardening against her, as well as against the trials that lay ahead of me.

Now I knew at least what to expect. The chief porter, Kleméntiy, with his huge moustaches was no longer intimidating: I could almost detect a twinkle of welcome in his deep-set eyes. And old Dasha of the dormitories left me in no doubt that she was delighted to see me back. The familar austerity of the study-room was no longer chilling, merely indifferent; Fräulein Schmiedel's gruff voice, Mílochka's supercilious looks and Fatima's slyness, though they made me writhe inwardly, no longer made me wonder what it was they found wrong with me. When I first came, I felt weak and small, and at the mercy of hostile forces all around me, and I was beaten down by them like a corn stalk by a heavy rain storm. Now, like the corn that rises up again when the sun comes out, I was regaining my vitality. I discovered my inner resilience. Curiosity, playfulness, desire for adventure were returning.

Our movements within the school were rigidly controlled. We moved between the class-room, the dining-room, study-room and dormitory, using always the same corridors at the same time. There was no question of wandering freely from one room to another between lessons or meals. If we wanted to leave the study-room to go to the lavatory, we had to ask permission from the governess on duty, using the established formula. We asked the German governess: '*Kann ich nach oben gehen?*', although the lavatories were not upstairs but on the same floor. We asked the French governess, more realistically and simply: '*Puis-je sortir?*' The word '*sortir*' being almost identical with the vulgar Russian word for lavatory caused a certain amount of amusement, but we dared not show that we were amused, dared not betray that we knew the vulgar word.

The lavatories were at the end of a long corridor which ended with a large, low-silled window overlooking the school garden. The doors of several class-rooms opened on to it, and half-way along its length was broken by a wide staircase leading down into a second vestibule and up to the assembly hall. In the evening the corridor was lit by a single electric bulb placed above the stairs, so that it was almost dark at both ends. The younger girls did not like making the trip to the lavatory on their own and usually went in pairs. I often paired with Tania or Stassia.

These brief moments of freedom had to be used. My first idea was an obvious one – to race one another to the end of the corridor, stopping just in time to avoid going through the window. My second was to creep upstairs to the top floor and peer into dark, empty class-rooms and through the clear windows of the assembly hall down into the mysterious, late evening streets. Then, as I descended the stairs, while the unadventurous Tania waited on the lower floor, it occurred to me to get astride the handrail and swing myself over on to the other side – the narrow ledge overhanging the deep and wide staircase bay. I almost heard Tania gasp as she watched me picking my way down along the edge of that yawning precipice. But I was feeling as I had not felt for months – elated, admirably daring, more than myself again.

Tania, terrified, begged me not to do it. But it was not enough for me to have impressed her: she was too easily impressed. I had to demonstrate my prowess to Stassia and also to Yuzia, an older girl, who plaited my hair for me in the mornings. She was one of the few seniors from the big dormitory who was not 'stuck up' and who paid us visits in the small dormitory. She usually did this disguising herself as a ghost. She made herself almost twice as tall as she was – and she was a tall, slender girl of fourteen – by holding her arms outstretched above her head, covering herself from top to bottom with a dark shawl and placing her small black school cap on top. She came in moving her arms, so that the 'ghost' appeared to be nodding its head, and, running up to our beds, bent over us menacingly, a gaunt, faceless giant, over six feet tall. We dived under our blankets, squealing faintly, and she laughed, peeped through the folds of the shawl to show us that it was really herself, and ran back to her own dormitory before the matron or any other grown-up had time to come upon the scene.

The suggestion that we might play the ghost game in the corridor after we had finished our homework came from Yuzia, who, I suspect, felt, like myself, an urge to stretch her limbs and her imagination. On Mademoiselle Vinogradova's duty day she bravely volunteered to ask her permission for us to play in the corridor. Stassia and Tania were allowed to join us. Needless to say, we did not invite either Fatima or Milochka.

We made up the game as we went along. Stassia and I were the children of a wicked stepmother, living in a medieval castle. Tania was the nurse looking after us. Yuzia, the stepmother, forced us to go to a part of the castle which was haunted, hoping that the ghost would frighten us to death, and then she would inherit our fortune. Yuzia, in her double role of the stepmother and ghost, was to chase us when we entered her domain. It was this chase that provided the main thrill of the game.

Stassia and I, in our soft shoes, living our parts and impelled by a genuine terror, ran as if we had wings to our feet. But Yuzia could run even faster, and a touch of her hard fingers on our backs sometimes produced a scream which could be heard in the study-room. When this had happened a few times, Mademoiselle Vinogradova – for it was only on her evenings that we were allowed to play unsupervised – sent one of the girls to tell us that if we screamed again, we would have to come back and do something less exciting. But playing at ghosts without a single scream proved to be an impossible undertaking, and after a warning repeated on another occasion, we decided to think up some other game.

Here my wish to show my prowess as a climber found its opportunity for satisfaction. I suggested we should play at being a circus. Yuzia was to be the cruel owner of the show, Stassia a maltreated young dancer, and I a daring acrobat who stood up for her against the owner. Tania was offered the part of a clown, which she could have played to perfection because of her plump, awkward figure and sad, round face. But poor Tania had no sense of humour, and she could not bear to see me walking along the edge of the stairs on the outside of the handrail, which was after all the main point of the game. So, after one or two attempts to carry on with the game, mainly to please me, she dropped out altogether. We continued without her. Neither Yuzia nor Stassia, however, attempted to follow my acrobatic example, and that gave me a wonderful sense of superiority, a much welcomed prop to my self-esteem.

Tania had never really recovered from homesickness to any extent, and she looked as if she could not enjoy anything. 'She's always moping,' Fatima said of her, scornfully. Perhaps because she was so depressed an unfortunate thing happened to her soon after the start of a new term.

One of the conventions observed at the boarding school was that girls were not to ask permission to go to the lavatory immediately after a meal: to do this was 'bad manners'. That meant that sometimes we had to wait longer than we would have done otherwise. One evening, as we were finishing our French exercises, Tania whispered to me, asking if I would come 'to the end of the corridor' with her. I nodded, but as she got up to ask permission, Mademoiselle Vinogradova called us to her desk, to check up on our homework.

Neither of us was bold enough to do anything but comply. We filed up to the governess's desk with our books. While Mademoiselle Vinogradova was listening to my translation of a French passage, I became aware that Tania was shifting from one foot to the other and looking more and more anxious. Fatima was eyeing her sideways with malicious amusement. Suddenly we heard a faint rippling sound as if someone was using a teapot to pour water on to the floor. The governess was the last to notice that something unusual was happening. Tania turned scarlet, then pale.

'*Puis-je . . . puis-je sortir?*' she babbled and rushed towards the door even before the startled Mademoiselle had time to reply.

Fatima was shamelessly grinning. I did not know where to look. A pool on the floor where Tania had been standing drew the eyes of every girl in the room: a wave of agitation ran over the tables.

All the heads were raised; there was suppressed tittering and whispers.

'Girls, please be quiet,' said Mademoiselle Vinogradova, recovering her poise. 'Will one of you call Sasha and tell her to bring a mop?'

Two of the older girls ran towards the door.

'One is enough,' said Mademoiselle firmly. 'Rayévskaia, you can go back to your place now. Bazoókova, will you read and translate what you had prepared.'

I opened my arithmetic book on the page where some 'problems' were marked as requiring solution, but hard as I tried I could see even less sense in them than usual. Why for goodness' sake should anyone want to know how much faster a bath would fill if two taps were left running for five minutes, or one tap for eight minutes? My thoughts were on poor Tania and *her* problem: she had been gone for some minutes. Sasha, the maid, came with the mop and dried the floor, but Tania did not reappear. I could imagine what state she was in: her agonized recoil from the ordeal of returning to the study-room to face the furtive, mocking glances of the many girls who had witnessed her humiliating mishap. I felt the humiliation of it so acutely that I was suddenly seized with fear at the thought of 'There but for the grace of God go I . . . ' I jumped to my feet and, interrupting Fatima's reading (she gave me a devastating glance), went up to Mademoiselle Vinogradova.

'*Puis-je sortir, Mademoiselle?*'

'*Certainement,*' she replied, a little startled, forgetting to reprove me for interrupting.

I almost collided with Tania just outside the study-room door where the corridor ended and the light was at its dimmest. She must have been standing there for some minutes, unable to pluck up her courage to come in. For a second or two we stood, peering at each other. In semi-darkness I could see her large eyes swimming with tears and her mouth quivering pitifully. I felt a dangerous tightening of my own throat and knew that I had to act or burst into tears myself. I seized Tania by the hand, whispered: 'Come!' and we ran along the passage back to the lavatories at the other end.

We sat down on a low window-sill by the wash basins, and Tania at once broke into sobs, laying her head on to my shoulder, a shoulder not quite broad enough for her rather large head.

'I've prayed and prayed, oh, how I prayed to God to make it so that it hadn't happened . . . ' Tania sobbed. 'But it's real, isn't it? It *did* happen. You saw it with your own eyes? Tell me!'

I could not bear to speak, I merely nodded. I, too, was feeling bitter against God. Why could He not undo what had happened? It would have been such a small thing for Him; it was so desperately important to Tania!

'Fatima will never forget it . . . ' continued Tania. 'Nor will the others. Were they *all* laughing? Was Mademoiselle? . . . '

I was able to assure her that the governess showed no sign of having been amused by what had happened and that she had discouraged gossip and tittering. Gradually Tania calmed somewhat and, though still frightened and ashamed, seemed to accept the inevitable. Slowly, we made our way along the corridor towards the study-room. Twice Tania stopped, as if she were about to turn and run back to the refuge of the lavatory again. I put my arm round her shoulders, telling her that she could not stay there all night, and that Mademoiselle was sure to send one of the big girls to fetch her sooner or later — which 'would be worse'. In the end Tania marched into the study-room, looking as if she were going to her execution, and I, walking beside her, felt almost as if I were to be present at one. But all the turmoil inside us produced only a faint ripple outside. Some heads were raised and glances exchanged, but the heads were soon down again, intent on their books, no doubt aware that Mademoiselle was on the alert, watching them. Fatima was back in her place at our table, and she whispered to Mílochka, who sniggered just as Tania and I were squeezing ourselves between the form and the table to take our seats. The governess at once spoke to us, asking whether we had completed our homework, and telling us to go to our dormitory if we had.

Tania got ready for bed very quickly, pretending not to hear Fatima's sardonic mutterings at the wash basins. As it was Wednesday, and we were due for a change of underclothes on Thursday morning, she was spared the embarrassment of asking the matron for a set of clean things. The mishap, however, could not be concealed: Fatima guffawed when she heard old Dasha mumble in astonishment as she collected our discarded linen from beside our beds: 'Merciful Mother of God, these are soaking wet. How did the child manage? . . . '

Tania made no sound: she could cry almost noiselessly, but I knew by the slight shaking of her bed.

One morning soon afterwards I noticed her crying again in bed, while Dasha was fussing around, half-comforting, half-grumbling at her. Remembering the incident in the study-room, I at once thought the worst, and I was puzzled by her not getting up, although the bell clanged the second time, calling us to breakfast.

I was even more puzzled in the evening when I found Tania's bed empty and covered up, instead of being ready to receive her. Alarmed, I questioned Dasha.

'She's in the big dormitory,' mumbled the old maid and trotted off, clearly unwilling to enter into conversation.

In the big dormitory! I slipped in at the risk of being reprimanded and sent away by the 'big ones'. There was Tania, in bed, quite near the communicating door. She closed her eyes when she saw me. Was she pretending to be asleep? I could not quite believe that she might not want to speak to me.

'Tania, why have you been moved? What's the matter?' I asked.

She began to cry. I stared at her, bewildered. Just then one of the older girls came to the next bed and saw me. She scolded me for being in the wrong dormitory, told me Tania was 'all right' and that she would be up tomorrow. Still puzzled, I returned to my own bed.

'Been to see Pánova?' Fatima asked me, with a note of mockery in her voice. 'Know what's the matter with her?'

'No. What?'

'She's started her periods.'

'What's that?'

Fatima laughed derisively.

'You don't mean to say that you don't know!'

'Why should I pretend?'

'You *are* a baby! Just to make me tell you . . . '

'I'm telling you — I don't know!'

'I don't believe you. Anyway, it's what happens to all girls. You go to the lavatory one day; you look down, and there's blood . . . It comes out of you.'

'It isn't true! You're making it up.'

'You ask Pánova. That's why she's been transferred to the big dormitory. All the big girls have it.'

'But Tania is the same age as you and I . . . '

'Some girls start earlier than others.'

There was such ghoulish pleasure in Fatima's tone of voice that, however hard I tried to disbelieve her, the impact of her words struck me with an awful convincingness. What was this new threat, this inexplicable alarming thing which 'happened to all girls'? How soon was it going to happen to me? Tania was only a few months older and she had succumbed already! She was very unhappy . . . Why, why did it have to happen? And why only to girls? I wished again I had been born a boy.

If Fatima's 'revelation' was meant to upset and frighten me, she succeeded only too well. My next few weeks at the school were haunted by the fear that 'it' was going to happen to me any day. The subject was too dreadful to discuss with anyone. Tania's obvious embarrassment prevented me from probing her. Between the 'big girls', including even Yuzia, and myself stood an apparently insurmountable barrier of their superiority and my newness. Despite the communicating door between the dormitories, there was hardly any communication between us. The 'big girls' habitually ignored us. Mílochka was the only one whom they occasionally noticed and smiled at, and she made the best of her doll-like prettiness.

The musings aroused in me by Fatima's remarks were so confused that even if I had wanted to write and ask my mother what it all meant, I could hardly have put it into words. Anyway, I felt that perhaps my sister was the best person to ask, but as weeks passed and nothing happened, the alarming thoughts began to fade away.

Shrovetide week, the *Máslennitsa*, was rapidly approaching, and in my imagination I was already eating the delicious pancakes of buckwheat flour, richly flavoured with fresh butter and sour cream, and listening to the festive tinkling of harness bells as *troikas* galloped past our windows through the snowy streets. My sister, my brother and I would go for a ride in a *troika*, and Maxim would race other drivers and beat them. And when we came back with steamy breath and glowing cheeks, my mother would be there, behind the samovar, and my father in the rocking chair, smoking a cigarette, with a newspaper on his lap . . . My mother with a question on her lips: 'Did you keep yourselves well covered?' . . . My father silent, just glancing up . . .

On the morning my mother was to come for me I got out of bed, tense with anticipation. Fatima, who had just returned from the washroom, looked at me, and suddenly began to grin and point a finger at my face.

'See what she's got!' she shouted.

I passed my hands over my face but felt nothing unusual under my finger tips.

'What is it? There's nothing . . . '

'There is! There is! You're covered with spots. You have chicken-pox!'

'I haven't!' I shouted, alarmed, because Mílochka had been taken to the school sick-bay a few days previously with red spots all over her face. Stassia and Yuzia came up and stood staring at me, silently.

'You have!' Fatima shouted, triumphantly. 'She has, hasn't she? Look at yourself in a mirror if you don't believe me!'

Barefoot, I ran across the cold floor to a looking-glass by the linen room door. Alas! Fatima was right: my face was covered with red spots. Yet I felt absolutely nothing. How could I be ill if I felt nothing? Surely, just having spots could not prevent me from going home!

Old Dasha, alerted by Fatima's high-pitched exclamations, trotted up to see what was the matter. She raised her hands in a gesture of distress and commiseration and hustled me off to the medical-room. The nurse in attendance gave me one glance and said: 'Chicken-pox. She should go to the *lazaryet* at once.'

I protested that my mother was coming this very afternoon to take me home. The nurse explained that I could not travel because I might get a chill and because I was infectious. I still protested desperately, with bitter sobs. Old Dasha stroked my hair and whispered that there would be many more Shrovetide holidays in my life, next year and the year after that . . . Kondratiy, the junior porter, was summoned from downstairs. Dasha wrapped me in a blanket, tied a warm shawl over my head, and he carried me across the yard to the *lazaryet*.

It was a morning of proper Shrovetide thaw, not uncommon at the end of February in our part of Russia. The quilt of snow which had covered the high stacks of birch wood in the yard had almost disappeared, and what remained of it was half-transparent like opaque glass. The twigs on a tree by the sick-bay were dark and swollen with drops of water hanging from them. Innumerable sparrows chirruped and fluttered by the pools where the cobble-stones had sunk and formed a hollow. The air was permeated with the scent of melting snow.

I took a gulp of this soft, humid air with my sobbing breath: it might have been my last breath if measured by the extent of my misery. God was indeed unkind! Why did He send me this chicken-pox just on the morning when my mother was to take me home for a whole ten days? If I had to have chicken-pox, why not a few hours later when I could have had it in my own home, with all the comforts and compensations of my mother's and sister's presence and care? As if I hadn't had my share of unhappiness already!

My eyes were very sore and swollen when Mademoiselle Vinogradova came to visit me at the sick-bay. My tears flowed again when she told me that my mother had called and went away again, after asking her to tell me not to fret and that she would send me a parcel as soon as she returned home.

I never knew why my mother did not come to see me at the sick-bay. Perhaps she thought this would only upset me more, or decided to spare herself the ordeal of seeing me in a state of inconsolable grief. She may have been right, but I imagined she had been prevented from seeing me because I was 'infectious'. My self-pity became swollen by picturing to myself the pity she must have felt for me. My grief grew in poignancy at the thought that my brother was luckier than I and was now travelling towards home in my mother's company. Then it occurred to me that my mother might be quite contented in his company and not as grieved at leaving me behind as I had thought she was, and a bitter feeling invaded my breast.

Mademoiselle Vinogradova was sympathetic, but her bird-like cheerfulness jarred on me, and I almost disliked her for it. Seeing that I could not be comforted, she said she would send me some books tomorrow if my temperature went down to normal, and left, smiling. The nurse came, took my temperature and said it wouldn't go down unless I stopped crying. Later on, one of the maids brought me a light meal on a tray. I left most of it untouched and cried myself to sleep.

The next day the Headmistress came to visit me. She sat beside my bed, exhaling a faint fragrance of scent, her mid-blue silk dress spread about her chair, her small hands in black lace mittens folded on her lap, and talked in her gentle voice of the time when she was a little girl, a year or two younger than me, at the Institute for the Daughters of the Nobility in St Petersburg, and how a whole class of them were laid low with chicken-pox. 'Can you imagine, *dóoshechka*, two long rows of beds with a little girl in each one of them, her face and hands *absolutely covered* in red spots? Well, the doctor just stood there and laughed! What a spectacle!'

I felt too much reverence for her to do anything but listen, yet her story, especially the fact that the girls were younger than I, had the effect of reducing the intensity of my self-pitying mood, and of making me smile. The *Nachálnitsa's* manner, too, was much warmer than Mademoiselle Vinogradova's: she gave me a feeling that she really knew how I felt.

Later in the afternoon the Director came. I had not expected these important visits, and was both flattered and embarrassed by them. He did not tell me a story but gave me two oranges, then sat and looked at me with his kindly, humorous eyes. The sympathy which radiated from him nearly broke through the thin crust of resignation which had grown round my wounded heart during the day, but fortunately my respect for him inhibited tears.

I was kept in bed for a week, a tormented soul, longing for the intimacy and warmth no sympathetic strangers could supply, tantalized by the visions of Shrovetide celebrations at home. The dreary little room with the lower window panes painted white was a prison cell to me. The two oranges and some pretty Crimean apples on a plate were the only spot of colour which enlivened it and gave me pleasure. Anna Avdyéevna brought the apples. She came every day and turned my soul inside out by asking questions about my sister and home. But she also brought books, and as soon as my temperature was normal, I was permitted to read them and to escape from my prison into the world of *The Prince and the Pauper*, of *Tom Sawyer* and *Huckleberry Finn*. Hours passed without my noticing; dusk crept into the room; soon it was supper-time and the injunction to settle down to sleep. The light was turned out, but I remained awake, staring at the pale stars through the upper panes of the window which had been left clear.

I had always liked being alone at the top of an apple tree covered with blossom or in the clearing of a forest, bright with the green of young birch trees. But this was a new kind of solitude: in a room of a house where nothing was familiar and where no one slept but myself — or so I thought. Yet, strangely enough, I was not afraid. The fear that haunted me in those early years was not a fear of something real, that could happen, but of bad dreams. I would dream of dead people who rose from their graves and pursued me, or of white-clad ghosts coming to seize me. So often did I have such dreams between the ages of nine and eleven that I was terrified of going to sleep. I prayed to God to stop me dreaming them, and because my prayers were not answered, I began to have my first doubts concerning the kindness of God.

An unexpected effect of boarding school-life on me was the virtual disappearance of these dreams, as if the real stresses of separation and adjustment had literally pushed out stresses and fears due to imagination. At first I hardly noticed this, then I realized that I was no longer afraid of going to sleep but, on the contrary, welcomed it as an escape from grim reality. Nor did I remember my dreams as well as I used to: the clanging of the morning bell sent them scurrying away.

One dream, however, the last ghost dream I have ever had, stands out in memory as vividly as if I had it yesterday.

I returned to the school dormitory before the end of the Shrovetide holiday, saddened and matured by my experience of the unkindness of 'Fate' and of a new kind of solitude. Tania and Stassia had not yet returned; Fatima's and Mílochka's beds were some distance from mine.

In my dream I had the illusion of awakening in that very dormitory to a grey morning of unwonted stillness. I sat up and saw that on each empty bed there stood a new coffin. The coffins were brightly varnished and piled with brilliantly coloured flowers. Awed and fascinated, I gazed at the scene expecting the lids of the coffins to fly open and the dead in their shrouds to rise from them. I waited — but nothing happened. Suddenly a feeling of extraordinary relief came over me. I heard myself saying: 'This is a joke. There's no one in these coffins . . . I am not afraid any more . . . ' and I opened my eyes to the clanging of the morning bell in the real dormitory, on a real grey morning. Fatima and Mílochka were stirring and yawning in their beds. The other beds were empty. My fear of ghosts had completely gone.

With the Shrovetide holiday irretrievably lost to me, there was now only Easter to look forward to. It seemed very far away, and between it and the present there was an important date, March 23rd, my name-day.

On your name-day you prayed to your patron saint. Mine was Lydia, and my mother told me that she was not a martyr, merely a Roman lady of noble birth who became a saint. My mother declared that she had determined not to call any of her children after martyrs — that would be inviting misfortune. My sister, Maria, was called after Mary of Egypt, and my brother, Vladímir, after the saintly Prince of Kiev.

At school, as the day approached, I looked back with nostalgia on my past name-days. How mischievous I used to be in trying to find out in advance what present my mother was going to give me! I went as far as abstracting the key of a great oak chest which stood in the hall and digging among the spare rugs, lace curtains and shawls for a suspicious-looking parcel I had seen my mother deposit there after a trip to M*. How ashamed of myself I had been once when my mother discovered that I had opened the parcel and seen the splendid doll which she meant to be a surprise to me! It was one of the rare occasions on which I saw my mother looking really angry, and her face, as I saw it then, remained long in my memory.

On the Day I was given my favourite breakfast, curd cheese with sour cream and fresh French rolls. And for the main meal of the day there was, of course, the name-day *pirógh*, a large pie stuffed with minced meat and chopped egg; and another pie, a sweet one stuffed with apples, for tea, when children came to the party and brought boxes of sweets and gateaux in pretty boxes tied with ribbons.

At school nothing like this was going to happen. I had to rise with the morning bell and sit through the lessons in my class as if it were an ordinary day. Stassia and Tania were the only ones who knew and who congratulated me. I received a parcel from home, of course, and Fatima commented on this — just to make sure that I would not dodge offering her some of its contents. My mother wrote to wish me happiness and health: health was the main thing she seemed to worry about as far as we were concerned, all the time I can remember. She explained that she was not sending me a *piróqh* because it would not keep fresh long enough but that she would make me one when I came home for Easter. The parcel contained the usual supply of short pastries and sweetmeats. My sister, more imaginatively, sent me an album for picture postcards, which I had begun to collect, and filled the first two pages with pretty pictures of lambs and foals gambolling among forget-me-nots and lilies-of-the-valley. I was delighted with them.

Yet a real surprise awaited me when I took my place that morning beside Margóolina in the classroom. After one of the pupils had read the prayer and we had all sat down, I opened my desk and found a wrapped-up book with my name on it. It was a handsome Edition Rouge-et-Or volume, and on the fly leaf there was an inscription in a round, rather childish hand: 'To L. Rayévskaia from A. Saburova on the occasion of her Name-Day.' And underneath in smaller letters Anna Avdyéevna had written: 'You will be surprised how much French you will learn if you read half a page of this every night.'

I was conscious of blushing to the tips of my ears as I raised my head and met the governess's moist brown eyes gazing at me across the gap between her desk and mine, while the corners of her mouth curled up in a hardly perceptible smile. Just then the teacher came into the room and we all rose to our feet. A few seconds later the lesson began. While it lasted I avoided looking in Anna Avdyéevna's direction. I felt more embarrassed than pleased with her gift: I was quite unaccustomed to receiving presents from persons who were not members of my family, and did not know how to behave on such occasions. I was overcome with shyness, almost with shame at the thought of having to thank her for it. Shame was somehow linked with gratitude: in my experience, only the poor received gifts from strangers, and the poor — the beggars — showed gratitude in such a humiliating way. I wished the lesson would go on for ever and the moment of confrontation would never come.

But at the usual hour the bell clanged in the corridor, the teacher picked up her books and walked out, and the girls began to stream out of the class-room. Anna Avdyéevna was waiting at her desk — waiting for me to come up and thank her, I was sure. Clasping my hands in front of me in the correct way, I went up and made the correct little curtsey.

'Thank you very much, Anna Avdyéevna, for . . . the book . . . '

I could not even bring myself to say 'for the nice' or 'lovely' book, lest this praise would be taken as an expression of hope for further gifts.

'You will read a little every day, won't you?' she asked. 'I know you can talk French, but reading will give you a much larger vocabulary. You *will* read it when you are at home during Easter?'

'Yes, Anna Avdyéevna.'

'Is this a promise?'

I hesitated a moment: the prospect did not appeal to me at all. I wanted to forget the school and its tasks during the holidays. But although her lips were smiling, Anna Avdyéevna's dark eyes had a compelling look, and I dared not offend her. So I whispered: 'Yes,' again, and was glad when she let me go without asking anything more.

After the break I looked at the book again with the flap of my desk raised as a shield against curious glances. The story was about a family of children who travelled with a circus and lived in a caravan. There were many delightful pictures and the text did not seem too difficult. Yet mere guessing at the meaning was not going to satisfy me: I wanted to know the exact Russian equivalent of every unfamiliar word. I would need a dictionary . . .

Margóolina looked over my shoulder as she settled down in her place.

'Oh, what a nice book!' she said. 'Who gave it to you?'

'Never mind . . . ' I muttered, aware that I was blushing again.

'I know.' Margóolina looked very pleased with herself. 'I saw her put it inside your desk as we came into class this morning. I told you: you're her favourite. Everybody knows it.'

I was flattered despite myself, still innocent at the time of the obligations the status of a 'favourite' was going to impose on me. I was only just beginning to recover from the wounds which separation from home and a partial loss of identity had inflicted on me. To get such individual attention from the *dame-de-classe* went a long way towards restoring my sense of personal value. At the same time the teachers' praise of my work helped me to withstand the constant humiliation of an over-controlled existence. I did well in all my school work, probably because I was innocently eager for achievement, disliked making a fool of myself and had formed a habit of preparing work for my tutor before I went to school.

How well I remember the faces of the half-dozen masters and mistresses who taught us in my first year at school: the kind, soft-

featured countenance of Maria Ivanovna, who hardly ever failed to read
my compositions aloud to the class; the stern-looking, tetchy French
mistress, Vera Petrovna, with a complexion of yellow parchment, whom
we thought so irritable and who later died of cancer; the pretty German
teacher, Fräulein Kurz, who had dark down under her chin ('She shaves
every morning,' Fatima assured me). She was the only one who could be
coolly sarcastic at our expense, and would ask on returning an untidy
copy-book: 'Have you by any chance dropped your book in a chicken
run? These pages look as if chickens had scratched about on them.'
Only about her did I feel definitely that she did not like me. Nor did I
like the language she taught so condescendingly, with its unnatural
construction, the verb often coming at the end of a long sentence.

The French mistress could be sharp-tongued, too, but only when she
was annoyed. She flared up at me once for 'always asking irrelevant
questions'. To me my question was far from irrelevant. I had wanted
to know what happened to the boy in the story from which she had
dictated a short passage. The passage stopped just as the boy had climbed
up a tree to rob a rook's nest and the rooks swooped down on him.
Was not my question to be expected? But I was the only one who asked
it. The whole class sat quiet, incurious, startled at my boldness and
perhaps secretly pleased at my discomfiture.

Maria Ivánovna, who taught us history as well as Russian, did not
mind questions being asked. She did not object even to my contesting
that there had been no King Louis of France until Louis the Eleventh, as
nothing was ever said about the first ten in our history books. She
assured me, unemphatically, that they had really existed.

The masters were even more kindly than the kinder of the mistresses.
I never really liked sums, but I liked 'Adolphe', the arithmetic master,
a whimsical, bald-headed, bespectacled man with a walrus moustache,
who could not bear giving a pupil a 'six' mark because in a twelve-point
system of marking it meant that she had failed. He had a trick of calling
you out by reading your surname and Christian name in full from the
register with a mock solemnity. In this way I discovered the rather
exotic first names of my Jewish classmates. Surnames only were habitually used unless the girls became close personal friends; my being a
boarder precluded close friendship with a day girl.

Malyévich, the geography master, was also bald, but had a beard.
While 'Adolphe' paced the room between the blackboard and our desks,
gesticulating with a piece of chalk while he taught, Malyévich would
loll in his chair, eyes turned up at the ceiling, and drone on in a soft,

nasal voice, telling us about date palms in the Sahara, or mosses in the *tundra*. He hardly ever troubled to disturb the second-year girls on the back seats by asking them questions which he knew they could not answer – at least not until the very end of the term when they had to have some marks against their names in the register. Then he would make a day of it, calling them out one after another and asking each the same gentle question: 'What have you prepared for today?'

'About the Sahara' . . . or 'About tea plantations . . . ' the girl replied.

'Well then . . . what can you tell me about the Sahara?'

'In the Sahara there are . . . oases . . . ' she would begin with a desperate brightness. A long pause would follow.

'Yes . . . there are oases in the Sahara,' Malyévich would at last confirm softly. 'What else can you tell me about that famous desert?'

'It's . . . it's all covered with sand. Sometimes mirages happen . . . '

Another long pause. A few more questions would reveal that the girl retained hardly anything from all the lessons she had sat through during the term and that she had probably never opened her geography book.

'You may sit down,' Malyévich would tell her just as gently as he had put his question, and trace delicately an unmistakable 'seven' in the register against her name, and the girl would sigh with relief, for a 'seven' was the lowest pass mark in our school. The same procedure would be repeated with every 'second-yearling' until they all had a mark for the term, and Malyévich could discreetly leave them in peace for the next couple of months.

Bátiushka, the school priest, was an impressive figure, tall and broad, made to look even bigger by the long cassock with wide sleeves which he always wore. He had a brown beard and a thick mane of straight brown hair, brushed back and reaching down to his shoulders. His voice was rich and deep like a violoncello, and the stories from the Gospels sounded beautiful when told in that voice. I remember him telling us the story of the resurrection and describing how Mary Magdalene met Jesus in the garden where He had been buried, and mistook Him for a gardener.

'Jesus spoke to her and said "Maria!"' – *Bátiushka's* voice might have been the voice of Jesus Himself, from the intense emotion which ran through me like an electric current.

The drawing master, whom we called behind his back by his first name – Arkády – was a very different type of man: small, dapper, voluble and fussy. He spoke with a lilt, a singing intonation character-

istic of Moscow where he was born and had received his training. He
tended to boast of this and to criticize the speech of the Bielorussians.

'You all say *dz* instead of *d*,' he would tell us. 'In Moscow we speak
beautifully.'

He had little patience with the uninterested or lazy and would compare their efforts with the scratchings of hens. He was inclined to help
the more able or conscientious by adding a few expert strokes to an
insipid though honest attempt, thus transforming a pale ghost of a cube
or a pyramid into a substantial, life-like object. But instead of feeling
gratitude for such help, I was annoyed and discouraged by it. I would
much rather he told me how to do it instead of doing it himself. He had
changed *my* drawing out of all recognition, so that it was no longer mine,
and he did it with such enviable ease and speed. How could I ever hope
to achieve such a standard? And when he gave me a mark, was it really
my work or his own that he was assessing? I was not sure whether I
liked Arkády as much as the other masters — or whether I liked him
at all.

In Favour and in Disgrace

'The rooks are here again . . . ' A poem I learned almost before I could read began with these words. It meant that winter silence was over: the air was full of cawing voices and of flapping wings; the pale sky patterned with the dark tracery of their flight. I was standing at the window of the drawing-room, looking up at the birch tree tops in the Catholic church enclosure. The rooks have returned . . . from where? Were they the same rooks which made their nests in these trees last spring, before I went to school? Were they glad to be back? *I* was glad to see them because they came with the spring, and I was weary of winter for the first time in my short life. The joy of welcoming the spring had an undertow of sadness when I thought of all the bright winter days which I had spent indoors, at the school, with no toboganning, no building of snowmen, no sleigh rides . . . And next winter will be the same, and yet another, and another . . . It will go on for ever! I wished I were a bird . . .

I did not realize that I said this aloud and my sister was standing behind me. She put an arm round my shoulders. Her arm was soft; everything about Maroossia was soft: her hair, the look in her hazel eyes, her embrace, which enveloped but never held one fast. She had come from Petersburg for the university vacations and was already at home when my brother and I arrived from M*. She was thinner than when I saw her at Christmas, and I heard my mother remark that she spent all her allowance on books and theatre tickets instead of feeding herself as she should. She had certainly brought quite a pile of books with her which

looked different from the usual run. They were very small, had yellow
paper covers and the words 'Universal Library' printed over them.
I looked through a few of them. Almost all were translations of plays
by authors whose names were new to me: Maeterlinck, Ibsen, Haupt-
mann, Strindberg, Bjernson, and some of the novels of Knut Hamsun. I
asked her whether she had seen all these plays on the stage. She laughed
at my naïveté, then told me of the wonderful production of *The Blue
Bird* by Maeterlinck, which she saw when the Moscow Arts Theatre
visited Petersburg.

I listened wide-eyed as she described how all the things in the
children's kitchen came to life: the dough in the tub began to rise and
a large loaf of bread with a round face emerged from it; the sugar loaf
on the table stirred and began to sprout long white fingers . . . The
children in the audience, she said, squealed with delight.

'The children in the play went in search of the Blue Bird. They found
it in the 'Place of the Unborn' and carried it away in a cage, but
accidentally they opened the cage and the Bird flew away.'

'What a pity!' I said.

Maroossia disagreed. She explained that Maeterlinck probably meant
that imagination could not be kept in a 'cage' of any kind, and that the
Blue Bird stood for something that we must always pursue but cannot
retain – an ideal, a beautiful dream, perhaps . . .

I found her words disturbing: I wanted to believe that ideals could be
attained and beautiful dreams realized. And if she were right – and
I obscurely felt she might be – would it not be better *to be a bird* and
fly over town and mountains and forests, and look down on them?

'I would grow terribly dizzy,' said Maroossia. 'You know that I never
dare look down when I am on a bridge or a church tower. If I did, I
would probably throw myself over the edge.'

The bells on the Catholic bell tower began to toll. The sound was
more high-pitched than that of our church bells, more like a tenor
voice than a bass.

'Their Easter Eve service is tonight,' said my sister. 'A week earlier
than ours.'

'And this time I shall come to the midnight service with you,' said I.

Memories of 'first' occasions become, no doubt, overlaid with later
ones, but I believe that the *feeling* of that particular Easter has survived
in my memory more or less intact over the years. It *was* the first time
I was to be present at the midnight service, and I looked forward to

it with awe, as to a revelation of a great and all-important mystery.

The drive through the streets at night was in itself mysterious: I could hardly recognize the familiar shops and houses. The streets were full of subdued animation: people were walking along the pavements, all going in the same direction. There were some children among them, and many girls were wearing white dresses under their overcoats. I, too, had a white dress on, with a new, light-coloured coat over it.

As we drove up to the church, I was surprised to see how faint was the light in its windows. But people were streaming in through the wide-open doors.

'It'll be very crowded and airless inside. I hope you won't feel faint . . . ' said my mother.

Just inside the entrance we bought our candles. A beadle, who saw us arrive, motioned us forward and went in front, making a little path through the crowd, murmuring as he went: 'Be so kind . . . please . . . excuse me . . . ' Near the iconostasis the throng was much thinner, and we stopped there, to the right of the praying desk at which a deacon was reading from a book with many coloured ribbons between the leaves.

The church was in semi-darkness with only a few clusters of candles burning before the most venerated of the icons – a large image of Mother and Child, a Christ with one hand raised in blessing, Saint Nicholas with his staff. Above, the vaulted ceilings and the embrasures of tall windows were peopled with shadows which extended to the lower arches and the recesses behind them. A few more candles were burning in those recesses, and their flickering light now and again snatched a glint of gold out of the surrounding penumbra. Blueish wisps of incense smoke trailed slowly across the half-lit spaces between the dark recesses and the brighter part of the church where we were standing. The deacon went on reading and chanting: 'Oh, Lord, have mercy upon us!' after almost every sentence. His voice was mournful because Christ was still in His grave: the mystery of resurrection had not yet been revealed to the world . . .

People continued coming in, gently working their way through the crowd so as to be nearer the iconostasis, and although my mother made me a sign which meant that I must not go on looking round, I could not refrain from glancing at the new arrivals out of the corner of my eye. Among them I saw many familiar faces: Father Ioann's two grown-up daughters, Alexandra, with her husband and son, and Nela, the unmarried one; our family doctor, Mihailóvsky, with his wife and adopted daughter, who was so boring to play with; the garrison commander's two sons with whom I had danced so much at Christmas – they looked different without their grins – and . . . goodness! I had almost forgotten about him . . . Shoora Martýnov! He was craning his neck, looking in our direction over the shoulder of his mother who was wearing a large hat loaded with fruit and flowers. Should I have to kiss him if he came up to say: 'Christ is risen'? The prospect threatened to destroy my reverently receptive mood.

Meanwhile two priests and their attendants came out of the side door in the iconostasis and walked, swinging their censers and intoning prayers round the *plashchanítsa*, the table symbolizing the tomb of Christ. It had been there since Friday, the day on which He died, and people came during these days of mourning to pray before it and kiss the feet of the crucified Jesus embroidered in silver on the purple cloth. Now the priests lifted it and carried it, singing, through the Royal Gates into the Holy of Holies while people stood silent with their heads bowed. The Royal Gates closed. Inside, the prayers went on while we stood waiting, holding our candles, unlit but ready . . . What was happening inside these closed Gates? What would we see when they opened again? The minutes of waiting dragged . . .

Then, at last, the Royal Gates opened slowly, solemnly, and the procession filed out. A boy walking in front held up a large crucifix; behind him young men, who had now exchanged their dark cassocks for bright garments, came carrying banners with the images of Christ, His Mother and the Saints embroidered on them in coloured silks and gold. After them came the deacons in blue and silver vestments, with Father Ioann, the senior priest, in the centre of the procession, small and bent, yet impressive in his rich golden chasuble and purple velvet cap. The choir followed, singing in full voice a hymn glorifying Christ. The words were archaic Russian, yet familiar enough for me to understand their meaning:

'Oh Christ, our Saviour, the angels in Heaven are singing of Thy resurrection; grant us pure hearts so that we, too, can glorify Thee here on earth . . . '

Now little tongues of flame were springing up everywhere: people lit their candles from one another. The palms of their hands looked pink, half-transparent, as they sheltered the flames from the draught. The procession passed out into the churchyard and many of the congregation followed it. The rest stood waiting in the half-empty church, listening to the choir whose singing reached them in snatches as the procession walked round the church. Slowly the singing grew closer, louder, more jubilant . . . Here they were, coming back into the church, proclaiming at the top of their voices the miracle of the resurrection in the words which made my heart beat faster:

'Christ is risen from the dead, by His death He has trampled down Death and has given life to those who are in their graves . . . '

Father Ioann walked slowly up the steps before the iconostasis and turned to face us. Raising the crucifix which he held in both hands, he moved it to make the sign of the cross over the congregation, and said as loudly as his old voice would let him:

'Christ is risen!'

The middle of the church answered him as one voice:

'In sooth, He is!'

Father Ioann turned to his right and made the sign of the cross with the crucifix a second time, repeating: 'Christ is risen!' And the congregation on the left of the church replied in chorus: 'In sooth, He is!' Then he turned to his left, facing us; and, bending our heads to receive his blessing, we too answered him, loudly confirming the great good news he was announcing. The Royal Gates behind him were wide open and the main altar inside shone with white linen and gold. He turned and went inside.

The church was now ablaze with candelabras above and the candles in everyone's hands. The choir was singing jubilantly: 'Christ is risen from the dead!' A rustle and a ripple of movement was spreading through the church, a murmur of voices, saying: 'Christ is risen' and 'In sooth, He is!' The light of the candles made eyes shine and faces look young, and the emotion which I felt rising from somewhere deep inside me was not the ecstasy I had been hoping for but a kind of compassion, an urge to love everyone around me. Now Christ had conquered Death, no one, not even the little old woman with trembling hands whom I saw buying a very small candle on the way in, need be afraid of dying!

My sister was the first to exchange the three traditional kisses with me. The other members of the family followed her. The rare experience of being kissed by my father so confused me that I replied to his greeting by simply echoing his words 'Christ is risen', instead of saying 'In sooth, He is!' or 'He is risen indeed!' Smarting inwardly under this humiliating mistake — which my father most likely had not noticed — I turned away only to be embarrassed further by finding myself face to face with Shoora Martýnov. His mother stood beside him looking like a fourteen-year-old girl in her enormous hat. Both were leaning forward as if poised for immediate advance, and Shoora's small piercing eyes were fixed on mine. Instinctively, I stepped back and trod on my father's toes. He grunted in disapproval and I felt blood flooding my face.

'Christ is risen!' said Madame Martýnova to my mother. 'In sooth, He is!' replied my mother, stretching out her hand for a handshake. 'I wish you a bright, happy Easter.' — 'Thank you,' said Shoora's mother.

I curtseyed hurriedly to her, keeping my distance and wished her a 'bright, happy Easter'. Surely, they must understand that we do not embrace mere acquaintances! But Shoora's eyes were still persistently searching mine. 'Happy Easter!' he said and lunged forward. But Maroossia suddenly materialized between him and me. 'Happy Easter, Shoora!' she said, offering him her hand. And in the general movement of people towards the iconostasis, I managed to put more than one living obstacle between him and myself, a defence which he did not attempt to storm.

Other priests came out of the Royal Gates to bless us and to announce the news of the Resurrection, and finally Father Ioann appeared with a crucifix, and we all went up to kiss it.

'Christ is risen!' Father Ioann said to each of us in his tired old voice, and this time I remembered to reply 'In sooth, He is!' and touched the priest's cold, wrinkled cheek three times with my lips. I hesitated for a second whether to kiss his hand, as some people were doing, but decided not to do so. Hand-kissing — except women's hands by men — was somehow linked in my mind with servility: did not serfs kiss the hands of their masters in the not so distant past?

As we came out of the church and the dew-scented air blew into my face, I felt unsteady on my feet, elated, yet troubled at the same time. Christ was risen . . . yet I knew the joy I was feeling was not the pure joy of the Saints. It was tainted by guilt. I was wrong to evade kissing Madame Martýnova. Perhaps I should have kissed Shoora three times as well — because it was Easter. Why was I always thinking of him as very plain . . . more than plain . . . positively ugly? My brother had said that he looked like an ape . . . that he had a pig's eyes. I should not have such thoughts on Easter night. Christ was risen . . .

The sky was still dark as we drove home, but much more blue than two hours ago, and the stars were pale. The dawn was approaching, the morning of the day when Mary Magdalene went to visit His tomb and met the Man whom she mistook for a gardener. I seemed to hear *bátiushka's* rich voice: 'And Jesus said to her, "Maria!"' And she, recognizing Him, fell to her knees and cried: "My Lord!" Oh! if only

I could have been in her place and met Him in a garden, at dawn, on Easter morning, and heard my name spoken by Him like that!

The transition from church to domestic scene could have been an anti-climax to any sensitive creature if the Easter table had not so much resembled an altar. A pagan altar no doubt — for the offerings displayed on it were those of turkey and ham and sucking pig, of coloured eggs and a pyramid of sweet cream cheese — but there were also flowers: pots of fragrant hyacinths, and garlands of paper roses and evergreens pinned to the dazzling white table cloth.

We did not sit down to the 'breaking of the fast' — an experience no less exciting to me for never having fasted. My father poured out some Madeira wine, and I drank half a glass with the others, and we all had some *paskha*, an Easter egg, and a slice of *mazóorka*, my brother cutting himself a slice of ham as well. I felt the wine flow through my body, warming me inside, tangling my thoughts, calming my scruples . . . My mother kissed me on the top of the head and told me that I must not stay up a minute longer. In my room my sister helped me to undress — Aniuta, no doubt, was 'breaking fast' with the other servants — and I dropped off to sleep, thinking of tomorrow, *Easter day*!

I remember that Easter morning as exceptionally bright, the sky high and blue, with half-transparent shreds of cloud drifting across and melting as they went. I knew the wind was strong as soon as I opened my eyes because tree-tops were dancing and I could hear the excited voices of the rooks. After breakfast I went to the orchard to wish 'a bright happy Easter' to the trees. The ground was sodden, and my feet in ankle-high overshoes sent up little spurts of water as I walked between the fruit trees. The first lines of a poem were beginning to sing in my head.

> *This morning trees will dance and sun will smile,*
> *The rooks will fly around and shout for joy,*
> *For Christ is risen, and all that's mean and vile*
> *Must disappear from earth, and . . . and . . .*

I could not think of a rhyme for 'joy' and trudged through muddy grass and wet snow, searching for it and hardly noticing that my feet and legs were getting soaked.

'All that's mean and vile must disappear . . .' To me some of the underhand taunting and teasing of Mílochka and Fatima at school was 'mean and vile', and I tried to imagine them changed, transformed by having been in church on Easter night — but my imagination failed me.

Could those two girls ever be really affectionate and friendly? My own verses no longer sounded convincing to myself.

I crossed the orchard, pursuing the elusive rhyme and myself pursued by the inexorable rhythm of my verse. The log fence, darkened by many falls of snow and rain, was there for me to climb and look over beyond the edge of the cliff at the wide meadows which would soon be flooded by the Dniepr.•On that Easter Sunday they shimmered in the sunlight, grey-blue with dampness, broken here and there by large dark patches of last year's grass uncovered by the thaw. Half-way between that stretch of meadows and the horizon the curves of the river could be traced by the edge of the steep bank clearly emerging from the surrounding snow. I thought I could see the river swell and move, about to break its ice. When that happened, the waters would spread as far as the foot of our escarpment, almost as far as the blue ring of forest on the other side . . . The wind which came from there was full of the familiar, stirring fragrance of wet earth and melting snow. The wind was free . . . the river will soon have its freedom . . . the birds . . .

> *Would I be free and fly to Heaven*
> *On Easter Sunday, bright and blue . . .*
>
> . . . .
>
> *And sing my song to gladden you . . .*

A whole line was missing in this poem! What could rhyme with 'Heaven'? The uncompleted quatrain felt like a yawning chasm inside me, an emptiness almost of hunger. I was compelled to fill it, but with something that I really felt, something that was *true.*

> *If I were free and could take flight*
> *This Easter Sunday, blue and bright . . .*
>
> . . . .

I returned to the house by the back door which took me past the servants' room. Aniuta put her head through the door and said with an arch smile: 'There's a visitor in the drawing-room.'

She helped me off with my coat and overshoes.

'My goodness! Aren't your stockings soaked! What would *bárynia* say?'

As she was helping me to change them, I asked: 'Aniuta, who is the visitor?'

She smiled again.

'You'll see!'

She was so artful about it that I jumped to the conclusion that it would be a pleasant surprise. Could it possibly be my uncle Fyodor?

Breaking away from Aniuta's ministering hands, I ran to the drawing-room, flung open the door and nearly backed out again in my disappointment at finding that 'the visitor' was Shoora!

The effect my sudden entrance produced on him did not escape me. He stopped in the middle of what he was saying to my brother and stared at me for a few moments before he moved. Then, as if coming to life again, he seized an object which lay on a chair beside him and strode towards me, his eyes fixed on mine. His handshake was so strong that I screwed up my face, and with the other hand he held out his parcel with the words: 'This is for you!'

I took it awkwardly, thinking of the fretwork box he gave me at Christmas, which had since fallen apart.

'Shall I open it for you?' he asked eagerly.

I watched his fingers with thumbs curving far backwards as he untied the string. 'Thumbs that curve backwards denote a sensuous nature . . . ' my sister had read out from some book. What was 'a sensuous nature'? I vaguely knew — and disliked what I knew.

Shoora unwrapped the object he had taken out of the box. It was a large cardboard egg covered with shiny blue paper, the kind we used at school to wrap up our books, and overlaid with a fretwork pattern made of silver paper.

'An Easter egg!' he said with pride. 'I made it myself.'

My brother came up to look.

'Does it open?' he asked.

'No.' Shoora's tone of voice implied that the question was silly.

'What is it for, then?'

'What *for*? An ornament, of course!'

Try as I might, I could show no more enthusiasm for this present than my brother implied by his remarks. Among my toys I had a splendid bright red egg, the size of a baby's head, made of wood. It was made to be taken apart, and it disclosed a blue egg inside. That one contained a yellow egg and the yellow a green one, then another red, until in the end you came to a tiny blue one which did not open. When you put all the halves together you had a row of at least ten coloured eggs of different sizes, and you could play at selling them or pile them on a plate like the eggs on the Easter table. This cardboard egg with its silver pattern already coming unstuck in several places was of no use to me at all.

I was a poor hand at pretending and my spiritless 'Thank you very much' would have chilled the heart of any but the most buoyant of craftsmen. Shoora, however, showed no sign of disappointment. Looking as pleased with himself as if I had paid him the highest compliment, he stuffed the tissue paper back into the box, put the egg half-in as into an egg cup and placed the whole thing on the drawing-room table, evidently to display its beauty to all who might come in.

My brother bent over it to take another look.

'Is that what you do in your spare time, Martýnov?' he asked with a faint trace of mockery in his voice.

'Yes. And why not?' Shoora's tone was challenging.

'A bit juvenile . . . ' said my brother.

'Indeed! And how do *you* spend your spare time, pray?'

'I go for walks,' my brother said.

'Very healthy, no doubt! Polishing the pavements!' snorted Shoora.

I sat on the edge of a chair listening to this exchange with increasing astonishment and discomfort. To be discourteous to a guest as my brother was to Shoora was against all the rules of hospitality. Nor was it any less ill-mannered to be offensive, as Shoora clearly was, to one's host. I knew that Shoora was a year older than my brother and one class above him; until last Christmas they knew each other only by sight, and I understood they were not 'comrades' in the sense the word was used by schoolboys. Yet Shoora had asked my brother to his Christmas party, and he had been to our house more than once, and now he was here again, despite the fact that every time he came, my brother and he invariably got across one another, prodding and sparring and being sarcastic at each other's expense, until someone, usually my sister, managed to separate them. This enmity, which sprang up between them almost from the first meeting, grew more outspoken with every new encounter, and although I felt no tenderness towards either of the combatants, the combat itself distressed me.

This particular duel, however, had no time to develop into a proper verbal fight, for my mother and sister came into the room. Shoora was clearly soothed by Maroossia's appreciative comment on the ornamental qualities of his cardboard egg, and then we all went into the dining-room to have some food from the Easter table. Other visitors began to arrive, and soon the dining-room was full of people, chatting, clinking their glasses, being offered *zakoóski*, a slice of ham or pork, a taste of *Paskha*, a piece of almond shortcake or of a chocolate gateau. Almost all the visitors were men: women did not visit on Easter Sunday, but stayed at home to be visited by men. Most of the guests kissed my mother's hand when 'congratulating' her with 'the bright Day of Resurrection' — *Svyétloye Voskresyénie*. It struck me for the first time that the word for 'resurrection' and 'Sunday' was the same.

When the visitors had gone and we returned to the drawing-room, my mother noticed the cardboard egg occupying a place of honour on a table.

'Where did this come from?' she asked.

'Shoora Martýnov brought it,' said my brother. He always used this slightly contemptuous diminutive when speaking of Shoora out of his hearing. To his face he addressed him either as 'Martýnov' or just as 'you'. He added ironically: 'He made it himself, of course!'

'That's obvious,' said my mother. 'Do you see him often at M*?'

'Only occasionally during breaks at the *Ghymnásia*.'

'Yet he always comes to see you here . . .'

'He comes to see Leda, not me,' said my brother.

I blushed violently, expecting everyone's eyes to turn on me, including my father's, who, I was sure, would disapprove. But he was rocking himself gently in the rocking chair, smoking a cigarette and seemingly not listening at all.

'So our *króshka*'s acquired an admirer,' my sister said, smiling at me. She said this tenderly, but her tenderness did not compensate for the gentle mockery of her remark. I suddenly felt angry with her as I had never been before. I pushed away her arm which she put round my shoulders and ran out of the room.

My brother's tepid welcome did not deter Shoora from coming to our house several times during the Easter holidays. After exchanging a few bantering remarks with Vova, he usually found his way to the day nursery where I was busy with a new project — making myself a dolls' house. The success I had enjoyed with my Christmas presents to the family gave me a taste for making things with my own hands, and at once my imagination took charge, planning and visualizing on a grand scale. I decided to build a really large 'country house' with two drawing-rooms, one red, the other blue, and a suitable number of other rooms. Shoora, on hearing this, at once offered to make furniture for all of them.

He also helped with measuring out pieces of cardboard for the house, and drew and coloured the 'tiles' for the roof. Every time he came, he brought a few little cardboard chairs or beds which he had made at home. Like the Easter egg, they were covered with glossy paper and decorated with cut-out patterns of silver or gold, but his glueing once

again proved less effective than it might have been and the decorations
came unstuck even before the furniture could be used.

It was a new experience to have a boy of my brother's age ready to
share *my* interests and eager to help me to carry out *my* plans. My brother
had always imposed his plans on me: when we had played together before
he went to school, I had to play his games. I accepted Shoora's ministra-
tions with a slightly reluctant gratitude.

Then the 'building materials' ran short and the house was still
unfinished when I had to return to school.

My departure from home this time was made easier by the knowledge
that the summer vacation was only seven weeks away and that by my
mother's decision it was to be my last term as a boarder. I do not know
what decided her eventually: my pleading must have played some part in
it. Also she had heard from a cousin who had retired from the Army and
bought a *dacha* near M*, so that his only daughter, a few months younger
than I, could go to school there. My mother asked him and his wife
whether they would be prepared to take me *en pension*, and they consented to do so. To me, any change from boarding school appeared as
liberation.

'I think Zena, their daughter, has had very little proper schooling
because her parents have moved about so much,' said my mother. 'She's
an only child and probably rather spoilt . . . '

'What is her mother like?' I asked.

'Aunt Katia is an *institoótka*,' said my mother. 'It means she has led a
very sheltered life and knows little about practical things. She dotes on
Zena . . . Her father does, too.'

I found this last bit of information very intriguing. Fortunate Zena,
on whom her *father* doted! How different her father must be from mine.
Or was it I who was different? Somewhere deep inside me a dark
sediment of feeling which had never quite risen to the surface was stirred
by these thoughts. I was on the point of formulating an accusation, of
pronouncing a judgment – on my father, whose apparently complete
indifference to myself I had until then accepted as being a characteristic
of all fathers. Yet the idea of condemning him for this was so alarming
that I promptly turned the judgment on myself: it must be I who was not
the kind of daughter on whom fathers dote.

And yet . . . and yet! Was I not rather good at my lessons? After all,
most of my marks for the term were 'twelves'. And more than once I got
a 'twelve-plus' for my compositions. Besides, I was a poet . . . My

mother and Maroossia were proud of this — proud of me. Why was not my father? Perhaps he just did not like poetry? Perhaps he was like my brother who read historical novels about wars and religious persecution, or adventure stories by Fenimore Cooper and Mine Read, translated from the American? He might read Pushkin's *Captain's Daughter*, or Tolstoy's *Prisoner of the Caucasus*, but I had never known him to read 'Mtzyri', my favourite poem by Lermontov. Perhaps most men looked down on poetry as unmanly, and on poets as time-wasters, not to be taken seriously. My brother could earn my father's approval by being good at mathematics; I could not hope to earn it by being gifted in writing poetry.

Spring weather made the indoor life at the boarding school more irksome but less depressing than it had been in the autumn when the days were short and dark. Getting up at the sound of the bell was less of a brutal wrench when one could see a strip of blue sky above the roof of a house opposite. Even Fatima's and Mílochka's meaningless gibes seemed more silly than offensive when the sun was shining. Or perhaps I had become less sensitive, more tough and less liable to be caught unprepared? I certainly felt stronger than I had a few months ago.

The test of my strength, however, came from quite a different quarter and it all but shattered my newly won, fragile self-confidence.

When we assembled in our classroom on the morning following my return, Anna Avdyéevna greeted me with a smile which I felt was a special one for me. She did not speak to me until after the first lesson: there was not enough time: prayers had to be read and books prepared before the teacher arrived. But in the first break, as I curtseyed to her on my way to the passage, she smiled again and asked 'Are all your family well?'

I thanked her. Her brown eyes were bent on me with an expression of distinct benevolence: they were swimming in it as if in oil. I had noticed before this peculiar, moist or oily look in her eyes. The pale skin on her face also looked slightly oily.

'You are looking much better than you did before the holidays,' she said. 'You have more colour: you must have been out of doors quite a lot. It did you good. But I hope you've done some reading, too . . . some of the good French of Madame de Ségur. How far have you got in the story?'

Far from realizing what effect my reply was to produce, I blushed only a little while admitting my dereliction.

'I didn't read any of it,' I said simply.

The eyes gazing down on me were still moist, but their expression became mournful. The smile disappeared from Anna Avdyéevna's lips; her faint eyebrows went up in a painfully broken arch.

'You didn't read *any* of it?' she repeated as if she did not quite believe what she had just heard. 'After I had specially asked you?'

Aware that I had offended her in some incomprehensible way, and beginning to feel guilty, I tried to justify myself: 'You see, there was so much to do.'

'So much to do? The whole three weeks of the holiday?'

My face was now burning, and I began to stumble over my words.

'Yes . . . we started making a dolls' house and a lot of furniture . . . It took hours to . . .'

'I see . . .' Anna Avdyéevna tossed up her chin, a gesture the meaning of which was to become all too familiar to me in subsequent years. Her eyes were no longer benevolent and were looking over my head, at the far wall of the classroom. Her silence seemed to indicate that our conversation was now over. I waited a moment or two for a clearer sign of dismissal, but none came, so I dropped another curtsey and trotted out of the room, feeling thoroughly unhappy.

For several days after that Anna Avdyéevna remained seemingly unaware of my existence. While before she often used to entrust me with small but responsible tasks, such as taking a message to the staff-room or issuing books from the class-room library, she now called upon other girls to do these things. She would not meet my eyes when I looked in her direction, but gazed straight past me with her lips compressed and no trace of a smile. This was so different from her former, almost caressing manner towards me that other girls in the class also noticed it. 'I don't think you're her favourite any more,' Margóolina said to me. 'What have you done?'

I wondered myself. I had never before been subjected to this form of punishment, a punishment by complete withdrawal of attention, and I found it very painful. My suffering must have been pretty obvious, for at the end of the week, just when I was beginning to despair that my condition of ostracism was ever going to cease, Anna Avdyéevna allowed her eyes to descend from contemplating the ceiling of the class-room and to meet mine. Her gaze was still rather cold and distant but she seemed again to acknowledge my existence. And when at the end of the lesson I had to pass her desk on the way to the corridor, I felt I had to speak to her, to give her another, weightier reason for having neglected the holiday task she had set me.

'I forgot to tell you last time . . . last time you spoke to me . . . that it wasn't only making the dolls' house . . . it was also because I didn't have a French-Russian dictionary . . . '

Anna Avdyéevna said nothing for a few moments, her eyes fixed sombrely on mine.

'I would have been content if you had read even a few pages,' she spoke quietly, but with such force of expressiveness that I quivered. 'It is your utter forgetfulness of my request, your putting everything else before it that I found so inconsiderate. And you did not even think it necessary to apologize . . . '

I felt as if the ground were giving under my feet. Her accusation was true: I had not apologized because I believed that the explanation I had given exonerated me, as it would have done with my mother. At home, if an explanation was adequate, no apology was expected, and I had come to associate 'asking forgiveness' with an admission of guilt. I fumbled for words in an effort to explain further.

'I didn't think . . . ' I began.

Anna Avdyéevna cut me short.

'You didn't think! You —whom I believed to be so thoughtful and sensitive . . . who write poems and the best essays in the class! You *did not think* of the effects your actions have on others?'

I stood before her speechless, bewildered and distressed. Until that moment I had imagined that I had merely failed to carry out a holiday task, and perhaps deserved to be reprimanded for that, but I had not realized that I had also shattered an illusion. This realization was borne upon me with a devastating force. I suddenly saw myself through Anna Avdyéevna's eyes as a thoughtless, insensitive, ungrateful creature who deeply offended someone —a person who had behaved towards her with the greatest kindness and generosity. This revelation was so harrowing that I could no longer contain the tears which had been gathering deep behind my eyes for the last few minutes and were now beginning to burn my eyelids.

Anna Avdyéevna's face became blurred, the blue of her dress grew misty. I cried silently, not daring to move or speak. I was utterly humbled and ashamed of both my 'thoughtlessness' and my weakness, my inability to check this flow of tears. I felt as if I had made myself contemptible and disliked for ever.

Then, with a shock of surprise I heard Anna Avdyéevna's voice, soft and comforting, as her blurred face bent towards me and her misty blue figure came nearer.

'Now, now,' she said, 'you mustn't cry like this. I see you are really sorry for having caused me pain and disappointment. Where's your handkerchief? Dry your eyes as quickly as you can. The break is nearly over and ·the girls will be coming back into the classroom very soon now. You don't want them to see you crying . . . '

If Anna Avdyéevna had expected her words of reconciliation to have an immediate effect, she had overestimated her power. Sympathy always stimulates self-pity, and I reacted by a renewed flow of tears. Anna Avdyéevna's voice grew almost caressing.

'Don't, don't,' she said softly, laying a hand on my shoulder. 'It might be better if you ran along to the wash-room and put your face into a basin of nice cold water. Next lesson is only sewing, and I'll explain to Zoya Dmítrevna why you are going to be a little late – a headache, shall we say?'

The girls did, of course, notice that I had red eyes when I returned to the class-room, but some of them also heard the explanation Anna Avdyéevna gave to the sewing mistress when I did not reply to her calling out my name from the register. 'You still have a headache?' Margóolina asked me, sympathetically.

I nodded. I really had a headache now from having cried. But my dejection was less deep and my thoughts were no longer centred on the wrong I had done to Anna Avdyéevna but on the wrong she was prepared to do for my sake. She had volunteered to tell an untruth – I dared not call it a lie – to Zoya Dmítrevna, so that I should not be reprimanded for being late! This gave me enough material to ponder on, until I fell asleep in my bed at the end of that upsetting and bewildering day.

Summer Freedom

During my first two terms at the boarding school I refused to believe that I could ever be anything but intensely unhappy there. My mother's suggestion that I could 'get accustomed' to it filled me with indignation. I took it to mean that I could become so dispirited a creature as not to mind confinement in a cage. I liked to think of myself as someone never to be tamed, like the boy in Lermontov's poem 'Mtzyri', who was pining away because he was deprived of his freedom and who finally escaped from his monastery only to be found dying from his wounds in a forest after a fight with a leopard.

I must admit that this romantic vision of myself was rather blurred by the sober thought that there were no wild forests or mountains in the vicinity of the school, no tigers which would give me a chance of showing my courage by wrestling with them, and by the knowledge that the town streets, paved with cobbles, were of little use as a refuge for a fugitive. I disliked these facts but I could not ignore them, and it made my longing for freedom even more intense.

But as time went on and the pain of home-sickness abated, I ceased, almost without noticing it, to react to things and people as if I had been stripped of my skin. Probably because I now knew I would soon be rid of them, the personalities of Fräulein Schmiedel, of Fatima and Mílochka affected me less and less. I worked well in class and found satisfaction in learning and in the appreciation of my teachers. Except for occasional fits of giggles during lessons, from which most girls suffer, I gave little cause for Anna Avdyéevna to be displeased with me.

My last term at the boarding school passed off surprisingly quickly. My sister, on vacation from the university, came to take me home. It was a warm, overcast May morning, and we had been to the school garden to say good-bye to Mademoiselle Vinogradova, who was sitting with half-a-dozen older boarders, studying in the open air for their final examinations. As we were crossing the courtyard on the way out, my sister stopped to speak to a pale, languid girl who was reading by the open window of one of the class-rooms. Maroossia knew her elder sister and they exchanged a few remarks.

'How much longer have you got at the school?' my sister asked.

'Another whole year!' the girl sighed. 'My sixth as a boarder . . . It'll be your second,' she deigned to notice me.

'She's not coming back as a boarder,' said Maroossia. 'She's going to live with an uncle and aunt.'

I heard her say this with a curious detachment: suddenly I became aware of the fact that I no longer cared very much whether I came back as a boarder or not. A thought flashed through my mind: how differently I would have felt if these words had been said at the end of my first term! Then it would have been a triumph and a joy indeed. But now there was a faint taste of bitterness in my acceptance of this news, no longer new to me. The great turmoil of feelings caused by separation had subsided; the feelings themselves had all but burned themselves out; there remained only a realization that good things are less good when they come too late. Liberation meant less to a 'prisoner' who had learned to tolerate her imprisonment.

Yet it was good to wear my own *short* frock again, to let my hands take care of themselves instead of always remembering to clasp them in front of my stomach, to be free from bare walls and corridors, and from the rule of dropping curtseys to all the teachers and *dames-de-classe* I happened to meet outside the class-room. It was good to see the strips of fields running past the window of the train and the way they turned sideways and came to a point in the distance like the sections of a great open fan. Wafts of heavy scent blew in as we passed copses of bird-cherry in bloom. 'Are the apple trees still in blossom?' was my first question to Maxim who met us at the station with the phaeton.

A surprising piece of news my sister told me on the way home was that Shoora Martýnov was going to spend part of his summer vacation with us at our country house, Fyeny. Knowing that he and my brother did not get on at all well, I shared my puzzlement with Maroosia. She explained that my mother had had a letter from Shoora's mother, who had to go into hospital for an indefinite period and was worried about her son not getting proper care or company while she was away and his father at work. I asked what was Madame Martýnova's illness. My brother, who was travelling with us and did not take kindly to the news, growled: 'I bet she's having another of her mad spells.'

'She's had a nervous breakdown,' said my sister.

'It's just another word for the same thing . . . Shoora is mad, too,' muttered my brother. 'I hope he's not coming for the whole of the holidays.'

Without saying it, I hoped for that, too. We left our town house at B* a few days after my return from school. Nine months had passed since I last saw the country, and I was looking forward to going back with such keen anticipation that it was almost greed, an unwillingness to share my pleasure in it with anybody. I did not want to be distracted by visitors. As we drove up the avenue of lime trees towards the house, I got off the seat and stood on the step of the phaeton, so that I could see forward and back along the whole of its length. Last time I saw it the leaves were turning yellow, it had a farewell look; and now it welcomed me in its spring freshness, yet it was the same . . . the same! I was sure I recognized the very pattern of the shadows the trees threw on the ground beneath them, and I loved even the dust rising from under the horses' hooves, and the way it stood, faintly pink, in the air behind us.

We were now approaching the house. Here was the willow on the corner of the orchard, an old tree so thick with new shoots that my sister had used it as a refuge from visitors; afterwards it had become my watch tower. Soon the white-painted front of the wooden house with its columned porch and a veranda appeared in full view across the flower garden, its beds glowing with jonquils and daffodils. The lilac bushes by the steps of the porch were in full bloom.

Inside the house there were bouquets of lilac on the tables in all the rooms, the whole house was scented with it. It was the hour between light and dusk, to me a bewitching hour full of poetry. Outside, the light was soft yet clear: through the wide cut in the trees the distant meadows still showed green and the river steely grey. Indoors, the colours of the chairs, the carpets, of the lilac itself were dissolving into different shades of grey, changing into their shadowy selves. I ran out into the garden. The sun was setting in the west, but in the east the sky was also turning red, and I stood, puzzled, almost frightened, until

I realized that it must be the moon, rising to chase the sun off the skies.

> *That night the moon was early awake,*
> *And as she rose and raised her curtain red,*
> *She saw the sun about to go to bed,*
> *And cried: 'Oh, stay and tarry — for my sake!'*

'Stay and tarry . . . ' No, this will not do. 'Stay and tarry' is repeating the same thing. Surely the moon, Artemis, should be able to think of something better! The sun, Apollo, would hardly listen to such a feeble appeal. 'Oh, stay a little' . . . ? No! 'Oh, stay, beloved' . . . Could she really call him 'beloved' if she had never seen him before?

I strolled across the flower garden, oblivious of my surroundings, seized suddenly by my poetic daemon. As I turned into the lime avenue, two small figures materialized out of the shadows beneath the trees. I did not at once recognize them. They remained silent and I peered at them for a few moments. 'Mashka, Varka!' I exclaimed. Still without speaking, they nodded and giggled. For the next minute or two we continued staring at one another. Even in the dark I could see how much they were already tanned by the sun; Varka's nose especially was one mass of freckles.

'You've come!' Mashka said at last under her breath. And Varka added quickly and more loudly: 'There are lilies-of-the-valley come up the other side of the brook . . . '

My mother's favourite flowers! Wouldn't she be pleased if I brought her a bunch! Impulsively, I plunged forward.

'Let us pick some!'

They hesitated, hung back a little.

'It's dark by the brook . . . '

'There's the moon! What are you afraid of? Ghosts? There aren't any. Nothing can hide in the meadow. You should see the huge, long, dark corridors at the school!'

'Corridors . . . ' Mashka repeated in an awe-stricken voice. 'What are they for, these . . . corridors?'

'Why . . . to go from one room to another.'

'Haven't they got any doors?'

I was stumped by this simple question and used the speed of our advance through the shrubbery to avoid answering it. Just as we were leaving the shadows of the limes to step under the moon-drenched clouds of apple blossom in the orchard, Aniuta's voice reached us, calling urgently 'Lédochka! Where are you? Supper's ready! Come in to supper!'

We ran as fast as we could. The heavy dew on the grass soaked my shoes and stockings; Mashka and Varka, their feet bare, tucked up their skirts. The small gate which opened on to the meadow was shut with a bolt from inside. The girls did not want me to open it, but led me to a loose plank in the fence which could be swung aside, leaving an opening big enough for us to slip through.

'Pan Poznítsky doesn't know,' Varka said confidentially. Pan Poznítsky was my father's bailiff. 'If he knew he'd be very cross. He'd be cross if we undid the bolt before tomorrow morning.'

'Is Bronia home?' I asked, only half-wanting to know, for Bronia, the bailiff's son, was the only person I did not like meeting at Fyeny. Last summer he was still posing as a rejected lover, and I found his reproachful glances an embarrassment and a bore.

'Isn't yet . . . ' Mashka murmured, and I sighed with relief.

The lilies-of-the-valley by the brook were full of dew and fragrance, so young that their little cups were more green than white. We plucked them hurriedly, not one by one but several together, mixed with grass.

Back in the flower garden the lamp-lit windows of the dining-room threw rectangles of faint radiance on to the flower beds, snatching patches of colour out of the thickening dusk. On the veranda stood Maroossia, peering into the distance, her elbows on the balustrade, her face propped with both hands. At the sight of her Mashka and Varka melted into the shadows. I ran up the steps of the veranda and put my bouquet to my sister's face.

'*Króshka*, where have you been? Aniuta's gone to the stables to look for you.'

'I've been composing a poem, and then I've been picking these. I'm very hungry. Tell me, would Artemis call Apollo her 'beloved'? I know they could never meet because . . . but still, she knew about him.'

'Artemis could love no one,' Maroossia said. 'She was cold, cruel, she hunted animals for pleasure. She had Actaeon killed because he saw her bathing.'

'Why did she mind? And who was Actaeon?'

'He was a young man hunting in the woods and he came upon Artemis bathing with her women. She thought he was spying on them. She did not like being seen naked — it offended her chastity — so she sent her dogs . . . no, it was Actaeon's own dogs that tore him to pieces because she turned him into a stag.'

'What does chastity really mean and why is it so important?'
Maroossia demurred.

'It's . . . a kind of convention. A chaste girl is supposed to have
nothing to do with men.'

'Nothing at all? Not even speak to them?'

'Yes, she can speak to them, but never kiss or love them . . . '

'Men's faces scratch so . . . ' I said after a moment's meditation.
The French window rattled and my brother appeared silhouetted
against the lamplight.

'What are you doing here?' he demanded to know. 'We've been
having supper for the last half-hour.'

I held out my bouquet as we entered the dining-room, but it detained
my mother's gaze only for a moment: her eyes travelled at once down
to my wet stockings and shoes.

'You've stayed out in the damp all this time with your feet wet
through!'

'Mamma, smell this lovely scent!'

'You shouldn't have picked them so late at night. They'll give me no
pleasure if you catch a cold.'

After having had my feet bathed in hot water and putting on dry
stockings and shoes, I sat down to my favourite supper of buckwheat
kasha with butter and milk, and a compote of dried fruit. We would
have to wait for fresh fruit at least another month — and then it would
be wild strawberries! I thought I could smell my lilies-of-the-valley
above the scent of lilac which filled a vase in front of me, and I wondered
whether my mother was enjoying it and why she so often saw my
activities as a threat to my safety or health.

Three events stand out among the memories of that first summer from
school: my ride on Sultan, my brother's strange fight with Shoora
Martýnov, and a peasant wedding to which Aniuta took me.

Until then I only had an old pony to ride, but my mother at last
agreed to my riding a 'real horse' which, however, was only Moor, a
quiet animal without any initiative. He never tried to get in front of
another horse, trotted or galloped only when other horses trotted or
galloped and was impervious to any sudden stimulus which made other
horses shy. Even so, my mother was full of fears of what might happen
when I went out riding, and this made me nervous before a ride. As
a rule I got over it after a few minutes, but the effort of keeping my fear
under control often left me only half-able to control my horse.

Maxim was to accompany me on all my rides. He was a good instructor: he told me to keep the stirrup iron on the ball of my foot and never to pull too sharply on the bit.' You can make the horse rear and fall right over on his back if you do that,' he said. 'And if your foot is right inside the stirrup, it'll stay there when you're thrown, and you'll be dragged. Best to be thrown clean off.'

He had done his military service in the frontier guards, somewhere in the steppes of Southern Asia where wild ponies roam the countryside, and I could never hear enough about those days. He told me how difficult those ponies were to catch and how fiercely they fought, when captured, to get free again. I asked if he had ever tamed any of them himself.

'I didn't have the knack, *báryshnia*. There were one or two *Bashkírs* in our detachment who could do it. They knew the trick and they knew their ponies. You see, a horse that's born wild can't be broken the same way as a horse born domestic. They don't understand our language, to start with.'

'Did you ever ride them yourself, Maxim?'

'I sure did – after they'd been broken. They could go like the wind. So sure-footed they were too. Never a stumble.'

'Go like the wind!' This fascinated me. But the fastest I could get out of Moor was a medium-speed gallop. I hankered after my father's horse, Sultan, and I seized my chance when once Maxim decided to exercise him by riding him when he went out with me. My father was still in town, and I saw this as an opportunity not to be missed. As soon as we were well out of sight of the house, I asked Maxim if he would change horses with me. He argued that I would not be able to hold Sultan, that if my mother came to hear of it he would have a lot to answer for, but I pleaded with him so insistently that in the end he agreed.

We dismounted. Maxim changed our saddles – I was riding side-saddle – and lifted me on to Sultan's back. Trembling with excitement and apprehension, I threaded the reins between the fingers of my left hand, just as Maxim had taught me. Sultan danced on the spot while Maxim tightened the girth. He hardly had time to mount Moor when we were off at a gallop.

Sultan's gallop was so smooth and easy that at first I felt nothing but elation and pride. In a matter of seconds, however, he shot forward, leaving Moor a whole length behind.

'Hold him, *báryshnia*!' I heard Maxim's urgent voice, its sound blown away by the rush of air past my ears.

I needed both my hands to do this, but sudden alarm made me clutch the pommel of the saddle with my right hand, and I dared not let go. The cluster of reins in my left hand took all my strength merely to grip, I could not tighten them. Sultan laid his ears back and went 'like the wind'. I knew that the sound of Moor's hooves behind him was driving him to go faster and faster. I knew I could not possibly stop him. Trees, bushes, glimpses of earth and sky streaked past with a vertiginous speed. Thoughts raced through my mind even faster. Where was I coming to? How was it going to end? My mother had warned me . . . she was right . . . my father's horse . . . I should not have . . . am I going to be smashed to bits? Am I going to be thrown when Sultan jumps? When? Where?

An obstacle loomed ahead: a low shed or the remnants of an old corn stack . . . I could not tell: I could just see that the track turned sharply to the left and that someone was standing on the corner. What would Sultan do? Jump the obstacle? Swerve left at full speed? Shy away from the person who was standing there, still as a statue? Whatever he did, I could hardly hope to keep my seat. Staring fearfully ahead, I no longer listened to the sounds of the other horse behind me: I believed Maxim to be far behind. But suddenly Moor's head appeared close to my left elbow, a broad hand reached out and seized my horse's reins. Sultan's head was twisted sideways just as he was bearing down on the obstacle in front. He reared and tossed his head. White foam flew from his bit. Maxim turned him off the track and brought him to a standstill in the corn.

The person who had been standing motionless, watching our approach, ran up to us. It was Maroossia. She was breathless with alarm.

'What's happened? Why were you going at such a speed?'

Maxim helped me down and was changing the saddles.

'Can't think what's got into him,' he muttered. 'Been in the stable too long, that's why . . . Too fresh.'

My legs were trembling with the tension suddenly gone. I begged my sister not to mention the incident to my mother.

'But what *has* happened? I could see you from a long way off: one moment you were like dots on the horizon and the next you were bearing down on me. Did your horse bolt? You can't imagine how you frightened me. It's the second time . . . '

I remembered this strange remark, and when we were alone the same evening, Maroossia strumming 'My fire's burning in the mist' on the piano in semi-darkness and I sitting beside her, I asked her to explain its meaning. She told me that one summer on the estate, when I was eight months old and she in her ninth year, we were taken for a walk in the woods by my wet nurse, Matriona. Matriona was carrying me in her arms. When she saw there were a lot of mushrooms about, she sat me on the grass by a stack of birch logs and proceeded to pick them. Followed by my sister, she went further and further into the forest until they lost sight of me. Maroossia became very apprehensive. She asked Matriona to go back, and they made their way towards the clearing in the forest where they had left me — but there was no child there. Was it the same clearing? It had the grass and the stack of birch logs — yet there were many such in the woods. 'I could swear that's the place!' Matriona said. Maroossia was so terrified at the thought of losing me that she could hardly speak or move. She imagined that gypsies or wolves must have taken me. 'Matriona began to shout, to call you by your name — as if you could answer her! And then, as we stopped and listened for a moment — a miracle! We heard your voice! We ran towards it and found you sitting under that stack, "exclaiming", as Matriona described it, talking to yourself — or to things around you in your own language — perfectly happy!'

'I'm glad I wasn't crying,' I said, complacently. 'You see, I wasn't afraid of the forest even then!'

Shoora Martýnov arrived at Fyeny half way through the summer vacation and stayed a fortnight. During that time he followed me about and tried to share in all my pursuits. When I played in the pile of sand by the veranda, making mountain roads and forests with bits of branches and grass, he incurred my brother's mockery for helping me to plant them. When we played at 'Kazaks and Brigands' with my brother and our cousin Vera, who was staying with us at the same time, he invariably went all out to capture me, leaving Vera to be caught by my brother. This seemed to please my brother, who found Vera a willing victim. She would shatter the air with her screams and alarm my mother who was not accustomed to such violent displays of emotion, as neither my sister nor I were given to screaming.

Vera was the same age as myself but in some ways much more sophisticated. She shocked me by confiding that she did not really love her parents because they did not love her, and much preferred her younger brother and sister. She disturbed my conventional views on feminine beauty by declaring that her ideal was an English Miss with red hair and green eyes. Because at the time I was reading *The Three*

Musketeers and had begun writing a novel about Henri Quatre and Marguerite de Valois, I maintained that a French girl with black hair and flashing dark eyes was *the* ideal, but I began to have doubts about it from that time on. Because Vera was such a screamer I could not take her seriously, but the effect of her personality persisted for a time after she had gone.

Shoora's visit ended in a rather disturbing way. Although my brother and he sparred and teased one another continuously, giving one another contemptuous nicknames — Shoora nicknamed my brother 'Baldwin', a play on the Russian word '*baldá*', a blockhead — they had never shown real anger with one another. Then one morning, the day before Shoora was due to leave, something happened.

We had a full house that fortnight and my brother was sharing his room with Shoora. It was in the mezzanine, across the landing from the room I was sharing with my sister. I was still in bed, in that delightful, indeterminate state between sleep and waking when the body is almost weightless and the mind just aware of the sunshine pouring in and the jubilant birds outside. I was about to sink into a dream again when the sound of shuffling and bumping close to our door brought me back to the surface with a jerk. I thought I heard my brother's half-stifled voice telling someone to 'leave me alone' and 'let go'. Then there was some more shuffling and grunting.

I sat up in bed and was about to speak to Maroossia when I saw that she, too, was awake and on the alert.

'It must be Vova and Shoora! What *are* they doing?'

In a second we were both out of bed and on the way to the door, but before we reached it, we could hear footsteps hurrying up the stairs. They were to quick to be my mother's, but the voice we heard was certainly her voice. She sounded deeply alarmed.

'Don't open the door!' my sister whispered, but I had already pulled it ajar. My brother and Shoora in their pyjamas were confronting my mother who was in her dressing-gown with her hair in *papillottes*. Their faces were flushed, my brother was scowling while Shoora smiled a contorted smile, trying not to look at anybody.

'I'm sorry, Elisaviéta Matvyéevna,' he muttered. 'We were just wrestling . . .'

'You had your knee on his chest and your hands round his throat,' my mother said, short of breath. 'What kind of wrestling is that?'

Vova growled something to the effect that he would have sent Shoora flying down the stairs if she had not come up just then, then brushed

past her into the bathroom while Shoora sidled back into their
room. My mother came into our bedroom and sat down, visibly
shaken.

'That boy is dangerous . . . quite unbalanced . . . ' she said. 'I do
believe that if I hadn't come up in time, he might have strangled our
Vova . . . I wish I had not asked him to stay . . . '

My brother would not tell us what caused their quarrel except that
Shoora's teasing had made him lose his temper, so it looked as if it was
he who had started the fight. This was most unlike him: as a small boy
he was not a fighter and he disliked taking physical risks. I had never
forgotten how he sent me up on the roof of the house to get his arrow,
and from that time on I suspected him of not being really 'brave'. He
knew he could tease me with impunity because I could not really hurt
him, and when in exasperation I would rush at him with my fists raised
to strike, he would throw himself on to a sofa and hold his feet up in
the air, to keep me at a safe distance. It was not until a year or two later,
however, when I entered the phase of criticism and re-appraisal
characteristic of adolescence, that I began to tell him he should have
been born a girl, and I a boy.

Without Shoora and Vera life at Fyeny flowed much more evenly.
Our next diversion was provided by a wedding in the village. My mother
gave a dress to the bride, and Aniuta, our maid, was going to the
wedding. She asked if she could take me with her and my mother
consented.

The village church was tiny, whitewashed inside and out, with an
iconostasis of painted wood and primitive icons. The bride's white
dress set off her deeply sunburnt face and hands. The bridegroom wore a
red sateen shirt and black trousers tucked inside high boots. I noticed
that the bride's eyes were swollen. 'With crying . . .' Aniuta whispered
into my ear. 'Oh, Lord! how she cried when they were plaiting her hair
this morn . . . '

'Didn't she want to marry him?' I whispered back.

'I'll tell you afterwards . . . '

> '*There's something knocking and stamping hard . . .*
> '*See, Mother dear, who's in our yard?*'
> '*They've come for you, Daughter, they've come for you,*
> '*And for the goods that you bring with you!*'

This song had been pursuing me all the morning as I wandered about
the orchard where it adjoined the kitchen gardens of the cottages. The

lilt of the song was nostalgic, the words reflected a mood of conflict — the girl's fear that the bridegroom's friends might not come to fetch her for the wedding ceremony and the hope that, if they failed, she would remain at home with her mother. The song was familiar to me from early childhood: my brother and I knew the words and sometimes we teased Aniuta with it, singing it to remind her that she was still unmarried at the age of twenty-two.

I had heard that village mothers-in-law often maltreated their sons' wives, and I wondered whether this particular bride had cried so much because she expected this to be her fate. I stared closely at her as she stood there with her eyes downcast. What was she thinking? Did she really mean it when she repeated after the priest the promise to honour and obey her husband? I saw the priest putting a ring on to her finger, and another one on the bridegroom's. I craned my neck, trying to see what they did next. The priest joined their hands and led them round the praying desk three times, while two sturdy young men followed, holding crowns, heavy and bulging like Russian bishops' mitres, over their heads. Why?

As I watched the ceremony, I became conscious that I, too, was being watched — by a small barefoot child dressed in nothing except a white linen shift. Holding on to his mother's skirt, he was staring hard at me: it seemed that to him I was more of a spectacle than the crowned couple in all their finery. But as soon as I met his gaze, he dropped his eyes and edged away to hide behind his mother.

The procession that made its way back to the cottages from the church door was very different from the orderly cortège that arrived there less than an hour before. It sprawled and straggled all over the wide, dusty street, eddying and spilling over into the neighbouring yards and gardens. The bridegroom's friends, with their jackets off and thrown over their shoulders, had picked up their accordions and were playing and singing as they went along. The girls in bright head scarves linked arms and led the way, laughing and cracking sunflower seeds. The older men, joining in groups, were talking loudly with guffaws of laughter. Only the newly married couple and their parents walked demurely and quietly in the middle of the road, but no one looked solemn any longer and the bride was smiling.

Aniuta and I walked alongside the girls who offered us sunflower seeds. My skill in shelling them was vastly inferior to theirs. They put them between their teeth: there was a cracking sound and instantly the husk was spat out and the kernel eaten. The girls hardly seemed to use their hands at all, and to be eating the seeds all the time. When I tried to imitate them, I found I was chewing the husk as well as the seed.

I recollected Aniuta's promise to tell me more about the bride.

'Why was she crying this morning? She's quite cheerful now.'

The girls stopped giggling among themselves and listened.

'She's got to cry to keep the bad luck off,' Aniuta said. 'And she'll be leaving her own father and mother . . . '

'Where is she going to live then?'

Aniuta indicated a cottage a few yards ahead of us.

'But it's almost next door to her parents!'

Aniuta shrugged. We were about to enter the bride's former home. We stepped over a high threshold into the *syeni*, a windowless, unheated room which divides a Russian peasant cottage in two parts – the best room and the 'black' *izba*. A young calf was lying on some straw in the far corner of the *syeni*, but, hemmed in as I was by Aniuta and the girls, I could not get across to stroke it.

In the cottage best room red geraniums in pots and muslin curtains screened the two small windows, but the sunshine outside was so strong that the low-ceilinged, white-washed room looked cheerfully light. Several wooden trestle tables, put end-to-end, stretched right across it with plates and many dishes of food displayed on them, among which pigs' trotters in jelly drew my attention. They looked like large lumps of glass with objects captured and immobilized inside them. There were also dishes of eggs, sliced salt herrings decorated with rings of onion, piles of boiled potatoes, salt cucumber and beetroot, and many loaves of bread. Several dishes were piled with rolls of a peculiar shape, patterned as if with scales.

'Fir cones,' Aniuta told me. 'You've got to have them. They bring luck.'

We all sat on wooden forms: there were no chairs. Aniuta and I had the seats of honour on the left of the bride who was sitting beside her husband. On his right sat his parents, and opposite us the parents of the bride. Her father picked up the nearest bottle of vodka – several of them stood between dishes of food all along the table – and asked us to hold out our glasses. 'No, no,' Aniuta said warding off his hand, '*báryshnia* can't have any, and I never take it either . . . !'

Our host protested strongly: we had to have 'a drop, for the newly-marrieds' health and happiness'. A chorus of voices supported him. I was curious to have it. Aniuta, flushed and flustered, had her hand forced. Someone put a plate piled with food in front of me, and urged me to take a sip from my glass, half full of an almost colourless liquid. I did so, and something like a ball of fire travelled right through my middle down to my legs and feet. It was a pleasantly alarming sensation, and as it ebbed away, I suddenly thought it funny and began to laugh.

'Eat something, lovey, eat!' Aniuta urged me.

Meanwhile, all the men in the room, glass in hand, shouted: 'Bitter, bitter! *Górko, górko!*' and would not drink until the young couple kissed each other. The men went on shouting this at intervals, and I began to feel sorry for the bride and bridegroom who could not settle down to their food, but had to wipe their mouths with the back of their hands and go through the ritual of a ceremonious kiss every time. The guests then drank, smacked their lips and declared: '*Tepiér sládko!*' – now it is sweet.

Voices were getting louder and faces redder when Aniuta leaned across the table and whispered to the bride's mother that she had to take me home. As we rose to go, hands stretched towards us pressing fir-cone rolls upon us.

'For your Papa and Mamma, *bdryshnia*, and some for yourself and your brother and sister. From the bride and bridegroom! They'll bring you luck.'

We went home by a short cut through some cottage gardens and a hole in the fence which gave access to our orchard. Aniuta looked uneasy as we approached the house.

'You didn't have much of that vodka, lovey, did you?' she asked.

I told her that I had had half a glass, which I thought she knew.

'But you don't have a headache, do you, dearie?'

I confessed that I felt a little dizzy. She assured me that I would be all right in a short while. She did not want my mother to get worried, she added. I told her I would say nothing about it unless my mother asked me. Aniuta sighed. She could not have made her wishes plainer, and I did not want to be scolded.

My mother and sister were reading on the veranda when I walked up the steps, my arms full of fir-cone rolls.

'These are for you — from the bride and bridegroom!'

'Why this shape?' my mother wondered.

'Something to do with fertility,' my sister said. And she began to talk of old customs, superstitions and remnants of pagan rites among Russian peasants, which she was studying in a seminar at her *Koorsy*. The many seeds of the fir-cone might stand for a large harvest of corn or a large family of children. Throwing confetti at the bride and bridegroom must have the same origin. And in some parts of Central Russia they had a marriage custom of serving the newly-wed with an omelette on their first morning as man and wife. The assembled relatives watched the husband cut the omelette. If he cut it crosswise it meant his wife was a virgin when he married her, if he made a circular cut, it meant that she was not, and all her family were disgraced.

'What a barbarous custom!' said my mother. 'Our Bielorussians here are much more civilized.'

I remember this conversation, I think, because for a moment I identified myself with the bride, and was shocked by the cruelty of this custom. Vaguely I knew what virginity meant and I accepted the unspoken assumption that a girl should remain a virgin until she was married. All the same, my sympathy was with the girl who had been 'seduced', rather than with her husband who maltreated her on that account. But the whole subject of sex and marriage was not yet a matter of much interest to me: it seemed too prosaic compared with what happened before marriage — a meeting between two kindred souls and their falling in love.

For this I required the most romantic setting — France in the times of King Henry of Navarre — which of course I found in *The Three Musketeers*. I was still enough of a child to make the couple in my story begin as children, high-spirited, mischievous, always on the look-out for adventures such as I myself should have liked to have. In the course of the story they grew up, fell in love and became engaged to be married — but the character in my story who fascinated me most was King Henry himself, whom I hero-worshipped after reading Dumas. The boy in the story was a page of his, and the girl his ward. I suspect Henry of Navarre was to me an ideal father-figure who treated the two children as I wanted my father to treat me. He could be strict with them, but most of the time he was kind and gay, and able to share in their fun and some of their adventures. The boy, also called Henry, was passionately devoted to him. And so was I. With them I led a life of pageantry and excitement, for which a part of me must have craved.

But most of myself was deeply involved with my native countryside. I had composed my first poem one spring morning when I was eight years old. Perhaps if I had not had Pushkin read to me when I was very young, I should not have conceived that love for words arranged in rhythmical, rhymed patterns, which now compelled me to put my feelings and thoughts in the form of verse. Perhaps if my mother had not been impressed by my early poems and had not shown them proudly to her friends, my first attempts at writing poetry would have remained my only ones — mere scribbling in a child's exercise book, to smile at when one happened upon it in later years. How can one tell? Personally, I have a feeling that it was not all nurture. The intense emotion which things of Nature – flowers, cornfields, streams, clouds, stars, swallows – aroused in me pressed for expression, and poems were a means that lay at hand. No doubt, if we had been a musical family I might have chosen music as my means: in fact, I always sang my poems while I searched for the best words and rhymes before putting them on paper. But when I tried to learn the piano I found it slow and laborious, whereas verse meters came to me easily and almost unerringly after the first few attempts. My verse improved so rapidly that at the age of eleven I was already smiling at the inexpert poems I had written when I was eight. I learnt pages of Pushkin and Lermontov by heart with ease; reading poetry aloud became a passion. To me it was music and painting combined and brought to a perfect art: music of words, rhymes and rhythm, evoking images of Nature and people in action as vivid as life itself.

Only the women of my family showed an interest and appreciation of my literary pursuits. My father ignored them. The only occasion when I heard my mother speak to him of my poems, he remarked that 'everyone writes poetry when they are young – even I did!' This seemed to me so incredible that I assumed he was joking. My brother, on the other hand, seized upon my poems as an ideal means to tease me with. He used to get hold of the exercise book in which I wrote them and which I tried to keep in a secret place, and read them aloud in tones of exaggerated pathos. Or he would lisp and babble like a very small child, conveying in this way that they were very babyish stuff. This drove me frantic and often ended by my bursting into tears.

That summer I found an unexpected ally in my father's young secretary, Dimitry Aleksyeich, or Mitya, as we soon came to call him. He would chase my brother and rescue my poems from him. He came to help my father with some letters and stayed a week. He wore his hair a little longer than was customary and had gentle, deferential manners which pleased my mother. She told us that he reminded her of Lensky, Oniéghin's poet-friend. In fact, he confided to her and me that he, too, wrote poems, so I let him read mine. He declared them to be 'quite remarkable' and offered to make a book of them — typed, of course, not printed. I was delighted with the idea, and let him take away my precious exercise book when he went back to B*.

Every morning after that I expected a parcel in the post, but it did not arrive until three weeks later. It was well worth waiting for. My poems were typed on thick, glossy paper, each with a vignette around it, so that each poem was set in a kind of frame. Mitya contributed an introduction in verse, in which he called me 'a fellow-traveller to Parnassus'!

But his conception of what was due to me as a poet did not stop at this. He had the idea that my portrait ought to accompany my 'book', and when we returned to B*, he persuaded my mother to let him take me to a photographer. He took me to Perelmuter, who had photographed us as children several times before, but this time he was not permitted to have his customary way. Perelmuter was Jewish, as were most of the men who ran their own small businesses in my part of Russia. He was lively, chatty, and plausible — I had believed him when he told me to watch for a little bird which would fly out of his black box. Now, of course, I was too old to be told such tales. Anyway, Mitya had his own ideas on how a young poet should be photographed. He removed the traditional palm in a pot from the rickety bamboo stand and made me lean on the stand with my elbow, propping my chin with one hand. Screens with clouds painted on them were arranged behind my back. I was not to look at the black box but 'into the far distance'.

A few days later he arrived at our house with an air of discreet satisfaction and produced a fat envelope from his breast pocket which he handed my mother with a bow.

The photographs! I ran up to look. My mother examined them critically. They were quite large, and — a most unexpected thing — they were partly in colour! My hair had been given a yellowish tinge, my eyes and the bow in my hair were the same shade of blue, while my lips and cheeks were lightly touched in with carmine. The bamboo stand had disappeared, and my elbow was supported instead by a large crescent moon coloured the same shade of yellow as my hair.

My mother looked doubtful. 'Did Perelmuter put the colouring in?' she asked.

'Yes . . . with some advice from me. You see, he's not exactly what you would call an artistic photographer.'

'He made her look older than she is,' said my mother.

I did not know what to say. The imagined and the real never coincided — that I had already found out — but the impact of this discovery would continue to be distressing for years to come. That portrait was not at all my idea of what a young poetess should look like. But Mitya was so eloquent in its defence, that shortly before I left home for school, it was framed and standing on my mother's dressing-table.

A Family not Like Ours

The recurrent experience of parting from my mother had blunted the sharp point of pain and turned it into a dull ache, tinged with nausea. As I went to bed in an austere, small room in Uncle Vladímir's house and closed my eyes, it was the image of my own room at home with its warm colours and shaded lights that sprang up before my mind's eye. At that moment I missed the place more than any person in it. Homeliness was entirely absent from this household, and I sensed it from the moment my mother and I crossed my uncle's threshold.

I remember well my introduction to the Martsinóvsky family. My uncle was short and stocky with a bullet-shaped head covered with thick, greying hair cut *en brosse.* He had a short moustache and his colour was high. His eyes were deep-set with no spark of humour in them. Aunt Katia was short and plump, and she walked with tiny steps, like a ball rolling. She had small, pale-blue eyes which did not rest on you but darted about as she spoke to you. In any case she hardly spoke at all during that uncomfortable forty minutes we spent over the tea table with them. Neither of them smiled once the whole time.

Zena, their only daughter, was also unsmiling and silent. Taller than her mother by half a head, she had a broad Russian nose, an un-Russian head of coarse light-brown curls and large, round eyes. She sat close to her mother and watched me sombrely across the table, rather as one would watch an unpredictable, possibly dangerous animal.

She turned red in the face when my mother addressed her, asking what class she was in at her school, and failed to reply. Her father answered the question for her.

'She's in the second class . . . really ought to be in the third, like your Leda, but with all the moves and changes we've had following the regiment . . . well, she's had no chance of proper schooling. She'll have to work hard to be moved up next year.' He stressed the words 'work hard' and looked at his daughter, who seemed to take this as a reproof and was on the point of tears.

'In my *Ghymnasia* we count our classes backwards,' I chipped in. 'I'm in the fifth.'

My mother must have noticed Zena's distress and suggested that if we had finished our tea, she might show me my room.

The corners of her mouth still drooping, Zena looked at her mother. I heard Aunt Katia whisper: 'Go!' Reluctantly, Zena dragged herself off her chair and led the way through the red plush drawing-room and a chilly hall to a small bedroom, the window of which opened on to a rather neglected garden. The room contained a small work table with a drawer, a narrow bed, a small wardrobe and two chairs. There was a shelf for books and a mirror over a wash-stand. I was aware that Zena was watching me while I looked the place over. Neither of us said a word until I went to the window and looked out into the garden.

The house stood on a hillock and the ground fell away steeply from the edge of a flower garden, fringed with syringa and lilac bushes. I could glimpse a stream at the bottom of the drop, and beyond it the gently rising slopes of another hillock over which young birches grew freely with plenty of space between them. Though my heart was heavy with the sense of approaching separation, I felt soothed by this spectacle and glad that the repellent, blind window-panes of the boarding school dormitory would no longer stop me from looking out on the world outside.

'Can one bathe in your river?' I asked Zena.

'Yes.' Her voice, which I heard for the first time, was low and a little husky.

'Can you swim?'

'No.'

'Is the river deep?'

'In some places.'

'Shall we go out and have a look?'

'If you like.'

We made our way between half-empty flower beds to some earth-and-wood steps which descended towards the stream.

'A boat!' I exclaimed on seeing one tethered to a pole at the corner of a small landing stage. 'Is it yours?'

'Yes.'

Was she ever going to say anything more than 'yes' or 'no'?

'Can we go in it?'

'I don't know.'

I felt suddenly annoyed, irritated by her lumpishness and lack of any effort to be hospitable or pleasant.

'Why don't you know? If it's yours, surely you can go in it?'

Zena, who had been looking merely glum, now turned sulky again. 'There are no paddles,' she muttered.

'Haven't you got any, anywhere?'

She did not reply.

'I suppose you don't know,' I said waspishly. 'Do you know anything at all?'

Zena reeled back as if I had struck her, and glared at me with her mouth skewed.

'Don't you dare say such things to me!' she spluttered after a pause of stunned silence.

'I didn't *say* anything, I merely *asked* you,' I retorted. 'Perhaps you don't know the difference . . . '

Zena suddenly recovered her full voice and her power of speech.

'You're showing off!' she shouted. 'You're mocking me because I'm only in the second class at a private school, and you're in the third at the *Maryínskaia*. It isn't my fault, it isn't! It's mean of you to tease me about that.'

It was my turn now to be surprised.

'I didn't mean that at all . . . ' I began.

'Yes, you did! You *are* mean! I'll tell my mother . . . '

Tears were beginning to trickle down her cheeks. I shrugged my shoulders and turned away. I felt embarrassed, annoyed, but not really sorry for her. It was ridiculous to be so touchy and to cry like a three-year-old.

I heard her scramble up the steps and knew she was running back to her mother, but made no attempt to detain or to follow her. When I could no longer hear her footsteps I sat down on a backless wooden seat by the landing stage and gazed at the scene before me. The birch trees clustered thickly over my head and the water at my feet looked deep and dark. The sluggish stream seemed hardly to be moving, and the only sign of a current was the slight bumping of the boat against a pile of the landing stage. The air was still, and the occasional yellowed leaf which detached itself from the branches above floated slowly down before it finally landed on the surface of the river and began to glide along with it. I was suddenly overwhelmed by a feeling of ineffable sadness: it was like a sensation of nausea and it made me double up on my perch. The dark water, the yellow falling leaves meant the end of summer . . . and of freedom – the beginning of another year of trial away from home. My first encounter with Zena did not augur well. I wondered what she was going to tell her mother. I did not like my uncle or his family on this first meeting, and I felt they were not going to like me. I wondered why my mother had chosen this household to put me into. She had told me, of course: because they were her relatives, and I should be 'well-looked-after' and have a companion of my own age. A companion indeed! She – my mother – wanted me to be 'looked after' well, no matter how unhappy I was in myself! Not having yet experienced any physical deprivation, I felt happiness was preferable by far, and that my mother was wrong in putting material well-being first and happiness second. I was making this judgment and condemning my mother without yet formulating my thoughts in words.

I do not know how long I sat there staring at the river and the yellow leaves floating past before I heard my mother calling me. She was standing at the top of the steps in her grey suit and hat, and the dull ache inside me suddenly mounted and ended in a stab of pain as I realized that the moment of parting was upon us.

I went up to her. She was looking grave.

'Did anything happen when you were with Zena?' she asked. 'She seemed upset when she came in from the garden, but she won't say anything.'

This surprised me. I had expected Zena to complain at once to her mother. But perhaps she would tell her when they were alone . . .

I told my mother that nothing really happened and that I thought Zena took offence far too readily. She shook her head and said that this might be true and that Zena, being an only child, was probably spoiled, but that I should try for my own sake to make friends with her.

We returned to the house and soon afterwards my mother said good-bye to my uncle's family and myself. With great difficulty I managed to prevent my distress rising to my mouth and eyes: my throat was blocked with it. I did not want the Martsinóvsky family to see me crying. My uncle's buggy and horse, a strawberry roan, were waiting outside the porch. I watched my uncle get into the buggy with my mother: he was accompanying her to the station. I was on the point of asking: 'Can I come, too?' but, fearing refusal, remained silent. The young coachman shook the reins and the pink horse gingerly trotted down the slope towards the open gates. From the house porch I watched the buggy climbing up the opposite slope and roll away in a cloud of dust along a grey ribbon of a road, which went winding across the burnt yellow of the fields covered with stubble. Soon it became a mere dot against the faded blue of the sky, but I lingered in the porch, reluctant to turn round and meet the stare of those two pairs of eyes: Zena's and her mother's.

I did not eat much at supper that evening and my aunt inquired some- what acidly whether her food was not to my taste and what I was accustomed to eat at home. I replied that I was not hungry. But it was also true that I did not like her food, and that I was at that age a small and fastidious eater.

I shed some tears in my bed that night. In the morning, Mavra, a strapping, youngish woman, the family's *bonne-à-tout-faire*, came to wake me. I took to Mavra at once: in contrast to her employers she looked straightforward and almost cheerful.

'Get up, *báryshnia*, the *samovar*'s boiling,' she told me. 'And Stan's getting the horse ready to take you to school.'

It was arranged that Stan, the coachman, would take Zena and me every morning as far into M* as the corner of a certain boulevard, which was about the same distance from our two schools. At the end of the school day he was to meet us at the same place and drive us home.

On the way out that morning Zena remained silent and morose. Concluding that she was still resentful because of my remarks yesterday, I decided to ignore her, and, diverted by the pleasant drive, almost forgot about her. Home-sickness receded into the background before the excitement of returning to school as a full-fledged day pupil, of seeing Anna Avdyéevna and my school-mates again.

That summer, with the help of my sister's dictionary, I had managed to read most of Madame de Ségur's story about the circus children, and I was looking forward to showing my *dame-de-classe* the list of words I had learned and to earning her approval.

To walk along the street in M*, unaccompanied by any adult, was exciting – almost an adventure – enhanced by my wearing a new uni- form. No longer was I trammelled by the long skirt or made self-conscious by the white cape and sleeves, worn by the boarders. Quite a number of girls dressed like myself in a brown serge dress and a black pinafore were walking in the same direction: girls alone, girls in pairs or in small groups, some with satchels on their backs, others swinging their book-carriers on their arms, chattering, laughing, calling out to one another. Suddenly I saw Margóolina, my desk companion of last year. She, too, saw me, and stopped, her mouth half-open in surprise.

'What! You, Rayévskaia?' she said. 'You're no longer a boarder?'

'No, I'm not, thank goodness!' I replied cheerfully. 'I'm now living' at my uncle's and I'll be coming to school every morning, just as you do.'

She said nothing, but as we walked on together, she glanced sideways at me now and again, as if still uncertain of my identity. Only later did I understand that the attentions she used to lavish on me were inspired by the fact of my being 'different', no matter that the difference was mainly one of uniform.

We were met at the main door by Kleméntiy, the senior porter, who looked rather pleased at starting the new school year. You could never catch Kleméntiy actually smiling, but you could always tell by his face whether he was pleased or faintly disapproving. He told us, as he held open the door, that '*báryshnias* of the fifth class had their coat stands in the second hall, Kondratiy's.' So Margóolina and I, and other fifth formers found our way through a part of the school I had not been in before, and were greeted by Kondratiy, the junior porter, the same Kondratiy who had carried me to the *lazarýet*, such a long time ago, it seemed! He showed us where to leave our hats and told us how to get to our class-room. It was on the second floor, next to the one we had during the previous year.

Anna Avdyéevna was standing just inside the class-room door and we all curtseyed to her before coming in. She smiled with the whole of her face when my turn came and her eyes appeared to be swimming in oil. As she looked me up and down, I wondered in some confusion whether my dress was too short or my shoes not properly cleaned.

'You've grown inches!' she said.

We waited for her to tell us where and with whom we were to sit this year. I was given the equivalent of my old place in the second row on the window side, but my desk companion this time was to be Mania Bábina. I knew that she had finished last year with top marks in all subjects, obtaining what was called 'a round twelve', which meant that she had done better than I, who had eleven marks in two subjects, arithmetic and German. Mania was blonde and had grey eyes, unusual colouring for a Jewish girl, and she wore her straight hair in a single plait which reached below the small of her back. She was a quiet, hard-working, serious-looking girl who hardly ever smiled. I, on the other hand, was subject to fits of giggling during lessons, and Anna Avdyéevna might have decided to pair us, hoping to neutralize this propensity of mine which even she had sometimes found infectious.

I had not had many contacts with the day girls while I was a boarder, as we took our midday meal in our own dining-room while they ate their sandwiches in a passage outside the class-rooms. Now, perched on a low window-sill in this 'corridor' — which was in fact a kind of loggia, all windows on one side and class-rooms on the other — and chewing Aunt Katia's rather dull sandwiches, I felt really one of them. Several of them came up to me, to comment on my transformation from a boarder to a day pupil. And as often happens in such small communities, mixed, yet closely bound by common interests and pursuits, I learned a lot about its various members, without asking questions and hardly remembering who had told me what.

Liolia Tálina, plump and cheerful, with a plait of hair as thick as a rope — she was the singer of the class and her sudden bell-like laughter made every head turn towards her and alerted the *dames-de-classe* along the whole corridor. Her mother lived, with Liolia, apart from her husband — an unusual and intriguing fact. Katia Kign, tall, slightly stooping, with a delicate complexion, dark eyes and dark hair — she was rich in her own right because she was an orphan: both her parents died within a few weeks, the mother from consumption, the father from heart failure, trying to stop a runaway horse. Surreptitiously, I searched her face for a stamp of tragedy, but she looked quite ordinary, a serene, well-behaved, rather silent girl; a great contrast to her cousin Lena Kazanóvich, who always chattered. Lena made me think of a very large baby dressed in girl's clothes. Her movements were clumsy, her cheeks pink and round, her mouth always moist, and her face habitually wore a look of startled innocence, intensified when she was detected in a fib. Tonia Rosen, 'the baroness', was the untidiest and perhaps the best looking girl in the class. 'Her father is the Leader of the Nobility' . . . but Tonia clearly did not care about her status or her appearance.

The two Komaróvskayas — *not* sisters, but both Polish and Roman-Catholic: Liuba, plumpish, soft-voiced, dark-haired, with eyes like black olives; Masha, short, flaxen-haired, grey-eyed and determined. 'These two are always making up to the teachers and to Anna Avdyéevna,' was the comment. Olia Rodiónova, whom I knew before I went to boarding school . . . She looked sleepy most of the time. Fatima and

Stassia in their boarders' uniform were also there. I was glad to see Stassia again, but felt sad when she told me that Tania Pánova had left to go to an Institute in Petersburg. I could not imagine Tania happy in an Institute. A newcomer was Alma Fibikh, a German girl, who failed to pass into a higher class and whose face shone with health and cleanliness. 'Her father teaches German in the higher classes. It'll be awkward when he comes to teach us. He'll have to be specially strict with her or everyone would think he favours her . . . ' And besides Mania Bábina and Margóolina, my former desk-companion, there were three more Jewish girls in the class, whose first names only they themselves seemed to know. Epstein, the smallest girl in the class, very plain, with black fuzzy hair and small restless eyes which darted about like little black mice whenever she was called upon to say what she had learned. 'She learns everything by heart, word for word,' I was told. 'She's always on her own, never talks to anyone . . . has nothing to say . . . But she's very near the top of the class, especially in sums.' The other two, Ginsberg and Rashal, had a great deal to say to one another, so much that Anna Avdyéevna had warned them they would have to sit apart if they went on talking during lessons. The two were bosom friends. Rashal had a deep voice, like a man's, and a straight narrow face; Ginsberg was a good-looking, smiling girl who seemed older than most of us, more of a young girl than a child.

With these girls I was going to spend half the day during the best part of every year for the next five or six years! I did not mind this, I was quite looking forward to it.

But the evening of every day, except during school holidays, I was to spend with Zena. How long was that to go on for? I certainly could not envisage years and years of that!

One of a straggly group of girls, I walked at the end of the school day to the corner of the boulevard where Stan, the coachman, was to wait for me and Zena. She was already there, sitting in the buggy and looking like a storm cloud.

'Look at that sulky girl there!' one of my companions said to me. 'And the funny pink horse!' Then, seeing that I was about to join the object of her comment, she giggled and hurried off with a wave of her hand.

Deciding to be friendly, I asked Zena what the girls in her class were like.

'Horrid,' she muttered. 'Nearly all of them Jewish.'

I recollected my mother saying that all the Jewish girls who could not get into my school because of the 'five per cent quota', went to the private school of Madame Zalyéssky, which was Zena's school. But before I could say anything more, Zena turned, glowering, towards me.

'What was that girl laughing at? What did you tell her about me?'

'I didn't tell her anything.'

'She looked at me and laughed. Why did she?'

'You'd better ask her!' I retorted, my irritation getting the better of my best intentions.

'You're saying this on purpose! You know I can't ask her!' Zena's voice was now pitched on the note of angry tears.

'Nor can I. I've told you already that I don't know.'

A tense silence followed. I kept my eyes on the road before us as we drove out of town, following the bank of a small stream. There was a touch of late summer freshness in the air, and the grassy bank was still speckled with tiny flowers — the magenta of 'Virgin's tears', the pale yellow and blue of 'Ivan-da-Mária', the bright, glossy yellow of 'Chicken Dazzle'. But the pleasure I took in it was spoiled for me by Zena's pent-up, hostile sense of outrage and my own annoyance at her touchiness. So that was how it was going to be! This stupid girl would be always taking offence at every word I said, watching out for every glance or gesture she could take as an insult or a reason for complaint.

There was pea soup and a rather dull meat course for dinner. I ate very little of either, and was conscious of both my uncle and aunt watching me. 'You don't seem to be very hungry,' my uncle said at the end of the meal. I confirmed that I was not.

'That won't do,' he said. What was it in his voice, I wondered, which made it greasy without properly oiling it? It made me wish he would gargle or use a bottle brush to clear his throat.

'That won't do,' he repeated. 'You can't live without eating. Your mother wouldn't approve if she knew. I think I'll drop her a line and see what she says.'

'Perhaps cousin Lisa makes special dishes for her,' said Aunt Katia ironically, in her thin, mosquito voice.

I flushed — not with embarrassment but with anger. I noticed that Zena was enjoying the scene. As soon as the meal was over I escaped to my room and wrote to my mother, telling her how much I disliked the Martsinóvskys' food, and asking her to arrange with my aunt that I should be given a glass of milk and a slice of rye bread for my supper, instead of having to eat a regular evening meal. I added the description of my first day at school and of Zena's behaviour on our journey.

My anger having spent itself in the process of writing, I settled down to my homework. I had to do preparation in three subjects: arithmetic, geography and history, and as I pored over my books, I looked up now and again to rest my eyes on the green of the garden outside. Between one such glance and another, the green of the leaves and the red of the scattered clumps of dahlias faded, and the air grew dim with approaching dusk. I saw Zena walking slowly between the flower beds, her tousled head hanging down, her arms clasped behind her back. She was making her way towards the steps descending to the river. She seemed to be looking at her feet, but just as she was about to disappear over the edge of the slope, she turned her head slightly and I saw the glistening white of her eye. I was sure she had glanced at my window. She was curious to know what I was doing all on my own.

Suddenly restless, I got up and went through the front door into the vast court-yard, partly short grass, partly beaten earth. As I came down the steps of the porch, I looked back at the windows of the house, still unlit, and noticed at one of the windows a small white face peeping through. Aunt Katia. Were these two determined to spy on me?

At the far end of the yard there was a swing of a kind common in Russian villages. It consisted of a long stout plank and four lengths of rope. Two people could swing on it, standing at each end of the plank, but one person could get it moving while standing in the middle with one foot forward. That was what I liked doing, and I knew that I could push the swing as high as it would go, to the very limit of safety. If the plank rose higher than the beam to which the ropes were fixed, it could go right over it backwards and fall like a rearing horse over its rider.

I got on the swing and began to work it, gradually increasing its speed. With my back towards the house I was gazing westward, along the shallow valley of the stream almost invisible between its grassy banks and bushes of alder. From the dip at my uncle's gate, the ground rose gently, coming up against the sky and cutting off farther view at a distance of about a mile. Just there a single birch tree was poised on the bank of the stream, the whole of its graceful, dishevelled silhouette outlined against the sunset sky. I had noticed it on the way from the school: it had a kind of presence, it was isolated, like myself, it spoke to me as a friend. I told myself that I must visit it, make myself known . . . I greeted it silently across the fields, with every rising thrust of my swing in its direction.

Every upward thrust carried me into the golden region of the sky where I lost sight of the ground. I imagined I was about to take wing and fly out into that golden world where there was no night. The sun was always travelling that way, so there could be no night there. I could follow the sun right round the world. If one always lived in the sunlight, there could be no sorrow, no envy, no resentment – only joy and happiness . . .

'You've been a long time on *my* swing,' said a voice behind me.

I knew it was Zena, so I did not trouble to look round. I stopped working the swing and let it slow down to a standstill. I got off and only then, looking my cousin full in the face, gave back as good as I got: 'I suppose you're afraid I might *eat* your swing?'

Zena was not very ready, with her retorts. Her lips quivered, her eyes blinked, but only when I was already half-way across the yard did I hear her shout: 'I'll tell Mamma!'

I did not reply: I felt scornful of Zena and her futile threats. What did she think her mother could do to me? She could of course refuse to keep me, and my mother would have to find somewhere else for me to live. She would not like that – but then – she should have known!

Friends and Enemies

She should have known! But did she, in fact? I doubt it, for if she had known, she might have decided against letting me take such a close look at an unhappy marriage and a disunited family.

I soon noticed that my uncle and aunt never went out together and hardly ever spoke to one another. When my aunt had to mention her husband to someone else, she did not speak of him by name but as 'he'. 'He' lived and slept in his study which contained a bed, a large, yellow bureau with a roll-top and some guns and swords displayed on the walls. My aunt shared a large bedroom with Zena. The two spent most of their time in that room, and the sitting-room was used only when they had visitors, which was rarely.

I did not often see my aunt occupied, except in the garden tying up plants. Cooking, cleaning and even shopping were all done by Mavra, the *bonne-à-tout-faire*. Mavra had an appendage in the person of her illegitimate daughter, Hovra, a wispy, flaxen-haired child of about six years of age. Stan, a lad of twenty, looked after the horse and did some gardening. As for my uncle, I think he took his retirement as an excuse for complete inactivity. He would sometimes stand outside the wood-shed, watching Stan sawing up wood for the stoves, or walk across the flower garden and look over the edge of the slope at the river below or more likely at the boat, tied up by the landing stage. Most of the time however, he kept to his room and, to judge by the sounds of snoring which issued from it in the afternoons, he probably slept there quite a lot of the time.

I could only explain this strange situation to myself by assuming that my uncle and aunt had had a serious quarrel a long time ago and had never made it up. I even drew the conclusion that Zena's obvious unhappiness was linked with her parents' quarrel. What I found difficult to understand was her habit of drifting aimlessly about. She would not read, or colour pictures in a book, or row a boat. I often saw her in the evening wandering through the deserted garden, with the child Hovra following in her wake, or sitting on the swing, her feet on the ground, her head lolling, while the same child pushed the end of the plank, making it move gently to and fro. She looked bored and only half-alive.

It is perhaps not surprising that I was glad to escape from this sad household by going to school in the morning and loth to return to it after school. I do not think I was mistaken in believing that Aunt Katia disliked me and that Zena shared her mother's feelings. My aunt, I was sure, resented the fact that I would not eat her food and that I was doing so well in school, while her Zena was backward. Zena was hostile because of the clashes we had had and because she thought I looked down on her. As for my uncle, I believed him to be indifferent, so long as Zena did not complain of me. If she did, I was sure he would blame me for the quarrel.

All this made me feel as if I were living in enemy-occupied territory and I was at ease only when I withdrew to my room, though even there I was not sure I was safe from intrusion. I was rarely disturbed, however: Zena and her mother stayed at their end of the house, and the only person who knocked on my door at supper time was Mavra, bringing me my milk and bread, with Hovra clinging to her skirts and gazing at me in wonder with a pair of owlish, sleepy eyes. She never saw '*báryshnia* Zena' so assiduous at her books.

I found work the best way of escaping from depression, and my taste for it increased as time went on. Preparation for the next day lessons took me two or three hours every evening, and I was also writing my 'novel' about Henri and Margot at the court of King Henry of Navarre. I rationalized my fondness for writing by telling myself that children could write for children much better than grown-ups, because after all *they* knew at first hand what children liked to read. Reading for pleasure took the rest of my time, and I now quite enjoyed reading in French and German, with a dictionary.

All this might make me appear as a bookworm, but I was far from being only a reader and writer of words. The urge to use my body was almost as strong in me as the need to use my mind, and during the months of attending school I badly missed what I had done at home: walking, riding and climbing trees. Organized games did not exist in Russian schools when I was a child; even boys' schools had only gymnastics and the 'Sokol' drill, developed by the Czechs. In my school we had gymnastics without apparatus of any kind twice a week. We were also taught ballroom dancing, and often danced in the intervals between lessons. But that was not enough for me, and by Saturday afternoon — we had classes on Saturday morning — I was longing to be out in the open air, doing something physical.

On my first Sunday at the *dacha* I made an excursion up the valley of the little stream and had a good look at the solitary birch tree which until then I had only seen from a distance. At close range it proved to be a very comely tree, and as it had been my habit at home, I spoke to it and told it how much I liked it and that I would come again to visit it.

I should have liked to explore the birch groves on the opposite bank of the river which crossed my uncle's property, but there was no bridge and I did not want to ask my uncle for the use of his boat and oars, for fear of being refused. Even if I were allowed to use them, I was sure Zena would protest and claim them as her own, for, like her mother, she was morbidly possessive with regard to every bit of family property, and she watched me unremittingly for any sign of trespassing.

This state of tension between us was brought to a head by a trivial incident which, however, proved an important turning point in our relationship, and perhaps in the development of my own character.

In the far corner of the flower garden there was a pile of sand which may have been put there for Zena's play or for sanding the paths. I was still enough of a child to like playing with sand, and one Sunday morning I spent an hour making hills, caverns and winding paths in the side of this neglected pile. I left it to go in to lunch, after which I went to read in my room. I was sitting at my work table in front of the window and, as I raised my head from my book, I saw Zena in the flower garden, crouching in front of the sand pile, busy with a stick.

I leapt up from my chair and rushed through the garden door and across the flower beds with a speed that the Furies might have envied. Zena, with her back turned, did not hear me approach until I was standing right above her. She had dug up all my constructions and was aimlessly pushing the stick into the sand heap, making deep, round holes.

'Why did you do that?' I asked, enraged, but trying not to shout.

She started, then looked up at me, her sad baby face distorted in a grimace, half-smile, half-tears.

'You've no business to make things out of *my* sand,' she said.

I was so angered by what she had done that this silly reply left me speechless. Instead of telling her that she was 'a silly baby', I pushed her, and she sat back on the ground in a most undignified way. From that position she could not retaliate, and she knew it too, for she did something I never expected a girl of twelve to do in the circumstances. She broke into a howl of outraged impotence, while I stood looking down at her with scorn and disgust.

She was heard in the house. My aunt appeared in the window. My uncle came out of the garden door and walked across to us.

'What's the matter?' he asked in his 'unoiled' voice. 'Why are you crying, Zena?'

'She . . . p-pushed me . . . ' Zena wailed.

My uncle turned his blood-shot eyes at me.

'She smashed something I had built,' I said. 'I didn't push her very hard and she *isn't* hurt.'

'Come indoors, Zena,' said my uncle. 'It might be better if you two keep apart.'

He led her away, still weeping. Zena looked so miserable when she cried that for the first time I felt a pang of pity for her, and a touch of remorse. The image of her crumpled face and red eyes pursued me as I made my way up the valley to walk off the anger I was still feeling, as well as pity. Silly baby! She had looked so ridiculous when she sat there, bawling with rage . . . It was easy to make her look ridiculous because she was so backward. It was almost too easy . . . hardly worth while . . . And now my uncle and aunt would scowl at me for the rest of the week, and probably write to my mother and complain, and my mother would write me a reproachful letter — all this because of Zena's stupidity and touchiness.

I walked as far as my birch tree, stopped under it and put my arms round its smooth, while bole. It rustled faintly in the breeze; its leaves fell around me like a shower of small, golden coins. I imagined it standing there, stripped and alone, all through the autumn and winter months, and the snow so deep round it that I would not be able to get across to visit it, and I pitied it as I pitied myself.

The dusk was gathering when I returned to the *dacha*. My uncle came out of his room as I was passing his door.

'Look, Léda,' he said, 'I'm responsible for you to your parents. This is not the country round your estate where you know every peasant, boy and girl. I won't have you going out for long walks in the dark.'

I replied that it was not dark when I went out. He told me that I must be inside the gates *before* it got dark.

I hurried off to my room. So that's how it was going to be! They would keep me in now! They were determined to make my life with them as unpleasant as they possibly could. They were my enemies. And I would have to live in their house for years . . . perhaps until I finished school.

My glass of milk and two slices of rye bread were waiting for me on my work table. I grew calmer while I was eating, and soon afterwards got ready for bed. I closed my eyes, but Zena's face was still with me: I could not stop thinking about her. She was tiresome and silly . . . but need she be my enemy? I could hardly hope to get her parents to like me, but perhaps I could do something to make Zena like me better than she did? And in a sudden surge of determination I decided that I could, and would.

This was a clearly reasoned-out and conscious decision. I promised myself that I should not say in front of Zena anything that might wound her *amour propre*. I would talk to her as to a younger sister, rather as my sister talked to me. If need be, I would help her with her homework. I would show her the nice corners on the estate which I had discovered and kept secret. I would never again lose my temper with her. Having settled it all in my mind, I went to sleep much relieved.

I do not know whether it is uncommon to make a decision of that kind at the age of twelve. What surprises me even now, when I look back on it, is that I was able to adhere to it so firmly and consistently. I have made such decisions in later years but have never again succeeded in changing the character of a relationship so radically as I did that with Zena.

It was not easy for me. I had to curb my pride before I could take the first step towards a rapprochement, and then to control my natural spontaneity and watch my own behaviour almost as closely as I watched Zena's.

On our way to school the following morning I told her what lessons I was going to have and described the teachers and some of the girls. Zena listened, silent, unsmiling, incredulous, as if I were telling her some kind of fairytale. She did not volunteer anything herself about her own school. When I joined her again after school, she met me with a

glance from under her brow, half-mistrustful, half-hopeful – an expression I had often noticed in the eyes of a maltreated dog. I was very
compassionate towards animals; to see them suffer wrung my heart.
Zena's glance affected me in the same way. I smiled at her, and slowly,
irresolutely, she smiled back.

As we drove along the bank of the stream, I pointed out my birch
tree and told Zena I often came to visit it in the evenings. 'There are
no other trees near it: it must feel lonely sometimes,' I added.

I had not expected the effect my words would produce on Zena. Her
eyes filled with tears.

'Well,' I said hurriedly,' next time I go to visit it you'd better come
too. With both of us there, the tree will have quite a party!'

Zena suddenly laughed. Her face was a strange sight: eyes brimming
with tears, mouth distended with laughter, shoulders shaking, locks of
curly hair dancing on her forehead.

'Yes, quite a party!' she repeated. Then, raising her head and looking
straight at me, she said with a kind of passion: 'I knew you went to that
tree every evening! I saw you!'

So she *had* been spying on me! I was surprised to feel so little annoyed
at my suspicions being confirmed.

'I don't go the same way *every* evening,' I said. 'Sometimes I walk
along the river. I wish I could get over to the other side . . . '

'In the boat?' said Zena.

'Could we?'

'Pinky' meanwhile was climbing the track leading to the house and
Hovra was running to meet us, so that she could get a ride of a few
yards, perched on the step of our buggy. I knew I should feel sorry for
Hovra, and I was in a way, but like everybody else in the house I
regarded her mainly as a nuisance. She received many more slaps than
caresses from her own mother who complained that the child always got
in her way. Aunt Katia suspected her of pinching sugar from the sugar
basin, and Hovra was not allowed into the living-rooms unless accompanied by her mother. So Hovra tried to follow her mother everywhere.
When driven off by her, she would attach herself to Zena, who seemed
to be flattered by her devotion and treated her as if she were a little
slave, protectively, yet capriciously.

When we came into the dining-room my aunt took a sharp look at
Zena, and as they left the room together I heard her ask: 'You've been
crying? Has she been saying things to you again?' I did not hear Zena's
reply but saw her shake her head. My aunt returned and took her place

at the table. She still glanced at me with suspicion, but looked puzzled rather than annoyed and I felt incredulous and elated at having gained my first victory.

My confidence grew as I began to receive proofs of Zena's increasing trust and affection. At the same time I noticed that her parents' attitude towards myself became more, rather than less, suspicious and disapproving. Naïvely, I had assumed that they would like me better when I got on better with Zena, but I soon came to realize that it was not so at all. The quirks of human nature revealed themselves to me in all their alarming, chilling complexity. My aunt's acid comments on my appearance and conduct became more pointed and frequent. My uncle began to interfere in whatever Zena and I did together, under the pretext that Zena should play less and work more.

'It's all very well for you,' he would say, 'you're clever. But our Zena will get stuck in her class for another year if she doesn't work much harder!'

Did he, by making these remarks which hurt Zena's pride, hope to break up our friendship? This thought, incredible as it seemed, occurred to me but I noticed the way Zena looked at her father when he was speaking. Certainly, her anger with him was not projected on to me, and unpleasant as it was to be the object of this grown-up hostility, I found I could brace myself against it with Zena on my side.

Zena was not unintelligent but quite exceptionally uninformed and unread. I discovered that she did not know any of the stories which had been my staple diet from the age of five or six — Pushkin's folk-tale poems, Hans Andersen's fairytales, and later Lermontov, Gogol and Tolstoy. Her imagination was a virgin field for me to scatter seeds over, and I could not help myself scattering them in some profusion. At that time I was devouring historical novels by the dozen. They were mostly foreign history. Although I read some novels by Zagóskin and liked *Yuriy Miloslávsky* very much, the descriptions of life in pre-Petrine Russia held no romantic appeal for me. Aesthetically, I was repelled by the pictures of the bearded boyars in their long, heavy coats, and by the low-ceilinged houses with tiny windows in which they immured their women. I imagined them as always indulging in gluttonous eating and drinking, or occupied in poisoning or beheading one another. Russian history was acceptable to me only up to the Mongolian invasion; after that it was something to be regretted, almost to be ashamed of. Foreign ways of dressing and behaving as I saw them in pictures and knew them by description, had the appeal of 'something different' much more elegant and sophisticated, and I was fascinated by foreign history, especially that of France and of England. I became an addict of Victor Hugo, Alexandre Dumas and Lord Lytton.

In my games with Zena I improvised incidents and conversations in which she had to participate, but she seemed unable to improvise her part and I had to tell her what to say. Often it was very heavy going, irritatingly so, and I had to exercise much self-control not to let fly at Zena on such occasions.

The time for such games was usually Saturday evening — on weekdays I had my homework to do, and Zena was kept at her books by her jealously watchful parents. But on Saturdays she begged to be allowed to sleep in my room, so that we could act our dramas without being disturbed or disturbing anybody. Her mother reluctantly agreed to that.

I remember one evening when we were enacting a scene from *Ben Hur*. We were already in bed — Zena propped up on the pillows and I standing up, draped in a sheet and declaiming some sort of speech in which I addressed Zena as 'my gracious lady'. Suddenly the door was held ajar and my aunt's head poked through. Startled, I shrieked and fell on my knees. Zena accused her mother of frightening me, of creeping in on us, of spying . . . She told her that she had interrupted me in the middle of an important speech and spoiled our scene. Aunt Katia defended herself: she only came to remind us not to stay up too late. Thus I became the cause of a quarrel between mother and daughter which did not improve my standing with Aunt Katia.

From *Ben Hur* to King Henry of Navarre and Marguerite de Valois. Of course, I had to act the king, or rather Prince Henry when he was still the heir to the throne of Navarre — Zena was too passive a person to play the part of a man.

I told Zena that Prince Henry had been brought up in relative poverty in his native Navarre, and that Margot was a capricious and proud beauty who at first treated him disdainfully. Zena could *be* capricious, almost tyrannous with Hovra, and proud enough in her own way, that is, quick at taking offence; but she could not, for the life of her, *act* a proud beauty with me; could not provide me with a foil I needed in this fantasy of rejection and eventual triumph which became my dominant theme for the next two or three years.

'You must flash your eyes at me when you're saying this, Zena.' Zena just gazed at me, her round eyes anything but disdainful. 'You must stamp your foot!' A feeble effort at stamping without a trace of anger. 'You must rush out of the room!' Zena made a brave attempt but fumbled with the door handle. And so it went on. Frustrated in action, I turned again to writing. My so-called diary had begun with recording real happenings, but soon I felt this to be repetitive, too ordinary and dull. I began to write a fictional diary, which became the story of the courtship of Margot de Valois by Prince Henry of Navarre.

A whole series of incidents would be written during the week and ready for acting out on Saturday — and yet again I would be frustrated by Zena's passive compliance, by her inability to sound convincing when I put words into her mouth. But she must have found some pleasure in all this, for throughout the months during which this game continued, she never once refused to play.

'Reality' however kept breaking in and had to be dealt with to the best of one's ability.

One afternoon, early in the autumn term, as I came out of school in company of other girls, a familiar grey uniform on the other side of the street caught my eye. A small group of *Ghymnasia* boys were standing there, watching the entrance to our school, and as one of them moved, I recognized the slouching gait and long swinging arms of Shoora Martýnov. He took off his cap to me, then crossed the street to my side. My companions, with half-concealed but unmistakable signs of amusement, hurried forward, leaving me to shake hands with him. I knew I was blushing and felt angry with myself and with him for causing me this embarrassment. He walked with me all the way to the crossroads where Stan was waiting with the buggy and Zena already sitting in it. I took my leave from Shoora as quickly as I could, and we drove off, while he stood on the kerb, smiling, cap in hand.

This happened before the improvement in my relationship with Zena, and I was expecting her to make some disparaging comment. She merely asked: 'Who was that ugly boy?'

I replied that he was someone my brother knew.

'He's your admirer, isn't he?'

'What has it to do with you?'

'Does he meet you outside the school every day?'

'He met me today, that's all. Anyway, it's not your business.'

'What an admirer to have!'

I was very annoyed because Zena's remark echoed my own feelings and, I suspected, also the views of my schoolmates. When next day Shoora was seen again outside our school, they tittered and nudged me:

'There's your admirer, waiting for you!' He certainly looked ungainly and odd with his close-cropped, acorn-shaped head, his small eyes and his peculiar walk. I could not understand how he had managed to get to his observation post so soon after the end of his lessons, unless he ran all the way. The boys' *Ghymnasia* was at least ten minutes' walk from ours, and our lessons finished at the same time. I did not want him to escort me every day and to appear to accept him as my 'admirer'. What was I to do?

One thing I could not do was to tell him bluntly to stop waiting for me outside the school. However annoyed and embarrassed I felt, I could not bring myself to do or say what I knew would hurt him. I was quite capable of saying hurtful things in the heat of the moment, as I did with Zena and my brother, but I could not do so with deliberate intent. This was going to prove a source of painful misunderstandings in my later relationships with men. Men, I discovered, could rarely believe that when a woman did not reject them outright, she might be merely being compassionate. They would rather believe that she was reluctant to admit that she reciprocated their passion.

Few admirers could have had less encouragement than Shoora received from me. When he joined me outside the school, I hardly spoke to him and I walked so fast that even he had to lengthen his stride to keep pace with me. Yet, once I had let him carry my books, I could not withdraw this privilege without giving a reason, and so he took them from me as if by right, and I appeared, in my schoolmates' eyes, to encourage his attentions. They, on their side, all scuttled as he approached, as if to show me they did not want to be *de trop*, whereas what I wanted least of all was to be conspicuous, walking alone with Shoora.

Would I have reacted differently if my 'admirer' were not Shoora, but some elegant and handsome boy? Most probably I would have been flattered and might have enjoyed it, for I was as much aware of beauty in human beings as I was of beauty in Nature — even if my ideal of male beauty at the time was a young man with long locks of hair and the feathered hat of a sixteenth century cavalier. I found it almost painful to look straight at Shoora.

Our brief encounters were apparently not enough for him. One Sunday afternoon I had the shock of seeing him arrive in the company of my brother at my uncle's *dacha*. Knowing how indifferently the two got on together, I even felt a faint trace of admiration at the thought of the devices Shoora must have used to induce my brother to bring him along. My brother rarely came to see me: he was a studious boy and had heavy assignments to prepare every evening. Besides, he was always ready for food, and at my uncle's house he could not count on a really good meal. Incredible as it was to us, the Martsinóvsky family were stingy with their food: there was never an abundance of cold meats, cheese, jams and pastries on the tea table, such as we had at home. 'She watched every spoonful of jam I took,' my brother said about Aunt Katia.

Shoora appeared quite unaware of the lack of welcome at my uncle's house. He helped himself unconcernedly to one piece of bread-and-butter after another and talked away as he ate and drank his tea, while Zena and her mother listened and watched in unsmiling silence, and my uncle grunted now and again and muttered: 'Nothing to boast about!'

He was referring to Shoora's stories about his school: the ingenious ways in which the boys baited the German master, the stupid answers some of the boys gave to the masters' questions, the tricks they played on one another, and such like. Shoora seemed not to notice that the Martsinóvsky family were not amused by these stories and that Aunt Katia was obviously disapproving. On my part, I felt responsible for his being there and thus included in the family's disapprobation. I knew I did not deserve it, and felt annoyed with everyone in the room, including my brother who — weak character that he was! — had allowed Shoora to come with him.

Next moment I felt grateful to him when, soon after tea, he said they ought to be starting for home. Shoora protested that 'there was no hurry', but my brother insisted that he 'still had a lot of geometry to do'. They bickered for a while but as none of us said a word to suggest they were welcome to stay longer, they took their leave in the end.

'That Shoora of yours has got an appetite!' my aunt said as she helped Mavra to clear the table.

'He's got a queer shaped head,' said my uncle. 'An odd boy, altogether.'

These comments were milder than I was expecting, but I made the excuse of unfinished homework to spare myself hearing more. In the quiet of my room I opened the fat exercise book in which I was writing my novel. I began:

'Henri saw from his window that Margot was picking flowers by the big fountain which thrust its silvery spears into the air under the weeping willows of the park. At once he decided to join her . . .'

Outside, in the thickening dusk the flower garden looked battered, strewn like a battlefield with fallen leaves, and the half-denuded trees were bending over them with agitated autumnal gestures. I wished passionately, almost with tears, that I were Henri or Margot, living in the sixteenth century and picking flowers by a fountain in the park of a French château on a hot summer day. I did not mind whether I was one or the other, boy or girl, so long as I was not myself, not in this house, with these dour, unfriendly people. I wished Shoora were not a very plain schoolboy in the fifth form but a dashing young cavalier from a book by Dumas. I wished my brother were an ally of mine instead of an unhelpful occasional visitor . . .

I embarked on a dialogue between Henri and Margot and wrote on until I was tired and wanted to go to bed. But although my discontent was stilled by the effort of using it creatively, the scenes I described did not quite compensate me for the drabness of my real surroundings, did not make me forget who I was and where I lived. Pangs of regret that my fantasies were not reality made me turn in bed many a time before I went to sleep that night.

Next day and all through the week Shoora met me outside the school, and on the following Sunday he arrived at my uncle's *dacha* on his own. My first impulse on seeing him — from my perch on the swing — striding up the drive, was to flee and hide myself, but I got no farther than half-way across the yard when I realized what little chance of escape I had. It was easy to find anyone in my uncle's grounds, denuded by the late October winds.

I went into the house and told Zena as calmly as I could: 'Shoora Martýnov's come.' 'What, again?' she exclaimed. 'Yes, again. I didn't ask him to come.' 'I know,' she said, sympathetically.

My aunt, however, was not in the least sympathetic; and my face must have shown what I was feeling, yet again Shoora appeared unconscious of the tension he was causing and stayed, talking, until it began to grow dark.

He came again the following Sunday rather early, before I had time to finish my homework. As the rest of the household avoided him, I was left alone to entertain him, and I found his undiluted company a strain. I also felt cheated of all the things I could have been doing if he were not there: reading, writing, playing with Zena . . . After he had gone, Aunt Katia pattered into the drawing-room.

'Is he going to come every Sunday?' she asked.

I told her I did not know and that I wished he would not.

'Why don't you tell him that you can't spare the time . . . that you have your homework to do?'

'I can't . . . he might not believe me . . . ' And I added in desperation: 'I wish *you* would tell him!'

Aunt Katia puckered her small forehead.

'Very well, I will. Next time he comes,' she said. She seemed rather flattered by my appeal for help.

I awaited next Sunday with some trepidation. It was a rainy day and immediately after lunch I went to my room and tried to concentrate on my geography lesson. Mavra putting her head through the door made me jump. '*Paních* Shoora's here,' she said, and he walked in.

'I've come a bit earlier,' he said, 'so that I can start back before it gets dark.'

My guilty conscience made me stammer as I invited him to sit down. We hardly had time to exchange a few words when my aunt burst into the room like a ball flung by an angry hand.

'Monsieur Martýnov,' she addressed him in a high-pitched voice, her pale-blue eyes darting glints of steel, 'your coming here every Sunday interferes with Léda's school work and makes her sit up late into the night after you've gone. I am obliged therefore to ask you to stop your visits to my house from now on.'

She rattled off her piece very fast and rolled out of the room as quickly as she had come, leaving us standing face to face, but with our eyes averted from one another. My face was burning, and I felt so guilty and ashamed of my double-dealing that I could not bring myself to speak or to look at Shoora for what seemed an interminable time. At last he made a sound, clearing his throat, and a quick glance showed me – for the first time since I had known him – that he was thoroughly embarrassed and at a loss what to say or do. His mouth was skewed in a forced smile and his voice was hollow when he spoke.

'Well, that's that. I've been shown the door . . . a pity! The little witch meant it. Your aunt is dreadful, isn't she? I'll have to say au revoir. . . '

He wrung my hand so hard that I bit my lip. 'A pity!' he repeated, and went out with a last glance at me, the glance of hopeful devotion which made me feel sorry for him and annoyed at the same time.

Remorse at having caused him pain wore off fairly soon: it need not have happened if he had been more observant and tactful. But the shame at my hypocritical silence when he blamed my aunt for prohibiting our meetings – while she did this on my request – remained with me for a long time. Blood would rush to my face whenever I thought of it.

Shoora continued meeting me outside the school, but sometimes I contrived to evade him by getting out a little earlier than usual, or by inducing Stan to meet me at the school entrance and to pick up Zena at the corner where he was supposed to wait for us both. It made life much easier to have Zena as an ally.

Compensations

That winter frosts came before the snow and suddenly the river below
the steep bank at the end of the garden ceased to flow. It had been dark
and sluggish for days, choked with fallen leaves and so visibly cold that
merely looking at it made you shudder. The boat had been hauled out
and carried up the steps and into a shed in the yard by Stan, with
Mavra's help.

'There's ice in it,' said Mavra, as she shook water off her large, red
hands. 'The water's as thick as beer.'

Zena and I had watched it hopefully for days. Then one Sunday
morning we saw that the water was no longer moving.

'It's frozen!' Zena shouted, rushing down the steps to take a closer
look.

I followed her. From the landing stage we each stretched a foot to
test the motionless brown surface. It was hard! But would it take our
weight?

'We can try,' I said.

We raced back to the house for our skates. But Aunt Katia proved
unexpectedly adamant in refusing to let us use them until the frost had
held out for at least three days. Zena was in tears. Her mother's eyes
turned on me with an unmistakable reproof. I knew that, as usual,
she held me responsible for Zena's increasing zest for more adventurous
play.

I went out again and talked to Stan who was in the yard, sawing wood
for the stoves. He told me that he had crossed the river on the ice

this morning and that it was quite thick. I kept my knowledge to myself until lunch time when my uncle noticed that Zena's eyes were red and asked her what was the matter.

'Mamma won't let us skate!' Zena burst out passionately.

'Why not?' My uncle did not look at his wife when he asked this, and she did not reply.

'She says we must wait three days for the frost to hold out,' said Zena with tears in her voice.

'Why *three* days?' my uncle asked again. This time no one answered him. Aunt Katia looked ruffled like a small angry hen, while tears began to trickle down Zena's cheeks. I proffered my piece of information about Stan crossing the river this morning, and was rewarded by an immediate hopeful look on Zena's face, but stabbed by a wrathful glance from Aunt Katia. My uncle decided we should be allowed to skate but not to go beyond the limits of the estate, and that Stan should be on the look-out in case anything happened.

For the whole of the following week while the frost held out and the snow continued to hold off, skating possessed us. As soon as we got home after school, out came our skates and down we raced to the river, despite Aunt Katia's protests that we should have our meal first. We simply could not afford to waste this last half-hour of winter daylight.

I was even more of a beginner on skates than Zena, and at first we staggered along, clinging precariously to one another. Then I discovered that if I ran as fast as if I had *no* skates on, I could keep my balance, and, at the end of the run, coast a long way without losing my grip on the ice. Stopping was the hardest thing of all, and often the easiest way was to fall. I fell so frequently that I soon had two large permanent bruises on my knees.

It grew dark more quickly by the landing stage where the river was overshadowed by a high bank and the trees. Farther down the stream the ground flattened out into open meadows, and there it remained light considerably longer. We preferred to skate on that part of the river although it was outside my uncle's property. The child Hovra was usually sent out to summon us home. She would stand on the landing stage under the dark trees and call out in her shrill little voice, telling us to 'come quick' because she was cold and afraid. But, heartlessly keen on our pleasure, we pretended not to hear her. In the end Stan would be sent along, or my uncle himself would come to the edge of the bank and in his hoarse voice demand how many times we had to be

called before we came? Then we knew we had to come, even though I
told myself that 'Uncle could do nothing to me', and Zena asserted that
she 'wasn't afraid' of her father. We clambered up the steps with our
skates still on, and came into the dreary dining-room – our stockings
damp to the knee, our hands numb, but our bodies and hearts glowing
with exertion and the joy of it. For the first time since I had come to
live with this family I saw Zena looking happy.

On Sunday we skated all day, coming in only for meals. We ventured
some way along the river, discovering regions hitherto unknown and
inaccessible because they lay at the back of other people's property.
On our side of the river there were orchards and kitchen gardens, but
on the opposite bank the countryside seemed uninhabited, with birch
woods climbing up the low hillside. The trees had lost all their foliage
and the pale-blue sky shone gently through the delicate tangle of their
boughs. The ground below was a patchwork of gold, brown, faded
green and the silver of frost. The air was sharp and sonorous: it carried
the swish of our skates and the sound of our laughter over the top of
the trees – or so it seemed to us. The pain of early rising for school, the
drudgery of sums, the grumbles of Aunt Katia were forgotten – the snow
was going to hold off for ever!

This bliss lasted a week. It was a dark morning when we were roused
from our sleep and saw the garden, the yard and the surrounding fields
obliterated under a white pall which had fallen on them during the
night. The branches of the birch trees drooped under its weight, and
it started falling again as we drove to school. It was our first sleigh
ride of the year and Pinky wore a collar of little bells, but this distracted
us only briefly from the distressing thought of 'no skating from
now on!'

The snow continued to fall, off and on, throughout the week. The
overcast sky made the daylight short and it was dark by the time we got
back from school. We waited impatiently for Sunday. If the snow were
light and dry, Zena could perhaps persuade her father to let Stan sweep
a track for us on the river ice. But it was damp and sticky, only fit for
making snowmen with. Zena's toboggan would not run on it down the
gentle slope from the house to the gate.

During lunch my uncle teased Zena about her miserable looks.
'Perhaps now you'll find time to do some homework!' he said. She
burst into tears. Aunt Katia looked daggers at her husband.

'Cry-baby . . . ' he muttered and stalked out of the room.

When we returned from school on Monday we noticed that something

had been happening in a small meadow at the side of the entrance gate.
The blanket of snow which covered it had turned grey and looked hard
and shrunken. Stan had talked in riddles as he drove us home: there was
going to be a surprise for us, he said, not tonight, but perhaps tomorrow
or the day after — that is, if God sent us some hard frost during the
night . . .

A day or two later the layer of snow on the meadow, watered several
times over, was transformed into ice. It was not so hard or smooth as
the ice on the river, but it could be swept easily and it provided us with
a quarter of an acre of skating space for the rest of the winter. I could
hardly walk up the staircase at school for the pain in the calves of my legs.

All schools like to show off their pupils and Russian schools were no
exception. Preparations for a 'spectacle' to take place just before the
Christmas holidays had been going on for some weeks. Girls were chosen
from the higher classes to sing, recite poetry, play the piano and act a
scene from a play. At the end of the show there was to be a *tableau
vivant* in which some of the younger girls, dressed as flowers, angels,
or butterflies, were to appear.

When Anna Avdyéevna told me I was to be one of these, I was thrown
into a state of apprehension mixed with a feeling of being flattered by
her choice. The apprehension was much stronger than the pleasure, and
the more I thought of the prospect the more I dreaded it.

I have never quite understood why it is that some children — or adults
for that matter — are paralysed with fear at the thought of facing an
audience, however small, even if they have to do a minimum of talking
or acting. What are the threats that haunt them on a subconscious level?
A primitive memory of the power of the evil eye? A suspicion of a sneer
behind the benevolent smiles of the spectators? A striving after impossible perfection and the fear of falling below the high standards one sets
oneself? Whatever it is, it has had me in its grip for as long as I can
remember, and it took me many years to learn to control it.

On this particular occasion I hoped to make my aunt's lack of co-
operation a pretext for not accepting the honour of being chosen. But,
to my surprise and dismay, Aunt Katia declared herself quite willing to
make my dress of goffred paper, stipulating only that I should be dressed
as a bluebell, not as a forget-me-not, as Anna Avdyéevna wanted. It
was easier to make, she said, and it would not matter from a distance
so long as the colour was blue. Anna Avdyéevna agreed, and my fate
was sealed!

Not so long before, Zena would have been jealous of the attention her mother was giving to my affairs and envious of my being chosen to appear in a show. But now she was pleased on my account, wanting to help in the making of my dress and eager to see me on the stage. This made me feel that, having won her to my side by conquering my hostility towards her, I should be able to win another victory over myself and make myself look forward to my ordeal. I might have succeeded better if this occasion for enjoyment had not become over-night the cause of a new discord, as often happens in unhappy families.

Zena wanted her mother to come with us to the school show. Aunt Katia declared that she had nothing to wear for such an occasion and refused to come. Uncle Vladímir grumbled about sending Stan and the horse to town twice on a winter night: he could not possibly be kept waiting for two or three hours to bring us back. Zena was quickly reduced to tears and I felt I was being blamed for bringing it all about. In the end my uncle decided *he* had to come with us, and on the night of the show we drove to town – the three of us squeezed into a sleigh meant for two – feeling not elated but miserable, and burdened with a large cardboard box containing my dress on our laps.

Our spirits rose a little when we saw the brightly lit windows of my school and were met outside by the porter Kondratiy who carried in my cardboard box and held the door open for us.

In the entrance hall Kleméntiy greeted us and told us that 'the young ladies who take part in the show' were 'requested to report at the ladies' common room', while the visitors had to 'proceed to the second floor hall'. Zena gave me an encouraging smile as we parted on the first floor landing.

In the women teachers' common room, some of the older girls were helping the young ones to dress. There was already quite a cluster of 'flowers' and a few 'angels' ready to take their place on the stage when the time came. Mílochka was there, demanding attention, complaining that her wings would not stay upright. One of the 'seniors' quickly slipped my paper dress over my head and used some hairpins to fix my crown of artificial bluebells, specially ordered in a shop recommen-ded by the school. Remembering the many occasions on which reality proved very different from what I had imagined, and anticipating disappointment, I allowed myself only a brief glance into a looking-glass. To my surprise and pleasure I hardly recognized myself – so much had my appearance been changed by my fluffed-up hair which Aunt Katia had put into paper curlers the night before.

We were told that we could listen to the recitations and piano numbers from the back of the stage so long as we did not show ourselves —but the admiration I felt at the courage of the performers did not have the effect of increasing my own, any more than the contemplation of other people's misfortunes makes our own easier to bear. Inexorably, the testing moment came. The curtains closed on the last piano player and we were hustled on to the stage and arranged in tiers. The angels had to stand on forms and the flowers were clustered in front and at the sides. We were told to stand absolutely still and try not to move even our eyes while the *tableau* was being displayed. I thought I felt my paper dress rustle with the thumping of my heart.

Slowly the curtains parted. I saw row upon row of faces, smiling faces, whispering lips . . . Were they laughing at us? . . . Talking about us? . . . The Headmistress and the Director were in the front row side by side. She was beaming and he, too, looked very pleased. Even Vera Petrovna, the stern French mistress, was smiling, while Anna Avdyéevna wore one of her coy expressions, her chin down, her eyes searching and coming to rest on me. In one of the middle rows I could see Zena craning her neck, and my uncle beside her —short, greying hair, coppery complexion, a fleshy nose. For the first time it struck me that they looked alike.

The *tableau* lasted two minutes: it felt like an eternity to me. As soon as the curtain was drawn, fond parents and friends burst on to the stage from the sides, praising and petting their offspring. I suddenly felt sad, deflated: there was no one there to make a fuss of me. Zena was too shy to come behind the scenes.

One of the older girls asked me whether I wanted to change, adding that we could keep our fancy dresses on if we wanted to.

'I should keep yours on: you look very nice in it,' said a voice I knew well behind me. I flushed with gratification as I turned to look at Anna Avdyéevna, who added: 'There's an empty seat beside me. You can, if you like, watch the end of the performance from there . . . '

Undiplomatic, and thinking only of Zena's disappointment if I failed to join her, I murmured that I had a cousin and an uncle in the audience.

'Oh . . . ' said Anna Avdyéevna, her chin going up, her eyes becoming veiled. 'You'd rather be with them . . . of course.' And with a swish of her skirts she left me standing there, feeling more forlorn than ever.

The drive back was even more unpleasant than the drive out. There was a head wind and it was snowing: the wind forced wet snow into every gap and chink in our bonnets and overcoats, melting inside them and finding its way to our bare wrists and necks. I was thinking of Anna Avdyéevna, of her displeasure and my embarrassment, wondering how I could have behaved differently without offending her or hurting Zena. Pinky went at a snail's pace and we got home very late. My aunt was sitting up for us, her face colourless like an unleavened bun.

'Well, what was it like?' She addressed herself to Zena and me, ignoring her husband as usual.

'We-ell . . . ' said Zena, dissatisfied. 'We saw Léda only for two minutes!'

'How long did you expect a *tableau vivant* to last then? Half-an-hour?' her father scoffed.

Zena flushed and went out of the room with her eyes full of tears. Aunt Katia followed her. My uncle grunted and, with a shrug, withdrew into his own room. Left on my own, I picked up the glass of milk and a slice of rye bread left for me on the table, took it to my room, and, as I ate it, pondered on this depressing ending to an exciting day. It could have been so different if my uncle and aunt had been different people. Zena, I knew, was changing, but her parents remained stubbornly the same. Could grown-up people ever change?

I felt sorry for Zena, and my pleasure at the approach of Christmas was somewhat dimmed by picturing her sad and alone on her skates, without me to keep her company.

This second Christmas at home from school was made memorable by two events: I was able to hold my own on the skating rink, and I met my sister's devoted man friend for the first time. My sister, my brother and I went to the skating rink together. I remembered it as a magical place where I was taken as a young child and given rides in a sliding chair by my reluctant elder brother. The clockmaker's shop where the tickets were sold was a huge glass box up a flight of steps, and it was full of clocks which went on swinging their pendulums and ticking away at different speeds and paces, just as they did before. There was the same amiable little man with a round face and a pair of round spectacles behind the counter, and, as before, you could not hear what he said to you for the noise made by the clocks. The rink, enclosed by high banks, had the same greenish-blue ice, only it looked somewhat smaller and the trees around it taller than they had been. Everything was much the same as before except myself — because now I could skate!

My sister and I skated together, our hands linked, our arms criss-crossed. My brother skated separately: he had always been self-conscious about family groups. There were not many people at the rink: we had plenty of room to ourselves.

Vova glided up to us as we were turning round at the far end.

'See who's come,' he told my sister. 'Kolia Avílov. He's just put on his skates.'

I suddenly felt my sister holding back, making my progress more difficult, and I glanced at her in surprise. She looked flurried. Was it because of the young man whose arrival my brother had announced? He now skated up to us, checking his speed smartly as he took off his cap.

'Maroossia! How nice to see you! May I introduce myself to your sister? Your brother and I have already met.'

Kolia was a tall, plumpish young man with very fair hair, rather pasty complexion and kindly, tired-looking eyes behind thick spectacles. He was wearing a short black tunic with green piping and small epaulettes, the uniform of a student of the Institute of Rail and Road Engineering, one of the most selective schools for Higher Education. I knew that young men had to pass stiff examinations and be extremely good at mathematics before they could be accepted as students at that Institute. When they qualified they earned some of the highest salaries in the professions.

Kolia spoke to my sister softly, with a smile, saying something about skating in Petersburg. She shook her head, as if rejecting whatever it was he was offering. She accepted his arm however for a turn round the rink, and I, left on my own, ran forward and began practising 'eights' in the middle of the rink. Skating, I felt, was the nearest approximation to flying . . .

Kolia accompanied us to the house, and I wondered whether my sister would ask him in. She seemed to hesitate. Just then our sleigh drove up bringing my mother with her shopping. Maroossia had to introduce our companion. My mother invited him in to tea. He accepted — and stayed to supper. This kind of thing happened quite often at our house and other similar houses in Russia: people who 'dropped in' were asked to stay to a meal in the middle of the day and the invitation was frequently extended to tea and supper. There seemed always to be food to spare, even in quite modest households.

That night I asked my sister whether she liked Kolia. She replied:

'His eyes are always red like a rabbit's . . .' and left me puzzled, wondering what it was she really felt for him.

During that Christmas holiday Kolia Avílov 'dropped in' quite often at our house. So did Shoora Martýnov. It was left to my sister and myself to entertain them. As it happened, Shoora frequently entertained us all by reading extracts from his favourite poems. One of these was Alexéy Tolstoy's satire on Russian history. Alexéy Tolstoy was a contemporary of Tsar Alexander II, and had been his childhood companion in play and study. This, however, did not prevent him from growing into a free-thinker and an iconoclast. He was a 'Westerner': much that had happened in Russian history angered and disgusted him. He had no patience with the Slavophils who toned down and romanticized the barbarities of Russian life before Peter the Great. The poem Shoora liked reciting dealt in a burlesque vein with various events which in text books on Russian history were represented as highly creditable and even glorious; it emphasized their brutality, stupidity or falseness; and Shoora's reading made every point tell, though he often spoiled the effect by gloating too obviously over the hypocrisy of the official version.

These readings usually took place in my father's absence from the house. Shoora was not inhibited by the presence of my mother, though she did not really approve of the poem or of his manner of reading it: she had her own views on Russian history which resembled those of the Slavophils. I heard her say more than once that Peter the Great's reforms were 'criminal' and that he did much harm to Russia by forcing her off her natural course of development. My own sympathies were on the side of the 'Westerners', but I, too, disliked the violent, despotic ways of Peter the Great. As for Alexéy Tolstoy's poem, I sensed in it a cynicism which made me uncomfortable, and Shoora's sneering manner aroused resistance in me, making me reluctant to smile and encourage him. This spurred him on to greater efforts until my brother would put his hands over his ears and tell him to 'stop shouting like a peacock'.

I preferred quieter evenings when Shoora was not there. Kolia Avílov would ask my sister to 'play something on the piano', and when she agreed, they would go to the ballroom, half-lit by the lamp in the adjoining room, and Maroossia would play some simple 'romance' while Kolia sat close by, watching her. I would creep in and sit in the rocking chair by the window — they did not mind that — and when the music stopped, I could hear Kolia's voice talking on, softly, like a burbling brook, with a brief, infrequent answer from my sister.

During that holiday I discovered that Kolia could draw rather well, and I asked him to do some illustrations for my novel about Henri and Margot. Ready to oblige, he agreed, and I watched him, excitedly, trying to make my fantasies concrete. He succeeded better than I had — I could only draw faces in profile — but once again the drawing, the realization of something imagined, proved to be quite different from what I wanted to see. All the same it made me like Kolia more for having tried, and it looked most impressively professional.

My friendship with Zena made my return into the bosom of the Martsinóvsky family more tolerable. Her evident pleasure and eagerness on seeing me helped me over the first few dreary evenings of settling down.

Anna Avdyéevna, too, seemed pleased at seeing me back, but she had a special smile as she looked me up and down.

'You've grown again,' she said. 'Isn't this dress getting a little too short?'

I was conscious of her looking at my legs and wondered what was the matter with them. I knew they had changed shape gradually since I had started skating: my calves were getting bigger. Otherwise I was only vaguely conscious of the changes in my developing body. I liked using my body in the ways I enjoyed — for climbing trees, dancing and riding — and I was proud of being able to do these things well, but I felt no interest in it apart from its athletic achievements. Somewhere behind this there was an attitude unconsciously and imperceptibly acquired that using my femininity as a means of attracting attention was undignified, almost contemptible. If I was to be liked, I wanted to be liked for being myself — a whole person, and not merely a girl of a certain shape with this or that colour of eyes or hair. This wish was combined with my holding in mind a classical ideal of beauty against which I measured my own appearance and found it wanting in almost every detail. I examined my face in the looking-glass and felt I would like to change its lower half, leaving the upper half more or less as it was. I was always disappointed in my own photographs. My mother often said: 'It isn't like you at all,' and once Shoora, who happened to be present, smiled a proprietary smile and remarked: 'Her expression changes so quickly: no photograph can catch it on the wing. Anything static is false as far as she's concerned.' I felt flattered despite myself: it meant I did not always look as awful as I did in those photographs.

In any case our school regulations did not encourage personal vanity, and Anna Avdyéevna was punctilious in applying them and adding some of her own. She insisted on all of us doing our hair more or less the same way and allowed no embellishments in the form of combs or ribbons. Our brown serge dresses with high collars had no trimmings except a narrow white edging round the neck which had to be fresh every other day, and our black alpaca pinafores had no flounces on the shoulders or on the bottom edge. Anna Avdyéevna tolerated no exceptions or deviations on that score.

Critical and dissatisfied with my physical appearance, I was obtaining some compensation from my growing reputation as 'a writer', 'a poet' and 'an explainer' of lessons. This was a function into which I drifted gradually, rather puzzled by discovering that some of my schoolmates were able to memorize the contents of a lesson better by listening to me 'explaining' it, than by reading it to themselves at home.

Often a few minutes before a lesson was due to start someone would appeal to our *dame-de-classe*: 'Anna Avdyéevna, may I ask Rayévskaia to explain the lesson? And when, receiving a nod from her, I would begin re-telling, to the one who had asked, what I had myself prepared at home, a little group would assemble round my desk, listening hard, trying to retain at least the gist of it, so that they would not be completely at a loss if 'called out' by the teacher.

Often I was also asked by my classmates how to begin — or finish — an essay. This flattered me and amused Anna Avdyéevna, who nearly always permitted it.

In January we had two days when frost reached twenty-five degrees and we were told there would be no school while it lasted. Zena and I skated in bright sunshine, the sharp air cutting our breath, our heads swathed in *bashlýks*, our mittened hands tucked into fur muffs. This year I went home for the Shrovetide holiday and when I came back to my uncle's house at the end of February, the fields and birch groves around it still looked wintry, but something undefinable was already in the air, telling us that spring was not far off. Day by day the signs grew more visible: the snow in the fields changed from white to faint grey; the brittle sound of frozen branches stirred by the wind grew softer as the thaw set in; the breeze itself brought with it new, more subtle scents. Then, suddenly, the air filled with the cawing of rooks — and we knew the spring had arrived.

While the ice on the river could still carry my weight, I used to cross to the other bank and go off on solitary expeditions through the empty fields and birch groves. These excursions, knee-deep in snow, did not attract Zena, and I had to admit to myself that this suited me very well. The sky, the trees, the whole of the countryside were closer to me when I was alone among them, the excitement of discovery was sharper, the enjoyment more intense. As I trudged through the soft snow, I began to sing, the shape of a poem gradually forming in my head . . . or was it in my breast? The whole of me seemed to be involved, vibrating with emotion. I would stop and stare at the pattern of branches above my head, at the blue sky and white clouds shining through them. I would listen to silence, the seemingly absolute silence of woods under the snow, and hear the faint crackling of a small branch breaking, the soft thud of its fall, and then — was it possible — the hardly audible gurgling of water, very near, almost under my feet. I searched — and there it was! — a thread of a tiny brook finding its way through the snow crust towards some bigger brook, still bound and concealed under the ice. I would follow it a few paces, clearing its course of twigs and lumps of ice, then continue on my way, elated, as if I had really helped the spring to advance. Birds flew overhead, wild geese or cranes, calling as they flew, and a longing sprang up in me, a sharp access of wanderlust, which so often came to haunt me in later years. Pain and joy mingled; rebellion against being only human suddenly made my eyes burn with tears. I thought of the hours, days and years I was to spend in class-rooms, lecture-rooms, all kinds of rooms, imprisoned between walls, chained to my tasks, when I would much rather wander in strange countries, under new skies, in places with beautiful names — such names as Sorrento, Amalfi, Sevilla . . .

> *I wish I could fly with the birds*
> *To a far-off country where the sun never sets,*
> *Where men are free, not driven like herds*
> *Into stuffy rooms — these restricting nets! . . .*

These solitary walks were vivid emotional experiences, enriching and restoring, even though they made me feel more acutely the contrast between what was and what could have been. The atmosphere of my uncle's house was depressing, and it seemed that for Zena the only way of escaping from it was her relationship with me.

Zena did not like reading or school work; if she had any friends at her school, they lived too far to visit her. She became very dependent on me and lent herself willingly to my inventions and fantasies, the passivity in her nature responding to the initiative in my own.

I thought up a new game which took the form of a romance between the King of Rome, Napoleon's son, and his cousin, Princess Pauline Bonaparte. Having made a jump from the seventeenth into the nineteenth century, from the court of Henry IV of France into Napoleon's court, I did not hesitate to make havoc of history by re-arranging dates and events to please myself and by ignoring the facts that did not suit me. My own part in the game was that of the principal character, François-Charles-Joseph-Napoleon, the King of Rome, the Duke of Reichstadt, l'Aiglon — and Zena was Pauline, my cousin. The year was 1827 and I was sixteen, but the great Napoleon, my father, was not dead. He was still the Emperor of the French and we still lived at the Tuilleries and spent summer months at Fontainebleau. France was the mistress of Europe, and my mother, Marie-Louise of Austria, still a loyal wife to Napoleon I. Pauline in my story was the daughter of Napoleon's beautiful youngest sister, Pauline, who married the Prince of Borghese, and she was my parents' guest at Fontainebleau. We rode and walked together, we had quarrels, explanations, reconciliations, plans for the future and scenes of jealousy. My father sometimes called me to order, reminding me of my duties as the future Emperor. The brilliant court with its splendid marshals and diplomats was always in the background, but though proud of my birth and status, I was also an adolescent rebel, defying its conventions and demands.

Thus, parallel to my sober, hard-working school life with its trials and rewards, its restriction of freedom and compensation in achievement, this other, fantasy life went on, half-secretly satisfying a need for which there was no provision in real life. Was all this built up to satisfy my deepest and least conscious need for the all-powerful yet loving father, to whom I wanted to be as precious as Napoleon's son was to him? I collected all the picture postcards I could find in which they were represented together, and I pondered over them wondering longingly — could not this tender Napoleon have been my father in some previous life? I almost came to believe in reincarnation and transmigration of souls. Surely one life was not enough for everything we wanted to feel, see and do?

Once again my diary became a record of imaginary events, of scenes and conversations which took place between the young Napoleon and the Princess Pauline. It had become, in fact, the diary of my *alter ego*. The material never lacked, and page after page was filled with it. Soon what I described was no longer happening even in play: the royal romance continued only on paper.

Yet however much I became engrossed in my fantasy, the frontier between the imagined and the real never became confused. All the time I knew that I was I, and Zena was not Pauline, and often I felt annoyed at myself and at her for not helping me to forget it. I gave her a rendez-vous under the birch tree; she was to leave the 'palace' in secret, and suddenly there was excitement, an expectation of adventure in the air . . . But Zena rarely managed to escape her mother's or Hovra's observation. 'Where are you going?' one or the other would ask her. She would answer evasively, but Hovra would attach herself to her, and — if driven off — would watch us from a distance. There could be no real rendezvous with Hovra watching us, and the fact that Aunt Katia also knew of it completely shattered the spell.

Nor could Zena really act the Princess. She had a kind of inertness, a lack of sparkle which baffled me. Despite all my prompting as to what she had to say and how, or perhaps because of it, her responses were never convincing and often made me fling up my arms in despair.

When we were not Prince Napoleon and Princess Pauline, we were teaching ourselves to swim. A little beyond the landing stage the river was shallow with a sandy bottom, and after splashing about in it fruit-lessly for some days, we hit upon the idea of using a skipping rope as 'reins' to guide and support one another in our efforts to stay afloat. We practised this in turn until one day Zena let the rope go and I found I did not sink. I shouted: 'I'm swimming!' and Zena laughed and answered by a shout of confirmation, proud of her part in my success. It was only a few strokes, but it was real, all the same.

Zena's success followed closely upon mine, and soon we were sufficiently sure of ourselves to swim across the river in the deepest part. This added an extra dimension to our existence. Zena especially became keen on bathing. As the days grew hotter, she would run to the river as soon as she had returned from school, and she had to be called several times before she agreed to come out of the water and eat her meal. Often her body was covered with goose-flesh and her teeth were chatter-ing when she finally came in, yet she denied that she was cold and stubbornly ignored her mother's insistence that it 'couldn't be good for her'. Her father would on occasions suddenly become aware of what was happening, and from the edge of the high bank would shout to her to 'come out at once and get dressed'. But as often as not Zena and I were left to our own devices.

We got the sculls out of the shed and taught ourselves to row. We spent long evenings in May boating up and down the river by ourselves. Although Zena did not talk about it at the time, I knew she was unhappy and I wondered how she would fare when I left her for the long vacation, at the end of May.

A Summer of Crises

Our class-room library did not consist entirely of translations of Charles Dickens. It included some modern Russian fiction, among them books for young readers by a woman writer, Lydia Chárskaya. She had written several books about the same child, a girl of ten or eleven, a motherless tomboy, who lived in the Caucasus, dressed in Circassian clothes, rode fiery horses and was much indulged by her father — a kind of heroine who could not but appeal to me. So that summer — my second summer vacation from school — I arrived at Fyeny loaded with books by Chárskaya, in addition to a French and a German book, selected for me by Anna Avdyéevna.

One afternoon my sister suggested that I would do better if I came for a walk with her rather than go on reading 'that trash'.

Surprised and hurt, I protested that the story by Chárskaya I was reading was not trash at all. It was unusual for my sister to express herself so strongly about other people's preferences.

'Not trash?' she repeated. 'Look what Chukóvsky says about her.' And she put a copy of *Ogonióк* on the table beside my book.

Standing on my dignity, I ignored it and continued reading my story. The heroine had just been sent to a boarding school in Petersburg, and she was as unhappy there as I had been in mine. Her wild locks had been twisted into tight plaits and she had to wear long dresses instead of a *beshmiét* and trousers. She was planning to run away.

My sister went for a walk without me. After a while, feeling curious, I picked up the magazine, turned over a few pages and saw the article entitled 'Chárskaya'. Reluctantly, I began to read. Chukóvsky, one of the leading literary critics of the time, wrote in a light, witty, bantering style, all the more effective for not appearing to take his subject too seriously. He pictured to himself, he said, Madame Chárskaya sitting down to write one of her books. She had in front of her a typewriter which had only a few keys. These keys were labelled with sentences such as 'a fainting fit', 'a storm of tears', 'fell into each other's arms', or with punctuation marks, such as three dots and an exclamation mark. Madame Chárskaya, he assumed, would hit these keys more or less at random for an hour or so, and – hey, presto! – another book was ready to go into print! The only difference between all these books consisted simply in the number of exclamation marks or fainting fits they contained.

Appalled and distressed by this exposure of my favourite author's triviality, I went on reading all the same, and by the time I had finished the article, the glamour of Chárskaya's world had turned into ashes: I knew that Chukóvsky was right. I was suddenly and permanently cured of my infatuation with 'valueless' literature.

Soon afterwards, looking through the pile of my sister's small yellow books, I came upon one called *The Gadfly*, a translation from the English, yet by an author with a strangely un-English name – Voynich.

I must resist the temptation to retell the story, the impact of which on my mind was as dramatic as some conversions of sinner into saint. Only in my case the conversion was from a traditional faith to unbelief, from conformity to rebellion, and it took place almost overnight.

Conversions, it is said, are never really sudden: a hidden ferment must have been at work in my mind for some time before it happened. As a young child I questioned the goodness of a Deity who allowed the innocent to suffer and who created apparently useless and dangerous animals – such as crocodiles and snakes. I began to wonder whether my own faith was genuine when I found that I could not 'move mountains', and I was disappointed at failing to experience the ecstasy I was reaching out for at the great religious services of Christmas and Easter. Still I continued to hold on to what I had been taught, even while I pondered over it and asked unanswerable questions. The traditional beliefs were still sacred to me, and I felt hurt and offended by the derision with which Shoora Martýnov and my brother talked about the rites and teachings of the Orthodox Church.

That summer, before I read *The Gadfly*, I remember asking my mother whether she really believed that the bread and wine we received in

Holy Communion did turn into Christ's flesh and blood during the prayers which the priest read over them at the altar. As I waited for her reply, my brother, who was in the room, guffawed with laughter.

'I'll tell you what really happens,' he said. 'After he has given you your spoonful of bread and wine, the priest goes into the Holy of Holies, so-called, and gobbles up all that remains in the cup, and then most likely takes another drink from the bottle behind the icons.'

I jumped up gasping with indignation, appealing to my mother to stop him blaspheming, and I ran to my room where I wept with distress and horror at what I had been forced to hear. I wondered whether by hearing what my brother had said I had participated in his sin, the unforgivable sin against the Holy Ghost. It was dreadful to suggest that a priest could get merry on the wine of the Eucharist. But could it be true? Forbidden thoughts, like these, driven underground, persisted in returning . . . they were doing their insidious, corroding work.

Perhaps if I had not come upon *The Gadfly* then, my crisis of belief might have been delayed by a year or more. But suddenly, in a flare-up of intense compassion for the principal character of that novel, I discovered that I shared all his feelings and convictions: his hatred of authority, his devotion to freedom, his anger at the injustice of God and men and his love-hate for his father. Arthur Burton was as real to me as if I had met him in real life. I admired him for his strength and pitied him for his vulnerability. I was in love with him and I also identified myself with him. I pitied his father, too, and longed for them to forgive one another and to be reunited: I wanted love, not duty, to prevail. Perhaps when I wept passionately over this book I was grieving for my own unattainable father. But at the time I would have smiled, incredulous, if anyone had suggested this.

Through the alchemy of imaginative identification what had happened to a fictional character in the Italy of the Risorgimento had become immediately relevant to what was happening to me. Arthur Burton lost his faith because he had found that the priests of his religion had betrayed his trust; I lost mine because I thought I had discovered that what I had been taught as truth was not true. The Gadfly fought the Austrians, the oppressors of his country; my country, too, was oppressed — by the monarchy and its servants. Therefore I also should do something to fight the monarchy. The Gadfly was a hero, terribly wounded by men and Fate, therefore all revolutionaries must be unfortunate heroes, deserving admiration and respect.

This, too, was not a sudden discovery. In 1912, the revolution of

1905 was far from forgotten, and from conversations around me I gathered that most, if not all, university students were revolutionary or 'red'. My sister, whose opinions at that age I took on trust, spoke of 'the revolutionaries' with a sad and respectful fervour. In her small, very attractive voice she would sing the 'funeral march' of the revolutionaries: 'You fell, the victims of a fatal strife . . . ' and the affecting words and melody went straight to my heart. She herself, and her university friends, all spoke with contempt of the students who held monarchist views: they were either fops to whom they referred as 'white coat-linings', or anti-semites, described as 'black hundreds'.

My father, of course, served the monarchy as a provincial governor but I do not recollect him at the time expressing any political views. If I had thought of it at all, I must have assumed that he disapproved of 'the Reds' just as he disapproved of pogroms or of drunks – because they created disturbances and disorder. My mother disliked violence for whatever cause, and spoke of 'the terrorists' with horror and of the Imperial family with compassion. I remember her saying that governing Russia was 'a cross' which the Tsar and his family had to bear. It was a duty imposed on them by their birth, and they had no choice but to accept it. The Empress Alexandra was 'a tragic figure'; after having waited for years for a son, she at last gave birth to one but he was a haemophilic whose life was threatened by the slightest cut or scratch, which could cause him to bleed to death. The Tsar was 'a kindly man of simple tastes, devoted to his wife and children'. He would 'willingly give up his throne if his sense of duty were less strong'. His reign had been 'bedevilled by the double disaster of the war with Japan and the revolution of 1905'. He and his wife were 'not to blame' for these misfortunes: they should be 'pitied and prayed for'.

I felt that my mother's views had a great deal of truth in them, except for the idea of 'bearing the cross', which laid stress on a submissiveness against which I revolted. Why could not the Tsar share his burden with a popularly elected parliament, I asked. 'The Russian people are not ready for it,' my mother said. 'The majority of the peasants are illiterate.' 'Then teach them!' cried Shoora Martýnov. 'They'll never be educated as long as monarchy lasts.' He was all for a republic, for 'getting rid of the Románovs' and 'despatching Nicholas, the Fool, to the land of his ancestors'. I demanded hotly to know whether he would also murder the Tsar's innocent children, and, to provoke him, held up and kissed the portrait of the young heir to the throne. Contemptuously magnanimous, he replied that he would 'let the brats go' on the condition that they renounced all their rights to the throne.

Shoora was not a Gadfly; he was not a revolutionary I could fall in love with, yet he must have played some part in making my 'conversion' possible. When it came, it was overwhelming, and for years afterwards I could not read certain chapters of that novel without tears of pity, bitterness and pain.

I wept so much over it during that first reading that I had to hide myself, and I could not talk about it even to my sister. I suddenly saw the 'liberation' of my own country from 'tyranny' as a glorious task I ought to set myself. I saw myself as a young terrorist throwing a bomb at the Tsar . . . But would it not be much simpler to shoot him, first securing my father's revolver? If I killed the Tsar, I could not even be hanged, because of my age. And in any case his death would mean the end of monarchy: the revolutionaries would at once take over, and I would be acclaimed as a heroine, one who opened the way to liberation.

When I shared this fantasy with Vera, who was again our guest that summer, she was very matter-of-fact about it. She pointed out that it was very difficult to shoot straight with a revolver and that in all probability I would miss the Tsar. Even if I killed him, she did not think 'liberation' would immediately follow. 'They would at once put the young Alexéy on the throne, and you wouldn't have the heart to kill him, would you?' she said. I had to admit that I would not.

Vera's day-dreams were of a more personal kind. She told me she was determined to be an actress and have a lot of beautiful dresses, and that to achieve this she was prepared to run away from home, for her parents, she thought, would never let her do what she wanted. I had neither reason nor wish to run away from mine, but from an early age I had a passion for wandering on my own — which produced another crisis in my life that particular summer.

We drove out to bathe in a small river some few miles from home, my mother, my sister, Vera and myself. After a swim Vera and I got dressed before the others and the two of us started walking along the river bank towards a mass of floating logs we could see in the distance. As we came closer we saw that it was timber floating down the river and that the logs covered it from bank to bank. Immediately it occurred to me that we could cross the river by walking on them, and Vera needed no persuasion to agree that it would be fun. I leapt on to the nearest log, Vera followed. The log dipped under my weight and began to roll; quickly I stepped on to the next one, expecting to find it firm — and only just managed to keep my balance. The log was slippery and the water covered my feet. Fear gripped me, but I had just enough presence of mind to turn back at once and to shout a warning to Vera. She had already realized the danger we were in, and in a few seconds we were back on the bank, our feet soaked and our hearts thumping.

I told Vera that I had thought the logs would be like a raft and that it was stupid of me — but I still wanted to get to the other side and explore the forest there. Further up the river there was a small, one-man ferry, and I led the way towards it. I heard my sister's voice calling after us, and I shouted back: 'Soon!' or some such word just to reassure them. We jumped on to the ferry just as it was pushing off and, between us, we had enough kopecks to pay our fare to the other bank.

The forest was mostly birch and fir, and we plunged into it and walked on without giving a thought to where we were going. My impulse was to get to a place 'where no light could be seen between the trees', for only there did I feel I was in 'real forest'. Vera shared some of my excitement, although she remained a little uncomprehending and confessed to being somewhat afraid. 'What if we lose our way?' she asked. I replied that we could then sleep in the forest — it was warm and the ground was dry — but that I was quite sure we would find our way back however far we went.

We went too far, and though we did find our way back to the ferry, it was after some hours of wandering. We had to walk all the way home, and it was quite dark when we arrived.

The first thing I saw as we approached the house was the figure of my sister fluttering among the flower beds. She walked quickly towards us and spoke in a whisper as if afraid that we might disappear again if she raised her voice. Her first words were: 'Thank God!' and then she told us that my mother was 'beside herself' with anxiety on our account. I asked apprehensively whether my father knew of our disappearance. Maroossia told me that he had gone on horseback with the bailiff and one of the workmen to search for us in the forest.

I rarely saw my mother look as severe and solemn as she was when she met me that evening. Having satisfied herself that we were both unharmed, she told Aniuta to serve us with some supper, which we ate in penitent silence. I was anxious to get into bed as soon as possible, not only because I was very tired, but also because I dreaded facing my father when he returned from his search. My mother let me escape upstairs, but when I was in bed, she came up and spoke to me.

She said I had behaved in a most thoughtless way and caused her hours of anxiety. I protested that she need not have worried, that I could always find my way out of any forest, and had proved it many a time when we went for picnics or mushroom-gathering in the past. She replied that losing my way was not the only danger, and again I argued that wolves did not attack people except in winter when they were hungry and went in packs. As for the gypsy stories, they were all nonsense. Finally she told me that some men, escaped convicts or deserters from the army, could be more dangerous than wolves, and still I remained unconvinced and uncomprehending — for it never entered my head that men could or would attack girls sexually.

I remember her actual words because I was struck by the obvious effort it cost her to tell me. 'Haven't you seen paragraphs in newspapers . . . about girls violated by men?' she asked me.

I was startled into silence. I did recollect having seen such paragraphs, usually in small print at the bottom of a page. I had felt vaguely disturbed by them, but not sufficiently interested, it seems, to ask what 'violation' meant.

My mother now explained that 'violation' meant sexual assault, rape — and that a girl wandering alone in solitary places ran the risk of being assaulted in that way. She made me promise that I would never do so again.

Shocked and speechless, I let her leave the room without asking the question I might have asked if she had been less upset and more accessible. Why, I wondered desperately, should any man want to impose himself in that way on any woman or girl? Were such men criminals or madmen? If so, the danger was real, and not merely another example of my mother's habit of worrying excessively about the health and safety of her children.

I remained awake a long time, battling with a wave of mounting depression. Did this mean that I was no longer to enjoy my solitary explorations of the countryside I loved so much? That I could no longer pursue the experience of being 'in possession' when I was deep inside a forest, utterly alone and feeling utterly safe? That I would never rediscover the emotion, verging on ecstasy, of being one with Nature? It felt as if the world had suddenly become an alien place: all the sweetness and splendour had gone out of it, driven out by this grim revelation.

Preoccupied as I was with these feelings and thoughts, I was yet on the alert, listening to the sounds of the searchers' return, fearing whatever might happen when my father came back that night. I wondered whether he might not come upstairs to speak to me. He had never done so in the past — but this time . . . after what my mother had told me . . . Anything was conceivable after that.

Hours seemed to pass before I heard the sound of horses' hooves outside my window. The returning searchers spoke softly: I could not hear what was being said. I guessed rather than heard the horses being led away, footsteps of someone walking up the steps of the porch, movement and conversation in the house. Someone started walking up the stairs leading to the mezzanine, too lightly for it to be my father's footsteps. Nevertheless I sat up in bed tense with anxiety. The door opened quietly and my sister came in. She started slightly when she saw me sitting up in bed, and asked why I was not asleep.

'They're back?' I asked.

My sister nodded. I could hardly bring myself to ask what 'they' said, meaning of course no one but my father.

'He asked whether you'd been found,' my sister told me. 'He's now talking to Mamma in her room.'

She began to get ready for bed without lighting a candle as if she knew that I would rather not be seen. I was glad to have her in the room and relieved that she did not say anything more, except to tell me to go to sleep. I found that I could not talk even to her about the thoughts and feelings which were oppressing me.

She spared me the news I was to hear next morning and which was to haunt me with guilt for many a month. While they were riding at random through the forest in search of Vera and me, one of the horses put its foot through a molehill and broke its leg. The horse had to be destroyed.

This outcome of my adventure so horrified me that for a time I could not even give way to my distress and remorse: I could not cry. Why, why, I kept on asking myself, should an innocent creature die owing to my thoughtless behaviour? A horse, too, one of my favourite animals! It felt too much like punishment, a lesson, intended for me . . . But as I was now a non-believer, who could have intended me to learn this lesson? My mother would say that the punishment and the lesson were sent me by God, and this thought added fuel to my smouldering anger with Him. What kind of God was He, who made *others* suffer so that *we* should profit? How cruel He must have been to sacrifice His Son in order to 'save' mankind! Long before I read Dostoyevsky, I felt, like Ivan Karamazov, that I did not want to be saved if someone had to die for it — even if that 'someone' was only an animal.

My mother must have been aware of the state I was in and refrained from piling coals of fire on to my head. She decided I needed a change and suggested I should go with Vera to my Uncle Fyodor's house where

Vera was to join her parents after staying with us. I seized upon this offer with the eagerness of a criminal given the chance of escaping from the scene of his crime. I saw my beloved Fyeny through dark glasses, and for the first time in my life found no joy in my familiar surroundings.

My uncle's house at G* was always full of people in the summer, for his Polish wife had several grown-up step-children by her first marriage, and, being a generous woman, she enjoyed them coming to see her with their families and staying as long as they liked. It was a good place to be in, for Aunt Stefania was devoted to children and her devotion showed itself in providing them with plenty of good things to eat and leaving them to their own devices. To be noticed as little as possible was just what I wanted in my mood of self-dislike and remorse.

That summer the interest of the gathering was centred on the newly-married couple, Nina, Aunt Stefania's youngest daughter and the only child of her marriage to my uncle, and her husband Vladisláv. Nina had just completed a course in Russian language and literature at the Bestoózhevskiye Koorsy in Petersburg, where my sister was a student, and I was puzzled by her having chosen to marry Vladisláv, who was an officer in one of the privileged Guards' regiments. I had been accustomed to hearing my sister and her student friends talking scornfully of the military whom they considered to be brainless and uneducated. I assumed that Nina, a very independent and intelligent young woman, shared these views, and I remembered her saying that when she had finished her course, she would like to run a school of her own. Vladisláv was a languid young man, rather plain, and, in my eyes, not sufficiently attractive as a husband. Why, I wondered, did Nina choose to marry him?

I shared my musings with Vera who then solemnly imparted to me a secret — she did not say from whom she had learned it; Vladisláv had threatened to kill himself unless Nina married him, and this was the reason why she agreed to be his wife. 'He swore he would marry her when she was only a schoolgirl of thirteen, and he a cadet in a military school. She said 'No' for years, but then it came to a head — and, after all, she could not let him die, could she?'

Knowing how vivid Vera's imagination could be, I did not quite believe this story, but even so, it added piquancy to my observation of the couple. I noticed a change in Nina's personality. I used to be a little afraid of her because of her forthright, almost brusque ways. But now she was subdued, and, strangest of all, she *waited on* Vladisláv!

The ideas I had at that time concerning relationships between the sexes belonged more to the days of chivalry than to modern times. I assumed that a man showed his love for a woman by doing his best to serve her, forestalling her wishes, being courteous, tender and respectful. As far as this couple were concerned, these roles seemed to be reversed: it was Nina who insisted on doing everything for Vladisláv, and it was he who seemed to expect to be served and adored. I was puzzled and quite disappointed in Nina.

Vera's own family provided another diversion from my personal preoccupations. It was not a particularly pleasant family. Her father, a colonel in the Army, was a smallish man with pince-nez and the manners of a martinet. Her mother had a precise, imperious voice and a coldly observant eye which made me feel nervous of her, as I knew Vera was. Vera's elder brother, Pyetia, a cadet in a military school, talked out of the corner of his mouth and looked at his sister and me down his nose. Her younger sister and brother, Ánichka and Andríusha, were charming enough, but they always needed to be entertained — a task which their mother expected Vera to fulfil. As Ánichka usually burst into tears if she lost a game, Vera and I did our best to evade this obligation. I saw what Vera had meant when she told me that her mother favoured the younger children and was severe with her. It struck me as a very strange thing that a mother should dislike one of her children, and Vera and I discussed this in whispers late into the night without finding any definite answers to our questions.

I returned to Fyeny a fortnight later with none of my problems solved but feeling somewhat wiser than before.

Being a Favourite

In the wake of that disturbing summer came a disturbing beginning of a new term in my third year at school.

I remember the bitter-sweet flavour of the first evening on my return to Uncle Vladímir's and Aunt Katia's melancholy house: sweet because of Zena's pleasure in seeing me, bitter because of the suspicious and unfriendly look in her mother's eye, and of the scene which followed on our absconding from the house immediately after supper.

After nearly three months of separation Zena and I felt like talking to each other without witnesses — or rather, Zena was eager to hear all about my doings during that time. We slipped out through the garden door into the gathering dusk and walked to the far corner of the grounds where there was a rickety garden seat behind some berberry bushes. Zena did not have much to tell me. She had stayed at the *dacha* all the summer, and bathed and swam, it seemed, for most of every day. I told her of Shoora Martýnov's and Vera's stay at Fyeny, of our escapade in the forest and my visit to Uncle Fyodor's. The only thing I could not bring myself to tell her was the fate of the injured horse. Zena listened avidly. When I finished, she sighed and said she wished she could have been there, too. I told her she must come next school holidays.

'*They* will never let me,' she said, meaning her parents.

'Why not?' I asked.

'They're supposed to love me so much that they can't let me out of their sight,' said Zena.

Startled by the bitterness of this remark, I protested, without complete conviction, that surely her parents loved her and would want her to enjoy herself.

'Not they,' she replied with increasing bitterness. 'All they want is to keep me here, watching their beastliness to one another.'

I was shocked into silence, appalled not by her judgment on her parents, which I felt to be just, but by the desperate feeling behind her words, as if of a trapped animal. I could find nothing to say which would console her in this desperate situation except to fall back on our long-standing game. I reminded her of her role as Pauline Bonaparte, and of myself as her devoted cousin, Napoleon's heir, who had come back to her after a long absence abroad. I quoted to her the French proverb about love: '*L'absence pour l'amour est comme le vent pour les flammes; il éteint le petit et allume le grand . . .* ' I took her hand and suggested she should look up at the stars — a spectacle supposed to induce a peaceful, contemplative mood. She responded, and we both leaned well back, with our faces turned up to the sky. It was almost black and so richly bespangled with patterns of light that we fell silent and remained silent for a couple of minutes. Then Zena asked, dreamily: 'What is that large greenish star?'

'Probably Venus . . . or maybe Hesperus, the evening star . . . ' I was guessing.

'And where is the Great Bear?'

The Great Bear was the only constellation I could identify with any certainty, but I did not immediately see it. It could be just behind us . . .

Determined to locate it without moving from our seat, we leaned back farther and farther, and suddenly the seat tipped backwards and we were lying on our backs in the long, damp grass. A moment of stunned silence, then a burst of laughter. We laughed with such abandon that we could hardly get up from the ground, could hardly stand on our feet. And the more we laughed, the funnier it seemed. Our stunned moment of silence had been funny . . . the very name 'Great Bear' was funny . . .

'Where is it . . . the Great Bear? . . . ' Zena insisted among peals of laughter.

'There . . . behind you . . . a saucepan with a long handle . . . '

'Why – a saucepan? . . . The Bear . . . '

We could hardly speak for laughter during the next few minutes, and the sudden appearance of Hovra who must have crawled through the bushes, did not detract from our mirth. She told us that *bárynia* sent her to find us and tell us that she wanted us to come indoors.

As we came into the poorly lit dining-room with its oil-cloth covered table, Aunt Katia frowned at us across her patience cards. Zena and I glanced at one another and again began to laugh. This had nothing to do with Aunt Katia but she took it as a personal affront. She turned on me.

It was I, she said, who had taught Zena to laugh at her mother. I led her out into the garden when she should have gone to bed. I stopped her from doing her homework by inventing all kinds of games. I kept her out in the dark and the cold and would be the one responsible if she caught a bad chill.

This torrent of accusations caught me unawares and I stood there, speechless for a few moments. Zena, on the other hand, suddenly furious, sprang to my defence.

'Will you leave Léda alone?' she shrieked. 'Why are you always picking on her?'

Her voice must have carried across the drawing-room to my uncle's study. We heard his door open and his heavy footsteps coming towards us. Aunt Katia pressed her pale lips together, drew herself up and pattered out of the room. My uncle appeared in the doorway.

'What's happening?' he asked, glancing round the room.

'Nothing . . . ' Zena muttered, without looking at him.

'How — nothing? I heard you shouting.'

'I'm not shouting now.'

'That's not a proper answer to give your father. What's got into you today? You're not like that when you're on your own with us. There's a bad influence on you . . . not too far to seek.'

'It's you — no one but you!' Zena's voice broke, half-shout, half-sob.

'What? What are you saying?'

But she ran out of the room and I followed. My heart was beating fast with the violence of this scene. It was distressing, yet gratifying as well. Zena, so much on my side that she was able to stand up to her possessive parents! Zena suddenly showing that she had enough courage and intelligence to see what was happening and to protest against it! And I knew her parents were right when they said that it was my 'fault', that it was I who had shown Zena the way. Whatever guilt I felt at causing this scene, it was strongly overlaid with a sense of triumph.

The beginning of the new term was disturbing because I was to lose my favourite teacher, Maria Ivánovna, who was to be replaced by a man teacher, Konstantín Danílovich Shimkóvich. It was the tradition of our

school to have women teachers replaced by men as the girls passed into
the middle and upper forms. Boys' secondary and high schools had no
women teachers at all. The education authorities must have had reasons
for this, though I never heard them made explicit. It was probably
assumed that men were better disciplinarians, which would apply more
to boys than to older girls, who were on the whole very well behaved in
my type of school. Be that as it may, there was unconscious wisdom in
this practice — for adolescent girls, as well as boys, had to be helped to
grow away from their mothers.

I was very attached to María Ivánovna and grateful to her for being
so appreciative of my literary efforts, and I feared the testing that was
to come with a new teacher who had the reputation of an ogre. He was
said to possess the sharpest, the most sarcastic of tongues, and he would
taunt a girl for days with her mistakes, referring to them in and out of
context. We heard that he enjoyed reducing girls to tears. If other
teachers had favourites, he was given to picking out victims; once he
took a dislike to a girl, he was said never to change towards her. What if
he took a dislike to me? What if he decided that my compositions were
no good? I was half-expecting this to happen, unconsciously assuming
that Shimkóvich would set as little value on my achievements as my
father had always done. And living as I was with the unsympathetic and
critical Martsínovsky parents, I badly needed appreciation and praise to
strengthen me against self-doubt and fear of ridicule.

I remember how quiet the class was when Shimkóvich came in to
give us his first lesson. As he called our names from the register, he
glanced at each girl as she half rose from her seat to indicate that she was
present. He then proceeded to explain what we had to prepare for our
next lesson with him, speaking in a husky voice with a distinct 'seminary
accent', and we could stare at him as much as we liked.

In appearance he was very unlike an ogre — slightly less than medium
height, slender, with thin, almost emaciated features and a yellowish
complexion. Later we came to know that he was suffering from cirrhosis
of the liver — he had been a heavy drinker in his younger days — an addiction to which some of his irritability might have been due. His straight,
light-brown hair was brushed back from his forehead and he had a small,
well-trimmed beard. I thought he looked a little like Chehov.

Having finished his exposition, Shimkóvich leaned back and looked us
over with a benign air.

'Who would like to repeat in her own words what I've just explained
to you?' he asked.

This was quite a usual procedure, and there were always a few pupils, myself included, who volunteered to summarize for the benefit of the class and perhaps for further clarification what the teacher had been telling us. But this teacher's redoubtable reputation had inhibited us to such an extent that no one stirred. Even Lena Kazanóvich, the madcap who seemed to enjoy being laughed at, remained seated.

Shimkóvich looked quizzical, raised his eyebrows at us, professed himself surprised at our lack of ability or courage. Would he have to call out names, he asked.

I was aware that Anna Avdyéevna, as well as many of my classmates, were looking at me: I had often volunteered to re-tell Maria Ivánovna's exposition. Some of the girls began to murmur my name. The teacher's glasses flashed in my direction; behind them I met a pair of smallish, lustreless eyes.

'No one brave enough?' he taunted, savouring his contempt.

I was afraid of being laughed at, but being accused of cowardice was even more intolerable. I rose to my feet. Shimkóvich pushed his spectacles up his forehead; his eyes without them looked tired and almost kindly.

'You would?' he asked with sudden amiability. 'Well . . . begin.'

He had been telling us about the place of the peasant poet Koltzóv in Russian literature. I did my best to give him the gist of it. Shimkóvich did not interrupt me, only nodded his head once or twice. When I had finished and was told I could sit down, he made no comment on my effort, but wrote something in the register. No teacher ever gave marks for 're-telling' a new lesson, and the whole of the class was agog to see what it was.

There was a scramble to get at the register after Shimkóvich had left the class-room. Elbows dug into ribs and heads collided as the girls jumped on to the rostrum and crowded round the table. A mixture of pride and fear kept me from joining the curious crowd; I waited for them to tell me. I did not have to wait long. Ania Bielynóvich turned a smiling face and a pair of wide-open eyes towards me.

'He gave you a twelve!' she announced in a stage whisper. 'Good for you!'

Other girls were staring at me too. One asked anxiously: 'Are we to have marks for re-telling now?' Another declared that Shimkóvich terrified her. 'Did you notice how angry he was getting because people didn't volunteer at once?' 'Obviously he's chosen you as his favourite,' said Mania Komaróvskaya with tight lips. 'Well done!' commented

Katia Kign. Anna Avdyéevna said nothing but I could see that she was pleased. 'She's afraid of him, too,' whispered Liolia Tálina, and broke into irrepressible giggles.

I felt excited, relieved, elated by passing this test – surely it was a proof that the praise Maria Ivánovna had always given me so freely was genuine and not influenced by her personal liking for me. But the elation soon subsided and I began to wonder what would happen when Shimkóvich set us an essay to write.

As a rule we were given the choice of three subjects: a semi-abstract one, asking us to discuss some general statement; a more concrete one, such as a description of a journey or a visit to the theatre; and a third, related to what we had been reading. Themes with a philosophical bias, such as 'What would you consider as a worth-while purpose in life?' stimulated me most, but I was also fond of commenting on characters in fiction, especially if they were personally attractive to me.

As luck would have it, one of the subjects Shimkóvich set us for the first lot of essays we had to write, happened to be 'The Character of Pechórin in *The Hero of our Time*.'

Pechórin was one of the few characters in Russian classical literature whom I admired and was eager to discuss. Because he was misunderstood and unhappy, I was ready to forgive him his persecution of the ridiculous Grushnítskiy and his cruel treatment of Princess Mary. I knew that Lermontov was supposed to have been influenced by Byron when creating this 'Byronic' character, and I mentioned this briefly in my essay. The rest of it, however, became an apologia for Pechórin. I explained that he behaved in the way he did because he had been cruelly treated during his most impressionable years, and I accompanied my argument with many quotations from the original.

The hour we were allowed for writing was barely enough to put down all I wanted to say, though I wrote fast and easily. Shimkóvich set us our subjects and went out, leaving us in charge of Anna Avdyéevna. But when he returned the essays had to be collected, whether finished or unfinished, and he took the pile of exercise books away, to the accompaniment of faint moans and sighs which made him smile dryly and drew a warning hiss from Anna Avdyéevna.

We had to wait over a week before he brought them back, and everyone in the class sat up, tense with anticipation, when he walked in with a stack of many-coloured exercise books under his arm. Everyone was trying to guess whose book was on the top of the pile because, as a rule, it would be the one to be discussed. With Maria Ivánovna it was usually

the best essay, that is, one of mine. But Shimkóvich was unpredictable:
he might even open up by castigating the writer of the worst essay.

As he picked up the book, I recognized it as mine and held my breath.
'This is a very interesting essay,' he began.

Was he being ironical? My tiresome body reacted by a ringing noise
in my ears and a tingling sensation spreading from my head to my toes.

'The writer has obviously fallen under the spell of the character she
discusses,' he continued. 'There's nothing funny in this,' he remarked
sharply, glancing over his spectacles in the direction from which a faint
titter was heard. 'She has treated the subject seriously and was able to
express her views with a commendable clarity and even eloquence. My
point is that she has taken the character's opinion of himself at its face
value, and I do not happen to agree with her. Our disagreement merits
discussion . . . '

He went on for the next quarter of an hour, reading extracts from
my essay and adding his comments to each quotation. In his opinion
Pechórin was merely a poseur and a trouble-maker, an egoist who cared
for no one but himself, an unscrupulous Don Juan who gave himself
Byronic airs. Wealthy upper classes, he continued, produced such types
by the dozen in Lermontov's day, and the poet meant to satirize them,
but perhaps he was not quite single-minded about this. Such types
should be shown for what they are — mere drones, of no use whatever
to the community. They 'go mad from too much fat' — *z zhíroo
biésiatza* — Shimkóvich savoured this crude popular saying as he quoted
it, and for a moment I felt an intense dislike for him. By the time he had
finished talking, my apologia for Pechórin was torn to shreds, and I was
shaken and burning with confusion, yet obstinately unconvinced.

Shimkóvich laid my essay aside and started on another. I was now
sure that I would not get more than ten marks for it — something that
had never happened before. I also knew that I should never be Shimkóvich's favourite and that I was not going to like him. For however much
I admired revolutionaries, it was not on account of their 'usefulness to
the community' but because of their courage in defiance, their rebellion
against 'the oppressors' and the terror and pity which their destiny
aroused in me. My view of life was deeply and passionately romantic:
the French revolution was right in deposing the king, but I admired also
the aristocrats who went to the guillotine with flowers in their button-
holes and a smile on their lips. Shimkóvich's scornful reference to the
'upper classes' struck me as spiteful and in bad taste. I recollected what
my sister had told me: he was the son of a village priest and the grandson

of a peasant; he had received his education at a village school and a
seminary, and he was proud of it. My sister got on very well with him,
but then, she worshipped Tolstoy who believed in simple life and
dressed as a peasant.

These thoughts and many others whirled through my head while the
teacher's voice droned on, commenting on more essays, causing blushes
and shamefaced grins to appear on many faces. He stopped a few minutes
before the break to set us our task for the next lesson. As soon as he had
left the room, the monitors pounced upon the pile of essays and began
distributing them. Some of the girls pretended to be so frightened of
seeing their marks that they peeped inside their books and hurriedly
closed them again. Others boasted of unexpected successes. 'I've got a
ten, I've got a ten!' Liolia Tálina sang and giggled excitedly.

Alma Fibikh stuck a sharp chin into my shoulder trying to look into
my book as I braced myself to open it.

'Oh,' she said, 'A twelve minus! And what a lot of writing underneath!'

It looked incredible but it was true: Shimkóvich had given me full
marks with only a minus for what he pleased to call my 'mistaken
conclusions'. Half a page below was covered with small spidery writing
in red ink, more or less repeating what he had said earlier in the lesson.
To me, however, it was the last sentence that mattered — 'Although in
my opinion the writer has failed to prove her thesis, she has considerable
literary resources at her disposal.'

I thought the two Komaróvskayas looked disappointed and wondered
why they seemed to be so eager to see me fall from grace. They always
vied with one another to do things for Anna Avdyéevna, and it must
have hurt them to find me regarded by everyone as her 'favourite',
without apparently doing anything special to merit this. And now the
most exacting of our teachers was on the way to singling me out as his
best pupil! They clearly felt this to be terribly unfair. Yet I did not see
how I could be blamed for what was happening. In fact, I could have
told them that being Anna Avdyéevna's favourite was far from an
unmixed blessing, and I was soon to discover how awkward could
become the role of Shimkóvich's best pupil.

Of course, it was flattering to have my essays read aloud to the class
as examples of good writing; gratifying to be complimented on the
quickness and appositeness of my replies to questions on literary
subjects, even when these compliments were so wrapt up in circumlocution as to be almost incomprehensible. Shimkóvich often used clerical

turns of speech and mannerisms of pronunciation peculiar to the seminary, but as he was clearly doing this deliberately, no one found it
ridiculous. In any case his pupils feared and respected him too much to
giggle during his lessons, unless he himself gave us a sign that his remarks
were intended to make us laugh.

To be called out by Shimkóvich to recite before the class was flattering, but to be called upon to read a long poem before the assembled
school including the Director and the Headmistress was simply terrifying. The occasion was an anniversary of Lomonósov, a poet and
scientist of the eighteenth century, and the poem his 'Ode on the
Usefulness of Glass'. Shimkóvich seemed to take a personal pride in the
achievements of this man, who was the son of a fisherman on the shores
of the White Sea, and who walked all the way from there to Petersburg
in search of education. In my young eyes, however, Lomonósov's poems
were not poetry at all but mere naturalistic tracts in verse form. One
read them at school only because one had to, and privately made fun of
their old-fashioned, church Slavonic, pre-Pushkin language.

When Shimkóvich's choice of reader fell on me – as everyone in the
class seemed to expect – it was like a seal set on my status of a 'favourite'.
I was the only one caught unawares and my first reaction was dismay.
I dared not refuse and my silence was taken for consent.

Shimkóvich gave me the book and asked me to practise memorizing
and reciting it at home. I memorized it quickly enough but could not
concentrate on any other of my tasks because of my preoccupation with
the coming ordeal. A couple of weeks passed. My mother came to M* to
do some of her Christmas shopping and found me in a state of such
anxiety that it worried her.

'Why don't you tell him you would rather not do it?' she asked.

I explained that I could not give him the true reason. What reason
could I give him?

'Say that your voice is not strong enough to carry across the big
assembly hall; tell him that anyway his ode is so boring that people
would fall asleep while you're reciting it!'

I do not know whether my mother meant me to follow her advice
literally: she could not have known in what reverence Lomonósov was
held by our teacher. Be that as it may, feeling unable to stand the strain
much longer, I plucked up my courage to stand up in class and ask
Shimkóvich to release me from the task of reciting the ode to the
assembled school.

When I gave as my reason the weakness of my voice, Shimkóvich looked quite unconvinced, so hurriedly I trotted out my mother's unfortunate remark about people falling asleep. Shimkóvich's face darkened and took an intimidating hardness of expression. In a dry, hostile voice he began to speak of another great Russian, Krylóv, whose fables were so well known that quotations from them became a part of the common usage. He mentioned the fable about a mighty oak and the acorns scattered on the ground beneath it. An animal, which need not be named, he said, having eaten the acorns, began to dig under the tree, undermining its roots. We were all reaping the benefits of Lomonósov's scientific labours, but some of us were ungrateful enough to talk slightingly of his work as a poet.

I stood behind my desk as he delivered himself of this tirade and the eyes of all my classmates were fixed on me. When he had finished, I sat down utterly crushed and silent with confusion. Some of my classmates would have tittered if they dared but the spectacle of Shimkóvich's wrath froze them into silence and immobility.

As soon as he had left the room, however, they began to laugh and whisper among themselves, and Liolia Tálina broke into uncontrollable giggling.

Anna Avdyéevna tapped her desk to call the class to order. I dared not look in her direction, afraid of seeing my humiliation reflected as pity in her eyes. The break bell rang, and I mixed with the others to get out into the corridor as soon as I could.

A little crowd surrounded me, sympathizing, expressing their indignation at the teacher's rudeness. Ania Bielynóvich told me with her usual bluntness that I was a fool to have backed out of the task Shimkóvich had assigned to me. 'He'll never forgive you for that,' she said. 'It's the end of your being his favourite,' she said.

Mania and Liuba Komaróvskaya must have thought so, too: I detected a glint of triumph in their outwardly commiserating gaze.

'I hope he won't carry on as he did today — I mean taking revenge on you,' said Mania, and I felt she was hoping he would do just that.

At the next lesson Shimkóvich offered the recitation of the ode to Liolia Tálina, and, naturally enough, she accepted. Liolia had a much better voice than I for this task. It was strong and sonorous: she often entertained us in lunch break by singing Gypsy 'romances'. Her rehearsals in front of the class were models of correct recitation, and Shimkóvich smiled approvingly as he listened to her.

However, Mania Komaróvskaya's secret hopes concerning his treatment of me were not fulfilled. He did not start persecuting me — he just

ignored me. It was Liolia whom he now called upon to answer his more
subtle or provocative questions, and it was she who re-told the new
lessons after he had explained them to us, and got twelves for her efforts.
My pride suffered but still I did not regret what I had done. Even when
the celebration was in full swing and I was sitting in the audience,
listening to Liolia's model recitation and the applause that followed it,
impressed by the apparent simplicity and ease of this performance –
even then I had not a moment of doubt that I was much better off where
I was than on the rostrum.

A few weeks went by. The Lomonósov anniversary and the incident of
the ode receded into the past; Liolia was no longer in the limelight.
Gradually Shimkóvich was again becoming aware of my existence.
Incredibly – for I had accepted his reputation as an unforgiving man – I
found myself restored to my former position as 'the best pupil' in
Russian literature and language, and to the doubtful privilege of being
Shimkóvich's favourite.

It took me longer to forgive him, and to have my self-esteem even
partially restored. His quotation from Krylóv continued to rankle, the
humiliating comparison was difficult to forget. Nor could I forgive
myself for repeating my mother's remark about people being put to
sleep by Lomonósov's ode, which so angered Shimkóvich. I felt my
mother was to blame for this, and my belief in her wisdom was shaken.
But I was also aware that I had somehow profited by this unpleasant
experience: an irreparable catastrophe proved to be only a temporary
eclipse. It was both a warning for the future and a source of reassurance.

I told myself that I must control my impulsiveness and spontaneity,
but this did not come easily to me. Self-doubt often led me to acts of
self-display and rebellion against 'rules and regulations' which alarmed
and upset Anna Avdyéevna. When I broke some minor prohibition she
had issued to the class, she would tell me that 'everyone has to obey the
rules' and demanded to know why I should be 'an exception'. I had an
answer ready on my lips – a passionate affirmation of my right not to
conform: 'Because I am one!' But the fear of ridicule prevented me
from voicing it. The *dame-de-classe* must have read the challenge in my
face and, aware that she was losing control over me, tried to regain it
by forceful means, and brought about a head-on collision between us.

One morning we came out of the assembly hall where we had a gym
lesson to return to our class-room on the floor below. It was opposite
the women teachers' common-room, and we were to walk past it
in absolute silence. I was paired with Ania Bielynóvich with whom I

had a 'matey' relationship, half-teasing, half mutually protective. It happened that Ania turned and spoke to a girl behind her just as we were passing the common-room door. She did not see Anna Avdyéevna emerging from our class-room, and to warn her, I gave her a quick prod in the ribs. She turned fiercely towards me but checked herself on seeing the *dame-de-classe*. With some difficulty I suppressed a giggle.

I was hoping all this had passed more or less unnoticed, but as soon as we were inside the class-room, Anna Avdyéevna called us to her desk telling us to bring our French reading books. These were the anthologies of French classics, and we had started reading *Le Cid* by Corneille.

'You will learn these fifty lines by heart before you go home this afternoon,' she told us, marking them in the book.

Ania shrugged and seemed ready to accept this without protest. I asked Anna Avdyéevna why she was giving us this task. She replied that I knew quite well: it was for talking to Ania in the corridor outside the common-room door. I asserted that I had said nothing to Ania. The *dame-de-classe* insisted that I was responsible for a commotion which could be heard in the common-room and that my punishment was deserved. I refused to comply.

While this was going on, the class was very quiet, listening, and Anna Avdyéevna's face became flushed. She dropped her voice to tell me that she would not allow me to leave until I learned these lines, but that I could make use of the next period to learn them because the sewing mistress was unwell and would not be here.

I returned to my place quivering with anger, blood pulsating in my temples and filling my head with a roaring noise. I sat and stared at the open book on my desk, seeing only a blur. When the mist cleared from my eyes I began to read automatically and read the same lines several times before I could see any sense in them.

> Car enfin n'attends pas de mon affection
> Un lache repentir d'une bonne action . . .

She *was* expecting me to repent . . . to submit . . . but submitting to punishment would look like admitting that I had lied when I denied my guilt. That was unthinkable — a humiliation and an act of cowardice which I was quite unable to contemplate. I did my best to calm myself and went on reading without attempting to memorize what I read. The Cid's noble refusal to compromise fortified my determination not to yield to Anna Avdyéevna's threats or persuasion.

The hour dragged, yet the sound of the bell announcing its end made me start. The class-room was immediately filled with the noise of the desks being opened and shut and of books being pushed into satchels in preparation for going home. I heard Anna Avdyéevna asking Ania whether she had finished memorizing her lines, and Ania's reply, 'Not quite . . . not all of them.' All the same, she went over to her and recited them, Anna Avdyéevna gently prompting her through the stumbling progress of her recitation and finally releasing her with a friendly: 'That'll do, you may go.'

The class had emptied by that time and I stood up and started packing my books. Anna Avdyéevna came over to me and asked whether I was ready to recite my lines. I told her that I had not been learning them.

'You persist in refusing?' she asked softly, her eyes on mine, her chin tucked into her neck.

'I won't be punished for something I haven't done,' I said, trembling inwardly with indignation.

I remember the flattering phrases she used in an attempt to break my resistance. Need I be so uncompromising? she asked. Didn't I have an excellent memory? Could I not learn these fifty lines in half an hour? It would 'cost me nothing' to do what she asked. Finally she said that if I promised to learn it for tomorrow, I could go home at once.

Exasperated, I blurted out that I was not going to promise anything and that I had to go at once because my cousin, the coachman and the horse were waiting for me, and she had no right to punish them by keeping them out in the cold.

'Wouldn't you promise for their sake, if not for mine?' she insisted.

I shook my head. She looked me up and down with an expression on her face which might have been grudging admiration.

'Incredible!' she murmured. 'What stubbornness! I suppose you pride yourself on your strength of will . . . Very well, you may go. You might change your mind by tomorrow.'

How little she knew me! My pride was certainly involved in this contest but it was not stubbornness, a mere determination not to give in, which kept me resisting her demand. It was the feeling that I just *could not* do her bidding. I suppose early Christians felt something like it when their tormentors tried to force them into denying Christ. I believe I would not have given in even if physically tortured; I might even have preferred that to the prolonged emotional torment which was Anna Avdyéevna's method of coercing me.

The following morning she watched me from behind her desk with a curiously gentle gaze, as if seeking to conciliate me, almost pleading with me to relent. This disturbed me deeply; I tried to look as if I were indifferent, but was conscious that the expression on my face was strained and false. At the end of the first lesson, as I passed her on the way out, avoiding looking at her, I heard her murmur: 'What strength of will!' She was teasing me, trying to be playful! I felt baffled, annoyed, almost contemptuous of her tactics.

During the break Ania asked me whether I had learned my lines. I told her I had no intention of taking the punishment I had not deserved. Other girls were listening to our conversation, some with approval, some merely curious, the two Komaróvskayas obviously condemning me. Anna Avdyéevna was, no doubt, aware that our contest was being watched. At the end of the day she spoke to me again.

'I have been waiting for you to come up with that piece of French recitation . . . ' she told me.

I remained silent.

'Does this mean that you are determined to defy the rules of class discipline?'

Still I did not reply. She went on to say that I was putting her into an impossible position, setting a very bad example to the class, that if everyone refused to accept their punishment . . .

'For something they haven't done?' I broke in indignantly.

'Even if they hadn't done it, they should be able to accept my decision for the sake of the rest.'

This kind of reasoning seemed to me monstrous. I just stared at her. She made her last appeal.

'Will you change your mind about this?'

'I can't.'

She looked at me for a few moments as if studying me, then jerked up her chin and turned her head away in a gesture of arrogant dismissal. This used to make me feel very small and worthless in my early days at school, but now it stung me into an even angrier rebellion.

'Very well,' she said. 'I now see I've been mistaken in you. You can go.'

As I walked away, her words rang in my head, pursuing me. Mistaken in me? Mistaken in me! Whatever did she mean? What crime had I committed? Why should she speak to me as if I were an outlaw? Much as I tried to persuade myself that I did not really care, I was hurt by Anna Avdyéevna's parting remark and could not get it out of my mind.

The way she behaved towards me after that made it impossible for me to forget. Although she was facing me in the class-room at a distance of a few feet, she managed to look as if I were, in a current Russian phrase, 'a mere empty spot'. She ceased addressing me personally, including me only in her general directions to the class. When it was my turn to be a monitor, she gave me a cold stare and handed the blue rosette to Ania, instead of me. She told the two Komaróvskayas that she was displeased with the class for not inducing me to submit to her punishment. Her campaign of attrition against me finally culminated in an act of revenge which only these two devoted handmaids of hers failed to condemn.

It was the three hundred years' anniversary of the Románov dynasty. Our school, founded by the Empress María Fyódorovna, wife of the Emperor Paul I, and maintained from the funds of the 'Empress María's Department' was busy preparing to celebrate this event. There was to be a gala evening with recitations, singing, dancing and *tableaux vivants* on the stage. Arkády Miháilovich, the drawing master, conceived an ambitious scheme of having the portraits of the early Románovs drawn by pupils of the school, to adorn the walls of the assembly hall. To my surprise he chose me to do the likeness of the Tsar Alexéy Miháilovich, the second Románov, a feat of which I had not thought myself capable. I should have known that, in any case, a few masterly strokes from Arkády's own hand would, in the end, put right whatever blemishes I had despaired of correcting by my own honest efforts.

The gym mistress however was not going to be outshone by a rival 'artist' on the staff: she decided to produce some traditional dances. She taught us ballroom dancing and noticed Liolia and myself dancing together in a mock-dramatic way. Not being a disciplinarian, she laughed at that, and it must have given her the idea of choosing us to dance a Boyar dance at the prospective celebration.

For some reason dancing before an audience did not alarm me as much as reciting in public, and I agreed at once. Soon Boyar clothes were found for us, and we dressed up in the lunch break for the first 'dress rehearsal' of our dance. Liolia and I had been practising it on our own for over a week, and now many of our classmates joined the gym mistress in watching us.

I rather fancied myself in my *kaftán* of dull gold brocade, wide blue trousers and red leather boots. I set my fur cap rakishly on the side of my head, having done my best to conceal my hair. Liolia displayed hers, throwing her huge plait forward over her shoulder. She acted as a provocative beauty, a part that came naturally to her, arching her eyebrows at me, leading me on with flicks of her handkerchief. As I circled round her, I saw from the corner of my eye that Anna Avdyéevna had entered the room and was watching us from the doorway. 'Let her look!' I thought, triumphantly. 'Let her see how well we dance and how I am enjoying myself despite her confining me to limbo!'

It was gratifying to hear our audience clap when we finished our dance. Alexándra Ivánovna looked very pleased and told us we would not need much more rehearsing.

As we slowly jostled one another through the doorway on the way back to our class-room, I saw Anna Avdyéevna going up to the gym mistress with a purposive air. She did not rejoin us until the lesson began, an unusual thing for her to do, and I noticed that she looked rather flushed. I wondered vaguely what she had been talking to the gym mistress about, but I remained unsuspecting of what was afoot.

On the following day I happened to pass Alexándra Ivánovna in the corridor. I greeted her with the usual curtsey, but instead of smiling and nodding back, she stopped and, taking my arm, led me aside. Then, in an embarrassed and apologetic way, she told me that to her regret the Boyar dance had to be left out of the programme of celebrations. I gaped at her, hurt, uncomprehending.

'Left out? But why?'

She explained with the same embarrassed air, actually blushing as she did so, that Anna Avdyéevna had vetoed my taking part in the celebrations and that she, as her colleague, could not go against her in this matter.

As I listened to her, my eyes began to burn with tears of indignation and outrage. I escaped to the cloakroom where I spent several minutes gasping for breath and thumping myself on the forehead to punish myself for my weakness and to stop the onset of tears. This was revenge! Anna Avdyéevna has allowed herself to sink as low as that! She was determined to make my life at school intolerable. She had become my enemy!

I managed to wash my face and get back to the class-room just before the teacher entered it. Anna Avdyéevna gave me a look of cold disapproval from behind her desk. Our eyes met for a fraction of a second, and I knew that she knew that I knew . . .

I sat through the lesson in a state of complete absorption with my bitter thoughts. Fortunately, I was not 'called out' and so was spared the humiliation of displaying my unpreparedness. At last the bell rang for the five minutes' break. I waited until the class-room emptied, then went up to Anna Avdyéevna, who had just risen from her chair. Trying hard to control my voice, I asked why she had refused her permission for me to dance the Boyar dance.

She pretended to be surprised at my question. Avoiding my eyes, she asked, didn't I realize that taking part in these important anniversary celebrations was a privilege, and that I, by refusing to conform to school discipline had disqualified myself for such an honour?

'So this is your revenge?' I blurted out.

She did not deign to reply, just raised here eyebrows at me and sailed out of the room.

Until this incident I had managed, although uncomfortable under the cloud of Anna Avdyéevna's displeasure and disapproval, to continue leading a fairly normal life at school. The excellent relationship I had with most of the teachers, as well as the knowledge that my classmates, with a few exceptions, were 'on my side' provided consolation and support. Her 'act of revenge', however — for I continued seeing it as such — gave me a bad shock. I felt her persecution to be so unfair that merely to think of it made me ill. The strain under which I was living began to show in my appearance, in loss of appetite, and in lapses in concentration during lessons.

I could not conceal from Zena what was happening; then Aunt Katia commented on my lack of appetite. Zena must have whispered something to her because she suddenly questioned me about Anna Avdyéevna.

I was in no condition to pretend that all was well, and when my aunt heard of the incident of the Boyar dance, she became suddenly belligerent and declared that it was her duty to intervene. She was going to write to Anna Avdyéevna.

I did not know whether to beg her not to, or to welcome it. What was she going to say? I had little hope that anything she could say would improve the situation, yet did not feel strong enough to protest.

After half an hour's scribbling in frowning concentration, Aunt Katia showed me her letter. It ran something like this:

Highly respected Mademoiselle Sabúrova!

My niece, Lydia Rayévskaia, has told me that you had decided to punish her for some breach of discipline which, in fact, she did not commit. When she refused to accept the punishment, you began to express your displeasure by acts of petty persecution unworthy of a lady of your position and birth. This is having a very harmful effect on my niece's health as well as on her ability to cope with her homework, which I believe to be just as important — if not more so — as your idea of discipline. I should therefore be greatly obliged to you if you would cease worrying and upsetting my niece, who is, in any case, innocent of the transgression for which you are punishing her.

Yours respectfully, Ekaterína Martsinóvskaia.'

'I agreed to hand this letter to Anna Avdyéevna in school on the following day. I noticed that she flushed slightly as I placed it on her desk and that she did not open and read it in the class-room but took it away with her when she left the room during the break.

Since Mademoiselle Vinogradova had left the school to get married, Anna Avdyéevna had obtained her post of a boarding school governess, in addition to her duties as our *dame-de-class*, and had come to live in a room at the school, next to the boarders' study-room. We were all curious to see what her room was like but so far only the devoted Liuba Komaróvskaya had stepped over the privileged threshold once, when she was asked by Anna Avdyéevna to help her bring in some books. 'It has lots and lots of photographs in frames,' she whispered confidentially when her classmates asked her to describe what she had seen. We suspected however that she had not been much farther than the threshold: Anna Avdyéevna liked keeping her distance and her prestige.

I was startled that day when, on returning to the class-room after the break, she walked up to my desk and spoke to me. My schoolmates were startled, too, and on the alert to hear what she was saying, for they had been watching the feud between us and wondering how it would end. But Anna Avdyéevna spoke so quietly that only the two girls on either side of me. Fibikh and Bielynóvich, heard what she had said.

'She asked you to come to her room after lunch!' whispered Alma, her small round eyes grown even rounder with wonder.

'She'll saw away at you again,' was Ania's comment.

If adults could remember and be honest with themselves, they would concede, I think, that the emotions of childhood and adolescence are infinitely more intense than those of later life. The body can be overwhelmed by them; they are as much physical as mental, and can drain away all strength or double it, as the case may be. I dreaded this rendezvous with Anna Avdyéevna. As I stood outside her door about to knock, my reluctance to face her turned to physical nausea. I forced myself to knock. Her voice answered in French: *'Entrez!'*

As she came forward to meet me, she looked somehow different – not the official Anna Avdyéevna I was accustomed to see in class, nor the over-sympathetic comforter I knew in my early days at the boarding school. Her face seemed younger and softer, her eyes wandered over my

face with a curiously searching expression. She gestured me towards a
small sofa beside a round table on which stood several framed photographs, while she herself sat down in an armchair opposite and continued
looking at me.

The room was large, rather dark, with only one window overlooking
a corner of the courtyard. It was full of furniture: chairs, tables of
different sizes, *étagères* with photographs and knick-knacks. The end of a
brass bedstead covered with a white bedspread showed from behind
a screen. One of the photographs, of a young man in officer's uniform,
looked very much like Anna Avdyéevna. 'Her brother?' the thought
flitted through my mind. This sudden glimpse into Anna Avdyéevna's
private life had the effect of sapping my last line of defence.

'Your aunt's letter upset me very much,' said Anna Avdyéevna. 'She
accuses me of persecuting you. Is that the impression you gave her of
what was happening?'

My cup was already full when I entered the room, and now this
question, framed like an accusation, made emotion spill over the brim.

'My aunt could see herself . . . ' I began and could not continue.

'What could she see?'

Try as hard as I could, I was no longer able to hold back my tears,
tears of outrage and self-pity which had been choking me for days.

'That you were upset?' . . . I heard Anna Avdyéevna's soft voice,
muffled further by the noise of blood in my ears. 'But what about me?
Have you thought of the position in which you put me before the class?
You defied my authority in their presence. Now they know that this can
be done, how can I maintain discipline or keep the respect of your
classmates?'

I was in no condition to indicate that I could see her point, which
in fact I could, but even so, my sense of justice and my pride made it
impossible for me to say I regretted what I had done. Anyway, I could
not speak at all; I hid my face in my hands and sobbed. A swish of a dress,
a sudden giving of a cushion on which I was sitting and an arm round my
shoulders startled me into realizing that Anna Avdyéevna had sat down
beside me.

'Don't, don't,' she said, soothingly. 'There's no need to cry so . . .
We won't speak of it again.'

She drew me closer to herself so that my head rested on her breast.
I felt her breath on my hair and her lips touching my forehead. My head
swam with the heat of emotion, of tears and of her nearness. For a few
moments I felt as if I were going to faint. Anna Avdyéevna gently patted

my back. She produced a handkerchief and started drying my eyes as if I were an infant. I suddenly thought this ridiculous and began to laugh. Anna Avdyéevna laughed, too.

'What a child you are, really! Tears and laughter — all at once!'

Her comparing me to a child made me sober up at once. I found my own handkerchief, dried my eyes and stood up. My head was still humming, but the mist around me had melted away.

'You should bathe your eyes in cold water before you go back to your class,' said Anna Avdyéevna.

I let her guide me to the wash-stand and dabbed my eyes with a corner of her wet towel. Although all seemed well between us now, I was anxious to get out of this enveloping privacy as quickly as possible. I slipped out of her door, hoping I would not be noticed, as if I had been trespassing on a forbidden territory.

My Several Selves, Imaginary and Real

Lermontov wrote of his early passion, at the age of eight, for a little girl whose name he could not even remember. Yet he recollected as a grown-up man the turmoil and confusion into which her presence used to plunge him: at that distance in time he could still feel some of the violent emotion he had felt then. 'Passionate love at such an early age,' he wrote, 'denotes a nature rich in gifts for poetry and music.' As I read this, I envied him. I wished I could have fallen in love at the age of eight — but there had been no one among my early play companions who could possibly arouse such strong emotion in me. The demands of my imagination were always far ahead of reality.

In Russian *love* is a 'serious' word: it is never used lightly as it is in English. 'I'd love to come,' says one friend to another when invited to a party. 'Give my love to so-and-so,' scribbles another at the end of a letter. A Russian would reply to the invitation: 'I'll come with the greatest pleasure,' and he would write at the end of the letter: 'Yours with sincerest greetings,' or 'Please *bow* to your friend on my behalf.' He would regard it as an absurd exaggeration or as the height of insincerity to speak of *love* to mere acquaintances or friends.

I pondered on the meaning of love from quite an early age and knew that I loved my mother and my sister, all the animals on the estate, and all the aspects of Nature which surrounded me, and of other human beings probably the coachman Maxim. I realized slowly, with compunction and some anxiety, that I did not really love my father or my brother. As for my play companions, I was fond of some of them, while I merely accepted others, and I did not expect them to be more attached to me than I was to them.

As a small girl of nine or ten, I had been attracted by one or two handsome young men among my parents' friends who came to the house on New Year's day or on Easter Sunday, or who took part in picnics arranged by the Club. This awareness of male charm did not amount to much more than a fleeting, half-conscious need to be noticed by them, and a pleasure at any small mark of attention from them. Even at that age I tended to be selective: though I liked to dance with Monsieur Rodiónov and to read my poems to Mitya, I did not think they were good-looking and treated them exactly as I did any other adult of either sex.

If loving was a serious matter, 'being in love' or 'falling in love' was seen as an embarrassing thing which boys and men did quite often but which girls had to avoid at all costs. Bronia, our bailiff's son, had been 'in love' with me, but I felt most indignant at the suggestion that *I* could be in love with *him*. I declared in everyone's hearing that I could only fall in love with a prince.

'When you fall in love, *he* will be your prince, whoever he is,' said Nela, Father Ioann's daughter, a spinster of twenty-five.

'Never!' I retorted hotly. 'He'll have to be a *real* prince. I won't marry anyone else.'

My first experience of falling in love, brief as it was, occurred rather late to qualify me for Lermontov's 'nature rich in gifts of poetry and music'. Yet it was partly the effect of music, the highly exciting, dynamic music of Rossini, which made me crave for the company and conversation of the actor who sang the part of *The Barber of Seville*.

I was twelve at the time. A small opera company was visiting B* during my school holidays, and my parents took me to the première. I have no recollection of where my brother and sister were at the time; what I remember clearly is sitting between my parents in the front row of the stalls, emotionally on tip-toe with excitement and delight, as the orchestra galloped zestfully through the brilliant overture. Then the curtain went up and at once my imagination was set on fire. With innocent eye and ear I watched and listened; I participated in the actions of the characters, I took sides for or against them. I was captivated by the quick, gay and clever Figaro. I must have beamed with admiration when he came to the footlights, a tall, slender figure in red breeches and a bolero trimmed with gold braid, to sing his famous aria: 'Figaro here, Figaro there . . . ' I clapped furiously with the others as he bowed and smiled at *me!* The thrill I experienced at this mark of attention was so distinct and new in quality that it gave me a shock of surprise.

As I went to bed that evening, my head was full of tunes and visions of *The Barber of Seville*, the image of the barber himself persistently in the foreground of my recollections. I lived through the whole story again, wide awake, agitated with regret that it was all over, hankering after the repetition of the experience, after the concrete presence, the voice and smile, of the handsome young man in red and gold.

My excitement and pleasure were at their height again when a couple of days later I was taken to see *Rigoletto*. I enquired whether there was a baritone part in this opera, and awaited with tense anticipation the entry of the court jester, whose part I expected to be sung by the irresistible barber. Rigoletto, however, was not Figaro: he hobbled about the stage in a dark cloak, looking as if he really were a hunchback, and although I was impressed by his singing, and moved almost to tears by his distress on discovering that the girl he had killed was his own daughter, my feeling for him was not admiration but pity mingled with horror. There was no one in this drama whom I could admire: the duke was a scoundrel, the girl a silly goose. I went home saddened and vaguely disappointed.

It was the custom in provincial Russia for the leading citizens of a town to invite the visiting company of actors to their homes. My parents' house was open to them one evening and many came. As I entered the drawing-room buzzing with conversation, my mother was talking to a tall young man with hair as blond as my brother's. She called me up.

'Here's one of your great admirers — my youngest daughter,' she said. 'She's seen *Rigoletto* and *The Barber of Seville*.'

The young man smiled and, as I gave him my hand, kissed it.

'I'm greatly honoured. It's a joy to please someone whose judgment is fresh, fair and unbiased. You've seen both *Rigoletto* and *The Barber*? Well now . . . would you mind telling me which you liked best?'

'*The Barber of Seville*,' I replied without a moment's hesitation.

The young man laughed delightedly.

'I very much hoped so . . . But tell me . . . of the two baritones, which do you think was the best?'

I was nonplussed. I had compared the characters and their external appearance: it never occurred to me to compare their voices. Conscientiously fumbling for a reply, I caught my mother's eye on me, trying to convey something, but I was unable to guess what it was.

'Was the Barber's voice better than Rigoletto's or the other way round?' the young man pressed me for an answer.

'I think they were about the same . . . ' I ventured at last.

He looked disappointed, yet he laughed again.

'Didn't you recognize him?' my mother asked me afterwards. 'He was the Barber.'

'He! But the Barber was dark . . . with jet black hair!'

'He wore a wig on the stage. He wanted you so much to say that his voice was better than Rigoletto's.'

He was *my* Barber! And I had failed to please him! I could have wept with vexation and impotent regret, an early foretaste of many subsequent failures and regrets . . .

As I read Pushkin and Lermontov, I 'fell in love' with Oniéghin and Pechórin. These Byronic young men, handsome, elegant and disenchanted, fascinated me by their complexity. I was aware that part of their attraction consisted in that they themselves were apparently unable to fall in love, at least not until it was too late. No doubt, I thought, that was the reason for their unhappiness. I put myself in Tatiana's place and shared her humilation and distress while Oniéghin was sermonizing her in the garden. I went through agony with Princess Mary while Pechórin was explaining to her why he had been playing cat and mouse with her feelings. And then, my thoughts escaping my control, took the bit between their teeth: a secret voice whispered: 'But you are not Tatiana . . . not Princess Mary . . . you are different . . . perhaps if Oniéghin or Pechórin met you, they might have . . . ' Oh! what a triumph it would be! What deep satisfaction! Like striking fresh water from a rock and making a desert bloom! To open a world of love and happiness to the loveless and unhappy, to be the person through whom this regeneration is effected — an infinitely seductive, tantalizing fantasy — how many an adolescent girl is haunted by it, how many a young woman hopes to realize it in her own life? Even then I was vaguely aware that it was a dangerous fantasy and that the whole matter of loving and being loved was full of hidden pitfalls: I was aware of my own extreme vulnerability. My first love, my mother, had wounded me deeply by sending me away to boarding school and then ignoring my desperate appeals for rescue. Anna Avdyéevna, whom I began to love for the affection she showed me, had alarmed and repelled me by her excessive expectations and demands. Perhaps it was better, after all, to keep my heart on a tight rein. But my heart was leaping forward eagerly towards new experience. And again it was provided by a play.

A repertory company was visiting M* in the winter of 1914. Their repertoire included plays by Shakespeare and Schiller, as well as *La Dame aux Camelias* by Dumas. The school authorities could forbid us to attend any of the plays, and we were told through our *dames-de-classe* that *La Dame aux Camelias* was 'unsuitable' for us and we were not to try to see it. We could go to see Shakespeare or Schiller if we wished. My uncle was not very agreeable to sending the horse to fetch me from the theatre late at night, but after some discussion, he agreed to do it just once, and I chose to see *Hamlet*.

From the moment I heard the young actor, dressed entirely in black and wearing a medallion on a gold chain, utter the bitter aside: 'A little more than kin and less than kind . . . ' I was captivated and held under his spell for the duration of the play and for several days afterwards. I felt as if a deep affinity, almost a bond existed between us which made his conflicts, his doubts and sentiments my own. How can I account for the intensely moving effect these words had on me except by assuming that they touched off my unconscious resentment against my own father? Hamlet's rebellion against his parents was smouldering in my own breast. I had never had the courage or the opportunity of defying my father, and now Hamlet was doing it for me! His devotion to the father who died by his step-father's hand, coalesced with the image of an ideal father in my mind. Then came his monologue beginning with the familiar phrase: 'To be or not to be . . . ', so faithfully expressing my own agonized questionings on life and death, that in my adolescent arrogance I wondered why I had not written it myself. Moreover, these words were spoken by a young man who looked like the prince of my fantasies and for whom I felt an admiration and compassion verging on love, such as made me wish I could be his Ophelia, yet not fail him as she had done.

The final scene, the duel with Laertes and Hamlet's death, was a shattering experience: I wept bitterly over my own and my hero's death. So overwhelming was the impression the play had made on me, that for days afterwards I could not think or talk of anything else, and I could not talk of it without my voice breaking and my eyes filling with tears. I talked of it to my classmates, to Zena, even to my aunt, the least sympathetic of my listeners. My principal desire during the week that followed was to repeat the experience, however searing, to see my beloved prince live — and die — again. My aunt however declared that

I was making myself ill, as it was, about 'this Hamlet', and that I looked and behaved as if I had fever. On no account would she agree to my seeing the play a second time, and for once my uncle was in agreement with her, because he grudged sending the horse to fetch me. I told Aunt Katia that she 'just didn't understand what it meant to me', and withdrew into my room to rave and storm in solitude against the tyranny of 'the stupid and the insensitive' and to weep over my frustrated hopes, shutting my door even against Zena who wanted to comfort me.

My bitter and restless mood might have lasted much longer if, by a fortunate chance, one of the themes set to us for an essay in the following week had not happened to be: 'The Play that made the Strongest Impression on me.'

We had an hour to write it. During that hour I wrote fifteen pages, but when the bell rang for the break and the monitors began to collect our papers, my essay was still unfinished. I had not only re-told the plot, but described the actions, quoted the speeches, and poured out my own thoughts and feelings about the characters in the play. I wrote without stopping, my face flushed and hot, my eyes constantly filling with tears. It was a true catharsis, a stormy passage with the prospect of calm at the end. I was going to conclude with my own meditations on the theme of 'conscience does make cowards of us all', for it was the thought which disturbed me perhaps more than any other in the play so full of disturbing thoughts. Shimkóvich looked sympathetic, as I protested that I had not finished yet, while Mania Komaróvskaya stood irresolutely over me, a pile of bright exercise books held in the crook of her arm.

'You can add a postscript to it when it comes back from me,' Shimkóvich said with a smile, and I handed over my life blood to Mania, my throat tightening as I watched it being passed on to the teacher's desk.

When he brought our essays back a week later, my book was again on the top. 'This essay,' he said, 'is very interesting in that the author writes of Hamlet as if he were a real person she knew, not a character in fiction. She has taken his struggles and sufferings to her heart and is participating in them. Such sympathy with the main character may be the most direct way to understanding a great work of art, but *living* the character to that extent must be exhausting and can be very distressing. I hope it was not *too* distressing in this case . . . '

He began reading out passages. Everyone knew that it was my essay and some of the girls stole half-sympathetic, half-mocking glances at me. I sat without looking up, feeling as if I had been dragged out into a market place stripped to my skin. My apprenticeship for qualifying as an author was beginning in earnest. I did not yet see myself as the victim of a daemon that entices you to pour yourself into words, then flings the doors open to all the world to gaze into the exposed pool of your effusions and to throw stones and insults into it. But I was beginning to realize that the urge to put my experiences into words was becoming irresistible, and that its satisfaction could result in further strife and more pain. The very thought of exposing my writing to criticism made me writhe inwardly; the embarrassment of being praised was almost as painful. How could I write books that were to be read, and survive the ordeal? How could I reconcile my extreme vulnerability with the need to display some of my most intimate feelings to public examination? Which would prove the strongest, the revulsion from shame and pain, or the urge to make the inarticulate and the obscure revealed and clarified in words? I had no answer to these questions as yet, I had not even formulated them, but I already knew that writing was my vocation and that unless I followed it, my life would not be worth living.

My novel about the two children, Henri and Margot, who grew up and married at the court of Henry IV of France, was finished. It had been illustrated by the joint efforts of Kolia Avílov and myself, and typed on thick paper by the ever-obliging Mitya. A thick book, bound in lilac satin, it lay on my mother's writing desk where it was relatively safe from my brother's irreverent handling and sardonic comments. My mother proudly showed it to most of her friends and even lent it to their children who, she said, found it quite absorbing. I was proud of it, too, as a visible proof and token of my industry: had not some literary critics written that Russians always begin but never finish anything? This generalization nettled me into pledging myself, there and then, always to complete whatever I might begin, especially if it were a piece of writing. Having finished it, however, I hardly ever looked at it again, partly through fear of finding that my brother's jeers were justified, and that much of what I had written was so childish that it would make me blush for the person I had been.

My appreciation of literary style was developing so rapidly, that the aspiring author in me writhed with shame as the literary critic, my *alter ego*, turned over the pages I had written a year or even six months before. How could I have produced anything so naïve, so awkward, so utterly trite? Could I really have been so infantile? What if these pages fell into the hands of my brother, or of Shoora Martýnov? They would have every justification for laughing at me . . . That must not happen, no one must see them ever! But how to make sure of this? Of course, Pushkin burned some of his poems, Gogol threw the first version of the second part of *The Dead Souls* into the fire. Yet, somehow I could not bring myself to follow their illustrious example: these pages, covered from end to end with uneven, half-formed handwriting, were not just ink and paper — they were a part of myself I valued most, and I shuddered at the thought of destroying them. Why should I, I asked in self-justification. They might, after all, prove instructive as a story of one person's development.

I continued to live the double life of day-to-day reality and of romantic imagination, although my fantasy of being the King of Rome was beginning to wear thin. Perhaps, I told myself, it had been only one of my many incarnations. Still, I gazed at the portraits of the Duke of Reichstadt in his white uniform, blond, slender, large-eyed, full-lipped, and scrutinized it for resemblances between him and his father, and between him and myself. Why, I wondered, should I be so fascinated, so intensely moved by his fate unless there was a mysterious bond between his life and mine? It had not dawned on me — how could it? — that the bond might have been, as it was between me and Hamlet, my half-conscious longing for an ideal father, and the awe-struck pity for one who, in losing a father, lost all his brilliant future as well.

I wrote two long short stories at the time: one a pure wish-fulfilment fantasy about a girl being whisked off — in a dream — to Spain by a handsome matador; the other reflecting a basic conflict about love — that of dominance and submission. The young girl in the story has an accomplished and good looking man for a guardian, who is, rather improbably, only a few years older than herself. He treats her as a child; she hates him for this, then, to her distress and humiliation, realizes that she is in love with him. The story had a happy ending: she discovers that he loves her too, though somewhat *de haut-en-bas*.

Mitya, whom, as a fellow writer, I allowed to read this story, declared himself to be greatly impressed. He could hardly believe, he said, that anyone so young was able to describe transformation of hatred into love so convincingly. How did I know what it felt like? He seemed to take it for granted that at the age of thirteen I had not yet been in love.

Nor had I — except in my imagination — but the emotions I lived through when I wrote, or read, or looked at my favourite pictures were so intense and so contradictory, that I could not talk about them even to my sister, for fear she would show little sympathy or even smile at them. How could I explain why I felt so furious with my brother when he teased me by talking baby language to me, while a few hours later I would gaze at a Gérard painting of Napoleon playing with his son, and wish ardently to be that adored and precious infant? Why did I feel so indignant at the very mention of 'obedience' or 'submission', yet derive a curious, shamefaced pleasure from picturing myself as Tatiana to whom Oniéghin preached while telling her he loved her only as a sister? Writing was one outlet for these disturbing emotions, dreams provided another. One particular dream I remember from that period of my life haunted me for several years. Most people have a few such revealing dreams in their lifetime — often their meaning becomes clear only after years of experience and meditation.

I saw myself in that dream as a very young child, three years old perhaps, standing alone in some kind of starlit, featureless space. Soft air was blowing about me and nothing but the sky and the stars were in sight. I felt no fear — I was merely elated and expectant. Out of the luminous darkness a man rode on horseback, bent down to me, lifted me up, and set me before him on his horse, covering me with a part of his cloak. As I raised my head to look at him, starlight shone into my eyes and his face was only dimly visible, but I could see that he was young and handsome and was smiling at me. And I knew that he was my father. Overcoming my shyness, proud, delighted, full of trust, I pointed at a star above his head and asked him a question — I have no memory of what it was — and he replied, gravely, tenderly, while we rode on into the luminous night.

The dream was vivid, almost overwhelming in its intensity, and I awoke from it glowing with happiness, but an emotion verging on despair gripped me when I realized I had been only dreaming. Then I felt angry with myself for having had such a tantalizing dream. What was the sense of it? That wonderful dream father — what had he to do with my real father as I knew him? True enough, my father sometimes wore a long grey cloak and he rode a horse — but I dismissed these thoughts as quite irrelevant. I only wished I could dream that dream again. I never did.

I have wondered since if every girl carries an ideal image of a life companion in her unconscious, a husband who would also be a lover, son, friend and father in one? And whether every young man dreams of a wife who could combine the qualities of a mother, sister and mistress?

I was writing these stories and dreaming these dreams in the summer of

1914. I was also reading a great deal, and one of the books which fell into my hands was Leonid Andryéev's *The Seven that Were Hanged*.

I came upon this book by accident as I was searching for something in a chest of drawers belonging to my sister: it had been pushed in among some linen as if she had wanted to hide it. Everything about it — the print, the paper, the title page — were unusual, and I sensed that it must be one of the 'forbidden' books, printed secretly by the 'revolutionaries'. My sister flushed when she saw me holding it and quickly told me not to take it out of her bedroom. 'Read it here if you want to,' she said. 'No one else must see it.'

Once I started to read it, I had to go on. Its fascination was terrible. Andryéev described the behaviour, the characters, feelings and thoughts of five revolutionaries and two common murderers who had been condemned to death and were to be executed at the same time. Of the five revolutionaries two were young women, and it was the description of one of them that I found particularly affecting. At the trial and in the days preceding their execution she had no thought for herself, only concern for her companions and how she could make things easier for them, especially for one of the men who was terrified of dying and was in danger of breaking down at any moment. She made me think of my sister: I could imagine her behaving in such a selfless, self-forgetting way. I saw myself as more like the other girl, courageous but detached, going to her execution hand-in-hand with a common murderer while her lover was leading and supporting the other terrified criminal.

Before I read this story I had already believed that revolutionaries were heroes; now I saw them also as saints. Those who sent them to their death were blind or criminal, or both . . . Before I read this story I thought of my future as a writer; now, burning with compassion, pity and horror, I made an entry in my diary: 'I will dedicate my life to the struggle for the liberation of my country!'

Liberation from the power of a government my father was serving . . . In this obvious thought all the tangled threads of my fantasies and feelings might have come together: the tragedy of *The Gadfly*, the theme of *The Guardian* and his ward, my many identifications — with Napoleon's son, with Hamlet and even with Mtzyri. But they did not do so for me, at least not yet, at that time. Consciously, I had quite accepted that it was impossible for my father to share any of my interests, and that I existed for him only in so far as he had to provide for my sustenance and education. From early childhood I had become accustomed to being ignored by him; the only change that came about in adolescence was that I began to resent it, instead of just feeling constrained and uneasy in his presence. He had a disconcerting habit of not replying when one of us children asked him a question, and I was beginning to feel I wanted to break through this barrier of silence. When he was at home he would be nearly always reading a newspaper or working in his study. During meals he hardly ever spoke. On the rare occasions when I found myself alone with him, I could think of nothing to say. One such attempt at a 'break through' remained in my memory.

It was on an evening at Fyeny. We were sitting on the veranda, watching the summer lightning flare up every few minutes in the sky. The night was very dark and still, with the feel of thunder in the air, and my nerves were taut with the expectation of an approaching storm, with the excitement of this dramatic spectacle. Tree tops and clouds were suddenly snatched from the surrounding darkness, stood out, etched in black, against the white, pulsating sheet of light and disappeared again. I imagined that over there, far away, a thunderstorm was raging, trees lashed by heavy rain, houses struck by lightning — while to us, at this distance, it was all like a great, awe-inspiring pantomime, violent action without a sound to be heard.

I turned to speak to my mother and suddenly realized that she had gone indoors. My father alone was there: he was leaning back in a wicker chair, smoking silently. He, too, seemed to be watching the sky. For a moment, my need to communicate proved stronger than the fear of interrupting his meditations. I made some remark about the strangeness of the silent lightning and wondered why we could not hear the thunder.

My father did not reply. Perhaps he was so deep in thought that he had not heard me, or perhaps he did not like to say that he did not know the answer to my question. In another mood I would have accepted this as normal, but on that occasion I felt I could not leave it alone, and that I had to obtain some response from him. After a pause and in a voice unsteady with a mounting sense of humiliation, I tried again.

'This lightning seems to put out the stars . . . but of course some of the stars may not be there at all . . . The light from some of them takes several hundred years to reach us . . . the stars we see now may have disintegrated hundreds of years ago . . . '

Still my father said nothing. I had no doubt now that he thought me ridiculous, trotting out my recently acquired knowledge to impress him, yet I felt deeply hurt by his lack of response. At that moment my mother returned from the house, and I turned to her with an indignant question:

'Mamma, why does Father never speak to us? Why does he never answer when I ask him something?'

My mother stopped on the way to her chair, startled by the exasperation in my voice. The summer lightning flashed, lighting up for a moment my father, leaning back in his chair, my mother standing there, and myself — between them. I did not wait for her reply but rushed past her into the house and up the stairs to my room in the mezzanine, where I could let myself go in a passionate, silent denunciation of my father's unjust, contemptuous treatment of me. I wished the thunderstorm would come and the heavy rain pour down, so that I could throw myself into the battle of the elements and mingle my violence with theirs, and share with Nature herself the emotional tumult within me. I flung open the window and leaned out, gulping the damp, fragrant air and staring into the inky darkness, waiting for the throbbing light to flash again. I heard myself muttering: 'It's no use . . . no use whatever . . . never again!'

Half an hour later my mother came up to me. I told her I had a headache. She spoke, as she often did, of my being too highly-strung and of the storm in the air affecting me. Then she added that my father had said my remarks on the veranda did not require an answer, and that, anyway, he never talked much. This did not mean that he did not care for us — everything he did was really for our sake, for the good of the family.

I replied bitterly that I was sure he would not notice if I disappeared altogether. My mother said I was talking nonsense. My father had a great deal on his mind: he had important duties as a servant of the government and of his country.

'Duty, always duty!' I protested. 'Why should duty always come first? Why not love?'

My mother made it clear that she regarded duty as paramount to anything else: duty towards one's country, parents' duty towards their children, children's duty towards their parents. Love was something that could be added to it, but was not really indispensable. With that I passionately disagreed. To me duty was the synonym of compulsion, and it cut right across my idea of freedom. Love was the only compelling thing: what one did from love was a free act, what one did from a sense of duty was done under compulsion. 'Freedom' was a sacred word: it sanctified anything done in its name — even terrorism.

'Freedom can be used to justify licence and self-will,' said my mother. 'If duty is forgotten and order destroyed, chaos will follow.'

Was this one of her 'prophetic' remarks? Who could have linked it at the time with the news we read in the papers in July 1914? I hardly ever read the papers: they looked most unattractive, those columns of smudgy paragraphs smelling strongly of printer's ink. But on that day there were pictures on the front page, photographs of the Austrian Archduke and his wife assassinated at Sarajevo. The heir to the Austrian throne . . . I was surprised that somebody so obviously middle-aged could still be 'an heir'. A photograph of the family group with their several children wrung my heart. At once I imagined what I would feel if someone came to tell me that both my parents had been killed . . . But what about the killer? What did he feel as he prepared to strike, as he fired his gun at the smiling couple in the carriage, then tried to escape through the surrounding crowd? I could easily put myself in his place, for was he not one of those fighters for freedom, a patriot who wished his country to throw off the Austrian yoke?

My mother pronounced him to be 'a madman' who deserved the severest punishment because he had 'orphaned all those children'. My brother remarked that the children would, no doubt, be taken care of by the other Habsburgs, 'of whom there seem to be an inexhaustible supply'. He professed to feel no sympathy for either the revolutionaries or the monarchists, affecting a somewhat cynical, detached attitude towards all.

My father left Fyeny for the town on the following morning. Events followed in quick succession but with their impact still blunted, at least for me, by incomprehension and inexperience. 'General mobilization' meant chiefly that our Ivan would have to leave our service, that he might even have to fight in a war against Austria. But why should Austria fight us when it was a Serb who killed the Archduke? Then in a matter of days Russia was at war with Germany, with which she had had no quarrel.

Mitya, who briefly visited Fyeny on my father's behest, ostensibly to bring back some papers, but really to reassure my mother who was very worried by the turn of events, told us that 'the war could not last'. 'It'll be over in a couple of months,' he assured us. 'The Austrians are no fighters. Besides, all the Poles and Slovenes in their army will be coming over to our side . . . '

Mitya, being an only son, was exempt from being called up. My brother had a double exemption – as a university student and as an only son. Mitya begged my mother not to worry, telling her that my father did not want her to curtail her stay at Fyeny for his sake. But it was obvious that my mother *was* worrying. We heard her sigh as she went about the house. 'This war is a calamity,' she repeated. 'What is going to happen to us all?'

Ivan had to report to his contingent at M*. We were heart-broken to see him go. He moved from foot to foot as we wished him good luck, then suddenly started sniffing.

'Write to us, Ivan,' I said, myself on the verge of tears.

'Silly,' my brother muttered after he had gone. 'The fellow can only just sign his name . . . '

As a matter of fact, Ivan came back to us after only a few weeks in the barracks: he was not yet needed at the front. 'What was it like, Ivan?' we pressed him. 'Just ordinary, *báryshnia . . . paních . . .* ' He smiled his huge smile. 'Just as it used to be when I first went. Only the sergeant doesn't hit you across the mug as he used to. Sort of more friendly now . . . '

In fact, everyone seemed 'more friendly' to one another. We read surprising news in the papers: students and factory workmen were demonstrating their devotion to the fatherland: they walked in patriotic processions to the Winter Palace in Petersburg, carrying church banners and portraits of the Tsar. The Duma declared their full support to the war effort. Germany was now the enemy: there was no question of fighting the government while Russia was at war. And the fact that Russia was fighting on the same side as England, a constitutional monarchy, and France, a republic, was to me a matter of great satisfaction, almost of pride. These countries had the freedoms Russia should have: the freedom of speech, of public assembly, of religious creed; they were our allies, and somehow this made us participate in their 'freedoms'. Perhaps when the war was over we would obtain them, too, in our own right.

Goga Reingold suddenly arrived at Fyeny unannounced. My sister and I were on the veranda when I saw him coming towards us, threading his way between flower beds.

'Look, it's Goga!' I turned excitedly to Maroossia.

She raised her eyes from her book and became quite still like a bird suddenly aware of a mortal threat. Her face turned pale, then flushed deeply.

Goga was wearing the uniform of a second lieutenant in the Grodno Regiment. He was smiling broadly as he saluted us.

Apologizing for not having written to warn us of his arrival, he explained that 'things had moved rather quickly'. He was due to leave for the front tomorrow morning, so today was his only chance . . .

'You see, it's on my way, more or less . . . If I leave you tomorrow quite early, I'll catch up with my regiment at G*. Armies are cumbersome things, as you know . . . they travel at a snail's pace.'

He made it sound as if he were going on a pleasure trip. I gazed at him, trying to imagine *how* he would fight: would he use his revolver which he now detached from his tunic belt and placed on the table beside my sister's book? Or would he use his sword which he carried into the hall to hang beside the umbrellas? He came back, having also left his cap in the hall; his narrow, sensitive face was eager and smiling. He took a chair facing my sister's; very trim and slender in his uniform, his hair beautifully glossy and his finely arched eyebrows whimsically raised, he looked attractive and not much older than when I first saw him, a school-boy in a grey uniform coat.

'It's some time since we last met . . . Let me see . . . on the 22nd of May 1913, was it not? Now tell me about yourself — all you've been doing during that time?'

He leaned forward, clasping his hands together. I looked at his hands: they were not the kind of hands I could imagine in the act of killing. Nor was Goga the kind of man . . .

My mother's voice called from the house. I ran to tell her the news. 'He's come to say good-bye, then?' my mother said and went out hurriedly to greet him. I stood still where she had left me in a sudden realization what her words meant.

Of course! It was not just Goga who would have to shoot at the Germans: they would shoot at him, too. This farewell visit of his could mean that we were seeing him for the last time . . .

I now understood the emotion with which Maroossia saw him arrive. What were they talking about now? They had been friends from their schooldays: she used to meet him at the skating rink . . . skating was the only sport she was ever keen on. Was it because of Goga?

My unfinished, questioning thoughts kept me motionless in the empty hall where the voices of my mother and Goga conversing on the veranda reached me as mere patterns of sound without words or meaning. What was she saying to him? What *could* one say to a man who might be dead in a few weeks or even days?

I turned on my heels and on tip-toe, not wanting to be heard, ran through the empty rooms to the french window of the drawing-room and out into the part of the garden where a wide cut through the trees revealed a view of the distant river valley and the blue ring of the forest beyond. It was the view which never failed to exhilarate, to make me feel that however sad or stale life might be at the moment, *this* was something that could never pall, a beauty which somehow contained a promise of happiness and consolation. But this time the thought that pursued me was of death: somewhere over there, beyond that ring of forest was 'the front', and men like Goga, or like our Ivan, were killing and being killed in fields like these, the fields I could see from the window of my bedroom . . .

Since my conversion to 'atheism', or what I chose to call by that name, I had been thinking a great deal about death, usually in bed, before going to sleep. I lay awake, trying to imagine that final, inevitable moment, until utter terror gripped me and pierced my body with a needle-sharp sensation, half-shudder, half-pain. This breast of mine will struggle for breath, this heart I can hear thumping will grow silent, these limbs will go stiff and cold, and I shall be put into a grave to be eaten by worms! The thought horrified me, made me rear up with revolt. Why did we have to suffer this indignity? What was the sense of it all? If life had to end in complete annihilation, what was the sense of living at all?

When I returned to the house tea was being served on the veranda and everything looked ordinary and as pleasant as ever. Maroossia and Goga were talking of some of their former school-friends; of the evenings they spent rowing on the Dniepr and picnicking on its banks, of the fleeting encounters during lunch break in the main street of M*, where the boys' *Ghymnasia* was situated.

'Do you remember running into my old form master just as we were about to dive into Zavádsky's café?' Goga laughed. 'He was a terror, that man!'

'It was he, who —'

'Yes, it was. He failed me in maths . . . and that's why I'm wearing this . . . ' He twitched the lapel of his uniform tunic. 'If it were not for him, I should now be sitting in a lecture-room at the Petersburg University, listening to some kindly professor rambling on about the Code Napoléon. No other faculty but Law would have accepted me, of course . . . '

It was a general assumption and a standing joke among university students that only the least intelligent and the laziest of young people chose to study law: the body of codified law in Russia was barely a hundred years old.

'You would have made a very good advocate,' my sister said.

'I would indeed! I can go on talking for hours and say exactly nothing!'

My mother remarked that I was looking tired and suggested that I should go to bed. For once I agreed without protesting. As I said good-night, Goga stood up and clicked his heels.

'I may not see you tomorrow, Lédochka. Good-bye, and — whatever happens, remember no ill of me . . . '

This little phrase, so commonly used light-heartedly, nearly made me cry.

'Why?' I murmured. 'I know nothing bad about you . . . '

They all laughed. I gave Goga my hand; he raised it to his lips and kissed it.

So this was good-bye! Swallowing my tears, I walked up the steps of the winding staircase to the mezzanine, and got ready for bed without lighting a lamp or a candle. The bright moonlight outside threw the pattern of my window on the bedroom floor: the brightness was checkered with black bars, prison-like, sinister. I went to the window and flung it open to get rid of them. Then, seeking relief from emotions and thoughts which oppressed me, I followed a familiar urge: to get right outside and as high as I could. I stood on the protective bar of the french window and hauled myself up on to the roof.

The air was damp and fresh, and I shivered in my nightdress as I crouched beside a chimney-stack, my shoulder pressed against its brick still warm with the day's sunshine. All was still: not a sound or movement came from the faintly luminous distance where a light mist was trailing along the curves of the invisible river. I looked in vain for the twinkling fires around which peasant boys camped in the pastures with their horses. The even, white light which flooded everything from above seemed cold, relentless . . . Nature did seem to be indifferent to our sufferings, as poets and philosophers had said.

I threw back my head to look at the sky. How vast it was! A few stars were holding their own against the all-pervading moonlight. I thought of what I had learned recently: some of these stars were mere ghosts: they might have become extinguished thousands of years ago. The thought frightened me. If whole stars disappeared, could the life of a human being matter much?

By dint of gazing long at the sky I began to distinguish more stars, and, as my vision filled with light and space, a kind of peace descended upon me, and a notion of time fell away until a sound of voices talking reached me from below.

I glanced down: two figures etched in dark silhouettes against a background submerged in moonlight were strolling along the edge of the terrace. Maroossia and Goga! I could just hear their voices without distinguishing the words. I gazed at them, my breast aching with longing and compassion. What were they saying to each other? Could they be . . . was it possible that they were in love?

I saw Goga taking Maroossia's hand. I had seen Kolia Avílov do that, and Maroossia withdrawing it at once, embarrassed, almost annoyed. She did not take her hand away from Goga. He continued speaking in a low voice, then bent his head and kissed it. A few moments later they went in.

I slipped down the side of the roof and got inside the room a moment or two before Maroossia entered it.

'Aren't you asleep yet?' she asked, startled, as she saw me sitting up in bed.

'I've been on the roof,' I said.

She stood in the middle of the room looking at me. In her white dress, her face pale in the moonlight, she looked like the ghost of a bride haunting her bridal room. She knew I went up on the roof when I felt troubled or unhappy, and she was not sure whether it would hurt me to speak of it. But her own feelings were brimming over, and a moment later she was sitting beside me, her arms around me, her cheek against mine. She called me her '*króshka*', her favourite caressing name for me, and pleaded with me not to give way to sadness. We could not know what the future held for us – perhaps it was not as dark as it looked at present. Perhaps the war was not going to last . . .

I felt her tears on my cheek and knew that she, too, needed comforting. I could think of no consoling words, so I just held her tighter and let our tears mix. We stayed together like that for a few soothing tension-relieving minutes. Then she made me lie down, covered me up and kissed me on the head. After a time I went to sleep.

When I came down the following morning, Goga had already left. Maxim had driven him to the station to catch the early train to G*.

On the same day my father came to Fyeny for one night on his way to another part of the province. After supper my mother and he withdrew to his study and talked together for a long time; they were still talking when I put my head through the door to say good-night. After my father had left, my mother told us of her decision to take a house at M*, so that she could live with us for the duration of the war. 'Your father expects to travel a good deal, but he will come and stay with us whenever his duties allow it,' she said. We guessed that Father was far from enthusiastic about this plan, but that Mother, anxious as ever about our well-being, prevailed upon him to agree. Was she in this decision ruled by feeling or by her sense of duty? If the latter, then she must have felt her duty as a mother came before her duty as a wife. I never knew for certain, but it was most welcome news to me.

New Friendships, Expectations and Disappointments

The house my mother took at M* in the autumn of 1914 was smaller than our house at B*. It had a garden but no stables or dog kennels; the only animal we brought with us was my cat Kaly. Of the servants only Aniuta and Mitrofán, the newly engaged cook, came with us. Galaktyón, the old cook, Maxim, the coachman, and Piotr, my father's valet, stayed with him at B*.

Uncle Vladímir and Zena were our first visitors. While uncle was talking to my mother in the sitting-room, complaining of the rising cost of living and of the possibility that Stan, his coachman, might be called up, I took Zena to my bedroom and showed her my pencil drawings of the Duke of Reichstadt which I had copied from picture postcards. One of these was a sketch made of him when he was lying in his coffin, hands folded on his chest, a large star pinned to his white uniform, his features sharp and pointed, a lock of blond hair falling upon his forehead, wide, like his father's. I held it up for her to see, rather proudly, thinking of it as one of my more successful attempts at portraiture.

'Don't you think it's rather good?' I asked, fishing for a compliment.

Zena's eyes filled with tears.

'He died . . . What good is there in that?' she murmured.

'But . . . he looks beautiful . . . ' I protested.

'He looks better in that!' She pointed at the other sketch representing the Duke standing upright with his hand inside his half-buttoned tunic, his father's favourite pose.

'Well . . . yes,' I admitted, 'but more ordinary.'

Zena was not looking well. Her complexion was sallow with a greenish tint, her mouth drooped at the corners. I knew she was disappointed at my not returning to live with them, and I felt sorry for her. I visualized her trailing dejectedly from room to room, looking for something to do, or picking over her food, seated at table between her silent parents.

I told her that she must come and stay with us as often as she liked.

'If they would let me,' she murmured mournfully.

During tea my mother remarked that Zena seemed to have a poor appetite.

'She won't eat anything at home,' my uncle declared heavily.

'Why Zena! Living in the country with all that air and exercise? Doesn't it make you hungry?' My mother spoke cheerfully, but Zena's face grew tearful, while my uncle continued: 'Exercise! Fresh air! All she does is to sit in the water. True, it has been hot, but that doesn't mean you have to sit in the river all day. You can't get her out of it.'

'That is unhealthy, Zena,' said my mother. 'Why, my dear child, you're crying! We don't mean to be unkind . . . Your father's just concerned about you.'

'That's right,' said my uncle. 'Now she'll behave like a little victim — her mother's trick. I'm a brute, and she's an innocent lamb led to the slaughter.'

Zena rose from her chair and walked out of the room, her hands against her face. I followed her. She threw herself on to my bed.

'He goes for me like this all the time,' she sobbed, 'and all because he knows I love Mamma and don't love him.'

'But surely he does this . . . because he loves you, Zena?'

'Loves me! What kind of love is this? He's so mean, he won't give Mamma any money to buy me clothes. He says she can buy them out of her own money. Look at my dress! She made it herself from a piece she had in her drawer for the last fifteen years. Don't tell me it's pretty: I won't believe it.'

I did not think it was pretty, and so kept silent: to pretend in order to please was something I could never learn. But I promised to myself that I would try to get Zena to come and stay with us as often as possible, and make sure of my mother's and sister's support in that.

After our visitors had driven off in the familiar buggy drawn by the pink horse, with Stan on the box, my mother said to us that she had suggested to Uncle Vladímir that he should have Zena examined by a good doctor. He replied, however, that he did not believe in doctors, and that he considered Zena quite healthy.

My sister thought Uncle Vladímir should be persuaded to do what my mother had suggested, but I could not see her taking the initiative in that. She had just passed through a period of most painful indecision which left her nervously exhausted. The State examinations she took at the Petersburg University in order to qualify as a teacher had strained her health, and after she came home, she could not make up her mind whether she really wanted to teach, and where. I think my mother had assumed that she would obtain a post in our *Ghymnasia* and live at home, but even when the post was offered her, Maroossia could not decide whether to accept it. There were long discussions and emotional arguments between her and my mother; Maroossia talked of being independent and 'having life of her own'. I naturally wanted her to stay with us and was relieved when she finally yielded to family pressure and accepted the post at the *Ghymnasia*. But I had the sad experience of seeing her depressed and below par for weeks after that.

My sister was almost eight years older than I, and in my early childhood I saw little of her because she was at school in another town. When she came home for holidays, she gave me a great deal of attention: she liked dressing me in my winter clothes before taking me out, and I loved being whirled in her arms when she danced the waltz with me. Her tender affection enveloped me as if in a soft embrace, and I responded with a devotion which equalled only that which I felt for my mother. In those early years she seemed to be uncritical of me, and I of her. This mutual love continued throughout my first year or two at school. I received from her and accepted as my own her exalted ideas about the revolution and the heroes who fought the government in order to liberate Russia from its oppressive rule. Without yet having read a single line of Byron's verse, I shared her admiration for him as a fighter for the freedom of Greece, and a man who was irresistible to women, yet whom no woman could make happy. I fully entered into her feelings when she talked of the injustices and sufferings our great poets had to bear; I grieved with her over the deaths of Pushkin and Lermontov. And I drank her words when she described the operas and plays she had seen in Petersburg and Moscow.

But inevitably, as I grew older, differences in tastes and preferences began to appear. Some of Lev Tolstoy's ideas on social justice appealed to Maroossia's gentle nature — maybe even to the inferiority and guilt feelings which undoubtedly afflicted her. I remember her quoting Tolstoy in connection with the work of domestic servants. 'Tolstoy says that the servant's job is one of the least rewarding . . . Our Aniuta is not working for herself, in her own family or house . . . We all should do our own domestic work and live as simply as possible . . . ' This to me was less than convincing, and I watched with a touch of disapproval her attempts at helping Aniuta by going round the rooms with a duster. Why, I asked, should I waste time on dusting furniture when I wanted – and could – write poems? Anyway, I was inclined to share my mother's opinion of Tolstoy. She called him a hypocrite because he preached poverty and dressed like a peasant but in fact lived in luxury. Nor did I have a particular liking for Tolstoy as a writer. His characters were too much like the people one met in real life; his descriptions of their appearance and states of mind were too prosaic for my taste, his style too pedestrian. I wanted to meet unusual people, to be shown strange and exceptional aspects of life – and so I was fascinated by Dostoyevsky. If, as some critic had written, it was impossible for anyone to feel affinity with both these writers and one had to choose between the 'breadth' of one and the 'depth' of the other, I could tell myself that I had chosen 'depth' and feel rather proud of my choice.

I could not share my sister's fondness for walks in cemeteries. I accompanied her unwillingly: the beautiful trees and luscious grass growing among the graves made me think of all the dead disintegrating in the ground below. 'But that is what Tolstoy used to say when he was young!' my sister exclaimed. 'One should think of the peace the unhappy people find here.' 'The peace of death!' I mocked bitterly, for I regarded death as an outrage, an almost personal act of aggression on the part of God. 'We don't know what death is . . . ' said my sister.

'We know that it's the end of life!' I declared.

'The end of this life . . . that may be . . . ' she mused aloud. But I continued arguing against this, not knowing how passionately I wanted to be refuted.

In quite another domain our relationship changed in a somewhat unusual way. Partly by nature and partly because as a child I had played mostly with boys, I liked to be physically active and did my best to achieve fair competence in more than one kind of thing. I could ride a bicycle or a horse, play tennis, swim, row a boat, climb trees, skate and walk on skis. My sister was afraid of horses, could not swim, never learned to ride a bicycle competently, and was only good at ice skating. I have a memory of her getting on to a horse at a picnic, mainly to please me, and, as the horse began to trot, clutching at branches above her head, in an attempt to stop it. She was apt to lose her head in minor emergencies such as this, and I can still see her, in my mind's eye, careering madly on her bicycle down a short steep decline of the road near my uncle's *dacha*. 'Use your brake!' I shouted, but she did not do so and crashed at the bottom of the slope from sheer fright. Fortunately it was a soft, dusty road and she was not hurt. On another occasion, when the two of us and Zena were together in a boat, Maroossia was to push us off. She stood up to do this but held on so long to a post on the bank, that she could not recover her balance and fell helplessly into the river while the boat slipped away from under her feet. This kind of ineptitude puzzled me, made me feel sorry for her and want to help her as if she were, in fact, the younger sister, and I more of a brother than a sister.

The great timidity I sensed in her also puzzled me and aroused a wish to discuss it, to prove its unreasonableness. Whenever she herself or a member of the family was to go on a journey, Maroossia would grow anxious and her face would become blotched with red. With the arrogance of adolescence I believed that most, if not all, unreasonable fears could be conjured away by proving that they were unreasonable. Why, I insisted, need she be so agitated? 'We . . . (or he) might miss the train . . . ' In vain did I point out that there was plenty of time and that we had never missed a long distance train before: Maroossia's agitation continued and often ended in a sick headache. She used to have these sick headaches with an alarming regularity, and I, who was hardly ever sick, suffered with her in uncomprehending sympathy.

And so I came to feel protective towards her, and when we walked arm-in-arm on slippery, snow-covered pavements, I supported her by the elbow like a chivalrous *cavaliere servante* and warned her about the patches of ice on the road. I felt rather proud of my role. In winter she used to wear a little round seal cap, and because of that and for the reason that her nose was rather broad, I used to call her 'my duckling'. She continued to call me her 'mite' or '*kroshka*', although I was already an inch or so taller than herself.

I remember one particular walk when we talked of happiness. We must have talked of happiness more than once before, but on that winter evening I was, for no obvious reason, in an exceptionally heightened mood. It may have been the effect of the magical beauty of sky and earth after a very clear sunset. Its glow was still in the west, but above it the sky was faintly green and the snow on the road, roofs and trees was taking on the lilac tint of the increasing shadows. The familiar places had a look of mystery and promise.

'I don't know about happiness,' Maroossia said. 'It may be only a matter of moments . . . moments like this, perhaps . . . '

Moments like this! 'But I'm not happy!' I protested. 'This is beautiful
. . . but it only makes me crave for happiness all the more. Surely people
can be happy longer than just a few moments? Why do they talk of
'happy lovers' and of 'happy marriages'?

She glanced at me sideways from under her little fur cap, just like a
somewhat alarmed duck, her gentle brown eyes uneasy with doubt.

'I think happiness is very rare,' she said. 'People are too complicated
to stay happy for long . . . '

'But I want to be happy, I want to . . . I must be!' I repeated, my
distress mounting as I began to feel myself in danger of being convinced
by her words.

'What do you think would make you happy?' Maroossia asked.

'Oh, a lot of things. I want to travel – go anywhere I like – I want to
become a famous writer . . . To fall in love with someone who would
also love me very much and who would also be famous in some way, a
musician, perhaps. I would like to have children – no more than two, I
think . . . a boy and a girl. And . . . '

'You may have all these things and yet not be happy for long . . . '
my sister said.

'Why are you saying this?' I asked reproachfully. She was causing me
pain, an inchoate sensation tugging at my heart.

'Because I think it might be true . . . '

'She may be right, she may be right, and you are just being foolish,'
a small voice whispered inside my head. But I did not want to believe it;
I repeated to myself that much depended on my own will and determination. True, my dreams of travel had to be postponed and my chances of
meeting the 'prince' had been greatly diminished – the war was the
cause of that. But becoming a writer was something I could go on striving
for. My reputation as a 'poetess' was established at school; I was aware
of being pointed out to younger pupils in the assembly hall; one bright
girl from an upper form came up to me during the lunch break and
walked and talked with me for a full half-hour about literature – an
unusual and flattering happening. Shimkóvich, the most exacting of
teachers, now always praised my essays and read them in class; and
I was asked by the Director himself to write a poem for the school
concert which was planned in aid of the Red Cross and the wounded
soldiers.

I was proud of this, and told myself that although I could not hope to
equal Lermontov or Pushkin, I could become perhaps the best woman
writer in Russia. And with a touch of irony at my own expense, I re-

minded myself that my task would not be so very hard: there were so few women writers in Russia.

My mother and sister liked my poems and often asked me to read them to their friends. I doubt that my father ever read any of them, and as for my brother, he professed scorn for poetry in general and for female poets in particular. If he came upon a poem of mine, he would read it aloud in such a manner that it appeared ridiculous and false. Once he got hold of my diary and read passages from it in the same way. For the first few moments I was dumbfounded; to me, his behaviour was monstrous, not merely dishonest but dishonourable, like opening and reading other people's letters. Then I rushed at him to snatch my diary away, but he dodged round the table, still reading, and finally escaped into the sitting-room where he defended himself against me by throwing himself back-wards on to a sofa and lifting his feet in the air.

I knew that if I struck him, I would hurt my hands more than I could hurt him, so I called him a coward and said I despised him — and I meant it. I had suspected him of lacking in courage ever since he, as a boy of ten, had sent me, a girl of six, to bring down his arrow from the roof of the house. He would not ride a horse after having been thrown once and was not interested in any sport except ice-skating. I cannot remember having ever seen him do a dangerous or a daring thing. Heaven knows, time was to prove me wrong in judging him to be devoid of courage — but how was I to know?

I took my revenge on him in a way not many younger sisters could, and my mother was the one to suggest it, although she did so without any thought of revenge. My brother was a very able boy, but his best subject was mathematics and he found essay writing difficult. One evening in his last year at school, my mother found him worrying over an essay on some semi-abstract subject he had been set to write at home. She suggested he should ask me to write it, and after some hesitation, he swallowed his pride and did so. I enjoyed writing it, the more so as it proved that I was not as infantile and ridiculous as he chose to picture me. He copied my essay and was given a good mark for it, but was too self-conscious even to thank me for my effort on his behalf.

Despite his sedate, quiet manner in the presence of strangers, Vova was a highly-strung and sensitive youth. I remember him frantic with irritation, trying repeatedly to straighten a moderately straight parting in his hair, or standing before a full-length looking-glass, pulling at the tail of his school tunic and complaining in exasperation that the fold would not lie flat. He obviously hated the thought of not looking 'just right'. He was not handsome but had a fine forehead with well-marked, straight eyebrows and wide-set greenish-grey eyes. The extreme leanness of his face exaggerated the width of his mouth. His profile was long with a slightly receding chin, and it must have been that which made him declare, with a characteristic, self-deprecatory humour that he looked 'like an Egyptian dog-minder'. There was indeed some slight resemblance between his features and those rigid, two-dimensional figures represented on Egyptian frescoes with their arms extended, holding back elongated dogs which strain at their leash. His comment on himself showed a degree of critical detachment which was disarming, but I could not let myself be disarmed for long, always expecting him to return to attack.

I often wondered in later years whether members of a family ever really know one another. We all assume they do — but I believe this happens only when there is a deep affinity between them, such as existed, despite all our differences, between me and my sister. There was no such affinity between myself and the others, not excluding my mother, and my brother and father especially remained familiar strangers, whose actions and words I must have misinterpreted most of the time. Members of a family stand too close to one another, and this very closeness makes them myopic, prevents them from seeing one another whole, predisposes them to make more of one another's faults and weaknesses than of their virtues and strengths. They may be fond of one another, but they often reserve their respect for people outside the family circle. Familiarity, I believe, does not necessarily breed contempt, but it often distorts our view of those whom we see acting and talking only in the narrow framework of a home.

My brother, like my father, never condescended to talk to me as to an equal, but I knew that he sometimes confided things to my sister and my mother. He was a conscientious student, never took risks with his home work, but read little for interest or pleasure and was always greedy for food. I, for whom literature was a second life, thought him shallow, prosaic and limited to a degree. Yet, he finished school with a 'small' gold medal — that is, only one remove from the year's top finalist — and was admitted, on his school record, to the Polytechnical Institute in Petersburg, one of the most selective specialist universities in Russia.

I think he made friends fairly easily, but I also remember my mother saying that he often chose them among the boys of a less privileged background than our own. I remember clearly one of them, a serious-looking, quiet-spoken Jewish boy, 'Boma' Litvinov by name, of whom my mother approved, and whom I thought rather handsome with his sleek, black hair and wide forehead. Like my brother, he was good at mathematics and near the top of the class. I remember him quietly holding forth on the subject of the complete equality Jews enjoyed in other countries. In England, he told us, Disraeli, a Jew, had been a Prime Minister and a favourite of the Queen, while Mendelssohn, the composer, played the piano at the royal palace. I was much impressed by Boma's knowledge of such things.

The aspect of my mother's character of which I was most conscious was her worrying side. Our health seemed to be her main concern, and our future, in so far as it could be affected by the state of our health. My sister, she was convinced, had undermined her health by not feeding herself properly while she was a student at Petersburg. My brother's health worried her because he had an enormous appetite, yet remained as thin as if he had been starving all his life. As for myself, I could not, in her view, be really well because I was too restless and nervous. Despite being herself a reader and lover of the Russian classics, she would interrupt my reciting of my favourite poems by anxious remarks on the prominence of my thyroid gland.

If we planned some excursion or a trip on the river, her thoughts would inevitably turn to the possibility of accidents or mishaps: the sky looked stormy — a wind might spring up and the boat might overturn — my sister could not swim . . . Or we would all get soaked through and catch pneumonia. So persistent was she in foretelling various minor disasters, and — curiously enough — so relatively often did her forecasts prove correct, that we nicknamed her jokingly 'Elisaviéta the Prophetess'. This was my sister's invention: she had declared war on the family's 'addiction to gloom', and her way to do this was to make us laugh at ourselves. She invented ironical nicknames for all of us: my father was to be 'Vitaly the Silent'; my brother 'Vladímir the Saint' — a historical personage; myself 'Lydia the Martyr', an allusion to my tendency to make the most of my discontents; while for herself Maroossia reserved the most unlikely of titles, 'Maria the Harlot' — Mary Magdalene, of course. This made us all laugh, to her absolute delight.

At this distance in time, it is easy to see my mother's anxiety on our behalf as a foreboding of the dark things to come. One of her remarks has firmly remained in my memory. We returned from one of our boating trips very hungry to a lamp-lit, cosy dining-room, and my brother and I fell upon our food like ravenous wolves. Having finished his, my brother said he was still hungry, and more food was brought. My mother, who, as a rule, encouraged us all to eat more, shook her head and said: 'What is the matter with you today, my children? Can it be that you feel a famine is coming?'

'There you go again, Mamma — prophesying,' my brother replied, and we all laughed, but I remember a great unease coming over me, just as it had when my sister talked of happiness being only the matter of moments. Could that have been a foreboding, too?

I was often haunted by a sense of futility and a craving to escape — where to? I had no notion. On a golden autumn morning, transparent and absolutely still, the air chilled and fragrant like white wine, I walked to school up an avenue of maple trees which ran along the middle of our street. The large leaves of the maples had turned blood-red and amber-yellow, so that the path in front of me looked like a processional route richly adorned with banners. I felt its beauty intensely but my thoughts were fixed on its passing away, on the transience of all glory and the death of all things mortal. I felt a thousand years old and oppressed as if all the sorrows of the world were weighing me down. If all had to end in death, I wished I could die there and then.

When I was in these moods my sister told me I was suffering from *Weltschmerz*. Goethe, Lermontov, Byron, even Pushkin, had all suffered from it, she said; and every young person, aware of the evils and tragedies of life, suffers from it in some degree. The trouble with me was that I was having it rather badly. All the same, there were real and obvious reasons why we should feel sad and uneasy: our life had been made darker and poorer by the war. The only cinema in town had closed its doors; dancing was banned from public places; in school we knitted wristlets and gloves for soldiers, and in church, prayers were read for 'our valiant warriors'. Some of the older boys we knew had become cadets in military schools and were due to join the fighting forces in the near future. These play-companions, who were too young to be taken seriously, could be killed in battle in a matter of months. One simply did not know how to treat them.

Fairly early in the autumn we received the news that Goga Reingold had been killed in the advance on Prussia. It was hard to imagine him dead, and his last visit to Fyeny stood out in memory, seen like a painting in a frame. My sister appeared to take the news almost calmly, as if she had long prepared herself for it. 'Just think,' she said to me, 'he would have been still alive if he had not failed his school finals . . . ' I burst out in a passionate denunciation of the forces which allowed the question of life or death and all the waste and grief that go with it, to be determined by chance. Maroossia merely shook her head.

'Who knows that he hasn't escaped something worse?' she asked.

At home they saw me mostly in my depressed and discontented moods; at school, my other side, active and capable of enjoyment, came to the fore. Having lost my boarding-school friends in my second year at school, I became friendly with Mania Bábina, a Jewish girl with blonde hair and grey eyes, who was my desk neighbour. We maintained a friendly rivalry for the top place in the class, she leading in arithmetic and I in Russian. I found her a very sensible, quiet companion in school hours, but when I went to her home and she came to my uncle's, I discovered with surprise that she bored me. There seemed to be nothing we could do together except our home-work. Nothing I suggested could spark off her imagination. She could not swim and she was afraid to go out in the rowing boat. What dealt our friendship a final blow was my discovery that she did not know the names of the most common trees, to say nothing about her ever attempting to climb one. 'Is this a maple?' she asked, pointing at a lime. It seems that a kind of respect was the main ingredient in my pleasure in Mania's company, and this display of ignorance on her part brought her down in my esteem with dramatic suddenness. The streets of our town were lined with trees; there were several public gardens where Mania had doubtless walked many a time, yet she had so little interest in nature that she had never bothered to look at trees and ask their names!

In my third year I was paired in the crocodile with Ania Bielynóvich and sat next to her in the class-room, but when it came to dancing, I always chose Liolia Tálina. Musically gifted, Liolia had a perfect sense of rhythm, and I could trust her literally never to put a foot wrong. She was always gay and given to irrepressible fits of giggles with which she often infected us. She lived with her mother in a small flat on the second floor of an apartment house. Madame Tálina was divorced from her husband, and the story we all knew about this filled me with respect for this small vivacious woman with a brusque manner and rather deep voice. She had been married to a wealthy landowner in the district, who had led a gay life before he married her and had a reputation of a Don Juan. She was recovering from her confinement with Liolia when she surprised him making love to the nurse. Immediately, Madame Tálina had her luggage packed, picked up the infant Liolia and walked out. We never talked about this in Liolia's presence and did not know whether she had ever met her father. Madame Tálina was said to be very strict with Liolia, who was under instructions to come straight home after school. Liolia was thus led to practise mild deceitfulness in which she often needed our collaboration. If she happened to snatch a short stroll with an admirer from the boys' *Ghymnasia* – always a dangerous thing because she could meet her mother in the street – she would drag one of us up to her flat, whispering on the way: 'I'm going to say we've been kept waiting to change books in the library. You say it, too.'

I became friends also with Tonia Rosen, the daughter of the 'Leader of the Nobility'. I knew that the Leader was elected by all the 'nobles' of the province, including my father, but what his duties or functions were I had not the slightest notion and never troubled to find out. We teased Tonia with being 'a baroness': it sounded pompous. But there was nothing pompous about Tonia, and no one could accuse her of taking pride in her father's title. In spite of her good looks she seemed to be quite without vanity. She had a perfect 'Greek' profile, the bridge of her nose forming a continuous straight line with her forehead. Her hair was blonde, but her eyes were dark brown and her strong eyebrows velvety black. As we analysed our own and one another's appearance with the ruthless frankness of the very young, we decided that a Greek profile was much overrated and not such a thing of beauty as we had been led to believe, but that it had the virtue of rarity.

Tonia's weak points were her inability to keep her hair in place or her clothes even moderately tidy. Strands of hair were always hanging over her forehead and getting into her eyes. As for her clothes, she relied too much on pins instead of hooks and buttons, and the pins were not always safety-pins. Once as she was passing me in the class-room, I caught her by the corner of her pinafore, wanting to speak to her – and nearly ripped off most of her clothes. The pins which held her dress and pinafore together flew out, and there stood Tonia with a gap in her side, holding up her falling skirt, both of us laughing too much to do anything about it.

She was also extremely absent-minded. One summer afternoon Liolia and I were on the balcony of Liolia's flat waiting for her. We saw her coming along the street, late as usual. We called out to her. She waved back and shouted something about feeling very hot. Then she proceeded to remove her jacket, revealing that she was wearing no blouse but only a camisole and a lace 'front' under it. Hysterical with laughter, we could hardly speak and merely pointed, while Tonia gazed up at us, mystified. Only after she had walked up the stairs and we opened the door to her, did she realize that she had half-undressed herself in the street.

Two other girls who were friendly with Tonia and Liolia also became my friends. They were cousins, Katia Kign and Lena Kazanóvich. No two strangers could be less alike than these two: Katia, placid, quiet-spoken and studious, Lena excitable, voluble, mercurial and slap-dash. Katia was working up to the top of the class, only a few marks below Bábina and myself. Lena, though no less intelligent, never did any home-work and so lagged somewhere in the middle. Katia was always so attentive and well-behaved that I cannot recollect her ever being repri-manded by a teacher or a *dame-de-classe*. Lena, on the other hand, was frequently in trouble — for talking during lessons, for prompting or being prompted, for writing and passing notes, or for her provocative manner. Everyone knew that Lena had a passion for boasting and telling fibs. She could tell them brazenly, with an air of innocence and an assurance which was almost disarming. Occasionally she would get away with an unprepared lesson by richly embroidering on the scraps of material she had gathered from the teacher's explanation a few days before. She was resourceful but incautious and so was frequently caught out. She declared that she did not mind being punished at school by having lines to learn because her mother at home was much stricter than any *dame-de-classe*. Lena was an unusually big girl for her age and had a baby face, milky white and pink, with a pair of large brown eyes. She was rather proud of her hands, delicate and soft, with tapering fingers, more like the hands of a pampered young woman than of a growing adolescent.

Her cousin, Katia, was also tall but slender, and she had the habit of stooping which gave her a sunken chest. She was an orphan and had an elder brother who was at the *Ghymnasia* in my brother's class. Katia's mother had died of consumption; her father, a local landowner, died of heart failure as he ran in heavy snow after a pair of runaway horses. After a spell at the boarding school, Katia became a day girl and lived in a flat with her brother and a devoted housekeeper, who also kept house for them during the school holidays when they returned to their country estate. Katia's brother intended to run the estate himself as soon as he had left school. Katia said all four of us must come and stay with them in the summer holidays.

In the lunch break the five of us gathered in the downstairs hall, usurping a corner by the piano, and listened to Liolia's singing or danced with one another. Liolia was fond of the gypsy romances which I rather despised, but she would also sing Schumann's songs to Heine's words, some of which were among my favourite songs. I felt at the time that only tragic or truly tender emotions were worthy of being expressed in music: musical gaiety, especially of a popular kind, annoyed and

8

offended me. Katia could play the piano passably well, and whenever I could, I induced her to play Chopin's waltzes and nocturnes. I was particularly fond of the Waltz Number 7, and I was planning to write a novel about unrequited love and call it *The Seventh Waltz of Chopin*. But mostly Katia played ordinary waltzes for us to dance to. Liolia, despite her plumpness, was very light on her feet, so I preferred her as a partner to the others. We danced the waltz with abandon until she became giddy and giggly, and implored me to stop. But I, impervious to dizziness and proud of it, continued whirling her around, while an amused crowd of girls from other classes watched us getting more and more out of breath and eventually flopping down on any chairs that happened to be near.

With Tonia I danced the *dance d'apache*, partly borrowed from a film we had seen and partly invented by myself. To the strains of 'Tango Argentine', I pulled her roughly about, threw her over my arm and finally dropped her on the floor, pretending to stab her. By that time most of her hairpins were scattered and her dress was gaping at the side. This dance was much appreciated by our spectators who clapped and cheered us. Our success made us reckless and we began to talk about dancing our tango on the table.

The room where all this was happening was used for examinations at the end of the school year, and the only table in it was the huge 'examinations' table', covered with a heavy, green tablecloth. I had often pictured to myself with an inner shudder the scene when I, too, would have to draw my ticket from the urn – for examinations at our school were conducted as a kind of lottery. Each subject was divided into sections, and questions relating to these were typed or printed on slips of paper which the examinees drew in the presence of the examiners. The pupil then sat down with her 'ticket' and thought the questions over for about a quarter of an hour, when her name was called. Then she had to go up to the table and recite what she had prepared, facing a conclave of the Director, the Headmistress, the teacher concerned and several other teachers seated behind the table, any of whom could ask her questions on the section she had drawn. Fortunately, this ordeal was inflicted on the pupils only twice in their school life, at the end of the last but one, and in the final year.

The idea of dancing the tango on this important table appealed to our iconoclastic sense of humour, and, having posted Lena outside to watch out for possible adult intruders, we turned back the green tablecloth and climbed on to it, Tonia already giggling in anticipation. We took our stance and Katia struck the first notes of the 'Tango Argentine'. But we did not get very far. The anteroom door was flung open and Lena rushed in, hissing: 'Take care! The enemy's coming!' We only just had time to jump off, but could not manage to pull the cloth back over the table.

The enemy was a young *dame-de-classe* who had joined the school staff only that term. She was called Nadiézhda Miháilovna, had a fresh, supercilious kind of face and appeared to be devoid of humour. She was on the way to the *Nachálnitsa*'s flat, the door of which was at the far end of the hall. As she passed us, she threw a curious glance at the half-uncovered examination table, then at our faces which we were trying hard to keep straight.

'Do you think she'll tell Anna Avdyéevna?' Lena asked after the young woman had gone in. 'She looks the type that likes to make trouble.'

'What can she tell her?' retorted someone.

We soon knew that the woman had spoken because the following morning Anna Avdyéevna questioned Katia about what had happened in the examination hall 'during the lunch break the day before'.

Katia was a truthful person but not to the extent of giving away her friends. She merely repeated Anna Avdyéevna's question as if completely failing to grasp it. The *dame-de-classe* pressed her, and Katia told her, quite truthfully, that she had played the piano and the others danced — and that was all. Anna Avdyéevna got nothing more from her, and for some reason she did not question the rest of us.

The date of the concert at which I had to recite my poem was approaching fast. I had had several weeks to accustom myself to the thought of a public appearance and to write a poem suitable for the occasion. Verse writing was never practised at our school as part of Russian studies, and I was convinced that poems written 'to order' or for special occasions were bound to be vastly inferior to poems dictated by inspiration. I had discovered inspiration when I composed my first poem at the age of eight, and I knew it as a state of special awareness, of mounting excitement and the growing need to give my feelings a verbal and rhythmical shape. I was 'inspired' nearly always by something I saw in nature, and then I would move about in agitation, singing my lines, trying this word and that, elated when the word fitted perfectly, despairing when it eluded me. Indeed, often the experience was like wrestling with some force inside me, a voice insisting that I should express things for which I could find no words. The struggle set my head burning and my cheeks aflame; it set me wondering whether I *looked*, when possessed by inspiration, different from my usual self, and I wished I could see myself, or someone could see me and tell me what I looked like. Perhaps then people would realize what the *real* me was, and not be misled by my childish appearance into thinking that I was just an ordinary schoolgirl . . .

For the first time in my life I tried to induce inspiration by pondering on the theme of 'soldiers at the front'. The resulting poem of six stanzas was competent but hardly 'inspired' in my sense. I managed to express compassion for the men in the freezing trenches and a hope that the war would soon be over, with the sincerity I felt.

And I succeeded in controlling my nervousness well enough when the time came for me to recite my poem, even to the extent of being able to observe some of my audience. The Director was smiling into his beard, the *Nachálnitsa* was positively beaming, Anna Avdyéevna had a curiously intent and almost solemn look, Shimkóvich . . . There was a sad half-smile on his lips and a wistfulness in the tilt of his head which nearly made me lose the thread of my recitation. I remembered that he was said to be a sick man, and that my classmates assured me that he was 'in love' with me. Since my mother came to live with us at M*, he was a frequent visitor at our house.

My ears, which had been blocked by emotion when I started reciting, became unblocked and the long applause which greeted the end of my recitation sounded loud and good. Did I deserve it or were they applauding from kindness? If I were a musician I could get applause as often as I liked, every month or even every week . . . and I would know that I deserved it. But I had no gift for music-making, and this vision of glamour had to go the way of most day-dreams. Perhaps in my next reincarnation . . .

I joined my mother and sister in the second row of the seats. My sister's eyes shone tenderly as she whispered: 'You looked a very charming young poetess, *kroshka!*' I was not sorry that my brother was not there: he had begun his course at the Polytechnical Institute that autumn. And I was grateful for the absence of Shoora Martýnov who was also studying in Petersburg. I would have found his attentions very embarrassing under the eye of all the teachers and girls from all the classes in the school.

With my mother were Zena and Aunt Katia.

'I liked your poem ever so much,' said Zena, beaming at me.

'Yes,' said Aunt Katia. 'Only I know what some people would say . . .'

'What would they say?' my mother enquired with a touch of impatience.

'They'd say: "Here's a girl reciting a touching poem about the soldiers freezing and dying at the front, yet she's wearing a pair of diaphanous stockings." War poems and diaphanous stockings somehow don't go together.'

'I don't think for a moment they would say that!'

My mother sounded quite cross: Aunt Katia *would* spoil anyone's enjoyment. I too felt annoyed, but also guilty, aware that there was some truth in her rebuke. The stockings were my first pair of really fine ones, and I could not resist wearing them on that special occasion. But perhaps it was the wrong occasion? I almost wished my mother had advised me against it.

There was to be a dance after the concert and recitations; the ban on dancing was for once relaxed; it was, after all, a charity dance, and in a way private. Some young officers on leave, some cadets and older schoolboys were in the audience: they would no doubt stay after the show and partner the older schoolgirls. Liolia Tálina already had an officer friend, a blond, rosy-cheeked second lieutenant called Henryk Tomásov. Katia Kign's brother, Dima, was also there; he was a bovine-looking youth with a loud voice and laughter which made me feel uncomfortable. I wanted to dance and wondered who, if anyone, would ask me. I hoped not Dima, who would probably dance clumsily. My sister had told me that at such school dances introductions were omitted: young men asked any girl they wanted to dance with, so I need not worry about not knowing anybody . . . But what if nobody asked me?

There is no equivalent of the phrase 'wallflower' in Russian, but the feeling attached to the situation is the same as anywhere else. I loved dancing, I could dance well, and to have a middle-aged teacher who could not dance sitting beside me and doing his best to entertain me by his conversation, was not a substitute for being whirled around the room to the strains of 'The Hills of Manchuria'. Shimkóvich joined us as soon as we came down to the examination hall where the dance was held. For once his ironical comments, expressed with characteristic circumlocution, failed to hold my respectful attention. My eyes were following Liolia waltzing happily in Henryk's arms and Tonia being jerked uncomfortably in Dima Kign's embrace. I badly wanted to join them on the floor, and I feared that prospective partners would keep away as long as Shimkóvich looked as if he had secured my company for the evening. At the same time I wondered whether any of these young men would want to dance with me in any case. A small crowd of them were standing in the doorway, watching the dancing couples, trying to make up their minds . . . I avoided looking at them in case they would imagine that I was longing for them to ask me. If anyone came, he must be good-looking and a good dancer. I should hate to dance with someone who trod on my toes. But there were so few really good dancers among those who waltzed past me. Borís Orlóv, perhaps, with his straight back and arrogant air — but he had the reputation of being stupid . . .

The first waltz, my favourite dance, was over, and no one had asked me so far. I was doing my best not to look downcast, but knew that my face reflected all that I was feeling. Maroossia, who was sitting on the Shimkóvich's other side, could do nothing except look sympathetic, which only increased my self-consciousness. A few minutes passed, then the band struck a polka. Adolphe, the teacher of mathematics, bald-headed and bespectacled, glided over the parquet to my sister and bowed with exaggerated courtliness. With an emotion near to despair I saw her accept and realized that now I had to take full notice and give sensible answers to whatever Shimkóvich was saying to me.

Just then I caught sight of a tall youth in a *Ghymnasia* uniform tunic carefully threading his way between the chairs ranged against the wall and the whirling dancers and gradually approaching the place where we sat. I looked away quickly: he must not think I was expecting it, and it would be so humiliating if after all he asked someone else. Shimkóvich was saying in his slow, deliberately seminarist accents: 'I've never learned to dance . . . nor for that matter any fine manners. At the Seminary they didn't teach us any airs or graces . . . '

Without really looking, I saw that the tall youth had stopped in front of me and was bowing.

'Kavaliérov,' he introduced himself. 'May I have the pleasure?'

I glanced up quickly. Yes, he was speaking to me, not to a girl on my left. I nodded and rose, remembering at the last moment to say: 'Please excuse me', to Shimkóvich. The youth Kavaliérov put his arm round my waist and we joined the round of dancers.

Af fifteen I had grown out of liking the polka; I regarded it as a child-ish dance which I could only dance with abandon and enjoyment when acting a part for the benefit of my classmates. To stamp out its strong rhythms with a male partner whose sense of rhythm was clearly deficient was embarrassing and dissatisfying. The youth Kavaliérov had a very strong arm; he was taller than I by a whole head and he gazed steadily into my face with his dark, deep-set eyes all the time we were dancing.

He was very plain; his features large but somewhat flat, his eyes small, his mouth wide and his complexion sallow. There was a look of grave intentness about him which made me feel uncomfortable. He did not speak, and I wondered whether I should say something to him. But what could I say to a complete stranger which would not be so obvious as to sound inane? Should I ask him whether he had liked the concert? That would sound like fishing for a compliment. Ask him what class of the *Ghymnasia* he was in? He might dislike the question if he is still in the seventh class: he should be in the eighth . . .

The band finished playing the polka before either of us had found his tongue. Kavaliérov offered me his arm and led me to a couple of empty chairs, not back to where Shimkóvich was sitting. I saw my sister going back to him; they both searched for me with their eyes. My sister saw me, smiled and nodded. Kavaliérov was turning his back on them and still staring at me.

'My name is Fyedia,' he said, 'Fyedia Kavaliérov. Your sister knows my brother Leoníd. He's at the Military School in Petersburg.'

I replied: 'Yes, I think I've heard of him.' Then there was a pause.

'You write poems?' said Fyedia. 'Have you written many?'

'Not very many.'

'It must be quite difficult . . . writing poems . . . '

'Sometimes it is.'

'I should find it very hard if I had to. Mathematics is my strong subject.'

This was chilling. I could have replied: 'Then we have nothing in common', or 'Mathematics bore me', but it would not have been polite, so I said nothing. The band struck a *vienghiéiku*. Fyedia rose to his feet.

'May I?'

I submitted to my fate. How could I refuse without offending him?

He did not leave my side for the rest of the evening, and when dancing was over, he introduced himself to my sister and accompanied us home. As she was saying good-bye she said to him: 'Call on us some time, won't you?' He replied: 'With the greatest pleasure', and squeezed my hand so hard that I nearly gasped.

'Why did you ask him?' I turned on my sister as soon as the front door closed behind us and we started removing our coats.

'But how could I *not* ask him? He has been dancing with you all the evening, and he took us home. He would have been hurt if we just said good-bye, thank you, and nothing else . . . Besides, I know his brother.'

'I wish I hadn't danced with him the whole evening,' I cried. 'I wish you hadn't asked him to call. If he comes, don't expect me to entertain him! I don't want to, I don't, I don't!'

'*Kroshka!* What is the matter with you? Has something happened to upset you, or are you just over-tired?'

'Nothing! Nothing happened! Nothing ever happens, that's the trouble. No, don't try to comfort me. I'm not a little girl any more . . . '

I tossed in my bed, tormented with self-pity, my eyes hot and dry. As soon as I closed them, I saw the examination hall of the school, converted into a ballroom, looking festive with its shining parquet floor and all its wall lights draped in pink gauze. I saw the waltzing couples, Liolia laughing and chatting to her partner, Tonia languidly not-caring whether she kept time, Katia, solemn but obviously liking it, Lena muddling through with great aplomb. I saw myself with an elegant, handsome partner, perhaps a student of the Institute of Rail and Road Engineering, or a naval officer, dancing so well that people turned to watch us. 'There goes Rayévskaia, the poetess . . . What a nice couple they make!'

But even before I opened my eyes again, there intruded the memory of reality. Instead of the elegant partner, the uncouth Fyedia Kavaliérov. Instead of inspired dancing, a clumsy, jerky progress round the room. Instead of general admiration, perhaps a few amused glances from the group in the doorway, from others, sitting along the walls. My first success on the rostrum did not console me for the disappointment in my first dance. The dance seemed to matter more than the authorship of a poem. And I felt exasperated at the thought that I had acquired another very plain admirer, who, in contrast to Shoora Martýnov, was inarticulate, and whose favourite subject was mathematics!

Winning my Freedom

The winter of 1914-15 was dark and damp: the snow would not settle and was piled along the pavements in dirty yellow ramparts over which you had to climb if you were in a hurry to cross the street. The news that reached us from the front was now encouraging and now depressing. It looked as if the war was not going to be over in a year, as some had foretold but might continue indefinitely.

Preparation for lessons I had to do at home occupied at least three hours every evening. I went to bed late and found it very difficult to get up in the mornings: Aniuta had to call me more than once before I could wrench my head from my pillow.

The poem I had recited at the school concert was printed in the local paper under my name. I felt very proud of my first appearance in print, almost as early as Pushkin's or Lermontov's! I snatched at the copy of the paper when it arrived and gazed at the smudgy lettering with the intensity of a lover gazing at the beloved's face. How different it looked in print! How surprisingly compact and shapely! But even as I was re-reading it, my excitement was ebbing away. I could see its faults much more clearly; several weak rhymes, an awkward turn of phrase . . . but it was too late to improve it. My brief triumph was flawed with dissatisfaction and discontent.

I was in that kind of mood and deeply wrapped up in my thoughts when next morning at school I came down the stairs in the lunch break, on the way to the examination hall. The passage at the bottom of the stairs was poorly lit and I hardly saw the face of the woman who swept

8*

across it just as I reached the last step. I dipped a short, awkward curtsey and made for the door of the hall when the woman swung round and came towards me, her head high, her skirts swishing with the speed of her movement. I recognized Nadiézhda Miháilovna. She bore upon me with her characteristically arrogant air.

'You did not curtsey to me, Rayévskaia,' she said. 'The school regulations require you to curtsey to all members of the staff. Why did you not?'

My voice shaking with indignation at being so unjustly accused, I protested that I did so.

'Do you mean to say that I am not telling the truth?' she demanded.

'I mean . . . you may not have noticed that I did.'

She looked me up and down in silence, and walked off. I went into the hall. Katia, Liolia, Lena and Tonia were gathered round the piano. Liolia was singing '*Ich grölle nicht*'.

> *Ich grölle nicht, und wenn das Herz auch bricht*
> *Ewig verlohrenes Lieb, ich grölle nicht . . .*

'I do!' I growled, leaning over the piano and striking the lid with my fist. 'That beastly Nadiézhda Miháilovna!'

'What's the matter, Ziegfried?'

We have been learning about the Niebelungen, and my fair hair and fighting spirit earned me the nickname of Ziegfried. It was used interchangeably with 'Eaglet', for the members of our group of five knew of my fantasy of reincarnation and fell in with it.

I told them about my encounter with the governess. They were all indignant and sympathetic.

'She's bound to tell Anna Avdyéevna,' said Katia.

'I can just imagine what Anna Avdyéevna would say!' Liolia broke into giggles, somewhat inappropriately, I thought.

'Cheer up, my Gaetano!' said Tonia. 'Come and dance the tango with me.'

We danced the tango until the bell rang. Once in the class-room, a single glance at Anna Avdyéevna's face was sufficient to tell me that she had already been informed. She looked upset, but I felt I had been wronged and was determined to stand my ground. When the lesson was over, she called me to her desk.

'Rayévskaia, Nadiézhda Miháilovna tells me that you did not curtsey to her in the corridor, and that when she spoke to you about it you were discourteous.'

'I did curtsey to her, and I was not discourteous!'

'She says you were, and I want you to apologize to her.'

'I have nothing to apologize for,' I said icily, although fire was flowing through my limbs.

'I told her that she will receive your apology, and I insist on it.'

'You want me to apologize to someone who is entirely in the wrong and is throwing the blame on me?' I was trembling with indignation. 'I will never do it, never!'

'You *must* do it!' Anna Avdyéevna spoke with something like desperation.

But I, too, was in a desperate mood. Apology in my mind was the equivalent of asking forgiveness, an admission of being in the wrong, and the whole of my being revolted against such humiliation. I could imagine a smirk of satisfaction on Nadiézhda Miháilovna's pert little face as she watched me eating humble pie.

With my eyes fixed on Anna Avdyéevna's pale and agitated face, controlling my own agitation as best I could, I repeated that I would never apologize. For a few moments the two of us gazed into each other's eyes, she clearly taking the measure of my determination. Then she tossed her head and turned away from me. Released, I went quickly to my desk to pick up my books and leave the class-room. Two of my friends, Liolia and Tonia, were waiting in the corridor to walk home with me. They were curious to know what had passed between me and the *dame-de-classe*. I told them in some detail. They shared my indignation, but Tonia said: 'She'll do her best to make you do it, for certain.'

'Why should she be so keen on your apologizing to Nadiézhda Miháilovna?' asked Liolia, 'There's no love lost between them.'

'That's just the point!' Tonia looked her wordly-wise best as she said this. 'Anna Avdyéevna and the other woman are rivals. Our Anna Avdyéevna claims to have the best-behaved class in the school. Nadiézhda Miháilovna dislikes her and is determined to prove that this isn't true. She picked on you because she knows you're proud and would not give in on a point of honour, so to speak. She wants to embarrass Anna Avdyéevna.'

'What a disgusting plot!' Liolia could not help giving a nervous laugh as she made this remark. 'So Anna Avdyéevna will insist on your apologizing just to prove to Nadiézdha Miháilovna that she can make you do it!'

We reached the door of Liolia's block of flats to say au revoir. Some passing youths made the sounds of kissing as we exchanged the usual schoolgirls' embrace.

'Silly creatures!' said Liolia. 'Au revoir, Ziegfried. Don't give in to the dragons!'

Tonia and I continued along the darkening street. The snow was beginning to fall. We kissed au revoir outside the porch of her house.

'Be firm, my Gaetano!' she said, acting her Spanish part. 'I know you are brave. Au revoir!'

'Ziegfried', the 'Eaglet', 'Gaetano' — I needed all these *alter egos* to support me during the siege that followed.

Anna Avdyéevna spared no effort and neglected no kind of device to induce me to do what she desired in this triangular conflict between her, Nadiézhda Miháilovna and myself. She soon saw that mere insistence on her part was the least effective of weapons, so she tried persuasion on her favourite lines. The apology need not be formal, she said, Nadiézhda Miháilovna would be satisfied with just a few words on the first occasion I happened to meet her in the corridor. I just had to go up to her and say I apologized. This would cost me nothing, Nadiézhda Miháilovna would be pacified, and the reputation of *our* class as the best behaved in the school would be re-established.

'Cost me *nothing*?' I spoke with such force of suppressed anger that Anna Avdyéevna blenched. 'To apologize to her just to satisfy her ridiculous vanity? Apologize for *what*? I would be lying if I apologized! I would despise myself!'

Changing her tactics, Anna Avdyéevna tried to gain her ends by flattering and cajoling me. She appealed to my generosity. Her argument went something like this: surely I could understand what it meant to her? The whole staff of the school would know that she had no control over the pupils in her charge. She had been proud of the way her class had always behaved; this was the first complaint she had ever had from the staff about one of her pupils. And it had happened to be me, the pupil in whom she had always taken a very special interest. I was very much in the limelight, she told me: the school was proud of me. Such a minor concession on my part could not do any harm to *my* reputation, but my stubbornness was doing a great deal of harm to hers, and to the reputation of the class. If I apologized, people would respect me more for having admitted so courageously . . .

I almost screamed with exasperation that I had *nothing to admit*!

'Well, then,' she said, 'they will respect you for . . . for having done so in order to . . . restore my confidence in you . . . for my sake, if you like . . . '

I looked at Anna Avdyéevna with a sense of sudden illumination. It seemed as if something I had felt obscurely for a long time had become clear in a flash. She wanted me to sacrifice *my* pride to spare *her* pride.

The appeal to my generosity was the most difficult for me to withstand, but this last remark worked like a dash of cold water on hot metal; it made me harden. My own voice sounded strange to me as I replied with unnatural calm: 'I can't, Anna Avdyéevna.'

The siege continued for the best part of the week. The *dame-de-classe* kept me every day after the end of the lessons in the bleak, empty classroom to continue her pleading. She inveigled me into coming to her room during the lunch break. I returned home late, worn out and upset by her arguments and appeals. But although she occasionally reduced me to tears, my determination not to yield remained unshaken. As the struggle between us continued, its significance for me altered: from a clash of two kinds of self-regard it became a struggle for liberation, an all-out effort to free myself from a relationship which made upon me claims that I was not able to tolerate. Although I would not have used these words at the time, I became aware that I had been a victim of emotional blackmail, and that I had to break the bond between myself and Anna Avdyéevna in order to preserve my wholeness. I do not know how well she herself was aware of what was happening, but I believe that until the last moment she was hoping to win. The 'last moment', I think, was the occasion when I met the two *dames-de-classe* walking along the corridor together. I made a quick curtsey without looking up, and passed on. Anna Avdyéevna called me back.

To pretend I had not heard would have been an act of cowardice. I was already feeling cowardly for having passed them so quickly. I returned.

'Rayévskaia,' said Anna Avdyéevna in her most caressing tone of voice, 'I believe there's something you would like to say to Nadiézhda Miháilovna.'

I could never look straight at people I loathed, for my loathing seemed to invest them with an almost unbearable repulsiveness; and at that moment I loathed both the women standing before me. I hardly knew which of the two I loathed most.

'I have nothing to say to her . . . ' I spoke slowly and clearly.

'Not to *her*, Rayévskaia. You know very well you must refer to people by their names!'

'I have nothing to say to Nadiézhda Miháilovna,' I repeated, containing my mounting fury.

'Are you *quite* sure?' Anna Avdyéevna's voice was still sweet and fluting.

'Quite sure.'

I raised my eyes for a moment, just enough to see a kind of convulsion flitting across Anna Avdyéevna's face, while the other woman turned to her with a slight smile and a remark: 'Well, that settles it, does it not?'

'It seems so,' said Anna Avdyéevna in a cold, hostile voice.

They were talking as if they had made a bet on my response to their summons! I gazed them full in the face to show what I felt. Then, without another word or sign of dismissal both they and I walked off in opposite directions.

This was the end of the siege but not the end of the war. I realized it from the moment I saw Anna Avdyéevna's face on returning to the class-room. I had defied her in the presence of a rival; I had made it clear that my affection for her was not strong enough for me to accept humiliation on her account, that her power over me was not as great as she had imagined. In fact, I had won a victory: it was she, not I, who had suffered humiliation, and she was unforgiving. But neither could I forgive her for the torment she had been inflicting on me. The conflict had been long and painful, and now, after the break had taken place, I felt relieved, almost exhilarated, almost exulting in having an enemy. Now we were enemies she could make no demands on me except that I conform to the school regulations like any other girl in the school. I should not have to watch her face for signs of displeasure, or try to divine the tortuous workings of her mind in order to justify her expectations or fulfil her wishes. I was free to be fully myself at last!

Despite my masculine *alter egos* and my long game of 'prince and princess' with Zena during which I impersonated the prince, I had never been 'in love' with any of my female friends, not even in the form of an intense desire to please or serve them. 'Crushes' on teachers or classmates were not the fashion in Russian day schools for girls, and Anna Avdyéevna's demand for personal devotion to herself was imported by her from the Institute where she had been educated. I was brought up to feel that girls who talked of 'adoring' one another, or another female, were ridiculous, and when Margóolina made a fuss of me in my first year at school, I felt more embarrassed than flattered.

While my brother and his friends were my constant play companions, I accepted my feminine role naturally and without giving it a thought. They were generals, sailors or soldiers, and I took the part of a war nurse. But since my brother had gone away to school and I had to play alone, I began to pretend that I was a powerful masculine personality, a Caucasian Prince, or a French nobleman. Freud has a phrase for this: 'identification with the lost love object'. There was not much love between my brother and myself, but there could be little doubt that I missed him, and that by pretending to be strong and a male, I was compensating for the loss. Then as I played with children of my own age, some of them socially less privileged, I assumed leadership as if by right. If we all pretended to be Kazaks, I had to be the *Atamán*. Masculinity became in my mind a symbol for initiative, leadership and a degree of power over others, as well as a defence against the deeply vulnerable, and compassionate aspect of myself.

This proud image of myself had been well-nigh shattered by the experience of exile from home to boarding school. I was revealed to myself in all my vulnerability and weakness, and in my intense self-pity there was an admixture of self-contempt. But having passed through this ordeal, I knew myself better, and I felt stronger. My life with Zena and her parents added to this self-knowledge: I discovered that I could use my powers to modify my own conduct and so to influence the conduct of others. I found I was able to turn Zena from an enemy into a friend.

I was fond of Zena, but I did not think her particularly attractive, and my fantasy of casting her into the role of princess with whom I was supposed to be in love, was a pretext for inventing interminable dialogues, not the means of giving vent to my real feelings for her. It seems that in the manner of all writers, I was split between my characters: the passionate words I addressed to Zena could be addressed to myself by a 'real' prince, and they gave me the double satisfaction of being both speaker and listener, a giver and a recipient in one.

In our group of five no one assumed the leadership: we were friends and play-companions in the gayest, freest and most natural way. I assumed the masculine role only when dancing with Liolia or Tonia; Katia and Lena did so, too, because they were taller than the others. When we talked of 'love', it was always in relation to young men: Liolia with her flirtatious manner was quite irresistible to them. Katia was inclined to be 'serious' and too quiet to attract attention to herself; Lena, despite her size, looked too babyish; Tonia gave the impression of not caring for anybody or anything; I was rather ashamed of my admirers. Shoora Martýnov and Fyedia Kavaliérov, and shared with Liolia an infatuation with Moszhúhin, Polónsky and Maxímov, the film actors whom I had seen, of course, only on the screen.

Innocent of the meaning of 'love' between persons of the same sex, I saw Anna Avdyéevna's demands on me as a straightforward wish to have me in her power, and my revolt against it as the need to regain my freedom. If I had become aware that other emotions also played a part in her relationship with me, it was at first only briefly, during the scene of reconciliation which followed our last but one quarrel. It was the moment when she held my head against her bosom and comforted me as if I were a small child. That moment of surrender was followed by a strong inner recoil: I did not want such a situation to recur. Did I unconsciously wish it to recur? If so, I nevertheless did all I could to prevent it.

I am not sure even at this distance in time and with the knowledge I now have, to what extent the injury I felt so strongly that it made reconciliation impossible, was an injury done to my pride or to my affection for Anna Avdyéevna. The intensity of my revulsion could have been due to a disappointment in love. Whatever the cause, it made me realize by intuition perhaps above my years that further clashes between us were inevitable, and would be followed by further explanations, reproaches and reconciliations which I had found so exhausting and upsetting in the past. My gorge rose at the very thought of their recurrence. It was far, far better, I told myself, to have an enemy and to remain always armed, rather than make peace and live in an uneasy expectation of being attacked with your guard down, and perhaps at a moment when you were most vulnerable.

From that time on, until I left school to go to a university, Anna Avdyéevna and I hardly spoke to one another. I gave her few opportunities to find fault with me, as most of the time I managed to keep well within the school rules and regulations. She treated me most of the time as if I did not exist, but her disappointment in me must have been bitter and lasting, for now and again it broke through in some act of verbal violence which startled the class.

My classmates were of course well aware of this state of affairs between us, and, except for the two Komaróvskayas, were mostly 'on my side'. So were the teachers, who knew of the quarrel, and thought that both Anna Avdyéevna and Nadiézhda Miháilovna had been unreasonable in demanding an admission of guilt and apology from me with such uncompromising insistence. I knew this from Maroossia, who had described the split existing among the staff between the '*institóotki*' and the '*kursístki*'. Most of the *dames-de-classe* belonged to the former group: they were sticklers for manners and etiquette; they had a narrow outlook and little knowledge, except foreign languages. The teachers belonged mostly to the latter group and were women with a university education: they regarded the *dames-de-classe* as affected and rather silly. As for the male teachers, I realized from the remarks dropped by Shimkóvich when he visited us at home, that they all but despised the *dames-de-classe*.

Secure in the sympathy of the teachers, I had no fear that Anna Avdyéevna's animosity would do harm to my relationship with them. I was sure of them all with one exception: the *bátiushka*, our priest. Anna Avdyéevna had given up her duties at the boarding school and rented a room in *bátiushka's* house. A friendship sprang up between them which we regarded with suspicion. He had been fatherly and sweet to us when we were children who listened to him, open-mouthed, as he told us stories from the Gospels. But as we grew up and began to show signs of scepticism and ask awkward questions, his manner became more authoritative, his facial expression sterner. Disrespectfully, we wondered whether he would, if we confessed our misdemeanours to him, pass them, more or less casually, on to Anna Avdyéevna. Going to confession once a year was one of the school rules, and since I had lost my faith, confession had become to me an unpleasant and meaningless formality. I intended to drop it as soon as I had left school, but meanwhile I contrived to avoid confessing to *bátiushka* by going to our old friend, Father Ioann, at B*, during Easter holidays. I said nothing to him about my 'atheism' and he did not question me, perhaps because he was too old to be interested in the sins of the very young. In any case, he gave me a signed paper to say that I had been to confession, and I handed it over to *bátiushka* on my return to school.

If he resented my evasion of his pastoral supervision, he did not show it immediately: I was as good a student of his subject as of any other, and he could not but give me the highest mark. In the year of my break with Anna Avdyéevna he was instructing us in Church history, and one afternoon the subject of his lesson was the life of some Saint. This Saint was canonized, *bátiushka* told us, because his body was found 'untainted' on the sea shore, after having been washed up by the waves. Without any thought of provocation, I rose to ask whether the body was swollen, as bodies of drowned people normally swell up. Suddenly *bátiushka* turned on me in most un-Christian anger:

'Now, Rayévskaia, you're always asking provocative questions, attempting to throw doubt on religious truths. I won't have you mocking religion and leading your classmates into temptation!'

'I wasn't *mocking* anything,' I protested. 'I merely asked . . . ' But he silenced me by raising his voice.

'It is quite obvious to me that you are asking these questions with the intention of discrediting the Church witness, and I'm not going to tolerate it.'

Thrown completely off my balance by the unexpectedness and violence of his attack — for I genuinely wanted to know whether the 'untainted' body of the Saint had also resisted the effects of floating for days in the water — I was further shaken by Anna Avdyéevna suddenly joining in the attack. She rose from her seat and spoke in a nervous, high-pitched voice.

'Yes, I too have noticed for some time that Rayévskaia sits through your lessons with a sarcastic expression on her face . . . and I have observed signs of irreverence quite incredible in one so young . . . '

This intervention was most unusual and uncalled-for: in all my school life I had never seen such a concerted attack on a pupil by a teacher and a *dame-de-classe* together. Indignant as I felt, I knew it was useless to protest my innocence, to say that I did not *feel* sardonic during *batiushka*'s lessons: they could still assert that I *looked* it. My loss of faith was to me a serious and painful matter, not an occasion for priest-baiting or cheap amusement at his expense. Though I no longer believed in a personal God, I was, in the manner of Ivan Karamazov, still carrying on a dialogue with Him, holding Him responsible for all the evils and injustices of this world. And I still longed to believe in life after death, because a life which ended in complete annihilation seemed to me a diabolical joke the only dignified answer to which was suicide.

My mother had been saying regretfully that she wished I could discuss religion with a Roman Catholic priest: she thought they were better equipped educationally and intellectually than the Orthodox, and would be able to convince me of the error of my ways. But neither *bátiushka* nor Anna Avdyéevna knew anything of this: they merely detected 'irreverence' in my questions and in my facial expression.

'This cannot go on!' *bátiushka* finished grimly amidst the stunned silence of the class.

It did not go on, for from that day I refrained from asking questions during his lessons, and if his words were meant as a threat, it proved to be an empty one. We all knew that our Director, Ivan Kuzmích, was not on the side of 'the reactionaries', and if *bátiushka* chose to complain to him about our free-thinking tendencies, his complaints would most likely be dismissed with a smile. Nor did the Director approve of the *dames-de-classe*'s excessive attention to 'inessential details' of our appearance and behaviour: he let it be known, my sister had told me, that the staff existed for the pupils, not the pupils for the staff. The only harm *bátiushka* could do me would be to give me an 'eleven' mark for Religious Knowledge, instead of a 'twelve', which would have spoiled my chances of obtaining the gold medal, for which I was the favoured candidate at the end of the school course. Such an act on his part would have been dishonest, for he could not fault me on my knowledge: it would have been punishment for 'irreverent' behaviour, and behaviour was not his province at all. Anna Avdyéevna dealt with that, but anything except a 'twelve' for behaviour was an unheard-of thing in the upper forms of our school, and if she had the temerity to dock my behaviour mark, she would have to do a lot of explaining to our *Nachálnitsa*. Thus, I felt relatively safe, yet determined to avoid the repetition of the unpleasant scene in the class-room. Needless to say, this incident did not increase my respect for the clergy of the Orthodox Church.

However hard she tried to ignore my existence, Anna Avdyéevna could not resist giving vent to her animosity now and again. I soon realized that what annoyed her most was that none of my friends had changed towards me as a result of her disfavour, and that the class as a whole seemed to sympathize with me, or at least to remain neutral, with the usual exception of the two Komaróvskayas. She would have liked to see me ostracized and avoided like a plague, while I often found myself at the centre of a group – of my personal friends or of those of the class who came to me asking for 'explanation' of a current lesson. In addition to this, my 'fame' as a poet spread to the rest of the school and even some of the youngest girls came to know me by sight, and would surround me outside their class-room, clamouring for me to read them one of my poems.

One day the youngest of all pulled me into their class-room while their *dame-de-classe* was absent, and I talked to them jokingly from behind the teacher's desk. Anna Avdyéevna happened to be passing; she heard the children squealing with laughter and caught a glimpse of me through the half-open door. She swept in, her chin up, an expression of righteous indignation on her sallow face.

'Please leave these children alone!' She spoke in a husky voice.

The school bell was already tolling, so I followed her out of the room, waving good-bye to the puzzled and silent children.

'I forbid you to go into the infants' class-room again!' Anna Avdyéevna continued angrily. 'They must be safeguarded from a pernicious influence like yours!'

I could not have felt more insulted if she had struck me. I stopped and looked straight at her for a moment: I was capable of striking her then. My eyes must have told her as much because she dropped hers and swiftly went into our class-room ahead of me.

I discovered then that I could hate, and that I hated Anna Avdyéevna.

Thinking about Feelings

The war emptied the town of young men with the exception of older schoolboys, such as Fyedia Kavaliérov, or university students who came home for the holidays. I regarded schoolboys of my own age or slightly older as 'too young', and found them uninteresting or plainly boring. Schoolboy-and-girl parties with their games of forfeits, which usually meant kissing, annoyed me. I believed that only lovers should kiss, and my idea of a lover remained exalted. I still saw him as a kind of Oniéghin or Pechórin — a daemonic charmer, whose image was sometimes embodied in one of the most accomplished actors of the cinema. Early Russian films were highly romantic: their plots were frequently taken from famous novels; there was one made of *War and Peace*. My sights were set high, my appraisal of physical appearance very critical: I could admire only the handsome, the elegant, the well-bred, the sophisticated and the slightly wicked; and I could not fall in love without admiring — or so I thought.

The reality was very different. Fyedia Kavaliérov, who became an assiduous visitor at our house, was very plain and had no conversation whatsoever. Nor did I know what to say to him. To my great embarrassment he made me a present of an album for my picture postcards. It was bound in red velvet and had my initials, and his, forged in silver and firmly clipped to the binding. 'To L.R. from F.K.' It was there for all to see. It was no doubt quite expensive, and I knew that his parents were far from rich. They were *myeschάne*, that is, petty bourgeois, and we never met them socially.

My other 'admirer' and frequent visitor at our house, Shimkóvich, was a frail man of about fifty. He, too, made me a present on my name day — a beautifully bound and printed 'Academy' edition of a biography and poems by Iván Koltsóv. Proud of his own 'humble' origin, Shimkó-vich liked writers of peasant or petty bourgeois origin, and I knew he wanted me to come to love them as I loved the 'aristocrats', Pushkin and Lermontov. Dutifully, I ploughed through the Koltsóv book but failed to raise any enthusiasm for the poems, which were too folksy for my taste. Nor could I feel anything but pity for their author, the son of a village shopkeeper, who had lived a miserable life and died of consumption at the age of forty.

Shimkóvich would sit for hours at our tea table, eating almost nothing — for he was on a strict diet — and talking most of the time. Knowing that I had begun to teach myself English, he told us how during a short visit to Petersburg soon after the declaration of war, he met an English naval officer on one of the Neva bridges. The officer asked him a question in English, but our teacher of Russian had not been taught any modern language at his seminary. He replied to the officer in Latin, and to his delight they managed to explain themselves to each other in that language. Not only was he able to tell the officer the way to the Nevsky Prospect but they even exchanged their impressions of Petersburg.

Deeply patriotic, Shimkóvich hoped that Russia would come out of the conflict victorious and unshaken, and he wanted to see this with his own eyes. He knew, however, that his illness was incurable and wondered whether he would live long enough for that. I stumbled upon this discovery while amusing myself with a parlour trick, designed to look like an exercise in thought reading. Someone had shown me how to do it. You invited each person in the room to write a question on a slip of paper, to roll it up and put it into a hat. To these slips you surreptitiously added an extra blank one. The trick consisted in taking one of the slips out, holding it in your hand, unopened, pretending to concentrate, and then giving an answer to a non-existing question. Next, you opened the slip and 'read' aloud the invented question, while in fact memorizing the real one, written on the slip. As you picked up the next slip and 'concentrated' on it, you were really composing the answer to the preceding one, an answer you subsequently produced to everyone's surprise. And so until the end, by which time all the real questions had been answered, and the first, 'invented' question and answer had been forgotten. It was a trick requiring a good memory and some ability to act.

On that particular occasion I entered with zest into my rôle as a thought reader, yet when I saw what Shimkóvich had written on his slip, I felt a sudden stab of remorse. Here was I, playing this comedy, and the question he was asking was a very serious one: 'Shall I survive till the end of the war and see its results?' I had intended to disclose later on how the trick was done – now I dared not think of it. I closed my eyes, regained some control over my feelings, then answered slowly: 'You certainly will!', wondering whether my prophecy would be fulfilled.

I felt I was blushing and avoided Shimkóvich's eyes when he said how impressed he was with my gift for thought reading. 'I've never known anyone so young who could do it,' he said. My mother glanced at me anxiously: surely this kind of thing was a strain on my nervous system? Only Maroossia said nothing – until our visitor had gone.

'There were four of us asking questions,' she said, 'but I remember you giving five answers. It was a trick wasn't it? How did you do it?'

I told her and added that I could hardly bear the thought of Shimkóvich finding out. He would be hurt; I should fall very low in his esteem. I feared most of all that he might get the impression that I was heartless and frivolous enough to turn his grim preoccupation into a game.

My sister did her best to reassure me, but this incident put an end to my interest in parlour tricks for good and all.

My third 'admirer', Shoora Martýnov, was away in Petrograd studying at the Institute of Rail and Road Engineering. In the holidays, however, he haunted our house from morning till night, sharing his time between B* where his parents lived, and M* where he stayed at his former school lodgings. The smart student's uniform he was wearing did not improve his looks, and he had grown more revolutionary than ever in his political views. He never spoke of the Tsar otherwise than as 'Nikolai the Dunderhead'. My mother, shocked by the violence of his language, reproved him.

'You really ought to be more careful of what you say, Shoora! You may get yourself arrested for seditious talk one of these days.'

'If I am, I'll soon be out again,' Shoora smiled a self-satisfied smile. 'The Revolution will liberate me.'

'So you still expect the Revolution to break out?' my brother enquired, sardonically.

'Of course! Quite soon, in fact!' he declared.

During the Christmas holidays my brother brought a new friend to the house, a young man of rather striking appearance. With his sharply chiselled features, huge blue eyes and raven-black hair he did not look Russian at all. In fact, he was born in Russia, the son of an Austrian father and a Polish mother. His father, a naturalized Russian, taught German at the *Reálnaia* School at M*. The young man was called Evghéniy Preyer. I thought him very attractive in an unusual way, but wished he were taller and did not stoop so much. I liked his name — Evghéniy — like Pushkin's Oniéghin. My brother called him Zhenia. He was very shy and hardly said a word on the evening of his first visit to our house.

'Why does your friend Zhenia look so sad?' Maroossia asked my brother later that evening.

'He's a strange chap. He thinks the world's a horrible place and life's not worth living. He is a real melancholic,' my brother said.

'He looks a little like Vrubel's Demon at the Tretiakóvka,' said Maroossia. 'If he carried himself better, he could easily serve as a model for Vrubel's paintings of the Demon.'

'A *little* Demon . . . ' I spoke under my breath, but my brother heard me, and at once took up my remark.

'Yes! a romantic personage — and our little poetess will write a poem about him. There will be moonlight in it, and waving cypresses, and the scent of narcissi. It'll be all frightfully romantic.'

'And why not?' Maroossia asked. I flared up with annoyance, aware that my brother's arrow this time struck very near the mark. I *could* write a poem about Zhenia's face because its sadness intrigued and attracted me. I had not seen Vrubel's paintings, but I could imagine Zhenia as Lermontov's Demon, brooding over the ills and beauties of this world on his Caucasian rock. But my brother's irony was inhibiting.

Natural pride, as well as self-doubt, made me behave with reserve towards young men. I writhed inwardly at the thought of giving them an impression that I was pursuing them. This was reinforced by my mother's and sister's rather puritanical attitude towards so-called 'coquettishness'.

An incident remained in my memory. My sister's 'admirer', Kolia Avílov, often came to our house in the university vacations. He was 'in love' with my sister but his willingness to spend some time on drawing illustrations to my novel earned him my affection and gratitude. I did not, however, regard him attractive as a male: he had small, shortsighted eyes, wore thick spectacles and cropped his almost flaxen hair in the German style.

One evening, after we had all been talking rather excitedly at supper, and Kolia had stayed longer than usual, I was surprised and hurt to hear my mother remark that I had behaved 'flirtatiously' towards him.

'What do you mean? *How* did I behave?' I questioned in genuine bewilderment.

'You were shooting glances at him, your eyes sparkled and you talked to him in a coquettish manner.'

'How could I help my eyes sparkling?' I demanded to know. And deeply shocked to find myself so misunderstood by the women of my family, I left the room in protest.

Alone in my bedroom, I peered at my tear-stained face in the looking-glass. Anna Avdyéevna had told me more than once that my face 'showed everything I felt', that I 'could not conceal anything'. But what I felt for Kolia was no more than ordinary friendliness . . . how could my face *show* anything else? And I certainly had no intention of 'flirting' with my sister's young man! I was on the point of blaming my mother and sister for having *esprit mal tourné*, of seeing sex where there was none and of persecuting me undeservedly.

A few minutes later Maroossia followed me into my room and tried to soothe me, but the incident left a permanent impression, increasing my self-consciousness and inhibiting spontaneity. 'Coquettishness' became a danger to guard myself against.

That Christmas, the first Christmas of the war, university students whose homes were at M*, thought of collecting money for the Red Cross by taking around the 'Star' and singing carols. Some of the older schoolboys joined them, and Fyedia Kavaliérov was one of them. He suggested that I should come too, but I declined, wanting to avoid his company and his attentions. I had no doubt that he would use every slippery bit of the road as a pretext for taking my arm. The 'Star' duly came to our house, the choir sang, and we made our contribution. In the back row Fyedia's head showed above most of the others, but close beside him there was another face I knew — Zhenia Preyer's. The contrast between the two was most unflattering to Fyedia. Suddenly I decided that I would like to go with the choir, so that I could continue to watch that striking face.

While the choir was still singing, I started putting on my snow boots and overcoat. Fyedia watched me impassively, and as the group jostled itself out of the front door into the snowy street, I found him immediately at my side.

'So you've decided to come?' he asked me.

'Yes . . . The night is fine, and it isn't as cold as I had thought.'

The air in fact was very sharp, the sky clear and the whole scene drenched in moonlight. The snow glistened and squeaked under our feet as we followed the Star-bearers. I carefully avoided slipping so that Fyedia would not take my arm: I did not want Zhenia to think that Fyedia was a young man of my choice.

The students' Star was a great success. At every house they were received warmly and generously; they collected a fair sum for the 'wounded soldiers'. While the choir sang, I tried to place myself in a position from where I could watch Zhenia Preyer's face. Like myself, he did not sing: he was simply one of the Star's followers. He just stood in the back row, staring in front of him, his huge blue eyes shining in the candlelight, full of bewildered sadness like a fallen angel's. I wondered what sort of person he really was. What did he feel so sad about? Could he be happy if he were loved?

I made no attempt to speak to him, nor did he say anything to me during the whole evening, but I had had my fill of watching him. When the choir dispersed about midnight, Fyedia accompanied me home. The streets were empty and I did not mind so much his taking my arm. He remained silent until we were about to say good-night before our front door. As I turned to face him, I was struck by the look of resentment on his usually impassive face. His voice, too, sounded different, stifled and broken, yet harsh, as he blurted out: 'I know why you came with the Star tonight!'

I looked at him, startled and silent. This was a new Fyedia whose existence I had not suspected.

'You came because Preyer was there. I saw you looking at him all the time!'

Jealous emotion had quite distorted his face: he looked not merely plain but frighteningly ugly.

'I can look at anyone I choose!' I stammered. 'Good night!' And, turning my back on him, I pulled hard at the handle of the door bell.

My withdrawal was too much like a flight to be dignified, but my emotions, violently stirred, prevented deliberation. Surprise was immediately followed by indignation, and indignation by anger and something akin to shame. It had been stupid of me to underestimate Fyedia's capacity for observation and foolish to stare at Zhenia in such a conspicuous way. But it was also presumptuous of Fyedia, to say the least, to reproach me for this, and quite outrageous to make a scene of jealousy. Did he imagine by any chance that I reciprocated his feelings just because I was courteous to him when he came to our house? The incredible vanity of men! I had never encouraged, I merely tolerated him. Why did I have to accept the convention that a man could 'choose' a girl to burden with his attentions while a girl would be despised if she behaved in that way to a man?

Perhaps I felt so indignant because I sensed that this particular convention had become a part of myself. I had not yet liked anyone enough to want to show what I felt, yet I knew myself incapable of courting a man's attention, of doing anything at all in order to attract him. When I saw other girls transformed by the presence of a man, becoming excited and voluble, laughing excessively, hanging on his words as if he were the only person in the room capable of saying intelligent or amusing things, I felt embarrassed on their account, and on my own I could feel no respect for them.

Respect was to me a necessary part of friendship or love. I had yet to discover that lack of respect did not necessarily exclude affection: to me the two were absolutely incompatible. Love without respect, I would have said, was not 'real love'. And 'real' love was something that happened once in a life-time . . .

What name then had one to give the feeling Liolia had for Henryk, the young officer with the pink face and wide smile, who danced with her the whole evening on the night of the school concert? One day in the spring, the first spring of the war, Liolia missed a day at school. I called at her house on the way home, and she threw herself into my arms, sobbing: she had heard that morning that Henryk had been killed at the front. For several days Liolia appeared inconsolable. Then, to my surprise, I heard her laughing again as she and Lena Kazanóvich whispered to each other in the corner of the class-room. How could anybody recover so quickly from the loss of someone they had loved? I imagined my very life would end with the death of the person I loved. Or if it did not physically end, it could never be the same again: I was sure I would not be able to laugh, or dance, or be frivolous as I had been. If I were able to, it would surely mean that I had a shallow nature . . .

But how did I know that I was not in fact shallow? I knew I could feel strongly, even passionately, but could I feel *deeply* as well? And what did *depth* of feeling really mean? Did it mean constancy, or intensity, or both, and something else besides? Could depth of feeling be measured by the pain it gave you? And if I fell in love, how would I know that it was *real* love, that is, a feeling that was deep, passionate and constant, not a mere infatuation? I did not want to 'fritter myself away in small change', as a Russian saying goes: if I met someone I could love in that true sense, I would want no other for the rest of my life. So I told myself.

None of 'the four' with whom I was most friendly in my last years at school were particularly interested in my speculations on love, and through one of those quirks of adolescent secretiveness, I really preferred to keep them to myself. I did however try to talk about it to Zena when she came to spend the night at our house. I talked to her in bed, in the dark, grateful for the wide-eyed silence in which she so often listened to my speculations. In the dark I could only just see her eyes, but suddenly I became aware that they shone with something more than their normal brilliance. Then I heard her gently catch her breath.

'What is it, Zena? You're *not* crying?'

'No.' Her voice however belied her denial.

'Why are you crying?'

'I . . . I'm not feeling very well . . . '

She had not, in fact, been looking at all well since the end of the summer when my uncle complained of her spending too much time in the river. Her complexion, always rather pale, had acquired a greenish tinge, and my brother teased her about it, calling her jokingly 'our fresh young greens'. I had long ceased to think of her as a spoiled only child, the pampered daughter of her doting parents, and saw her now as she was, a pathetic, lonely girl, marooned on a desert island of a home, an object of dispute between her warring progenitors. The anxieties of war had intensified the already strong vein of parsimony in Uncle Vladímir's character, and he economized on everything, even on the trips Stan and the pink horse made from his place to the town. As a result of these economies Zena was often left to walk home from school, and was so tired when she arrived that she refused her evening meal.

'One more economy!' my brother commented sarcastically.

We all felt sorry for Zena and often asked Aunt Katia to let her stay the night at our house. Permission was given grudgingly, and we did not doubt that on the evenings Zena stayed with us, her parents ate their supper in their separate rooms.

On the particular evening I remember, Zena came to us straight from school by previous arrangement. She went to my sister's room to tidy her hair, complained of feeling dizzy and suddenly sank on to her bed in a fainting fit. My mother was seriously alarmed and made her stay in bed the following morning. When Uncle Vladímir came to take her home, my mother pressed him to take Zena to a good doctor. He resisted, saying that Zena was all right, she was 'just growing', that was all. And of course all that bathing in the summer had not done her any good. My mother then said she herself would take Zena to a doctor and pay his fee. Uncle Vladímir laughed. His laughter, like his voice, was affected by a permanent frog in his throat.

'Do if you must,' he said. 'I'm sure she's as strong as a heifer.'

Zena stayed with us for a few days after the visit to the doctor, waiting for the analysis of her blood to be made. She alarmed us by more fainting fits, and by the slow, lifeless cadences of her speech and movements. Then we had the doctor's letter addressed to my mother: Zena's complaint had been diagnosed as pernicious anaemia. She had to be treated at once; everything had to be done to increase the amount of red corpuscles in her blood. Her condition was serious: no time should be lost. Prescriptions for medicines and diet were attached to the letter.

Uncle Vladímir was shocked and bewildered by this news.

'But where are we to get it from, all that he says she must have: prime beef and calf's liver, and fresh fruit in winter? And even if we get it, the blessed girl won't touch it, I'm sure!'

Zena cried as she said good-bye to us, and turned a pathetic, imploring face towards me while Stan tucked her into the sleigh beside Uncle Vladímir: the snow was now lying thickly over the ground. She might have been going into Siberian exile, instead of to her home.

My sister and I went to see her the following Sunday. Zena was in bed, a plate of uneaten food on a tray beside her, and both her parents cajoling and scolding her because she refused to eat it up. It was the only occasion on which I saw them in agreement, but not for long. A few moments later my uncle was saying that no wonder Zena would not eat the food: it was abominably cooked, because Mavra could not cook and my aunt didn't know how to teach her, while Aunt Katia was looking daggers at him without speaking.

When we told my mother what we had seen on our visit, she decided that Zena must go somewhere where she would be looked after properly. A cousin of hers, another Martsinóvsky, was a physician attached to a famous hospital in Moscow. He was well-known for his work on malaria: he could use his influence to get Zena admitted to the hospital for the treatment she needed. There was a great shortage of beds because of war casualties, but my mother was sure that Zena would not get better unless she went away from home. She took the matter in hand, and Uncle Vladímir, now thoroughly frightened and humbled, agreed to everything she said.

We saw Zena off at the railway station. She was too ill to react to what was happening with much emotion. Her father was accompanying her to Moscow, while Aunt Katia either from economy, or from the inability of these two to co-operate in anything, was to stay behind. As silent tears streamed down her face, Zena repeated in a feeble voice: 'Don't cry, Mamma!' Uncle Vladímir's face by contrast was the colour of brick and his eyes bloodshot.

'I'll be back in a couple of days,' he told my mother. 'Can't afford the trip really, but I must see her settled. Cousin Iván, I dare say, will put me up for a few nights . . . '

Aunt Katia came back to our house and spent the night but would not stay longer. Her deep concern for Zena did not prevent her from also being concerned, somewhat excessively, we thought, with the house, left in charge of Mavra and Stan. 'You can't rely on servants these days . . .' she murmured. 'Without me there, young Hovra will get her fingers into every jam jar . . . Mavra is honest enough, but she indulges that child. And as for Stan, he'd go out with girls and leave the house without a man to guard it . . . '

After Aunt Katia had left us, we talked about the Martsinóvsky family with a sense of frustration, almost of hopelessness, and again promised ourselves to get Zena to come and stay at Fyeny in the school holidays. But this was looking too far ahead with too much confidence.

The preceding summer – before the war was declared – was a crowded one for me. First, Shoora Martýnov managed to get himself invited to Fyeny early in the holidays. Somehow it was taken for granted that he would. He had no real home of his own – his mother was a chronic invalid in a mental hospital.

His attachment to me persisted, apparently undiminished by distance or separation. He would stay in the room where I was, and leave it when I went out. During walks and picnics he was always at my side: if I climbed a tree, he would climb it also; if I scampered down a sandy cliff, he would follow, even when his precarious balance made him trip and slither. 'A rhinoceros pursuing a goat,' my brother would comment caustically. Shoora merely grinned and growled: 'Shut up, Baldwin! *You* would never dare!' which was probably true.

Shoora positively flaunted his subservience to my wishes. I told him I had been the King of Rome in my previous existence, so he began to call me 'Your Majesty', but to my annoyance would refer to me as a 'queen', not a king. His obedience to my commands was so much taken for granted by the whole household that I was expected to stop arguments between him and my brother. Shoora's voice was most penetrating

when he was excited, 'like a peacock's', my mother said, and she would
protest to him about this without him apparently hearing her. She
would then turn to me.

'Léda, do tell him to speak quietly!'

I did so, and at once he would lower his voice.

I accepted his company in my hours of leisure, but I also wanted to
work, which was impossible with Shoora always there. It was then that
I had the idea of making him into my secretary. I would dictate my
stories to him, instead of writing them myself. Shoora fell in readily
with this suggestion, and my mother approved, too, because 'it would
keep him quiet'.

Several of these literary sessions passed off smoothly enough. Shoora
sat at my desk while I walked up and down the room, dictating. His
sprawling handwriting devoured page after page of my note-books which
I liked to look neat and compact. I told myself with some irritation that
I would have to copy it all over again. Yet we were *doing* something, not
merely wasting time. But soon we began discussing what I was dictating
and arguing about some relatively trivial point, such as the best way of
dressing children. Little boys in my story were dressed in short socks
and sandals. Shoora declared perversely that when he had children, he
would 'put the boys into high boots'. I protested that high boots were
ugly and hot in the summer; he retorted that if children climbed trees in
short socks and sandals, they would scratch their legs.

We had had only about five dictation sessions and the story was far
from finished when one of these arguments ended in a most unexpected
way. Annoyed by what Shoora was saying, I declared that I was going to
punish him by cutting off some of his hair. He laughed. I seized a pair of
scissors, and snipping off a few hairs from the crown of his head,
scattered them over the page of the note-book before him. Suddenly my
hand was caught between Shoora's face and the book. He fell down on
it like a man parched with thirst falling upon water, pressing his mouth
to it, covering it with kisses. Petrified with shock for a few seconds,
I pulled my hand away and stared at him as he rose and stood facing me,
flushed, half-smiling, swaying slightly, as if he had indeed been drinking
something much stronger than water. Revulsion and fear surged up in
me, constricting my throat. The silence that followed was so charged
with emotion that it could not be borne for more than a few moments.
I turned and fled.

As if in a travesty of Paolo and Francesca's story, 'we read no more
that day', nor any other day. On the following morning I found a note

from Shoora on my desk. It contained three sentences: 'I could not help it. I love you. You are my life, my happiness, my *all*.'

As I read it, tears of anger sprang into my eyes. Why, oh, why, did he have to tell me this? It was the end. Never could I feel natural with him again! How wicked of him to thrust such a responsibility upon me! 'My life,' 'my happiness', 'my all' . . . It was far too early to be told this at the age of fifteen. I did not want to be, I *could* not be 'his life', his 'all': I was not able to give him any happiness.

Until that happened I had been aware of Shoora's ungainly appearance; now I could hardly bear to look at him. I feared finding myself alone with him lest he spoke to me again of his love and forced me to say that I could never return it. The fear of wounding him blended with a feeling of intense aversion, a physical shrinking, a sensation I had never before experienced in anyone's presence. I begged my sister never to leave me alone with him. She raised her eyebrows.

'But why not?'

'I can't bear it.'

'But you've been able to until now.'

'Something's happened. Don't ask me. I'll tell you afterwards . . . some time. But I assure you, it's serious. Please, please, don't leave us alone together!'

Maroossia promised, but did not always remember. On the first occasion when she walked out of the room where Shoora and I were reading at the same table, I was about to jump up and run after her. However, pride and the convention of 'good manners' held me in my place, tense and silent, in an atmosphere charged with agitated expectancy. I dared not raise my eyes from my book, convinced that Shoora's stare was fixed upon me and that he would speak as soon as I looked up. He cleared his throat. I leapt to my feet, and, forcing myself to walk slowly, went to an open window. My father's red setter was frisking about in front of the house, leaping over flower beds. I called him, and he came bouncing, put his paws on the window ledge and licked my hand as I stroked him. I heard Shoora's footsteps behind me, and again had to force myself not to move away. His hand stretched out beside mine and also stroked the dog who was wriggling with pleasure.

'You lucky devil,' he said under his breath.

Behind us the door swung open and my brother entered, announcing that we were going to have wild duck for supper. I waited a few minutes, listening to his distasteful account of how many ducks they had shot that morning, then left the room as casually as I could. I found my sister upstairs arranging her hair.

I reproached her passionately for having left me alone with Shoora after she had promised not to do so. 'But what *is* the matter?' she asked again. 'You used not to object to his company.'

I told her of the incident with the snippets of hair and showed her the note he had sent me, which, for reasons obscure to myself, I had not torn up. Maroossia read it and did not smile. 'Poor Shoora!' she sighed.

I was almost angry with her for pitying him rather than me. Should he have not spared me this? I asked. Why couldn't he be content with my friendship? What more did he want from me at this time of my life, from me *as I was*, for himself as *he* was? Didn't he — by telling me that I was his 'all' — make claims on my life? The whole of my nature revolted against such a monstrous claim. Yet I dreaded the moment when I should be forced to tell him that, and I spent the rest of that fortnight dodging being left alone with him, until I was able to leave Fyeny for Diédlovo.

Katia's invitation to entertain all four of us classmates at her country home came just in time. It was to be a rather unusual country house party, for there was to be no adult with us except the housekeeper. Katia's brother, Dima, aged eighteen and only just out of his school uniform, could hardly be regarded by our parents as old enough to act as host to four girls of fifteen. Yet they raised no objections, obviously confident that we would behave sensibly. And so we did, while thoroughly enjoying our freedom.

I can see the house at Diédlovo quite clearly in my mind's eye. It was built of wood, like ours, but had no upstairs rooms. There was a glass porch in front and a veranda at the back; not much of a flower garden, and the view from the back windows was cut off by a tall hedge of spruce. A soft track led to the front of the house, joining it to the highway and continuing into the stable-yard. Beyond the spruce hedge, vast orchards spread for acres towards the adjoining cornfields, and beyond them there was, as at Fyeny, the distant forest encircling it all.

When I arrived, the other three were already there. In the dining-room a long table was loaded with food, and Katia introduced me to *Panna* Rosa, the housekeeper, a quiet, youngish woman with a pleasant face, who presided over the samovar. She was, Katia told me, a daughter of a neighbouring smallholder, a *shliáhtich*; that is, her family belonged to the Polish petty gentry, of whom there were many in Bielorussia. These *shliáhta*, though hardly better off or more educated than the peasants, were very proud of their 'nobility', and their women always wore hats to go to church on Sunday, even if they had to ride there in peasant carts. They were Roman Catholic and spoke a mixture of Polish and Bielorussian dialect among themselves.

What do I remember from those days — almost a whole month of them — during which freedom reigned? Dima got up at dawn and was out in the fields, supervising his workmen, most of the day, for he took his apprenticeship in farming seriously. Then he suddenly went off to Petersburg — to visit his fiancée, Katia told us — and he stayed away for the rest of our visit, thus clearly showing that he had no interest in the company of mere schoolgirls. I welcomed his disappearance because he was in the habit of teasing us by telling farmyard anecdotes at table — a brand of humour I found distasteful.

Left to our own devices, we called ourselves the 'Republic of Five' and pleased ourselves entirely, which meant that we wasted the freshness of summer mornings by getting up late. We drifted over to the breakfast table on the veranda whenever we were ready, rarely all together, and ate whatever food we found there, under wire-mesh covers, protecting it from ubiquitous flies. The samovar and the coffee pot on a spirit lamp kept tea and coffee hot for late-comers. Then, as we yawned, and blinked, and stretched in the bright sunshine, Katia would appear and ask: 'Girls, what would you like to do today?'

My choice was always riding. We rode every day, sometimes twice a day. Katia generously let me ride her Bedouin, a horse which could not tolerate being overtaken. At first I was terrified of him because he would spring forward as soon as I was on his back and was very difficult to stop. Soon, however, I learned his ways and managed to stop him, once even when he had bolted, by taking him into a freshly ploughed field. We went on horseback to visit Katia's grandmother and her funny little aunt on a neighbouring estate. They were a curious pair: 'Auntie Olia', who was about forty, had never been away from her mother's house, and she was so afraid of thunder that she would run upstairs, bury her head in a pillow and weep when she saw a rain storm approaching. Young as we were, we thought her very childish. We loved our rides back through woods and fields in the dusk, the horses for once not competing but trotting peacefully side by side, while we sang the Pedlar's Song which goes so well with the rhythm of horses' hooves. We shared the chocolate bars Grandmamma gave us at parting and wiped our fingers on the horses' manes. And at the supper table we fell upon our food like hungry wolves, yet often had to stop eating because we laughed so much — riding invariably put us into a happy, laughing mood.

We did some silly things, of course. Once, as we lounged on the lawn, eating wild strawberries and cream, I threatened to put some down the opening of Tonia's blouse if she continued arguing with me. She did continue, and I carried out my threat, and then perversely locked her out of the house when she wanted to wash. We both laughed so much that we could hardly stand up. On another occasion, when we were riding in the forest on a very hot day and stopped for a rest, I stripped completely and danced round a tree, pretending to be a nymph. My companions were mildly amused but declined to follow my example: they only took off their blouses and long riding skirts. With the exception of Katia, we all rode side-saddle.

On the night of Ivan Kupála, the 24th of June, we watched peasant youths and girls jumping over a bonfire in the neighbouring field. They did this in pairs, a youth holding a girl's hand, and the point of this was that if the couple landed on the other side of the fire with their hands still joined, the girl would become the bride of the man. Ivan Kupála would see to that: St John's night was a magic night.

Liolia and I decided to jump together, but two village lads rushed to separate us and made us jump with them. I managed to pull my hand away before we landed on the other side, and Liolia's partner fared no better. But after that one of the youths was bold enough to approach Katia and ask her to jump with him. I heard *Panna* Rosa mutter under her breath: 'This Vanka has the cheek!' But Katia agreed, and when they jumped there were tremendous cheers on the other side, indicating that Vanka had been successful in retaining her hand.

Those who take the all-pervasiveness of sex for granted would be surprised to hear how relatively little we, five adolescent girls left to ourselves, were concerned with sex. We did of course talk about young men, mostly about film actors, famous at the time. We had our favourites among them: Liolia 'adored' Moszhúhin; I liked Maxímov, Tonia Polónsky. Katia and Lena expressed no preferences and declared themselves unromantic. As it happened, they were the first of us five to get married! We discussed our heroes' appearance, their behaviour as characters in the films, their attractiveness as possible lovers, but the words 'passionate' and 'passion' still meant to us little more than flashing eyes and prolonged kissing, the 'rest' being tacitly regarded as the prosaic aspect of married life or as a sordid mishap which sometimes befell servant girls or wild young women in avant-garde novels. I was quite sure that, like myself, neither Katia, nor Lena, nor Tonia had been kissed by young men except perhaps in the game of 'forfeits'. About

Liolia — remembering Henryk — I had some doubts but I knew she had very few chances of ever being alone with a young man.

We knew 'the facts', and I, for one, found them singularly unattractive — more than that, repulsive. I was not in the least interested in the physiology of sex. My own body was of interest to me only in so far as it could do what I wanted, that is: ride, swim, skate, climb trees, keep balance on a plank thrown across a stream, jump and run. When I was about twelve, I came upon the Latin tag *'mens sana in corpore sano'*, and determined to adopt it. It provided a good reason for doing the physical things I liked doing and a counter-weight to the studious side of my nature. My mother, holding the view that we should know 'the facts', chose the translation of August Forel's *Physiology of Sex* and of Otto Weininger's *Sex and Character* as suitable for this purpose. If her intention had been to put me off the subject, she could not have succeeded better. I found the two thick volumes of Forel particularly forbidding. My brother and sister had them first, probably much earlier than I did. When they were passed on to me, I took them to my room and put them underneath a pile of my school books. These had to take precedence over any reading I did in term time; I was always short of time: Forel and Weininger had to wait.

I remember looking at the portraits of the authors: the patriarchal, bearded and benevolent face of Forel, and the much younger, thick-lipped unmistakably Semitic face of Weininger. Someone had told me that he had been a woman-hater and had committed suicide. He regarded women as inferior to men, as creatures whose function was to submit and to serve men. Why, I asked myself, should I read a book I was bound to dislike, by a man whose face I disliked already? I could not even bring myself to begin. It may have been fear — the fear of being wounded or even finding confirmation of some of my own self-doubts. 'Later on . . . when I have more time . . . ' I said to myself, closing the book on that unpleasant face. But in fact I never got on to reading *Sex and Character*: there never seemed to be time enough for it. As for the *Physiology of Sex*, I made a determined effort to get myself interested in it. It was at least 'scientific' . . . Too much so! I found the descriptions at first repellent, then boring, and gave up after reading the first chapter. The books remained on my desk during the whole of my last year at school without my opening them again.

Whatever crumbs of knowledge I collected and retained from this attempt to inform myself, they aroused no strong emotion, stirred up no new line of thought. 'Sex' apart from 'love' made no sense to me;

without love, it reduced human beings to animals, and I was not yet ready to accept the animal side of human nature. I was unpleasantly surprised when I learned that the sexual act was not merely the means of ensuring the preservation of the human species, occurring only when children were desired. But the impact of this discovery was far less powerful than being told about menstruation when I was fourteen. This I really regarded as a monstrous imposition of Fate, or the Deity, or most likely the Devil himself. My mother made things rather worse by impressing upon me that when this condition arrived I should take no violent exercise of any kind. I stormed, and cried, and almost blamed her for getting me to be born a woman . . . But that summer at Diédlovo, at the age of fifteen, I was still free from 'the curse', and did not have to forego once the pleasures of riding.

Our last fling before we returned to our own homes was to drape ourselves in sheets and, late at night, drive on the *biegovýie drozhki,* the lightest vehicle in existence, through silent villages, howling, to make the inhabitants think we were ghosts. It was a complete failure: the inhabitants were fast asleep and did not even trouble to open their window shutters. No rumours were started in the countryside as a result of our escapade. But it was very exciting while it lasted.

The 'Republic of Five' was short-lived but memorable. Its experiences were never repeated, for that very autumn Dima got married, and Katia ceased to be the mistress of Diédlovo.

A Journey and a Romance

Of the countries I loved in my imagination the Caucasus was the first. I was very young when my mother read to me Tolstoy's simple story 'The Prisoner of the Caucasus'. As soon as I could, I read it myself, along with Pushkin's poem of the same title and Lermontov's stories and poems on Caucasian themes. In my solitary games, dressed in my brother's Circassian tunic and cloak, I pretended to be a Circassian prince, riding fiery horses. A few years later I shared Mtzyri's longing for freedom and learnt by heart whole passages from *Demon*. The power and beauty of Lermontov's verse took possession of me and made me long to see what he had seen and described – the places where he had lived and died.

Towards the end of that crowded summer my mother was to take a course of treatment at Essentuki, a spa in the Northern Caucasus, and I was to go with her. She decided on this because I had been having pains in my arms and legs which she thought might be due to rheumatism. Essentuki was *the* spa for such complaints. My father had gone ahead of us to Piatigorsk for a course of waters and baths. For some months his health had not been good, and he was able to obtain four weeks' leave to undergo this treatment. We were to join him later at Piatigorsk.

I was looking forward with great excitement to seeing the Caucasus and to my first long journey. We were to spend two and a half days on the train! Any new experience was welcome to me, and sleeping on the train was one of them. At the same time I wished I could stay awake all night, so as not to miss the countryside through which we would be passing. During the day I hardly left my seat by the window until it got too dark to see anything. Great stretches of forest in the early part of the journey, were followed by villages of grey log cabins, separated by their yards and cart-sheds. These gave way to more open countryside, to fields and meadows with isolated, white-washed houses, set among cherry orchards and hollyhocks. Bielorussia became Ukraina, and Ukraina became Novorussia, the true steppe, seemingly featureless but with a sunset sky which affected me like the music of 'The Swan Lake', nostalgic and enticing at the same time. On the morning of the third day the train began to climb the vast plateau of Pryed-Caucasia, and suddenly an apparition on the horizon changed the whole character of the country-side. At first one could not tell whether they were mountains or clouds. To see them better I thrust my head out of the window, ignoring my mother's protests. My eyes unfocused by the glitter of sunlight on leaves as the train rushed past the rows of tall Lombardy poplars, caught a glimpse of a white pointsman's cottage and of a slender, dark-haired woman chasing an infant, clad only in a short white shift. I gulped the bracing air of higher lands and told myself that for the first time in my life I was looking at *real* mountains. The train crept up and up, but they did not seem to come any nearer, they only became less like clouds, sharper, harder, more glistening.

I asked my mother, who had been to Essentuki before, whether the big summit we could see was Elbruss or Kazbek. She told me it was Elbruss, which could be seen quite well from Essentuki.

Our train was running late, and my mother was not pleased when the conductor told her that we would not be arriving at Essentuki before dark. I, on the other hand, was delighted. There were few things that fascinated me more than arriving at a new place in the dark. And so it was in this case. The contrast between the cosy smallness of the train compartment and the vastness of the balmy southern night into which we emerged, and then between the brightly lit station hall and the patchwork of light and shade under the acacia trees outside, where the jingling cabs were competing for our custom . . . an oriental face with a hooked nose and darting black eyes which peered closely into mine, and a voice with a strange, guttural ring demanding to know where we were going . . . being carried softly along a wide road fringed with trees to our 'destination' . . . or was it 'destiny'? I had never seen such trees covered with blossom at such an unseasonable time . . . I should never know who lived in those silent, shuttered houses standing so still beyond them . . . Why was the sky so black, with the blackness of velvet, despite

being filled with huge stars? Why did the stars quiver so? Why was the
air so soft and light that it made me want to rise on my toes? And what
was that fragrance, drifting out of the mysterious garden behind a stone
wall — a scent sweet and bitter, a blend of scents, such as I had never
met before? That scent! From the moment I first inhaled it it had become
for me the very essence of the South, instantly evoking the whole magic
of southernness.

Such a first encounter with a place in the dark can never be repeated.
The place you see in daylight is never the same place, nor does it become
so when the night comes again. You have now seen it in daylight and you
remember — the mystery is gone.

This did not mean that I was not delighted with the real Essentuki
when I walked out into the strong sunshine rather late on the same
morning, strolling beside my mother. It *was* different from any place I
had seen hitherto: acacias were flowering with incredible profusion,
there were trees covered with deep pink blossom the name of which I
did not know, the wide streets were crowded with well-dressed people,
and on the way to the park we met girls in Georgian national dress, very
beautiful girls with olive complexions, eyes glowing like coals and plaits
of raven hair hanging down to their knees. The park was large and shady
with a covered dais for open-air concerts, fountains, flower-beds and
many garden seats. A programme of concerts was posted beside the dais.
Music from Chaikovsky's ballets was billed for the evening. The conductor's name was Steinberg. 'A German or a Jew,' my mother said.

The same afternoon she took me to see one of the spa doctors. He
was a florid man with greying hair and suave manners. He took me
behind a screen where I had to lie on a couch while he felt my limbs,
asking where it was hurting. As he did so, he breathed heavily and
stared at me in the semi-darkness. I found this embarrassing and
unpleasant, and must have shown it, because he smiled reassuringly and
said there was nothing seriously wrong. He repeated this to my mother
but added that a course of mud baths and of drinking the Essentuki waters
three times a day would do me good. My mother was to have similar
treatment, and he wrote out prescriptions for both of us to take to the
thermal establishment.

I was curious to see what 'mud baths' really were, and was disappointed
that they were not baths at all. A friendly, sturdy Kazak woman, the
bath attendant, who wore nothing under her white overalls, took me
to a small room with no furniture except a wooden bench and a stool.
Stripped of my clothes, I had to lie on my back while she plastered my

arms and legs with steaming black mud from a tub. The mud was heavy and left me pinioned to my couch while rivulets of perspiration streamed down my face, tickling my cheeks and chin, driving me frantic with irritation. I decided that the legendary Chinese tortures must have included such refinements as these. The Kazak woman pattered in from time to time to see how I was faring and mopped my face with a towel, but almost as soon as she left me, the exasperating sensation as if of flies creeping down my cheeks was back again.

The effect of these 'baths' on me was fatiguing and depressing. My mother complained of my irritability. The truth of the matter was that, after the novelty had worn off, I began to feel disappointed with Essentuki. The place was crowded: at the restaurant where we took our meals we often had to wait to be served for what seemed to me an interminably long time. Many visitors were parents with young children; there were few girls of my own age and almost no young men: they were at the front. With Lermontov's *Hero of Our Time* in my mind I must have hoped half-consciously for a romantic meeting with someone like Pechórin. Essentuki, however, was not a place for wounded heroes but a spa for people suffering from rheumatic diseases and obesity. My mother drew my attention to a large number of fat Jewish couples in the park: Caucasian resorts had been opened to them for the first time because of the war. They all used to go to German spas, she told me.

She insisted that I should rest after lunch, which I found tiresome. In the late afternoon we usually returned to the park in time for the daily concert. I soon decided that these concerts were the best thing in Essentuki. The orchestra was large and, in my inexperienced judgment, it played very well. The conductor's selection of pieces was orthodox and middlebrow: the orchestra never attempted Beethoven's symphonies but acquitted itself creditably in such respectable works as Zuppé's 'Poet and Peasant', Strauss waltzes and Mendelssohn's 'Midsummer Night's Dream'. A novice in the art of listening, I responded to music on the plane of the senses and imagination: it painted pictures for me, it stimulated feeling, it aroused longings and increased my dissatisfaction with reality. After listening to Chaikovsky's 'Swan Lake' overture, I could hardly tolerate being recalled to the prosaic business of living by questions such as my mother would ask me on the way back to our hotel — for instance, had I remembered to drink my second glass of Essentuki water that afternoon?

I snapped back that of course I had, and she remarked that music was obviously bad for my nerves, to which I replied, it was not music but the perpetual talk about health which upset me. My mother would then come out with her favourite dictum about health being the most important thing in life, and I would retort that I would much rather have talent than health.

'Talent,' said my mother, 'is not much use without good health. Look at Steinberg . . . '

'What about him?' I asked.

She told me what she had gleaned from conversations with other concert-goers — in the intervals she always talked to people sitting near her, while I wished she would not. Steinberg, she said, was one of the conductors at the Maryinsky theatre in Petersburg. He was tubercular and northern climate was harmful to him, so he spent as much time as he could conducting in the Caucasus or the Crimea. No one knew how ill he really was, but he clearly was not very strong.

'Look at Steinberg' . . . I could not help looking at him unless I closed my eyes when he was on the rostrum. Before I saw him conduct, I used to regard conductors as something of a nuisance. They were just men gesticulating to music, distracting me from it, whose gestures were often ugly, sometimes funny, but never relevant to what was happening in the orchestra, as they seemed to come *after*, not before the sounds of the instruments.

Steinberg was the first conductor whose movements enhanced the impression the music produced on me. He was dignified, graceful and restrained. Aged about fifty, tall, with a slight stoop and greying hair, he had a lean face of a distinctly Jewish cast, yet without its less attractive features. When the audience applauded at the end of a piece, he turned and bowed with a look of melancholy pleasure which touched off some deep chord of sympathy in me and set me wondering what kind of man he really was. As I watched his stooping figure in black mount the rostrum evening after evening and stretch his arms like a priest over the heads of his receptive orchestra, this sympathy gradually developed into a feeling of passionate compassion. I wondered whether he was not in fact too ill to be doing all this standing about and gesturing, and whether he had to do this in order to keep the wolf from the door. Perhaps he could not afford to take a proper holiday . . . I tried to imagine the way he lived when he was not in the public eye. I began to weave a fantasy around him. He had a wife who was rather common and matter-of-fact and was not in the least interested in music. He found nothing to say to her when he returned home tired, after conducting. He had two children, a boy and a girl, aged perhaps sixteen and fourteen, who were always quarrelling and made a dreadful noise when he needed silence and peace. He felt alone in the midst of his utterly uncongenial family. If only he could live his life all over again, be young again! As he sat musing in a darkened room, he recollected a young girl's face gazing up at him from the audience when he made his bow in response to their applause. He could tell that she admired him, that if he chose to make the first step, she would be ready to love him . . . But how could he – ill and tired, and unhappily bound to his wife and family ? . . .

Love takes many forms, and my intense concern for Steinberg was a kind of love. I could not bear to miss any of his concerts, and I felt disappointed and anxious when, on some evenings, a handsome young man in Kazak uniform would stride on to the dais instead of him. I found this other conductor's brisk, energetic gestures almost offensive in their crudity and longed for the slower, softer movements of the older man. Why did he fail to appear? Was he feeling more ill than usual?

My mother would remark that he was probably resting, and I wondered throughout the evening and the following day whether it was only that. Then the evening came, the lights on the dais were switched on, turning the dark foliage around it into a harsh, theatrical green halo, and the musicians trickled on to the stage with their instruments. A tall figure in black walked up the steps and the audience burst into applause, making my heart leap with excitement. Steinberg was back!

From my conviction that he was unhappy arose, perhaps inevitably, my wish to comfort and console. What was the use of love, I asked myself almost angrily, if I did nothing for the person I loved? But what *could* I do? I could not even let him know how much I admired him. He was not even aware of my existence. I was unique among these hundreds who applauded him because I loved him, but to him I was only a blurred face in the crowd, indistinguishable from other faces . . . I came to feel that I *had* to do something to become someone to him.

I could not think of anything which would do justice to his qualities and express what I felt for him. I felt I could not write him a letter or hand him a bunch of flowers at one of his concerts, as some of the audience did. For some days I was a tormented and restless soul. Then one morning, on the way to the park, a florist's window caught my eye. It was filled with a variety of exotic-looking plants but in the centre stood a vase with a few *blue* roses – 'the colour achieved after many trials', said the writing on a card beside it. Fascinated, I stood and gazed at them. Blue roses – the flowers for him, rare, exquisite, strange, a little sad . . . My mind was made up.

It was to be a farewell present, for our three weeks' course of treatment had come to an end and we were due to join my father at Piatigorsk for the rest of our stay in the Caucasus. My grief at parting with Steinberg was tempered by the eager anticipation of seeing the place where Lermontov had lived and died. And anyway it was better than if Steinberg had to leave before me and I had to go on listening to concerts conducted by the other man. It was right, somehow, to give him flowers and leave the place on the following day, so that he would know my gift was entirely disinterested. The giving would be an act of pure homage, nameless and final, my only reward being that for a few days, perhaps, while the roses were still alive on his desk, he would remember the face of the girl who gave them . . .

My mother knew that I admired Steinberg and I did not attempt to conceal from her that I was going to give him flowers on our last night in Essentuki. She saw I was in a state of high nervous tension, and said nothing to ruffle me. We sat through the evening concert conducted by him, but before the final applause had died down, I left her and went out into the street along which Steinberg would pass on his way home. I bought two blue roses — they were expensive — and stood outside the shop, watching the gates of the park for the familiar figure to appear. My heart seemed to be beating in my throat and the tissue paper wrapped round the flowers quivered slightly.

The stream of people was slowly flowing out of the gates in eddies of twos and threes. Among them I saw my mother, and was suddenly afraid and angry at the thought that she might stop and watch me. I pretended not to see her, desperately pulled the paper off the flowers and held them to my face. Their fragrance was delicate and strange. I looked up, and my heart gave a great bound while my legs grew very limp. Steinberg was walking along the pavement on the other side of the street, *accompanied by a woman*!

This possibility had never entered my mind. I had braced myself for an act which, in my young pride, I felt to be an act of courage — because it could so easily be confused with the vulgar pursuit of a celebrity. But my imagination had pictured this scene as taking place in isolation, with Steinberg and myself alone, and only strangers passing by. Now there was this woman who would stand beside him, listening and looking while I offered him my flowers! Was she his wife? Or *another* admirer? Whoever she was, her presence changed everything . . . I remained on my side of the road watching them walking slowly nearer.

The small tornado of emotions which swept through me during these few moments was like a passage from Schumann's Piano Concerto in A minor. Wounded and rebellious, I was on the point of flight, but forced myself to go forward. Steinberg, in a grey overcoat and a felt hat — 'He feels the chill of the evening even in this climate', the thought stabbed me — stopped when he saw me approach. The woman stopped, too, holding herself a little behind him, effacing herself.

'For you . . . in gratitude for your music . . . '

I held out the roses to him. He took off his hat, looked gravely, attentively into my face.

'Thank you . . . thank you so much . . . '

His voice was deep and pleasant. I suddenly felt like crying. I heard his voice for the first time — and the last! I stepped off the pavement quickly and crossed the street, mixing with the drifting crowd. My mother was waiting for me a few yards away. 'What did he say to you?' she asked. 'You look so young . . . a mere child . . . ' I could not trust my voice to reply. I was thinking that if I had not gone forward, I would have shown myself to be a coward. My pride would have proved to be stronger than my love. 'All he said was "Thank you" . . . twice . . . ' I was still quivering from the effects of his voice. 'I must . . . I will . . . ' I said to myself, 'I will remember the sound of his voice to the end of my life.'

My father met us at the station in Piatigorsk. He looked thinner and was clearly very glad to see my mother. It never occurred to me that he might also be pleased at seeing me: I took it for granted that my presence there was a matter of indifference to him.

As we drove to the hotel, I was too busy looking at Piatigorsk to listen to my parents' conversation. The little town was quite different in character from Essentuki, more open, more animated. The mountains were nearer and bigger. Here were the streets through which Lermontov had walked, the very pavements, the trees, the houses on which his eyes had rested . . . I was impatient to see the site of his duel, the house in which he had lodged. Where were they? I turned to my father to ask this question but saw that he was listening to my mother, and waited. My mother was commenting with dissatisfaction on the distance of the hotel from the park, which we had just passed, and my father was looking very concerned, almost contrite. I was struck by the effect my mother's remarks produced on him, and suddenly felt I was on his side and against my mother in this matter. Feeling that way was so unexpected, so unusual for me, that I was made uncomfortable for the rest of the journey, and had not the heart to ask my question about Lermontov's house.

My mother looked no more pleased when we finally arrived at the hotel. I ran out on to the balcony of our room to look at the view but I could hear from there my mother's voice with its intonations of displeasure, and I caught a few phrases: 'This hotel is in the wrong part of the town . . . You know I like being near the park . . . Why couldn't you? . . . ' My father did not speak except once when I heard him say: 'The town is very crowded.'

A few minutes later he came out on to the balcony. I did not turn round but listened to his movements, wondering how he felt. He seemed to be re-arranging some chairs. The sun had set and southern dusk was thickening; the mountains in the distance had turned violet and one or two street lamps sprang into life and glowed green through the foliage. I could not bear the silence any longer.

'The view from here is very good,' I said.

My father cleared his throat. I hardly expected a reply but surprisingly, it came.

'Yes,' he said. 'I hope your mother will like it better in a few days' time. It is difficult to get rooms anywhere in Piatigorsk. No one can go abroad now . . . ' Then suddenly, irrelevantly, he added: 'I haven't been feeling at all well . . . tired most of the time . . . a sort of weakness.'

His voice broke. In the dusk I could hardly see his face, but his words made my heart turn over. Overwhelmed with compassion, I found I had absolutely nothing to say. This remote, reserved, silent man, *my father*, whom I regarded as immune from all human frailty, had suddenly come down to my level and was talking to me as to an equal!

This was a turning point in my feeling for my father: suddenly I ceased to fear him and saw him diminished, yet more lovable than he had been hitherto. I still could not call my feeling for him 'love', but I became able to put myself in his place, to see him as a person who needed sympathy, who could even seek it from *me*, young as I was. I also realized for the first time how deeply attached he was to my mother, and a thought entered my mind, which grew clearer and more definite as time went on, that in their relationship he was the giver and she the recipient. She was far more important to him than any of us, his children, while to her, I felt, we were more important than he.

Free from the daily torment of mud baths, I recovered my energy and the determination to drink as fully of the atmosphere of the Caucasus as was possible in the week or two that were left of our stay.

Lermontov's house on the edge of old Piatigorsk, a single-floor wooden structure with a porch and a few small rooms; a few pieces of furniture which he was reputed to have used; an old desk by the window on which he wrote: 'I can see Kazbek from my window . . . ' My prevailing mood of passionate compassion invested all I saw with a peculiar poignancy. Lermontov, who wrote at the age of fourteen 'I lost the count of my years, And strive to capture the wings of oblivion' and died at the age of twenty-six. He died unloved, unfulfilled, almost friendless, a fleeting visitor in this world . . . How could such a waste be justified? And now hundreds, no, thousands of young men were dying in the war . . . Compassion grew into a burning point of regret when I thought of Goga Reingold, who died in battle only a fee weeks after I had seen him alive. Gentle, chivalrous Goga —I would not let myself imagine how he met his death.

My thoughts swung back to Lermontov again, to his anticipation of the fatal duel in the scene of Pechórin's encounter with Grushnítzkiy. The site of the duel, a small patch of even ground amidst the mountain scenery, was tame in comparison with its description in 'The Hero of Our Time' and the image in my mind. There was no yawning precipice over the edge of which the body of the unlucky duellist would inevitably tumble to his death. Nor was it secret or inaccessible. 'It may have been different in Lermontov's day,' my mother remarked, aware of my disappointment. She complied with my wish to see and experience as much as I could, while my father, still a prey to lassitude, preferred to stay behind, sitting in a deck-chair and smoking on the balcony of our rooms, or on a seat in the park.

My mother and I went on excursions, a short one to a solitary place in the mountains from where an unimpeded view of Elbruss could be obtained, and a much longer one along the Military Georgian Highway as far as the highest point, a col where it begins to descend towards Tiflis. I should have dearly liked to go down into Georgia, but the rest of the road was closed to private travellers because of the war. On both occasions we travelled most of the way by horse-drawn vehicle and so had time to absorb the powerful magic of the mountain scenery rather than be stunned by it into a condition of speechless wonder.

A mountain meadow on the brink of a deep valley. The huge Elbruss, a perfect white cone glistening in the setting sun, its great mass dwarfing and dominating everything, seemingly so near, yet separated from us by a chasm full of dark shadows and rising mists. The extraordinary, exhilarating freshness of the air. A strange settlement of brown tents, friendly men in fleecy cloaks and tall sheep-skin caps, talking to our guide in a strange, guttural language. Hobbled horses around the tents and the dull jingling of their bells in the silence that magnified every sound. Large bowls of mare's milk which the men brought us, and the delicious sharpness of its taste, as fresh as the air we breathed . . .

On the long excursion, driving up the Military Georgian Highway, we were slowly, gradually drawn into the very heart of the mountains. They advanced upon us, getting closer and higher all the time, and as the wall of rocks on our right got steeper, the stream at the bottom of the ravine on our left retreated farther and farther into the depth of the chasm. The stream was the legendary Tiérek, a name I learned as a small child with my first poem by Lermontov, the 'Lullaby of a Kazak Mother'. Afterwards it appeared in almost every story about the Caucasus I had ever read. It had become a living thing to me, and this was our first meeting. It was to accompany us to the end of our journey up the defile. But where was the end? As we looked ahead, the mountains stood right across the way, yet when we approached we saw that they were on the other side of the precipice, and our road swung round a corner, clinging to a forbidding wall of rock. The dusk rose from below, and the first stars trembled in the sky above our heads while we were still climbing. My mother had been asking the guide a little anxiously whether we should get to the inn before dark. But I wished this ride could go on for ever, except that I was feeling sorry for the horses. Then, as the last gleam of sunset disappeared from the mountain tops, we turned a corner and saw our first human habitation, a flat-roofed house clinging to the mountain-side. Its windows shone with a yellow light in the rapidly advancing darkness. 'That's the inn,' said our guide. 'We've arrived at Kazbek.'

I did not know how tired I was until we sat down to our meal. Slender girls with long plaits of black hair brought us dishes of freshly fried fish. 'Trout,' said our guide. 'Straight from the Tiérek. Caught today.' It was my very first taste of trout, and it was delicious. Struggling to keep my eyes from closing, I finished my portion of *pilaff*, followed by a large slice of water melon. My mother urged me to go to bed at once, but I was determined to 'have a look at the night'. As I staggered out on to the porch, the sharp air blew into my face and in an instant I was fully awake. For a few moments I stood, shivering and gazing around me, then, as the laughter and voices inside the house impinged on my ears, I ran down the steps and walked along the road to get away from them. A wooden bridge hung over the stream on my left. I crossed it half-way and leaned over the parapet. Down below the Tiérek was foaming and roaring, a white-crested dragon flinging itself against the confining rocks. Above my head, between the jagged edges of the massive mountain walls, the luminous river of the sky seemed to be flowing in the same direction. This serenity above and the wildness below, with myself suspended between them, struck such awe into my soul that, despite my loss of faith, the word 'God' formed on my lips. If God had created this, was His purpose to overwhelm man? How could creatures like myself matter when set beside this immensity? Of what consequence was my puny life? Yet, it must be of consequence because it was *my* life! If I accepted my utter insignificance, I could not live. I might as well fling myself down this precipice.

I gazed at the foaming Tiérek beneath my feet, then at the sky again. A breeze, softer than the surrounding air, lifted my hair off my forehead and touched it like a friendly hand. My mother's voice called from the porch of the inn: 'Léda, where are you?'

I was brought back to reality by that breath of wind and that voice, yet needed a few moments longer to be able to meet it. As I lingered on the bridge without replying, my mother came towards me, looking quite alarmed. She began telling me that I was certain to catch a cold standing in the wind without an overcoat, but I could not bear listening to her, and walked past her into the hotel without replying.

Silently, I undressed and got into bed. I felt angry with my mother for being so out of tune with what I felt. Yet it was she who had opened the door into the enchanting world of poetry when she read Pushkin and Lermontov to me before I could read. I knew she loved poetry and nature — why could she not understand that my communion with nature was too precious to be intruded upon? How could she be so tactless as to talk of catching cold on such a night?

The next morning I looked longingly southwards, where the road began its descent towards Tiflis. The horses were being harnessed for our return journey. How I wished we could go on for many more miles, down into Georgia, to the coast of the Black Sea! I should have liked to cross the Caucasian mountains by the Military Ossietín Highway, said to be even more beautiful than the Georgian, and by the Military Sukhóom Road still unfinished and the wildest of all.

'Why so impatient?' said my mother. 'You have all your life in front of you. There will be plenty of time to do all these things.'

Plenty of time! As I stood on the landing of the railway carriage taking us back to Piatigorsk from Vḷadikavkáz, I wished things would happen

here and now, not in the indefinite time which lay ahead of me. I had
left my mother talking to a travelling companion about dull prosaic
things, and had come out on to the dark landing out of reach of their
voices. The train was careering down a sloping plateau, wildly jerking
and leaping like a runaway horse, filling the air with its clatter, emitting
ear-splitting shrieks. The moon, half-lost in the broken clouds, played
hide-and-seek with the countryside: mountains, trees, waterfalls would
appear in ghostly whiteness, then fade into shadows until the whole scene
became unreal as if in a dream. Swaying on my feet, clinging to cold
railings, I let thoughts and emotions rush through my mind, images now
light, now darkened,like this countryside fleeting past me. Life could be
like that, vertiginous, full of contrasts, of unexpected romantic incidents
. . . What has life given me in this beautiful, romantic setting, this
Caucasian scene? A tiresome course of mud baths . . . hours of lonely
contemplation of beautiful scenery but no one to share it with . . .
hours of listening to music and watching a much-admired conductor . . .
a strange condition of heart and imagination which could be called 'love'
if I were sure that love was like that . . . a state of passionate compassion
which embraced the sick conductor, my father, Lermontov and all the
strong men whose weakness I had intuitively understood and shared.
Did all this add up to *life*, about which grown-ups were always talking?
If this was life, it left my heart hungry and my imagination reaching out
for experiences and impressions that had been foreshadowed but dimly
in this, my first real journey. I had expected it to be a draught of intoxi-
cating wine. I found it more bitter than sweet; it left a sediment of
disenchantment and a thirst for more.

First Meeting with Love and Death

It was almost possible to forget the war in the Caucasus: the front was so far away. Back at M* we were very much aware of its nearness, especially when the news of the reverses on the Polish front and of the refugees streaming into Bielorussian villages and towns began to reach us. There was no question, however, of M* itself being threatened, and the term at the *Ghymnasia* started at the appointed time. My sister returned to her teaching and I to my studies: my brother was still with us because his autumn term did not begin until October. My mother was away for a short time staying with my father at B*. We seemed to be settling down to a winter of what I felt to be 'living at half-cock': the brightness of the present dimmed for the young by an indefinite postponement of most things the young crave for: change, exitement, new impressions, beauty, interesting social contacts. Some grown-ups of our acquaintance talked of 'life' as if it were a kind of present we were going to receive when we were ready for it; others in tones of warning, as if it were a harsh lesson we would be made to learn. 'Your life's only beginning: you have all your future before you . . .' or 'You don't know what "real" life is. It is not what you imagine', and so on.

It made me angry to hear them talk like that. The future might be good, but what of the present? *Nothing* worth while was happening to us in the present!

Then things began to happen. My mother arrived from B*, looking very grave. She called us all to her room and spoke to us in a low and troubled tone of voice.

'Your father has given up his post . . . '

If her manner had prepared us for bad news, this, as far as I was concerned, was the last I expected to hear.

We sat for a few seconds in stunned silence.

'Why did he do that?' asked my brother.

My mother explained that my father had been struggling for weeks with the problem of refugees. They had been pouring into his province from the villages and towns nearer the front, and there was nowhere for them to live and very little to eat. The movements of troops had clogged the railways and the supplies of food were not reaching our province in sufficient quantities. There came thousands of women, old people and children, many of them destitute and diseased. My father found that all the steps he was taking to relieve their plight brought very little result. He could not bear to see them homeless and hungry; his health was breaking under the strain . . . He resigned so that a younger man could take over from him.

My sister was the first to speak again. 'Perhaps it is for the best,' she said. My mother sighed and shook her head.

'I don't know how we shall manage without his salary. The estate only just pays its way.'

'There is my salary,' said Maroossia.

'Vova and Léda have still to get their university education . . . '

My brother asked where my father was at the moment. My mother told him that he was at Fyeny.

'What about the house at B*?'

'We may have to sell it.'

The questions I might have asked had been asked by others; those that really perturbed me I could not ask without revealing more of my feelings than I cared to put into words. Here was another proof that the image of my father I had built up from my earliest impressions was a false one! The man who spoke to me about his health on the balcony at Piatigorsk, and whose compassion for the refugees now made him give up his post, touched my heart in a way my father had never touched it in the past. I was so accustomed to think of him as strong and impervious to softer emotions that I needed time to blend the two images into one. And it hurt me to think that he could be so concerned about the refugees, yet had never shown much concern for me . . .

I was also distressed by the thought that our house at B* might have to be sold. I felt a sudden nostalgia for its sunny rooms, for my own bedroom overlooking the orchard, for the shape of the trees in it I knew so well — the tall pear tree which was my crow's nest, an old cherry tree on which I perched while learning my grammar. I could not imagine the house occupied by strangers and myself unable to go in.

I hardly had time to assimilate these shocks when we heard the startling news that M* was to become the seat of the General Staff Headquarters. The Chief of Staff, the Tsar's uncle, Grand Duke Nikolai, was to take up residence in the commandant's house, and accommodation would have to be found in private houses for several hundred of his entourage.

The excitement this caused among the town population spread to all of us; but the main subject of conversation among the older schoolgirls was the probability of visits from the young Grand Dukes whose photographs in uniform began to appear in shop windows and in newspaper kiosks. Liolia agreed with me that the Grand Duke Dimitry was the handsomest of all, but she liked also Igor and Oleg, the Tsar's cousins, sons of his uncle Konstantin, whereas I pronounced them loose-lipped and undistinguished. We all admired the appearance of Prince Felix Yusúpov and his young wife, the Grand Duchess Irina, a niece of the Tsar. We had heard that the Grand Duke Dimitry and Prince Yusúpov were close friends and that they both disapproved of Rasputin's influence on the Empress. This gave them an additional glamour in our eyes. The Grand Dukes were expected to visit the General Staff Headquarters, and Liolia and Ania Bielynóvich were all agog at the thought of meeting them in the street, or in the public gardens which adjoined the grounds of the Commandant's house, now 'the palace' of the Tsar's uncle.

M*, like many a town in that region, was situated on a high bank of the Dniepr, a large working-class suburb facing it from the opposite, low bank. 'The Ramparts' public garden was perched on the edge of a steep drop and might have been at one time a part of the town's fortifications. It was the town-people's favourite place for evening walks and it had a pavilion where a band used to play on Sundays in the summer. This entertainment ceased at the beginning of the war, not only because the garrison of the town with their band had been sent off to the front, but also because to enjoy anything at all was felt to be somehow improper and almost disloyal to 'our brave fighters out there'. This highly moral attitude, however, could not be maintained indefinitely, and in the following spring some breaks in the gloom were beginning to appear. The Duke's personal body-guard consisted of the Kazaks who brought with them their own band, and in the first spell of fine weather the inhabitants of M* were thrilled to read a notice, exhibited at the entrance to 'The Ramparts', which informed them that the Kazak band would be playing there on Sunday evenings. Their playing had a panache which the old band had entirely lacked, and the people of M* flocked to the garden to hear them. They were also hoping to catch a glimpse of some member of the Imperial family.

I recollect an occasion on which Liolia told me about her meeting with the Grand Dukes. Rather late one evening, she said, she was sitting on a bench in 'The Ramparts' garden when she saw the Grand Duke Dimitry and his cousin Igor walk past her. One of them said something to the other, and suddenly they turned back and came towards her. They sat down on either side of her and tried to engage her in conversation. 'I was so excited that I couldn't stop laughing most of the time,' Liolia told me. 'They asked whether I would like to come to the cinema with them, but of course I couldn't . . . Mamma would have been beside herself with worry if I didn't come back at the usual time.'

We all knew that Liolia's mother kept her on a very tight rein, and that she dared not be late home after school without asking her mother's permission and telling her exactly where she was going. I doubted very much that she could have been sitting on a bench in the Rampart gardens so late in the evening, and the whole story of her flirtation with the Grand Dukes sounded suspect to me. I knew her habit of embellishing and romanticizing every tale she had to tell, and found it somehow embarrassing. Did she tell us this in order to impress us? I could not bring myself openly to express my doubts. I merely told her that I wished I, too, had been there to meet the handsome Grand Duke Dimitry in the flesh. I carried his photograph in my satchel, and was immensely flattered when one of the women teachers to whom I showed it, asked: 'Is this your brother? He looks like you.' It was curious! There was indeed a likeness between us, especially in the upper part of the face, in the eyes and forehead. I recollected my mother telling me that I looked like the Románov family because she had gazed at the portrait of the Tsaritsa while pregnant with me!

As it happened, the only member of the Tsar's family I saw at close range was the Grand Duke Alexéy, the heir to the throne. That was in the second summer of the war. I was passing the cordoned-off part of the Rampart gardens adjoining the house then occupied by the Tsar, when I saw a boy in a soldier's long overcoat walk into it. He was accompanied by a tall man in a trilby hat and cloak, and a sturdy fellow in seaman's uniform. I at once recognized the *Tsesariévich*, who was always attended by his French tutor and his personal servant,

the sailor Doroshénko. The Grand Duke Alexéy was limping slightly and
sat down as soon as they reached the nearest garden bench. I recollected
that not so long ago he had had a fall which started a haemorrhage and
that he had lost a lot of blood before it could be arrested.

As soon as the Grand Duke and his companions sat down, a group of
local boys appeared from somewhere and started a game a few yards away
from him. It was a simple game called *zhgoot* (the strap). A handkerchief,
twisted to make it hard, was used as a striking weapon. The boys formed
a ring with their backs outwards. One boy was chosen to run round the
outside of the ring and to strike anyone he chose across the shoulders
with the *zhgoot*. This boy then had to chase the first one and wrest the
strap from him. The rôle of the others was for some to assist the escaping
boy, while the rest had to put obstacles in his way, thus assisting his
pursuer. There were shrieks and tussles and many dull thuds as the strap
came down on the boys' shoulders. The Grand Duke took a lively interest in
the game: unable to participate in it because of his station, or his lameness,
he was playing it by proxy, encouraging the players with gestures and
shouts: 'Faster, run faster! Harder, hit harder! That's a good one!'

He fidgeted on his bench and clapped the most successful runs. The
boys, though they were playing for his amusement, seemed to enjoy
themselves greatly: no doubt, they received money and gifts for doing
this. They were all boys from the 'town' schools, that is, children of
small tradesmen and artisans, and one Jewish boy was particularly
conspicuous among them, more vociferous, active and self-assured than
the others, behaving as if he were the leader of the group.

I watched this scene for a quarter of an hour, moved by its pathos,
an object lesson to all who envied the 'great', their exalted position
and their riches. Perhaps, I said to myself, my mother was right after
all, and health was more important for personal happiness than almost
anything else in life. The lame boy who could never safely enjoy the
ordinary rough-and-tumble, who could bleed to death from an
accidental bruise or cut — what was his life worth to him? I thought his
life would be tragic. He was barely twelve years old at the time: I could
not foresee the tragedy of his death at the age of fourteen.

We began two new subjects at school in the autumn term and a new
teacher was appointed to instruct us in them. The subjects were pedagogy and psychology, so the new teacher was immediately nick-named
'the pedagogue'. Until then all our male teachers were middle-aged.
This one was young, but like the others he was a *seminaríst*, that is, the

product of a training college for the sons of priests, who were preparing to be priests. Some of them, however, became teachers instead, and a school like ours preferred to appoint them rather than university men, perhaps on the assumption that they were less 'corrupted' by progressive ideas.

Evghéniy Rjevsky was good-looking in a raw, slightly uncouth way: long-headed and loose-limbed, he made one think of an overgrown colt. He stood over six feet tall, looked at the world with a pair of childlike blue eyes, did not know what to do with his hands and had a tuft of hair at the back of his head which refused to lie down. We took malicious pleasure in his obvious embarrassment when dealing with a class of adolescent girls. The less industrious among us decided at once that he would never have the courage to give them really bad marks, and so they need not do any work at all in his subjects. We watched him with ghoulish delight blushing and stumbling through his explanations. We felt he was defenceless and at our mercy, and we enjoyed our unaccustomed sense of power.

As for his subjects, I, for one, found them disappointing. I had been looking forward to studying psychology, to discovering the complex mysteries of the human mind. What we found in our text-book were dry descriptions of Fechner's and Wundt's experiments and a brief outline of the theories of Locke. It was meagre fare after the richness of Dostoyevsky. As for pedagogy, I had no intention whatever of becoming a school teacher. It was quite entertaining however to watch our 'pedagogue' teaching us how to teach when he himself so obviously lacked the teaching skill. Yet I could not for long remain amused by the spectacle of another person's torments, and soon my heart, always rather soft, became invaded by compassion.

Compassion was the emotion which I had come to consider as my principal 'enemy within the gates'. From my earliest years I had suffered agonies on account of abandoned kittens and puppies, and of starved or maltreated horses and caged birds. My distress at seeing dumb, defenceless creatures in pain was intense and lasting. Even now I feel a slight pang at one particular memory which goes back to my eighth or ninth year. My brother was determined to catch a small bird which we saw fly in and out of a hollow tree. It must have had a nest there, and one day, when it flew in, my brother told me to put my hand inside and take it. His own hand was not small enough. He lifted me, so that I could reach the hollow. As the captured bird squeaked and fluttered in my hand, so my heart fluttered with emotion: pride at having caught it conflicting with remorse and pity which made tears spring into my eyes.

In those early years human suffering entered my experience only through what I read. Having never seen dire poverty or incurable disease, I used to declare that I pitied animals more than human beings because animals, dumb and captive, could not complain or retaliate. It was through the pain of intense self-pity during my year at the boarding school that I learned to pity others and became able to put myself in their place. I also learned to what extent my capacity for compassion made me vulnerable, perhaps even open to exploitation, and I began to think of the ways of defending myself against it. By the time I reached adolescence, my defence assumed a characteristically rational form. 'Only the weak arouse pity,' I reasoned. 'One cannot respect the weak, so pitying someone leads to not respecting them. Pity, then, is a kind of alms one bestows on a person one feels to be inferior. One gives the alms and passes on as quickly as possible. And — to keep one's self-respect — one should not pity oneself either.'

Like many an adolescent — or for that matter like many an adult before me — I overestimated the power of reason and my own power in dealing with irrational urges in myself. It was not long before I became aware that the blend of amusement and compassion which the new teacher's struggles with his duties aroused in me, was becoming complicated by the addition of tenderness.

It was like a wave rising up from somewhere inside me when I saw him enter the class-room, and it took time to subside and settle down. He called out our names from the register in alphabetical order and glanced at every girl as she half-rose from her seat. As he called mine and my eyes for a moment met the blue flash of his, my heart suddenly started thumping with the fear that he would at once see what I was feeling. I dropped my eyes and tried to listen to his voice beginning to explain our next assignment. He cleared his throat and stammered a little. Then I looked up again — and again it came — that treacherous wave of emotion invading me, that stab of affection for his person, his long brown neck in a starched white collar, the tuft of hair at the back of his head, the red hands and vivid blue eyes. It was absurd, bitterly sweet and deeply alarming.

Back at home, reading through the boring pages of *his* text-books — how irrelevant it all seemed to the real stuff of psychology, to these floods and ebbs of emotion invading me — I thought of him, of what he might be doing at that moment. I wondered what he might talk about if I had met him outside the school. I wished I could meet him — but how? We had no friends in common, and anyway, his circle of friends would be quite different from ours; the only person in whose company we had ever seen him was another teacher — from the seminary. My mother had not met him, so I could not ask her to invite him to our house. In any case it was exceptional for teachers at our school to be on visiting terms with their pupils or their parents: it would have been so easy for the envious to accuse them of partiality. Shimkóvich was an exception: his boats were burnt, everyone knew that he was seriously ill and he did not care what anyone said about him. But Rjevsky! How tongues would wag if he came to our house!

Anyway, I was not at all sure that I wanted him to come. I should have liked to be with him alone, perhaps in the Rampart gardens, on one of those seats overlooking the Dniepr, in the shadow of lilac bushes, in the spring . . . I wanted to see his face lit up with animation close to mine, and his vivid blue eyes looking eagerly into my eyes; I wanted to be the only person he saw and talked to — not one of forty, in a class-room. And I imagined him falling in love with me, perhaps even having the courage to ask me to marry him, and my having to say 'No', while my heart was bursting with sympathetic pain. Because there was no question in my mind of a marriage between us — it was impossible. I had already mapped out my life: I would go to a university, take a degree in Russian language and literature, and become a lecturer in these subjects. In university vacations I would travel and write books. If I married, it would be someone very different from an awkward seminarist, a school-master in a provincial town, who would confine me to a life of narrow domesticity and the company of his seminarist friends.

No, I did not want him as a husband, I could not even briefly imagine him in that rôle. Nor did I picture him in my day-dreams kissing me or holding me in his arms. Why, then, did I long for him in this strange and irresistible way, so intensely at times that it made me weep in the solitude of my room? I longed to pass my hand over his hair, to see that obstinate tuft at the back smoothed down and ruffled up again under my touch . . . I wanted to tell him to take no notice of the silly giggling girls in the class-room, to say to him: 'Look, *I* am not laughing at you — I love you!'

Love him? Was this pressure of thoughts and images, this tender craving really love? Could one love a person one hardly knew? Someone so unlike the kind of man one wanted to love? A man to whom one could never confess one's love, whom one did not wish for a husband? What a bad joke, what a waste! Why should it happen to me? What was the sense of it?

These unanswerable questions I continued to ask in the poems I wrote about my love for Evghéniy, and I tried to answer them when I wrote letters to him, letters which I had no intention of ever posting. Into them I poured my tenderness and anger; derided myself for my weakness and foolishness; reproached him for his blindness and indifference; and bitterly accused myself of being merely in love with love.

I showed my poems to my mother and sister, assuming they would not guess who had inspired them. My mother, clearly fearing to offend me, said they were good but she liked my earlier poems better: 'those in which you write about Nature'. My sister, probably suspecting the source of my torments and inspiration, made no comment. Shimkóvich, who asked to see some of my 'more recent ones', read them slowly, then took off his pince-nez, swung it on his finger for a few moments, and finally said: 'Not like your usual writing . . . rather more like Nadson. I should say almost morbid . . . Have you been reading a lot of Nadson by any chance?'

I lived in fear that Anna Avdyéevna, or some of my classmates might notice that I was in love with the 'pedagogue'. To put them off the scent I often joined in the derisive comment on his speech and manners, still indulged in by some of the girls, though afterwards I felt ashamed of this 'betrayal' and my hypocrisy. I kept my secret from the members of our band of five as well: they all looked down on Evghéniy for being a seminarist, and I felt I would suffer in their esteem from this revelation. The only person I could talk to about my love was Zena: she had never seen Evghéniy, and so could not hurt me by criticizing him, nor did she have anyone to whom she could chat lightly about my confidences. She had just returned home after a long stay at the hospital in Moscow, still rather pale and easily fatigued, but with a normal appetite and well on the way to a complete recovery. She said she was glad to be out of hospital, but showed singularly little eagerness to return to her parents' house, and stayed with us for long week-ends.

Inarticulate and sympathetic in a depressed way, she listened to my outpourings after we had gone to bed, in a room where the only light came from the pale sky seen through the window. I could barely discern her tousled head against the blurred white of the pillow.

'What are you going to do then?' she asked in a tired voice.

'What *can* I do? Nothing, absolutely nothing! My love is just wasted . . . it's of no use to anybody . . .'

'It is of some use to you,' said Zena. A catch in her throat made me pause for a moment, wondering what my confession was doing to *her*. But my own feelings were pressing too hard on me to let me consider hers.

'It's of no use to him,' I continued vehemently, 'because he shall never know that I had loved him. It's of no use to me because it is just burning itself out in solitude, in pain and anger, and merely makes me desperately unhappy.'

'I don't see why you should be angry,' said Zena slowly. 'Angry . . . with whom?'

'With myself mostly — for falling so stupidly in love with such a . . . with the wrong person. Angry with him — for being what he is. Angry with Nature — for setting me . . . us . . . such a trap!'

Zena's response to this pulled me up with a start.

'I wish I could fall in love with someone,' she said in a low voice, full of tears.

I got out of bed and went over to her. She was crying quietly, her face undistorted by grief.

'Why, Zena? What did I say to make you cry?'

'Nothing . . . I think you're lucky . . . to be in love. I'm not in love . . . and I am unhappy. I think it is better to be in love . . . even if you are unhappy . . . '

My bitterness suddenly stilled by her distress and by the obscure wisdom of her remarks, I remained silent, sitting on her bed, stroking her coarse, tangled curls until she stopped crying. Then, more calmly, I said:

'I can't bear just loving him and doing *nothing* for him. You know what I can do . . . with your help. When the spring comes, I will give him a large bunch of white narcissi. We'll have to plan this: obviously, I can't give them to him myself . . . But you will help me, won't you?'

'Yes, if you tell me how.'

She sighed. I kissed her and returned to my bed.

I recollected that promise with a heavy heart when the spring came and Zena was not there to help me. A few days later she caught a chill on the way home from school; her father afterwards said she refused to wear a warm shawl over her shoulders when being driven in the open gig. 'As if a girl of fifteen would want to look like an old woman of fifty!' I thought indignantly. I could not help blaming Uncle Vladímir for what had happened. I felt that Zena should not have been sent to school so soon after her return from the hospital. She was not strong enough to stand exposure to bad weather.

We knew nothing of that until two days later. I was alone in my room, not concentrating at all well on a problem of algebra. Heavy rain was pouring down outside. My mother and sister were at the other end of the house and I could hear nothing except the noise of falling water like the rustling of a gigantic silk petticoat. Suddenly the front door bell clanged with a force such as no ordinary visitor would use. I sat up, my nerves taut, my mind an anxious blank . . . Who could it be? I heard the maid scurrying along to answer it, and got up and held my door ajar in order to hear better. There was a glazed veranda between the front door and the hall, and some of the drawing-room windows opened on to it. From my room, which adjoined the drawing-room, I could hear someone's heavy, shambling footsteps treading the length of the veranda and entering the hall. My mother must have hurried to meet the visitor because the first voice I heard was hers, asking in alarm: 'You, Volódia? What has happened?'

And the terrible, hardly recognizable voice of my uncle answered: 'I've come . . . come to ask you to my daughter's wedding . . . '

The appalling sounds that his grief tore from him made me close my door promptly and cover up my ears to avoid hearing those inhumanly raucous sobs. Surely he could not mean that Zena was dead? Yet what else could he mean by that phrase about the wedding? A white bridal gown? The bride of Christ? I dared not come out and meet him. Trembling from head to foot, I repeated to myself: 'It can't be true, it can't, it can't!' Several minutes passed. I gave a violent start when my door opened and Maroossia came in, looking grave, traces of tears on her face.

'Is it really true?' I asked her. She nodded.

'This afternoon. Her temperature was almost normal this morning. The doctor came to see her, said her lungs were affected and told them to keep her warm in bed. Towards evening her temperature shot up, she lost consciousness, and . . . '

'But why, *why*?'

'Her heart must have been weakened by her long illness last summer, by that anaemia. It couldn't stand the strain of high fever . . . It just gave out.'

Just gave out! I thumped my forehead with my clenched fist.

'Her parents are real criminals! It's their fault! They kept her short of everything . . . saving money to leave it to her . . . What's the use of it *now*? Poor Zena . . . dead . . . dead at sixteen . . . '

My sister sat beside me on the sofa, embraced me and begged me not to grieve so much. 'Perhaps it is better so . . . Zena has been unhappy . . . she might have had a life of unhappiness if she had lived.'

'But she would have had a *life* . . . now she has *nothing!* . . . '

'We don't know that,' said Maroossia stroking my hair.

Although she soothed me a little, I could not bring myself to come out to Uncle Vladímir that evening. His grief frightened me instead of arousing my sympathy. I doubt that he had noticed my absence. He had come to tell my mother because she was his first cousin, and more friendly towards him than his unhappy wife.

But during the next twenty-four hours I had to brace myself for a trip to their house to see Zena for the last time. I both wanted to see her and dreaded it, and I dreaded even more facing the desolation of Aunt Katia's and Uncle Vladímir's terrifying despair.

I had not visited the place for some time while Zena had been away in Moscow, and as we came up the rise leading to the vast courtyard, my eyes turned to the swing which I had so often shared with her. The posts were still in position, but the plank and the ropes had been removed. The thing was standing there, useless and vaguely sinister like a gibbet. The courtyard had a forlorn air; only the watch-dog rattled his chain and whined when he saw us. I looked at the house where I had spent many not very happy months: it seemed that the only good thing that had happened there during that time was the conversion of Zena from my enemy into my friend. And now Zena was dead. Could I have done more to relieve her unhappiness?

Uncle Vladímir met us in the doorway. One rapid glance at his face was enough for me: it was not so much changed as distorted by the blow that Fate had dealt him. His whole body had sagged under it, his thick shoulders were hunched, his neck drawn in, his gait weighted down as if with a heavy load. Aunt Katia appeared from her bedroom, her eyes swollen but dry, her face the colour of chalk. Tears began to flow down her cheeks as we all embraced her. Without speaking we followed them into the drawing-room. That room, which was hardly ever used when I lived with them because the Martsinóvskys so rarely entertained, was now made beautiful for Zena: with curtains drawn and *lampádas* burning before the icons, it looked like a chapel and smelt of incense and flowers. Zena occupied the place of honour under the icons, on a table covered with Aunt Katia's best linen sheets. She looked very much as she had been looking during the last few months, only her pallor was now tinged with yellow and the tip of her nose was no longer rounded but sharp. The look of weary bewilderment which I had so often seen on her face had disappeared: she was very calm, almost contented in her immobility. I came up close and stared at her face, wanting desperately to speak to her, to ask what she was feeling, to beg her to let me know what death was like. I thought of an evening some months ago when, half-jokingly, she, Shoora Martýnov and I had solemnly promised to tell one another whether there was life after death: the one who died before the others was to appear to the other two and tell them — 'if it were at all possible for him to do it . . .' I was sure Zena would keep her promise – *if she could*.

On the way back my mother talked to my sister while I listened with increasing exasperation.

'Your uncle Vladímir told me he had been saving all he could, so that Zena would have money of her own when she got married. He could think of no other future for her except marriage, and now all his hopes, all his plans for her are brought to nothing. It is tragic.'

'It might have been wiser to let Zena have some pleasure out of life while she was young,' said Maroossia.

'He could not foresee such a disaster,' said my mother. 'And I think Katia could have been more vigilant and more firm with regard to Zena's health. She let her do more or less what she liked. That bathing . . . '

My mother's evident wish to find excuses for Uncle Vladímir hurt and angered me, but I felt too depressed even to protest. When we got home I went straight to my room and tried to read what I had to prepare for next day's lessons. My efforts were of no avail. I leaned back in my chair and stared in front of me. Zena's face, as I had seen it only a few days ago, was imprinted on my memory, and I compared it with that other face which I saw reclining, peaceful and waxy, on a frilled, white, pitilessly hard pillow. I gazed at the closed, white-painted door of my room and wished, straining all my will power, that it would open and Zena would enter, as she had promised, to tell me that there was life after death. I, who used to be so afraid of ghosts, now wished a ghost to appear to me.

'Zena, do come!' I said aloud. 'Don't be afraid to frighten me. I won't be in the least frightened. I want you to come!'

The tension I felt was such that it seemed to spread to the very air of the room. My ears were ringing. I waited — but the door did not open and no one came. Perhaps it was too early to call, I said to myself; after all, she had only been dead these two days . . . her body was still in that darkened room in her parents' house. Her spirit might be there, close to me but unable to make itself visible . . .

Afterwards, I tried more than once to conjure Zena's spirit to appear to me by using all the strength of will I could muster. I was unsuccessful. Was I the kind of person to whom ghosts would not appear? Or was it, as I had suspected all along, because there were no ghosts, no life after death and no possibility of communicating with the dead? Zena could not answer my call because she was no longer herself but a weight of inert flesh, disintegrating under the weight of earth in a corner of a wind-swept and rain-soaked cemetery.

There was something about the image of a body I had known and touched and now knew to be decaying in the grave which aroused in me the feeling of intense revolt and indignation. I could not accept the finality of death, the meaninglessness of life which ended in death. What had been the meaning of Zena's life, or of her premature death? A child of unhappy, warring parents, she had seen little joy or pleasure while she was alive, and her death brought only grief and despair but no reconciliation between them. And if she had to die at sixteen, why was I privileged – if it was a privilege – to go on living?

I turned to my sister with some of these questions, hardly knowing what I hoped to hear from her. She was pained by the bitterness and violence of my remarks. If I did not believe in survival after death, she said, could I accept Tolstoy's idea that the way to impart a meaning to one's life was to do things for other people?

'Why always other people?' I protested. 'What about ourselves? Are our own lives any less valuable? It is all very well for Tolstoy to preach self-denial – he's an old man, he had lived a full life before he retired to Yasnaya Poliana and decided to live for others! I have my own life to live and I want it to be beautiful . . . I want to be happy . . . I want those I love to be happy too. I don't believe in self-sacrifice!'

The truth of the matter was that although I proclaimed myself to be an atheist, I could not really give up the hope of survival after death. I let myself think of Zena as being in some place where she was at peace with herself and could contemplate her past life and her parents with detached compassion. I liked to imagine that she was still fond of me. Perhaps, after all, she *was not allowed* to come and tell me what I had asked for. 'A country from which no traveller returns' . . . Perhaps that country was impossible to describe. But could she not just tell me that it existed?

My inner conflict continued. For weeks I dreamt of Zena being alive, of Zena looking ill and sad, and – a horrible dream – of Zena dead in a coffin with one eye distintegrating, bursting open and spilling on to her white dress.

When Shimkóvich, who had been a regular visitor at our house, sent a word to say that he was confined to his bed, my mother said: 'I wonder if he will get up again.'

It looked as if at the *Ghymnasia*, too, they did not expect him to return to teaching. Ivan Kuzmích, our Director, took over from him in my class. With a pang of remorse I had to admit to myself that I found him more stimulating than poor Shimkóvich with his astringent humour and his addiction to 'folk' poets, such as Nekrásov, Nikítin and especially Koltzóv. True, he had sometimes aroused my interest by asking general questions the answer to which was not to be found in our textbooks, and when the class remained decorously silent, he would turn to me with a smile, asking: 'And what does our little grandmother think about this?' — 'I'm not joking', he added, seeing that I looked disturbed and uncertain whether he was ironical. 'You do often speak as if you had half a century's experience behind you . . . '

Ivan Kuzmích did not flatter me as openly as that, but his eyes often turned in my direction when he asked one of *his* general questions. His lessons consisted of almost nothing else: he would start by quoting some lines from Tolstoy, or Pushkin, or Shakespeare, then invite us to say what we understood the author meant by these words. Frequently he would pull one word out of its context and challenge us to define it.

> . . . *a thought,*
> *A slumbering thought, is capable of years,*
> *And curdles a long life into one hour . . .*

'Life,' he would repeat slowly and solemnly, plunging his fingers into his long beard and surveying us with his piercing eyes: 'What is *life?*'

Needless to say, very few of us attempted the definition, and those who did rarely produced anything original. Iván Kuzmích must have derived plenty of amusement from our attempts, but he showed it only in his twinkling eyes: his mouth was well concealed under his beard. He did not slap down any feeble or muddled definition, he merely transferred his attention to the next speaker, and the next after her, until someone made a really creditable effort, and then he would purr his approval and go on to expounding and commenting on it for a little longer. I soon found myself among the few who received recognition from him, and I felt proud and relieved, for I had been passing through spells of depression and self-doubt alternating with spells of buoyant self-reliance.

These swings of mood are thought to be common in adolescence, but mine may have been intensified and made more poignant by Zena's

10

death and my unhappy love for Rjevsky. In my last two years at school I had moved to the top position in a class of eighty-four pupils (there were forty-two in my class and the same number in the parallel class, the two being treated as one form), and I retained this position without difficulty. I knew in my last year that I was the only candidate for the gold medal, while Katia Kign was the most likely pupil to get the 'right' to one. I was known to the whole school as 'a poet', and all the teachers, as well as personal friends, had praised my literary ability. Yet, on the threshold of university life, determined to make writing my main profession, I wondered whether all this was really true, and I compared myself to the ant in Krylóv's fable, a creature who was the object of pride and admiration on his own ant-heap, but remained quite unnoticed when he took a ride to the market on a hay wagon and began to display his strength by lifting wisps of hay. Could not this happen to me when I found myself at a university, among other students who were all gold medallists, like myself? I even wondered whether Shimkóvich would have said all the flattering things he had said about my work if he had not been 'in love' with me. The Director's encouraging nod was thus like a soothing balm on my exacerbated sensibility, and I looked forward eagerly to his lessons, feeling all the while that I was being disloyal to poor Shimkóvich, dying in his rooms half a block away from our school.

We visited him in small groups of twos and threes after lessons. His face was the colour of yellow parchment and he looked very frail, but as neat and composed as ever, his beard carefully trimmed, his hair brushed smoothly away from his forehead. He talked to us in his familiar way with characteristically measured intonations, in a voice perhaps more husky than in the past. There were three of us there on one occasion, Katia Kign, Lena Kazanóvich and myself, but as he talked, his eyes never left my face. We all sat awkwardly in a row on the edge of a settee. 'Like swallows about to fly away,' he said and smiled. That smile entered my heart and remained there like a great sharp splinter, making it ache whenever I thought of him.

When the Director, looking more grave than usual, entered our classroom one blustery February morning and began by saying: 'I have sad news for you . . . ' we knew at once that it was about Shimkóvich. He had died the previous night and the funeral was fixed for a date three days later, as was customary.

The upper classes of the school were told that they could come to the funeral. The funeral procession was quite long, but no relatives of the deceased were pointed out, and I wondered who was with him when he

died. I thought with remorse about an incident which occurred a few
months before, when at a school party he had offered me a posy of
flowers and I tried to decline accepting it. At school parties a stand with
posies of fresh flowers was usually put up. The men bought them as a
matter of course and offered them to girls before the first dance. I was
in a state of feverish excitement because I was hoping that Rjevsky would
ask me to dance with him. I was chatting with Ania Bielynóvich and one
of the Komaróvskayas when I saw 'the pedagogue' picking his way
through the crowd and coming towards us. He was wearing a new
uniform tunic with shining buttons, his hair had been too obviously and
frantically brilliantined, but the obstinate tuft was still rising up at the
back. His blue eyes were luminous and his hand felt a little rough as he
squeezed mine — for the first time since I set eyes on him. I trembled
lest he would now ask Ania or Liuba for a dance. But he took the posy
from his buttonhole and held it out to me. 'May I offer you this? And
would you grant me the pleasure of the first waltz?'

Would I not! I pressed the posy to my face, ostensibly to inhale its
fragrance, but really to conceal the flush of delight which I felt flooding
my cheeks. And then, out of the corner of my eye I saw Shimkóvich
approaching slowly, hovering on the edge of our group, and finally
greeting us all by shaking hands with each one in turn. He, too, had a
posy in his hand. He seemed to be waiting for Rjevsky to go, but as the
other man remained planted where he stood, Shimkóvich shuffled his
feet a little, fingering his posy like a public speaker fingers his watch
chain before beginning his speech. A desperate plea was running
through my mind.

'Don't do that, please! Can't you see that I have one already, and
that the other two have none? Give it to one of them, do!'

My embarrassment grew with the certainty that he was going to give
it to me, and the others, watching and waiting in silence, added to my
confusion.

'Will you accept this from a man who cannot ask you to dance?'

Impulsively, foolishly, I blurted out: 'But I have one already!'

As soon as I had said it, I could have bitten off my tongue. I saw that
Shimkóvich was taken aback and hurt. The softness which lit up his face
and stole into his voice while he was making his offer, had vanished,
and after an awkward pause he said with a touch of irony: 'Surely there
is no harm in your having two, as I can't claim a dance anyway?'

I took it, burning with shame at my tactlessness and the unfair distinc-
tion in being presented with two posies while my companions were still

without any. Luckily, the band struck the first bars of the waltz and I could turn to Rjevsky and to the long-anticipated experience which would reduce the distance between us to a few inches of air and the thickness of our clothes. I expected an electric shock to go through me as our hands touched, and was tense with fear that he, too, would feel it, and would know what I felt.

A current did indeed run through my body but it was mercifully earthed, and only a faint excitement persisted, which allowed me to waltz happily and almost without embarrassment. But the remorse remained: it gave my heart a twinge every time I swung past the doorway where Shimkóvich was standing, watching the dancers through his twinkling pince-nez. I had pinned one of the posies to my breast and held the other in my hand. It was awkward, for that hand rested on Rjevsky's shoulder and the flowers were touching his cheek. They were Shimkóvich's flowers, which added to the unfairness of it all. And the fact of being so near to the object of my desires — something which seemed so improbable when I had looked at him from my place in the class-room — suddenly dwindled in importance, was reduced to no more than a sensation of smooth cloth under my fingers, of an arm round my waist, and a faint smell of tobacco mingling with the fragrance of flowers.

I thought also of the occasion when I deceived Shimkóvich by pretending that I could 'read' without seeing the question which he wrote on a slip of paper and gave me to hold. He had asked: 'Shall I live long enough to see the end of the war?' And I replied: 'You certainly will.' and he looked so pleased and so impressed by my powers of clairvoyance. If there was life after death and if he now knew the truth, and saw me as I was, a vain creature, neither very honest, nor very brave, and besides hopelessly in love with a very ordinary young man, I hoped he would also know how genuinely sorry I was now for not having shown him all the respect and affection which I had felt for him. Why, oh why, I asked myself, with my throat constricted and my eyes burning but dry, why do we not remind ourselves more often that the people of whom we are fond can die at any moment, and when that happens, all we could and wanted to tell them, or do for them, would remain for ever not said and not done?

These thoughts goaded me into action when the spring came and Aunt Katia's garden was again filled with white narcissi, which she had also planted on Zena's grave.

'Yes, you can pick as many as you like,' she told me when I came to see her one Sunday. 'Now there's no one but myself to take pleasure in them.'

She had not changed much, Aunt Katia, since Zena's death, except for this letting up on what we called her stinginess. The loss of their only child did not bring Uncle Vladímir and her together; on the contrary they seemed more estranged. Aunt Katia came to see us more often and stayed longer, but her conversation was of trivial things, as before, and she seemed to spend her time at home reading light novels and doing a bit of gardening, almost devoid of human companionship but for Mavra, the maid of all works, and her daughter Hovra. It was a dismal house to visit, and I never stayed longer than I could help. I picked a very large bunch of narcissi, so large that I had to explain it, and I muttered something about distributing it among our several rooms.

In fact I gave half of the flowers to my mother and sister and took the rest to my room. 'You should put them out for the night: the scent is too strong,' said my mother. I ignored this. The scent was bright and incisive like the blade of a rapier. I sat and stared at a single flower, smiling at my thoughts. I saw it as a perfect symbol of hopeless love, its whiteness as the pallor of unacknowledged passion, the red circle round the centre as its fire almost stifled by neglect and the small yellow centre as the heart full of jealousy. A poem was forming in my mind: 'White, yellow, red . . . three shades of meaning . . . '

I threw myself on to my bed and repeated the phrase, lying on my back, staring at the ceiling. 'White . . . yellow . . . red . . . ' Each colour became crowded with associations. White became innocence as well as passion; it also stood for pride in suffering, for unavowed tenderness, for sadness and hopeless desire. Yellow stood for burning torments of secret jealousy, for restless, nervous, impulsive anger of unwanted love; it was the hate aspect of love. Red was 'a flame and a thirst', a fiery caress, the brightness of desire, the power of physical attraction — all these embodied in one flower, in the three colours of a white narcissus.

For an hour I tossed on my bed, paced up and down the room, plunged my fingers into my hair, and wrote, until all these meanings were packed into three stanzas of four lines. I reread them aloud and experienced a tremendous sense of relief from having given shape to so much turmoil within me in perfect anapaests and without a single weak rhyme. And it was *true*: I believed the words I had used were the nearest approximation to the intense and complex emotions that were tearing me apart.

On the following morning at school, while the others were dancing in the examination hall, I took Ania Bielynóvich aside and asked her whether she would do me a favour. She wanted to know what it was. I told her I wanted her to come for a walk with me that evening. 'Is that

all?' she asked, incredulous. I promised to tell her more when we met
after school.

My plan was to walk to the seminary at the far end of the town where
Rjevsky lived and to hand a bouquet of white narcissi to the porter, to
be passed on to him. I did not want to be identified as a pupil of my
Ghymnasia, so decided to disguise myself in my brother's old clothes,
trusting that the porter would take me for a boy. I needed Ania to
keep me company in this rather hazardous undertaking — for I hardly
dared imagine what would happen if a member of the school staff met
me wandering the streets of the town, dressed up as a boy. If Anna
Avdýeevna chose to dock my conduct mark even by one point, my gold
medal was certain to go to someone else!

Ania looked a bit startled when I walked up to her in the porch of
the cathedral church where we had agreed to meet. 'What on earth
. . . ?' she began, then, seeing in my hands a large object wrapped in
paper, which could not be mistaken for anything but a bouquet, she
said: 'Ah! I understand . . . ' and taking my arm, adjusted her pace to
mine.

She looked more and more ironically understanding as we made our
way through less frequented streets in the direction of the seminary.

'How can you make sure that he gets it?' she asked.

I told her that I had typed the name on a card and pinned it to the
flowers inside the wrapping.

'Even so, they might go astray.'

I told her to 'stop croaking'. Normally, I was amused by her teasing
but on that occasion it got on my nerves. I wanted Rjevsky to get these
flowers; I pictured to myself the expression on his face when he received
them — surprise, pleasure, embarrassment — if any of his colleagues
happened to be there. 'From one of your *ghymnazístkas?*' they would ask.
And he would blush, and laugh, and bury his face in the flowers, which
I had held against mine only a short time before . . .

The seminary buildings, like a monastery, were enclosed within high,
white walls, and one had to pull a handle of a resounding bell outside
its gates to gain admittance. My determination was almost shattered
by the noise. I was about to turn on my heels and run when the little
shutter in the door slid open and a bearded face demanded to know
what I wanted. I handed the bouquet to the porter with the words: 'For
Mr Rjevsky'. — 'From whom?' he asked. 'From a friend of his,' I
muttered and walked off as deliberately as I could, feeling the man's
stare on my back.

We had a lesson in pedagogy on the following day. I could not bring myself to meet Rjevsky's glance for fear that he suspected my secret and that my eyes would finally give me away. And I could not avoid seeing Ania's lips curl in an ironical smile whenever she caught me glancing stealthily at him. He, on the other hand, appeared supremely unconscious of the currents of feeling flowing around him, and carried on with his exposition of Fechner's theory of complimentary after-sensations in his usual genial manner. Was he just a little more pleased with life than usual? I saw no sign of his being in the seventh heaven of delight through having received a bouquet of white narcissi the night before, and I was disappointed . . .

But had I any right to be? Had I not wanted him to remain in ignorance with regard to the identity of the giver? Everything, postively everything in this one-sided love affair was to me a source of conflict and self-torment!

The Doors Open

Since he had given up his governorship of B*, my father spent most of his time at Fyeny, preferring us to visit him rather than come to us at M*. When he came, he often looked preoccupied and would talk to no one except my mother. These conversations usually took place when my sister and I were both at our school, and we knew of it only from what my mother told us afterwards. She said that my father was worried about the future. He had always lived on good terms with his peasant neighbours: he ran a model farm to show them the more up-to-date methods of land cultivation, and some of them had followed his example and accepted gifts of better seeds. He encouraged them to give up the custom of holding land in separate strips, and a fair number of families moved out of the village and settled down on *hoótors*, separate cottages on a few acres of their own. Shoora Martýnov declared that this policy was pursued by the government with the aim of splitting up the village community and making revolution more difficult, and he would argue with my sister who maintained that it also led to greater prosperity among the peasant owners. The movement, however, had been slowed down by the war, and the vicinity of the front brought its own disturbing repercussions. Army deserters were seen roaming in the district and there had been cases of arson on neighbouring estates. There was also shortage of labour, the income from the estate was shrinking, and having to run two establishments and make an allowance to my brother in Petersburg was proving a strain. My mother, however, made it clear to us that she had no intention of going to live at Fyeny, at least not until I had left school.

It did not occur to me at the time that these changes of fortune might affect my future. My final examinations were fast approaching. I managed to work quite hard despite my love-sickness and the emotional storms for which I found relief in writing, though often quite exhausted by them. I was nervous but no longer terrified of examinations, as I used to be years before. I found that I could accustom myself to any threat if I was allowed to contemplate it in imagination over a period of time. In this way I was able to control my nervousness during the examinations of the previous year. I did very well in them and in the course of my last year at school my position at the top of the class made it as certain as it could be that I would earn the 'large gold medal', the highest reward the *Ghymanasia* could confer and a sure way of entering a university. Katia Kign was next on the list as one to obtain 'the right to a gold medal', and Mania Bábina was to get the silver one. How did we know all that? I think the teachers talked about it in their common-room and these conversations somehow seeped through. In any case, the 'twelve' mark which stood against my name in the register in all subjects, could not but guarantee success.

I had little doubt that Anna Avdyéevna would have dearly loved to give me an 'eleven' for conduct but I also knew that she would never dare. I was sure of that since the incident of the drawing examination which happened in my last year but one. No one took that examination very seriously: we had no gifted artists among us, and the kind Arkády Miháilovich would give a good mark to anyone who tried to do her best. I was sure to get a 'twelve' because he knew I was top of the class in all other subjects and would not like to spoil the appearance of my last school report.

On that particular morning I came to school with my hair freshly washed and tied at the back with a black satin bow. As I was about to enter the class-room, Anna Avdyéevna, who was standing in the door-way, gave me one look and told me in a peremptory manner to 'go to the wash-room at once and do my hair properly'. Ribbons were allowed only to tie the ends of pigtails, and my hair was pinned up. I protested that I could do nothing with it when it had just been washed. My sister had helped me to put it up: if I untied the ribbon, I would never be able to gather it up again. All this was true, but she would not listen; she merely repeated that she would not allow me into the class-room with my hair like that', and she stood on the threshold, barring my way. I flared up.

'Then I shall have to ask the Director himself if I may go in.'

As I ran downstairs I could hear nothing but the noise of my blood pulsating in my head. Anger and sense of outrage were choking me. I knocked on the half-open door of the Director's study, heard his voice faintly, answering, and went in. He looked up at me with some surprise: he probably noticed that I was trembling.

'May I go in to the drawing examination with my hair like this, Iván Kuzmích?'

'With your hair like this? What do you mean? Why not?'

'Because . . . because Anna Avdyéevna says I mayn't. She won't let me in.'

His benign look changed perceptibly, darkening with annoyance.

'Of course you can go in,' he said. 'And ask Anna Avdyéevna to come down to see me.'

I curtseyed automatically and left the room. The two Komaróvskayas were outside in the small ante-room, waiting for me. They had run after me, I was told later on, because Anna Avdyéevna turned to the class, looking 'as pale as death', and said I had gone to the Director to complain of her. Now they walked upstairs, one on each side of me, muttering that I 'shouldn't have done it'. 'Done what?' I snarled back. 'It's wrong to complain of one's own *dame-de-classe*,' they said. 'I didn't complain: I just asked whether I could go into the class-room with my hair like this! She would have kept me out . . . made me fail the exam!'

The silence in the class could not have been more complete when I came in than if I had been the Director himself about to announce the results of the final examinations. Anna Avdyéevna was sitting at her table, not looking at me, but the eyes of all the girls were on me. This brief battle of wills left me deeply shaken, yet poised on the pinnacle of triumph. I crossed the room and gave her the Director's message.

As soon as she was out of the room, there was an uproar. I was surrounded and had to tell them exactly what had happened. The drawing master came in on this scene. He looked far from pleased at our lack of preparedness, judging us to be deficient in respect for his subject. When we got back to our places, he produced a small bust of Beethoven from his portfolio, placed it on his table, draped the stand with a piece of cloth and told us we had exactly fifty minutes to draw it. Just then Anna Avdyéevna returned from the Director's study. She had left the class-room looking very pale; she came back as red as beetroot. We could see it almost without looking at her.

We talked about it again after the exam. The two Komaróvskayas

were the only ones who were decidedly on the side of the *dame-de-classe*
and who condemned my action as 'disloyal'. My four special friends
were defending me while the majority of the class remained more or less
neutral, sympathetic to me and interested in our feud mainly as a
spectacle.

By a strange coincidence there was a witness of what had passed
between the Director and Anna Avdyéevna, and he happened to be our
frequent visitor and my devoted teacher, Shimkóvich. The men teachers'
common-room adjoined the Director's study, with a door opening on to
the same ante-room, and Shimkóvich came into it at the moment when
Iván Kuzmích was seeing Anna Avdyéevna out of his study. He heard
the Director say to her: 'I won't allow you to upset pupils during
examinations!' and Anna Avdyéevna looked flushed and very upset.

I have to admit that I felt not the slightest regret, nor a trace of
sympathy for Anna Avdyéevna; on the contrary, I was tremendously
gratified by the knowledge that in the Director's eyes my well-being
mattered so much more than the silly rules a *dame-de-classe* might choose
to impose. As for 'loyalty' to her, who had treated me so unfairly, the
idea struck me as utterly ridiculous.

During my last term at school, Anna Avdyéevna maintained an attitude
of icy politeness towards me and there were no more open clashes
between us. I felt for her a dislike tinged with contempt — of a kind one
might feel for an enemy one had conquered but not forgiven. 'She dares
not touch you,' said my friends, intending to flatter me. I merely
shrugged. They did not know how little this now mattered to me. The
approaching day of parting with Rjevsky preoccupied me even more
than the impending final examinations.

A few days after I had handed the bouquet of narcissi to the seminary
porter, Aniuta answered the door at our house and brought in a large
envelope addressed to me in an unknown handwriting. It contained a
sepia copy of 'The Red Boy' painting by Lawrence! Strange, that it
should be the same picture my sister gave me several years ago! There
was nothing written on the back and there was no verbal message.
Aniuta told me a boy whom she had never seen before, handed it in.
I was puzzled and not really pleased, though I liked the picture.
Maroossia, whom I had taken into my confidence after my expedition
to the seminary, suggested that the picture was from Rjevsky, sent me
in gratitude for the flowers. 'But he did not know they were from me!
And why this particular picture?' I wanted to know. My sister smiled.
'Perhaps it is a hint — that you are still very young . . . that a boy like

this is a more suitable companion . . . ' I must have looked very angry at this because she hastened to add that she was only joking.

But the sting remained in the wound, tormenting me. I raged inwardly against the handicap of my youth, angry with myself for being so young, for looking even younger than my age. So he could not take me seriously, he was thinking it was just calf love! But I could not even be sure that he knew of my love or was thinking of me at all! Life was not worth going on with, I felt. Suicide was an act of courage to be admired. It was far, far better to die before 'life' made a miserable coward out of you.

When my brother went to Petersburg, he left his small revolver behind, and I took possession of it. Between studying for examinations and writing 'letters' to Rjevsky, I would take it out, hold it on the palm of my hand and tell myself it was the easiest thing in the world to put it to my head and release the trigger. The thought excited and fascinated me. Evening after evening I would do that, yet all I did in the end was to write a long essay and call it 'A Suicide's Letter'. It expressed my belief that life was certain to disappoint and damage and distort the personality of the writer. Otherwise, why should it have been said: 'Those whom the gods love die young' . . . ? Hence it was better to put an end to it before these things happened.

Why did I not commit suicide then? Mainly, I think, because I feared the unknown, shrank from the possibility of merely wounding myself, and could picture to myself too well the effect my suicide would have on my mother and sister. And though I liked imagining the shocked faces of Rjevsky, of Iván Kuzmích and even of Anna Avdyéevna, and hearing in my mind what they would say about me with regret and remorse, some kind of faint hope was still flickering ahead, the hope that I might do something worthwhile with my life.

The final examinations took place at the end of May in brilliant, hot weather. The bird-cherry in the Rampart gardens was in bloom and the air was heavy with its penetrating fragrance, but we could not spare the time to go for walks. We were given from one to three days to prepare each subject, that is, to revise what we had learned during the year. This involved quite intensive reading. I preferred to work on my own, but when Tonia or Ania Bielynóvich asked me to combine with them, I was quite ready to do so. Helping my schoolmates gave me a pleasurable feeling of power; I was pleased with myself not because I was doing them a good turn but because I *could* do these things.

But I believe power over myself gave me the greatest satisfaction.

Even as a child of eight or nine I used to train myself to do things I wanted to shirk, such as washing my neck in cold water or going into a dark room to find matches for my mother. The most difficult thing was to refrain from running on the way out, when you turned your back on whatever might be lurking in the darkness, waiting to spring on you from behind.

I learned to control my nervousness during examinations and even enjoyed them in a somewhat paradoxical way *because* I had this control over myself. But I had been living for weeks in a state of high nervous tension, anticipating the strain of the last day at school, when our 'release' — *výpoosk* is the Russian word for this event — would be celebrated with prayers, the presentation of prizes and end in final farewells.

The day however came, as all days, dreaded or desired, inevitably do. On the occasion we still had to wear our uniform, but it was a 'parade' one, the white pinafore, of fine cambric trimmed with lace, over a brown serge dress. And our hair was no longer subject to regulations: many blossomed into curls, large bows and high combs. Everyone in the school, the staff and the girls, was assembling in the upper hall for the religious service. *Bátiushka* would give us his pastoral advice for the last time, then the Director and the Headmistress would take their turn to speak. Fortunately, no speeches were expected from us. Our medals would be handed to us, copies of The Gospels would be distributed, congratulations would follow.

And last of all there would be final handshakes. In agonized anticipation of saying good-bye to Rjevsky, I had not given a thought to what I would do about Anna Avdyéevna. In fact, I had decided long beforehand that I would ignore her, and then dismissed the thought from my mind. But as I was walking up the iron staircase — so memorable from my first day at the boarding school — I saw the *Nachálnitsa* descending it with a rustle of silk skirts, spreading a delicate fragrance of scent around her. She was dressed up for the ceremony, wearing her decoration, a little white cross on a blue ribbon, pinned to her chest. I stopped on the landing to let her pass. She stopped, too.

'*Dóoshechka* — my little soul —' she said. 'I beg you, do speak to Anna Avdyéevna on this day — your last day at school! Do say good-bye to her!'

Her mittened hand was on my shoulder and her kindly eyes searched mine with a beseeching look. I was startled, taken aback for a moment — how did she guess what I intended to do? Then all the suppressed bitterness and anger of the long-drawn-out feud rose up in me. Anna Avdyéevna had persecuted me because I would not be completely ruled by her. She had played on my feelings. I could not forgive her that. It would be hypocrisy on my part to give her my hand.

'I'm sorry,' I murmured. 'I can't.'

'Won't you try?' she pleaded.

I shook my head. I was so touched by her pleading that I was on the point of tears and could not speak. I would have even *preferred* to do what she was asking, but some force within me made it quite impossible. The *Nachálnitsa* seemed to realize what I was feeling and told me she had not wanted to upset me. She said softly: 'What a pity!' and kissed me on the cheek. Then she continued on her way down, and I tried to run upstairs but my knees were weak with emotion, stirred up in me by this meeting on the staircase. And it was concerned not only with the subject raised by the Headmistress but with something I did a few moments before. I had slipped a note into the pocket of Rjevsky's overcoat which was hanging in the main hall. It was foolhardy of me because I could have been seen by the chief porter Klementiy who was almost always there, or by anyone who happened to be passing through the hall. The school's best finalist, the recipient of the gold medal, caught putting her hand in the pocket of a teacher's overcoat! But I was in a desperate mood. As it was with Steinberg, the conductor, I could not bear the thought that my love for Rjevsky only gave me pain, and no pleasure or joy to him. I decided that he must know that he had been loved, even if he was not told by whom. I would throw my confession like a flower at his feet; he could trample on it if he so chose, but at least it would do something to him — flatter him, or make him smile . . . Yes, even an amused smile from him was better than nothing!

I wrote on a slip of paper: 'I loved you deeply, desperately, without hope — and you haven't even noticed it!' Without signing or putting it in an envelope, I waited around the hall — where we were supposed not to linger — until it was empty, then swept past the teachers' coat hangers and pushed the folded note into Rjevsky's pocket.

Though I made an effort to alter my handwriting, I knew I really wanted him to recognize it. He would not see it until the school-leaving ceremony was over, and then I should be out of the building, out of his reach — unless . . . But I was too painfully aware how improbable was this 'unless', and how useless any move on his part would be, even if he made it.

This knowledge was gnawing at my heart all the while the prayers were being said. We, the finalists, were lined up in front of the other pupils, facing the officiating priest. At a right angle to our group stood

the members of the teaching staff, with the Director and the *Nachálnitsa*
in the centre of the first row. My sister's gentle face showed above the
Nachálnitsa's shoulder, but I had to avoid looking at her, much as I
wanted to, because Anna Avdyéevna was close beside her. Nor could I
glance too often to the right of them where Rjevsky towered over the
other teachers, his long neck sticking out above their heads. I stared at
bátiushka and thought he was looking sternly at me, knowing me as an
atheist and a 'bad influence' on the religious among my schoolmates.

At last the climax of the whole ceremony was reached. Iván Kuzmích
read out the names of the pupils who were awarded the highest distinc-
tions, my name the first among them. I went up and he handed me a
small flat case, open to reveal a large medal in pale gold with the
profile of the Empress Maria Fyódorovna imprinted on it. We shook
hands, he congratulating me, and I curtseying and thanking him. Then
the *Nachálnitsa* embraced and kissed me with tears in her eyes. I would
have been more moved had I not known that tears came rather readily
to her eyes. Then I went aside and waited for the teachers to make the
first move. They all came and shook hands, and complimented me, except
Anna Avdyéevna, who stayed where she was, her face grey, unhealthy
and grim. My classmates went up to her and she spoke to them without a
smile. Many pupils asked the teachers for their photographs and gave
them theirs. I braced myself to ask Rjevsky for his. 'Only in exchange
for yours!' he said. His eyes shone like blue stars.

The whole crowd of us went into the adjoining class-room in order to
inscribe and exchange photographs. They were taken for the occasion
and provided the town photographer with a small yearly income.
Strangely enough, these photographs fared better at the hands of time
and fate than some other relics of my past. My early stories and novels
have been destroyed, but this collection of youthful faces and their
farewell dicta, written on the back, were preserved by my sister, and
I have looked at them since. How unexpected some of these written
farewells turned out to be! I was amused at Bábina, usually as quiet as a
mouse, producing a quotation from an unknown author: 'Those only
deserve happiness and freedom, who fight for them day after day!'
Ania Bielynóvich, a provocative critic in daily life, chose to be nostalgic,
and refer to our partnership in the publication of the class magazine.
Calling me by my Spanish nickname, she wrote: 'To dear Gaetano, the
retiring Editor, from his former (alas! alas!) editorial assistant. Remember our motto: *Liberté, egalité, fraternité.*' Alas, indeed! I had quite
forgotten it had been our motto; I even had difficulty in remembering

that we had produced a magazine. Tonia Rosen also called me her 'darling Gaetano', for was I not her partner in the 'Danse d'Apache'? 'Do not forget your loving Annunziata and be faithful to the end (faithfulness to the grave is a great virtue), and I will not forget you on account of a few bright moments.' Was she thinking of the moment when I put strawberries and cream down her neck? Lena called me 'dear Eaglet' and bade me remember our happy days at Diédlovo. But the most emotional farewell came from Sonia Ivánova, a girl who was outside our group of five, whom I visited during the summer holidays and who wrote: 'You are my dearest friend; my brightest and happiest memories are of you. My heart grows light when I think of your goodness to me. I love you very much. Remember our walks among the corn and in the meadows at B*.' I read this with a kind of shame, for I could not think of Sonia as my best and dearest friend.

And Rjevsky? He just wished me 'a bright and happy future'. Always the future, never the present! On his photograph he looked gay and sure of himself, quite free from the shyness and awkwardness that used to move me to such excesses of tenderness. I gazed at this false image of him, my heart aching with hopeless regret. On the back of my own photograph I had scribbled: 'Perhaps we shall never meet again . . . '

Was it really possible, was it conceivable that we never should? There must come a day, I told myself, when he would be proud of having that photograph and my scribble on the back of it!

'Life' is about to Begin

During our last term at school, we, the five friends, had discussed among ourselves our plans for the future and knew that some of us were going to continue our education in Petersburg. Liolia was to study singing. Her mother, not wishing to part with her, decided to move house to Petersburg. Tonia was to enter a Modern Languages College and be a boarder there, while I applied for admission to the Faculty of Philology and Russian Literature at the Bestoózhevskiye Koorsy where my sister had obtained her degree. Our admission, on the strength of our school records, was assured, and we promised ourselves to continue our friendship in the capital. Ania Bielynóvich told me that she, too, was going to study for a French degree in Petersburg, but Sonia Ivánova's parents decided to her distress that she was to go to Moscow. With most of our friends and brothers in Petersburg, we tended to look down on Moscow as provincial and somewhat barbaric.

Katia and Lena, the two cousins, seemed to have no plans, but soon after the school-leaving ceremony, they surprised us by announcing that they had become engaged to General Staff Officers, and Katia invited us to her wedding that very summer.

The town of M* had not been the same place since the General Staff made it its headquarters. A large number of middle-aged, apparently unattached men had descended on it and many were lodging with the town families. We had several friends among the 'Staff people' as we called them, who visited our house, most of them far too old to interest me. Anyway, the thought of marriage did not enter my head at that time, except as a day-dream for a distant future, with someone rather remarkable and quite different from the men I saw around me. The news of Katia's engagement shocked me, while the thought of Lena as a married woman just made me laugh.

It never occurred to me that Katia, who had won 'the right to a gold medal' would not continue her studies; I felt it was 'a waste' to throw away her achievement by becoming a mere wife. Besides, I regarded it as stupid to get married at the age of barely seventeen, before one had tasted 'freedom' and independence.

I was even more distressed when I met her future husband, a military engineer, Kozlóvsky. He was short, half a head shorter than Katia, and had black hair, a longish dark moustache and small, dark eyes behind glasses. Immediately I became convinced that he dyed his hair, was bad-tempered and was marrying Katia because she would inherit her grandmother's estate. We, as a group, regarded Katia as very practical but entirely without sex appeal, and we knew she had never had a flirtation with anybody. Katia herself told us that her fiancé was forty-four years old — old enough to be her father. What possessed her, I wondered, to agree to marry him, and in such haste! Of the five of us, I thought Liolia was the one to make an early marriage; Tonia would be next . . . not Katia!

Lena, her cousin, was a different matter. She told us dramatically many a time how much she disliked living with her mother and how beastly her mother was to her, so for her marriage was a way of escape. But she looked so incongruous in her grown-up clothes, with her face and body of an outsize baby, beside her pleasant, middle-aged husband that I had to look away when talking to them.

Liolia, Tonia and I went to Katia's wedding which was celebrated at Fyódorovka, her grandmother's estate. Our mood on arrival was very different from the carefree enjoyment of the previous summer. The more I saw of Kozlóvsky, the less I liked him, and my annoyance with Katia gave way to pity for her. Resentfully, I watched her fiancé ordering her about while she meekly submitted to whatever he wished her to do. The atmosphere of the place was subdued, unspontaneous, and the three of us agreed that it was more like a funeral than a wedding. Liolia however amused herself by flirting with the brother of Dima's wife. Dima, of course, was there and Olga, his wife, a cold arrogant woman, who, we understood, had made Katia's life impossible at Diédlovo.

I felt uneasy, not to say unhappy, the whole time I was there. Strange things were happening on the estate itself. Though Katia's grandmother was still the owner of acres of field and forest, local peasants were cutting trees in her forest without her permission and openly carting the timber through her own court-yard to their village building sites. 'We're obliged to tolerate this while the war is on,' muttered Kozlóvsky. 'Law can't be enforced in these conditions . . . But it will be, yes, it will be later on!'

The wedding was celebrated with some pomp. Semion, in a crimson satin shirt and a velvet cap with a peacock's feather, drove the couple to church in a four-horse carriage. After the wedding lunch, they were again driven off, this time in a Staff motor car, to M*, where Kozlóvsky had rented a flat. We heard later that the car broke down half-way to town and the newly-marrieds had to continue their journey by peasant cart and train. Motor cars were always breaking down in those days.

I returned to Fyeny in a dejected mood but was suddenly stirred into life by finding that we had a visitor — Zhenia Preyer. He had been to our house at M* more than once during the year, but had always remained so reserved and silent that I felt I knew him no better than the first time I met him. He was studying at the same Institute in Petersburg as my brother, and they drew close enough together for Vova to invite him to Fyeny.

I felt a certain amount of excitement at the thought of getting to know him better. One of our Staff friends had remarked about him that 'even when he smiled, he looked as if he were about to burst into tears'. I repeated this remark to my sister and asked her whether she thought Zhenia ever really enjoyed himself. She replied that she was sure of it. As she had had his company for some days before I arrived, I pressed on with my questions.

'What does he enjoy?'

'Nature mainly. He is also very fond of his dog and enjoys him a lot . . . '

'Does he *talk* about it?'

'Oh, yes, he does talk, but mostly during our walks together . . . not when other people are about.'

So he talked to Maroossia when alone with her! He trusted her but chose to remain a closed book to me. The thought gave me a pang, and immediately I put myself in the dock. Was I envious? I had never envied my sister before. But here was this young man of romantic appearance, nearer to me in age than he was to my sister and much more acceptable than either Shoora or Fyedia — and yet he preferred her company to mine! My immediate impulse was to withdraw, to make it more difficult for him to approach me. Not for anything in the world would I thrust myself forward, or attempt to compete with my sister. But it would have been the same if it were anyone else. I could imagine nothing more humiliating than competing with another woman for the affection or even attention of any man. If he had already chosen — and chosen badly — *tant pis pour lui* ! If my rival happened to be a pretty but stupid or frivolous girl, my respect for the man would dwindle to almost nothing. I might feel bitter or even cynical about such a choice. If, on the other hand, she were admirable in more than one respect, I would feel humbled and sad — and that was how I felt on this occasion, believing Zhenia preferred Maroossia to myself.

We all went for walks together: my brother, Zhenia, my sister and I. Zhenia usually walked beside my sister, and addressed his remarks to her. He talked about his dog, Jackie, whom he had left at home, telling her how intelligent he was and how devoted to him — 'the best friend he had in the world'. It made me think of Knut Hamsun's *Pan*. Like the hero of that novel, Zhenia loved nature, professed to prefer solitude to company and regarded his dog as his only real friend. Pan was fiercely in love with a proud girl who was bent on humiliating him, but he broke away from her and decided to move to a more distant part of the forest. As he was saying good-bye to her, the girl asked him for a favour, the gift of his dog. He promised this, then shot the dog and left its corpse on her threshold. I wondered if Zhenia were capable of such a gesture if he were really in love. I suspected he would not be: he had a rather weak chin and mouth. His forehead, eyebrows and eyes were magnificent: they could belong to a great poet or to Lermontov's Demon — but Zhenia was only *a little Demon* — he was to be pitied, not feared . . . I decided to write a story about him and call it 'The Little Demon'.

I watched him, to see how much he really enjoyed of what we could offer him at Fyeny. He liked rowing, so we took him on the river and treated him as an expert — which clearly pleased him. He was ready to prove his strength to do all the work with the oars, but Maroossia insisted that we should take turns to row in pairs, using one oar each. She soon found however that the effort defeated her. Good as she was in responding to rhythm in music and dancing, she could not keep in unison with another person when trying to row. With her and myself at the oars, the boat wobbled feebly from side to side, making no headway at all, and my brother at the tiller complained that we made steering impossible. With an apologetic smile, Maroossia would accept Zhenia's offer to replace her, and then Zhenia and I, sitting close together, our shoulders nearly touching, made the boat go forward at a spanking pace. I enjoyed sharing this sustained effort with him, and wondered if his pleasure in rowing was increased by having me beside him — but found it impossible to tell. As for myself, whatever mood I was in, being on the river, inhaling the fresh smell of water, watching its powerful, massive flow always had a soothing effect on me.

We knew our guest was fond of cycling: he cycled to Fyeny all the way from M*, undeterred by the cobbles of the highway or the deep sand of country roads. But I had left my bicycle at M*. What was the sense of cycling when there were horses available? I held forth about this in front of Zhenia who listened in silence. I did not suggest riding to him for fear he might decline, and I would feel snubbed and suspect him of timidity. However, next morning when I came down to breakfast in my riding habit, he asked me shyly whether he might come with me. He had only once been on a horse before, he said, but if he could have a quiet one, he might not fall off right away . . .

I was very pleased. As neither my brother nor sister rode, I would have him on my own and at last would be able to find out what sort of person he was.

He was certainly not a coward. He was ready to trot and even gallop on our first ride together. He was obviously uncomfortable trotting as he could not yet rise in his stirrups in rhythm with the horse's step, but he persevered, steadily and bravely, with a frown of concentration on his face. I did my best to pass on to him all the basic 'rules' Maxim had taught me about riding: 'Sit well back, hold your elbows close to your sides. Have the reins fairly short but don't pull on them. Never tug at the reins when you rise to the trot. Tuck your knees well into the saddle; hold your toes up and your heels down; keep your stirrup-iron under the ball of your foot.'

Conscientiously, Zhenia tried to follow my instructions; one thing he could not do was to hold his shoulders back. His natural posture was to hunch his shoulders, a habit which I felt he ought to be able to correct.

We had quite a few of these solitary rides together. I remember a luscious meadow where we dismounted and picked lilies-of-the-valley, and a boggy piece of ground across which we urged our horses — the animals, being wiser than us, refused to go, and we had to turn back. Once we lost ourselves and rode into the yard of some estate to ask our way; a woman who came out to speak to us looked us over curiously; I felt as if I were a person in a story . . .

Zhenia looked happy during these rides, yet when he made some remark it was nearly always pessimistic. We talked about the characters of our horses and he would go on to say that he liked animals far better than people. Animals *were* 'better': they did not lie or betray you, they were without guile, without vindictiveness . . . yes, even the wild ones, lions and tigers, killed only in order to survive. I was ready to agree, yet – just because his pessimism seemed so dogmatic and final – I was impelled to argue that not all people were bad and life must hold something good in store for us. He would not concede this, and it angered me. Perhaps, half-consciously, I wished that he would fall in love with me and find life worth living for that reason. But he showed no sign of falling in love with me: when we both patted a horse's neck and our hands touched, he made no attempt to hold mine. Nor did I find myself falling in love with him – partly because I was still tormentedly in love with Rjevsky.

Alone in my room, I would take out his photograph and gaze at it with the exasperated curiosity of an explorer who knows that he will never be able to penetrate this particular country. Perhaps if I had got to know him better this painful longing would have dropped away. He was, after all, a very ordinary person – and yet he had this power of making me weep, compose poems, write impassioned letters which he would never read, rage at myself and at him – and all to no apparent purpose, no gain of any kind either to him or myself. I was not even sure that what I experienced was 'real' love or being in love with love . . . How should I ever know? When real love came, how would I recognize it? This pain I was feeling was real enough – but was it the pain of *love*?

Zhenia attracted me but I did not fall in love with him: something was lacking in his personality which Rjevsky possessed – an impression of strength, perhaps? We both kept our reserve. After he had left Fyeny, I settled down to writing my story about him. The character of the girl in the story with whom 'the little Demon' falls in love had certain features of my own – it could hardly have been otherwise – but I think I was fairly successful in drawing the character of the 'Demon'. Anyway, when a few years later I showed that story to Professor Ovsiániko-Kulikóvsky, a leading literary critic of those days, he told me that although it showed the inflence of Hamsun, it was good enough to go straight into print. As it happened, it never reached the printers – by then, Russia was in the throes of Civil War and no printing was done except of military decrees and single sheet newspapers.

But when I wrote it at Fyeny the war with Germany was still in full swing and the Tsar's residence at M* gave the inhabitants a sense of relative security. That summer Shoora Martýnov did not invite himself to our country home, and my brother told us that he was spending most of his vacation in Petersburg. This was most unusual. Why did he choose to do that? My brother shrugged and murmured something about Shoora's 'dabbling in politics'. 'He'll burn his fingers if he's not careful,' he added.

The day when my new life was due to begin was now very near. A letter arrived informing me that I had been admitted to the Faculty of Philology and Russian literature at the Bestoózhevskiye Koorsy, and that the autumn term began on the 10th of October. My mother decided that we must return to M* well before that date, and my sister was to go to Petersburg a few days ahead of me to find a room on the Vassílevsky Óstrov, as near the Koorsy as possible. My parents had been having long conversations in my mother's room at Fyeny, and we guessed that Father was trying to persuade her to come and live there, now that only Maroossia would remain with her at M*. In the end, however, she came to M* with us, and things remained as they had been for the last two years. I believe she did this in order to be 'nearer the children' and because she wanted Maroossia to have the comforts of a real home. She told us that, however much she liked nature, she found life in the country rather limiting and boring; confidentially she admitted that she would miss the cinema – which only recently she had pronounced to be 'a horror'!

We knew she would have preferred my father to come and live with her and Maroossia at M*, leaving the estate in charge of the bailiff: she was worried by the rumours of arson and plunder of country houses in the district not very far from us. But my father must have felt that the estate required his personal attention. That summer he was more than usually preoccupied and more taciturn than ever. When he was not out on the estate, he would walk up and down the drawing-room and the adjoining dining-room, his hands clasped behind his back, his neck rigid, his eyes fixed on the empty space before him. There was an unseeing look in his eyes: he would pass me several times as I sat at the dining-room table, without noticing that I was doing something of which he strongly disapproved – reading while having a meal. His deep absorption in his thoughts alarmed me. What was he thinking about? Perhaps regretting that he had ever had a family? And I wished my mother would share her time more equally between Fyeny and M*, between him and us.

A kind of sad elation and excitement I felt at the prospect of living in Petersburg, clashed with the deeper sadness which descended upon me on the eve of our departure from Fyeny. I cannot honestly say that it was a premonition of still sadder things to come, but my mood that evening was unrelieved by even a small glow of hopefulness — an anticipation of eventual return which makes parting from a place one loves so much less wounding to the heart. My memory was thrown back to that other parting, when I went to boarding school, and had to say good-bye to every tree in the orchard at B*. A child then, a young girl now, I still wanted to take my leave from a group of aspens in the corner of a near-by meadow. I had climbed them so often, even quite recently; they were always whispering . . . that evening I imagined they were telling me not to go away. As I walked towards them through the long grass, a breeze blew into my face, lifting my hair off my forehead, bringing back another memory — of a game I used to play on my solitary walks, pretending that I had an assignation with my lover — Wind. Smiling at myself, I said: 'So here you are again! You've been away a long time!' and was strangely comforted by this invisible presence.

The morning of the day was even worse. I felt quite guilty when saying good-bye to the unsuspecting horses, who would be hoping for my visit and the tit-bits I brought them, tomorrow and for days afterwards. I walked quickly through the downstairs rooms where the empty chairs seemed to reproach me for my desertion by holding open their arms — they would remain empty for a long time.

A few minutes before we were due to leave everyone assembled in the drawing-room: the bailiff, Piotr, Ivan, Maxim, Galaktyón, Aniuta, the gardener, as well as our family. My parents sat down, all of us following their example, and for a minute or so there was complete silence in the room. I had never before troubled to find out the meaning of this 'sitting-down' ceremony before a journey, though it always brought a spasm of emotion to my throat. When my mother rose, everyone stood up and we began to say good-bye. My father was accompanying us to the station, and as Aniuta was also coming to M* with us, we had to travel in two vehicles. I went with Aniuta who was delighted to be going back to M*. She, too, was fond of the cinema! I asked her whether she knew why people always sat down before a journey.

'I reckon it's for trying to remember not to forget something, báryshnia,' she replied.

'Is that the only reason?'

'Well, the old people say it's for luck . . . '

For luck! Perhaps just to have a respite from the flurry and hurry of preparations — or, as in church, to have a brief moment for meditation and prayer? Meditation . . . as our buggy rolled along the soft, wide road where the shadows of great birch trees were already lengthening, I let myself think.

In a mood for self-examination, reminiscence and anticipation, aware of the present moment as something that was already a part of the past, I tried to see myself as I had been and as I was now, to sum up, as it were, my experience and discoveries, to find a patch of firm ground on which I could put both my feet — metaphorically — and say to myself: 'Here I stand, and from here I can start this "real life"!'

I was at that stage painfully — not at all triumphantly — conscious of my youth, and I knew that I looked even younger than I was. My fond teacher, Shimkóvich, had remarked on seeing my photograph only a year before that I was looking 'not a day older than thirteen'. But he had also referred to me in class, only half in joke, as 'our little grand-mother'. I had often felt centuries old, burdened with an infinite variety of experience — with all the emotions, philosophical musings, doubts and despairs that Dostoyevsky put into the mouths of Raskólnikov, Ivan Karamazov and Stavróghin. And had I not been hopelessly in love — a most maturing experience — with a man about whom I had no illusions, from whom I did not ask or expect anything in return? Before I was seventeen, I had written enough poems and stories to have the right to call myself an author, and the story I wrote about Rjevsky that summer, 'His Eyes', was unique in that there was not a single word of fiction in it. I prided myself on this absolute truthfulness, as if invention was an equivalent of a lie. I had been through the crises of belief, religious and political, and wrote in my diary, when I was thirteen, that I would dedicate my life to liberating my country from the Tsarist tyranny.

Yet what was I really at this particular moment of my life? An unbeliever still, but far less certain of my unbeliefs, and hankering, as in the past, for 'life everlasting'. I was hungry for life and love, and bitter when I thought of the 'love' I had experienced so far. I was still fascinated by the thought of suicide, seeing it as an act of self-assertion and courage, but was unable to carry it out — partly because it would have been cruel towards my mother and sister, but I felt it was weak of me.

The change in my feelings towards them was perhaps a measure of my emancipation. My mother had helped it by sending me away to boarding school, thus giving me the proof that I was not indispensable to her. Gradually, she ceased to be the source of all the comforts, emotional and physical, the haven of security and the arbiter of values she had been to me until that critical separation. Some of her judgments and principles I assimilated and made my own, others I rejected as uncongenial. Her idea of the primacy of duty, the duty of children towards their parents, of parents towards their children, and of nationals towards their country, went much against the grain with me — I identified duty with compulsion. Love, and service given out of love, came, in my opinion, before duty. My intense affection for my mother had become a kind of compassion: I felt sorry for her because she was growing older, heavier and afflicted with varicose veins, and I felt guilty at being irritated by her over-concern for my health. For my sister I still felt deep tenderness and respect, but these feelings were also tinged with compassion, for I had seen her in moods of anxiety and painful vacillation which puzzled me and made me wonder if she lacked strength of character.

I had no doubt that if I had committed my 'philosophical' suicide, it would have wounded them permanently. I also knew that my brother would not believe me capable of such an act of bravery, and if I had carried it out, I did not expect him to be broken-hearted about it. My attitude towards him had hardened into a conviction that I was completely misunderstood and unappreciated by him. He laughed at my writing and treated me as if I were still a child; he made me feel inferior by warning me not to attempt 'clever conversation' with his friends, as they would not be interested in what I had to say. I felt towards him a hostility which had in it an admixture of scorn — for did he not reject Dostoyevsky as 'unreadable' and prefer mathematics to literature? We had absolutely nothing in common.

As for my father — I had become almost resigned to the fact that the relationship between us could never be closer than it had been. The chance of renewing the fleeting contact that had been established between us when he spoke to me as to an equal on the balcony at Piatigorsk, had never recurred. The seed of compassion which was sown then, however, had grown and had driven out fear. I thought of my father now as a man who ought not to have had children: the love of a wife would have sufficed him. Now, in fulfilment of his duty he had to go on providing for us until we could stand on our own feet, accepting the fact that his wife felt her duty towards us had to come before her affection for him. I looked at him, as it were, across a gulf, doubting that my sympathy and respect could reach him.

Myself I saw as a disillusioned person. The apparent senselessness of Zena's short life and unnecessary death had burned a deep wound in

my soul: if that could happen to her, what right had I to expect that
things should go well with me? Yet I was passionately wishing and hoping
that life would prove worth living, and I was determined to live it as
fully as I could. I was making definite plans for the future: I was going to
work hard and do well in the examinations, so well that I would get on
the staff of the University lecturers as soon as I had obtained my first
degree. I would continue to write and make my name as a novelist and
a poet. The manuscript of 'His Eyes' was in my suitcase, and I promised
myself the bitter pleasure of sending Rjevsky a copy when it was
published. I would, of course, go to plays and concerts; because of the
war there would be, alas! no balls to satisfy my passion for dancing. My
sister had described Petersburg to me as 'a sombre city', full of mists and
rain, with snow sometimes falling in May, but I knew I was going to
like it, because it was the city where Lermontov and Pushkin and Dostoyevsky had lived; where Oniéghin and Raskólnikov, almost as real to
me as their creators, had walked the streets.

Aniuta's voice broke in on my thoughts. 'Here we are!' she said,
cheerfully. We had indeed arrived at the railway station. I said good-bye
to Maxim and the horses. My father came on to the platform with us.
I was the last to be embraced by him, and I noticed his eyes were moist:
he was, of course, upset at parting from my mother. I saw him standing
there as the train moved out of the station, holding his hat formally
above his head, while Maxim's broad smiling face loomed in the station
doorway some distance behind him.

The weeks of final preparations at M* flashed by. My brother and I
were to travel by a night train. One of our acquaintances on the General
Staff secured for us the tickets in a sleeping carriage reserved for members of the General Staff. The trains were few and generally crowded:
the officers of the General Staff were very obliging to their acquaintances
and friends, and obtained seats for them whenever possible. My sister was
already in Petersburg waiting for me to settle down in a room which she
had found for me. My mother came to the station to see us off. All the
way to the station and on the platform she was instructing us not to
forget to wear our goloshes in wet weather, to go to bed early and not
to neglect our food. She had heard that meat was getting scarce in
Petersburg; horsemeat was being passed for beef; she would remind
Father to send us parcels from Fyeny . . . I was feeling impatient, and
though sad at parting from my mother, wished that the moment of
departure would come sooner. We went into the carriage: it was
Wagons Lits Internationales, soft seats upholstered in strawberry coloured

damask, table lamps with pretty shades, a small lavabo compartment to share between two neighbouring coupés. My mother was satisfied that we would spend a comfortable night. Our luggage was on the racks and we stepped out again on to the platform.

Then, to our surprise, we saw Aniuta hurrying towards us. My brother saw her first and said with his characteristic phlegm: 'There's Aniuta! I wonder what she wants.' My mother turned and drew in her breath, alarmed. Aniuta trotted up and took a folded slip of paper from her pocket.

'A telegram came for you, *bárynia*, ten minutes after you'd left. I thought you might want to see it at once.'

My mother tore it open, read it, her forehead puckered, her lips pressed together.

'Who is it from? What is it about?' asked my brother.

'From Papa. He telegraphs "Don't send Léda off to ·Petersburg. Writing." That's all.'

The three of us stood, dumbfounded, Aniuta stepping discreetly aside. A feeling of bitter, undeserved injury flooded my breast. I looked at my mother and she looked at me.

'Why?' I asked.

'I have discussed this with him over and over again,' said my mother. 'He thinks the general situation and our own finances are so precarious that we should not take any more risks. But I don't agree with him. Everything has been arranged: you have your place at the university, the room has been found, Maroossia is expecting you. You are going.'

A station porter pulled the cord of a shining bell outside the main station entrance. The first bell! My mother embraced my brother and me, then made hurried signs of the cross over our heads.

'Get in quickly, the train is about to start!'

The second bell. My brother and I complied, getting into the carriage. We leaned out of the window. My mother looked upset but determined, with her lips pursed, her grey eyes anxious, Aniuta standing by her side. She repeated her admonitions.

'Wrap yourself up well when you go out in cold weather . . . '

'Yes, Mamma.'

'Try to go to bed early . . . '

'Yes, yes, I'll try.'

The third bell. The engine at the far end of the train exploded in a large puff of white smoke. The train started smoothly, slowly, almost soundlessly. As it accelerated and the platform began to slide backwards, Aniuta waved a handkerchief, and I could see my mother still making signs of the cross in our direction.

My 'real' life had begun.